DISTORTIONS OF
AGRICULTURAL INCENTIVES

DISTORTIONS OF AGRICULTURAL INCENTIVES

Edited by Theodore W. Schultz

Indiana University Press
Bloomington   London

Manufactured in the United States of America

Library of Congress Cataloging in Publication Data
Main entry under title:
Distortions of agricultural incentives.
Papers presented at a 1977 three-day workshop
sponsored by the Midwest Center of the American
Academy of Arts and Sciences.
Includes index.
1. Agriculture—Economic aspects—Congresses.
2. Agriculture and state—Congresses. I. Schultz,
Theodore William, 1902–   II. American Academy
of Arts and Sciences, Boston. Midwest Center.
HD1405.D57   338.1'8   78-3246
ISBN 0-253-31806-8   1 2 3 4 5 82 81 80 79 78

Contents

Preface

The poor rice and wheat crops in several major countries during the early seventies have given rise to an acute awareness of the importance of increasing the production of food grains. It is well known that the constraints on agricultural production are more severe in low-income countries than they are in most of the high-income countries. Thus it is understandable that much attention is being given to the agricultural production and food supply problems that low-income countries face.

A good deal has in fact been accomplished. Several additional international agricultural research centers have been established and the financial support of these centers has been increased markedly. There is a renewed emphasis on agricultural research nationally and by academic institutions. That more research is called for is clear from the *World Food and Nutrition Study* of the National Academy of Sciences, 1977. Large amounts of additional capital are also being allocated to increase agricultural production in low-income countries. Meanwhile, recent ample crops, mainly in the major exporting countries, have served to replenish food grain stocks.

The biological constraints on potential food production have been substantially reduced by the advances in agricultural research and by the availability of additional capital. But it has become increasingly evident that adoption of the research contributions and efficient allocation of the additional capital are being seriously thwarted by the distortion of agricultural incentives. For lack of optimum incentives it is not possible for farmers in many low-income countries to produce the potential supply of food.

I had the privilege of organizing a three-day workshop on Resources, Incentives and Agriculture in 1977. It was sponsored by the American Academy of Arts and Sciences. W. David Hopper, D. Gale Johnson, Marc Nerlove, Ruth Zagorin, and John Voss joined with me in developing the plan for this venture. Sir John G. Crawford assisted us through correspondence. The invited papers and comments were prepared by individuals with expertise on agricultural development both national and international.

A generous grant from the International Development Research Center made the workshop and this book possible.

I have referred to the American Academy of Arts and Sciences as the sponsor. More precisely, however, it was the Midwest Center of the

AAAS. It is worth noting that the Midwest Center also sponsored a seminar in 1976, the results of which appear in *Human Migration* edited by William McNeill and Ruth Adams (Indiana University Press, 1978), and a symposium, "Transforming Knowledge into Food" cosponsored by the Midwest Center and the University of Minnesota in 1977.

I have received useful advice and help from John Voss, executive officer of the AAAS, and from Corinne S. Schelling and Alexandra Oleson of the Academy staff.

I am especially indebted to Mrs. Virginia K. Thurner for very competent editorial assistance.

Theodore W. Schultz
January 3, 1978

PART I

CONSTRAINTS ON
AGRICULTURAL PRODUCTION

On Economics and
Politics of Agriculture

THEODORE W. SCHULTZ

Food and agriculture are meaningful words in any language. Food symbolizes the basic products on which people depend for their daily nourishment, and agriculture is the principal source of food. But what these terms connote differs greatly among countries and even within particular countries. The production, distribution, and consumption of food also vary widely as a consequence of differences in economic and political organization. No one can deal with all of these complexities simultaneously in an all-inclusive manner. Every study of food and agriculture necessarily entails simplifications. The literature abounds with simple analytical models and some of them are useful. For the purpose at hand it is instructive to begin with two polarized models, neither of which comes close to reality. They nevertheless call attention to the prevailing realities that lie between the two models. The first presumes a country in which all production and consumption consists of wholly self-sufficient farms and farm households. There are no markets. An analysis of the allocation of resources and of the utilization of the products under these conditions requires rather simple economics. The second model presumes a country in which all agricultural production is nationalized and all food is deemed to be a public good that is distributed free of charge to consumers. In this model political decisions dominate the allocation of resources devoted to agriculture and the utilization of food.

In between these two highly simplified polarized models, there are the intricacies of the market economy and that of the political economy. The role of farmers as entrepreneurs, the function of incentives, and the effects of policy are important parts of the reality in every country. But the economics and politics of food and agriculture are very different stories. There is an economic market which provides information on real costs, supply, people's preferences, and demand. There is also a political market that provides information about the demand of in-

3

fluential interest groups for political benefits, and I shall presently elaborate on several important attributes of it.

It is obvious that in many parts of the world there is not enough food. Clearly more food coupled with better nutrition is needed. It is also evident that in most low-income countries such additional food and improvements in nutrition depend largely on increases in and composition of agricultural production. But there are pervasive physical and biological constraints on agricultural production along with various unsolved environmental problems. Pereira and Steppler provide an overview of these constraints and problems. As every farmer and agricultural scientist knows, Nature tends to resist the food-producing endeavors of man. Nor is Nature on her own bountiful; on the contrary, she is, and always will be, niggardly. Although there is still much land that could be made suitable for farming, it is for the most part harsh land. The properties of its soil, climate, and biological environment are such that it requires substantial investment to make such land suitable for farming. With the exception of large irrigation and drainage facilities, most of the land-improving investments that are required to increase the productivity of both unused land and worn-out soils must be made by farmers.

FARM ENTREPRENEURS

Farmers the world over, in dealing with costs, returns, and risks, are calculating economic agents. Within their small, individual, allocative domain they are fine-tuning entrepreneurs, tuning so subtly that many experts fail to see how efficient they are, as I have shown elsewhere (1964). Farmers, although they differ for reasons of schooling, health, and experience in their ability to perceive, interpret, and respond to new events in their farm enterprises, provide an essential human resource which is entrepreneurship. On most farms there is a second enterprise, the household one, and from the viewpoint of economic activities, housewives are also entrepreneurs in allocating their own time and in using farm products and purchased goods in household production. This talent of entrepreneurship is supplied by millions of men and women on small-scale producing units; and on this score, agriculture is a highly decentralized sector of the economy. Where governments have taken over the entrepreneurial function in farming, they have been far from efficient in modernizing agriculture. Where governments have not nationalized agriculture, the entrepreneurial roles of farmers and of farm housewives are important and the economic opportunities open to them really matter.

Governments of many countries seriously constrain the entrepreneurship of farmers and of farm housewives and thereby reduce the efficiency of agriculture and the standard of living of farm families.

INEVITABILITY OF DISEQUILIBRIA

It is possible to specify conditions under which agriculture would have arrived at a long-run equilibrium. Under such conditions the economic activities of farm people would be that of traditional agriculture (Schultz 1964). Farming would be essentially routine. There would be no new technology, no alterations in land being farmed, in the equipment used, or in the labor employed. The productivity of each of the various agricultural resources would remain constant, and the demand could be such that there would be no changes in relative prices. Under these conditions, long-run costs, risks, and returns would be known almost with certainty. Accordingly, there would be virtually no entrepreneurial function; routine management would suffice.

But the agriculture under consideration here is not in such a secular, persistent equilibrium state. On the contrary, the transformation of traditional agriculture into an increasingly more productive state, a process that is commonly referred to as "modernization," entails all manner of adjustments in farming as new and better opportunities become available. The value of the ability to deal with disequilibria is high in a dynamic economy (Schultz 1975).

Two important inferences can be derived from the economic dynamics of agricultural modernization. First, *economic disequilibria are inevitable*. They cannot be eliminated by law, by public policy, and surely not by rhetoric. Second, the function of farm entrepreneurs in perceiving, interpreting, and responding to new and better opportunities cannot be performed efficiently by governments.

INCENTIVES

Despite the arguments in New Delhi early in 1966 calling for government prohibition of imports of high-yielding seeds, the minister of agriculture decided to import the new Mexican dwarf wheat seed (see Hopper's paper). Some 18,000 tons of this wheat arrived from Mexico in late spring of 1966. The new seed was well suited to the agriculture of the Punjab and to adjacent areas. The farm price of wheat in India was high. The increase in the yield of the new seed enhanced the profitability of producing wheat. The farm entrepreneurs of the Punjab quickly adopted the new seed because the incentives to do so were highly favorable. The wheat agriculture of parts of north India became impressively dynamic. Production increased rapidly. Landowners profited and real wages of farm labor rose. We called it a *Green Revolution* and then all too many "analysts" in India and abroad turned to making predictions about the unfavorable social side effects of this type of economic dynamics instead of searching for ways of duplicating the Punjab success in other parts of agriculture.

What is needed are many Green Revolutions that would increase agricultural production throughout low-income countries. They could be had, but they are presently suppressed by the lack of adequate incentives. The state of incentives is such that in many countries it is unprofitable for farmers to undertake modernizing investments that would increase the productivity of agriculture. Most of the papers in the volume deal with distortions in incentives and their adverse effects on agricultural production.

Two questions arise at this point. What is the incentive to which farmers respond? And, what is an *optimum* economic incentive? The first consists of economic information that farmers use in calculating their expected costs, including risks, against the returns they expect to receive. The result of this calculation is the *incentive*. An incentive in this context is the product of economic information from which the farmer derives his expectations. The cost expectations encompass the rate of interest, rent on land, payments for irrigation water, equipment, fertilizer, other current production expenditures, and wages paid for labor, including the value of the farmer's own time devoted to farming. On returns, the expectations encompass the value placed on the farm products to be utilized in the farm household and the expected price of that part of the production to be sold. An *optimum* economic incentive provides the information that leads producers to allocate resources in ways that result in a maximum of production that will clear the market at the price that maximizes the utility of consumers.

Governments, however, by various means often alter open, competitive market incentives. The agricultural production effects of what governments do is a measure of the value that governments place on that production. I present a simple threefold classification of countries, based on the differences in the economic policies that governments pursue: there are countries (1) in which agricultural production is neither overvalued nor undervalued, (2) in which it is overvalued, and (3) in which it is undervalued.

There are very few countries that fully satisfy the specifications of the first classification. The countries in which the economic activities of agriculture are overvalued are predominately high-income countries. Members of the European Economic Community qualify. High taxes are levied on cereal imports; these were increased again in 1977 to off-set the decline in world market prices.[1] Since World War II, the large increases in grain production in France have been in large part a response to the very high internal European Economic Community prices. Beef imports are restricted to the point that they are virtually nil. Milk is greatly overpriced; there is underconsumption, overproduction, dumping of butter abroad at large public expense. The production of costly sugar beets in temperate Western countries is a long-standing classic example of the overvaluation of a major agricultural product within a large set of countries. In the Orient, the vastly overpriced rice in Japan is still another case in point. The third classification consists predominately of low-income countries. Major agricultural products are undervalued and the adverse production consequences of this undervaluation are serious. Whereas high-income countries presumably can "afford" to indulge in overvaluing agricultural products, the food situation in many low-income countries is such that they can ill afford to forego the increase in agricultural products which is lost as a consequence of economic policies.

The economic implications of overvalued and undervalued agricultural production can be stated simply: where production is overvalued, the producer incentives are too high to be optimal; where it is undervalued, producer incentives are below optimum. The observable effects on production strongly support these implications. I shall concentrate on the adverse production effects of policies in low-income countries that undervalue agricultural production.

It is my contention that the unrealized economic potential of agriculture in many low-income countries is large. The technical possibilities have become increasingly more favorable, but the economic opportunities that are required for farmers in these countries to realize this potential are far from favorable. Thus, for want of profitable incentives, farmers are not making the necessary investments, including the purchase of superior inputs. I argue that interventions by governments are the primary cause of the lack of optimum economic incentives. Although it has not always been by design, the state of incentives in many low-income countries suppresses the economic opportunities of farmers.

The objective before us is to determine the conditions that are both necessary and sufficient to attain the optimum increases in agricultural productivity. It has long been obvious that better agricultural inputs and techniques are necessary. New forms of capital—equipment, machines, roads, irrigation structures, and storage facilities—are also necessary. But the availability of superior seeds, fertilizers, pesticides, and animals, along with the other forms of new capital, is not sufficient to achieve large increases in agricultural productivity. What appears *not* to be obvious is the critical allocative role that producer incentives play in attaining the optimum increases in productivity. Thus, because of wrong incentives the real economic potential of agriculture is not being realized. *This unrealized economic potential is a measure of a pervasive economic disequilibrium in world agriculture* (see D. Gale Johnson 1977).

Land and farm people have their limitations. The productivity of farm land could be enhanced by investment, and its distribution by size of farms, as well as the prevailing tenure, could also be improved. Then, too, the health and schooling of farm people are below par. But despite these limitations, land and farm people are not the cause of the pervasive economic disequilibrium that characterizes the agriculture of low-income countries.

Since the early fifties there has been real progress in scientific agricultural research oriented to the requirements of poor countries. But the utilization of the contributions of this research is being seriously thwarted by the distortion of producer incentives. Accordingly, although more agricultural research is clearly warranted, as called for by the *World Food and Nutrition Study* of the National Academy of Sciences (1977), it is presently not the major limiting factor in the production possibilities in many low-income countries. Meanwhile, large sums of external capital are being made available to such countries for agricultural development. The effective utilization of this capital is also being thwarted by the suboptimum and distorted incentives in agriculture. Because of the bad state of incentives, the misallocation of much of this additional capital is inevitable. Thus, having achieved real progress in agricultural research along with considerable additional capital for agricultural development, the primary constraint that presently accounts for the persistent disequilibrium, which is revealed in the low productivity of agriculture in many low-income countries, is predominantly the lack of optimum incentives available to farmers.

In bringing economic analysis to bear on this problem, there are three key issues, namely, the value judgments implicit in economics, an understanding of the reasons why governments treat agriculture as they do, and a general assessment of the agricultural production consequences of governmental policies. I shall consider each of these issues in turn.

ON VALUE JUDGMENTS

In coping with value judgments, it is both simplistic and all too convenient to assume that what a government actually does to agriculture is a clear and consistent reflection of the true social values of the country regardless of the economic consequences. The easy analytical road is to accommodate the purposes of government or, for that matter, to embrace any of the various internal special political interest groups. But to proceed on this road reduces greatly the utility of economics. This fact is obvious in the case of interest groups. Although corporations, labor unions, farmer organizations, and consumer advocates perform useful functions, they are not innocent economic agents, for they do conspire to exact benefits for themselves at the expenses of others in the economy. Clearly, when economics is used to serve special interest organizations, it sells economic analysis short. Although governments obviously perform necessary functions, to make economics subservient to them regardless of what they do to the economy is to take the heart out of the utility of economics. When economists merely accommodate governments, they serve only to rationalize what is being done and lose their potential as educators. When this occurs, and it can be readily observed, economists become "yes-men" in the halls of political economy.[2]

The analytical core of economics is sufficiently robust to estimate the production effects of incentives and to evaluate the losses in income that are a consequence of distorted incentives. Furthermore, the costs and the personal income effects of welfare programs can also be estimated and evaluated. Since inequalities in the distribution of personal income are an important welfare problem, an example of an analytical approach is as follows. The costs of improvements in nutrition and in health that the poorest of the urban families achieve as a result of the "fair price shops" established by some governments can be ascertained. If the food for this purpose is acquired by the government by procuring food grains from farmers below market prices, the adverse effect on agricultural production is a part of the implicit costs of providing food for the "fair price shops." However small or large the real costs of providing food grains for shops, there are also alternative approaches to reduce the inequality in the distribution of personal income. Whether the alternative approaches are less costly relative to benefits needs to be determined. Several papers in this volume deal with aspects of the welfare problem. Schuh's analysis is a major contribution in clarifying economic relationships between agricultural production efficiency and improvements in personal income.

Biases of economists aside, economic studies of production and of welfare and of the complex interrelations between them need not become stranded on value judgments. It is noteworthy that there are two academic styles for dealing with economic assumptions and value judgments. From the twenties to the fifties it was the style to question the assumptions of theoretical analysis and dispute the value judgments asserted to be implicit in the theory. This approach has been called, quite properly, "negative economics." Since then the emphasis has shifted to whether or not the implications of the economic theory, given its assumptions and value judgments, are validated by observable economic behavior. This approach has become known as "positive economics."[3]

It is my contention that economic theory and evidence tell a consistent story about the adverse effects of distortions in incentives on agricultural production and on welfare.

WHY MANY GOVERNMENTS
UNDERVALUE AGRICULTURE

It is not cynical to say that governments do what they deem necessary to survive. The individuals who govern are politically dependent on the support of particular population groups that make the regime viable. Economic policies are in this context a means to maintain political support. On the policies that are pursued, there is no lack of rationalizations by those in charge of the government and by the theoreticians that serve them. Although it is debatable how much governments learn from their mistakes, it is obvious that to the extent they do learn from their errors in economic affairs, they are slow learners compared to farmers' ability to learn from their experience. All too little attention, however, has been given to the factors that determine the learning function of governments.

As already noted, there is a "political market." The economic consequences of this market are very different from those of an open, competitive market which is not controlled by government and not manipulated privately. Economic theory is being extended to show the implications of the political market and to test the implications against observable behavior. The underlying assumption of this extension of economics is that the political market function is to maximize the political benefits that are demanded by individuals and groups of individuals who have access to and can influence the political market.

There are many "reasons" why governments undervalue the economic contributions of agriculture. These reasons are strung together by various ideologies, most of which have been "imported" from high-income countries.

Even though the rural population in low-income countries is much the larger, the political market strongly favors the urban population at the direct expense of rural people. Politically, urban consumers and industry demand cheap food. Accordingly, it is more important politically to provide cheap rice in Bangkok than to provide optimum price incentives for rice farmers in Thailand. For Thailand it is an easy policy to administer; as long as the country has an exportable rice surplus, an export tax on rice suffices. This tax has the additional political advantage of producing revenue for the government. Export taxes to acquire public revenue are more indirect in the case of state marketing boards. Even before the bankruptcy of colonialism, state marketing boards were launched on the assumption that they would be an efficient way to stabilize the agricultural prices of major export producers, especially throughout Central Africa. But they were soon transformed into internal revenue agencies. Having been vested with monopoly powers, they proceed to pay a low price to farmers and then to sell the product at the higher export market price. Revenue thus is forthcoming until the producer disincentives reduce production to the point where there is no exportable surplus.

Furthermore, the undervaluation of agriculture by governments is still being rationalized by an array of arguments that include the colonial heritage, the backwardness of agriculture, and its presumed low estate in contributing to economic growth. Agriculture in many low-income countries carries the stigma of having been the supplier of raw materials and of some food products that served the economic interest of the colonial powers. The view is still widely held that agriculture is inherently a backward sector; the presumption is that rural people resist modernization notwithstanding the occasional small "green revolutions." From the point of view of those who manage the political market, the lowly cultivator is viewed as indifferent to economic incentives because it is presumed that he is strongly committed to his traditional low level of productivity. Thus, the stage is set for the doctrine that industrialization is the mainspring of economic growth and economic policy is designed to give top priority to industry and this includes keeping food grains cheap.

Still another reason, often cited, why governments of some low-income countries turn away from agriculture relates to the presumed adverse effects of international prices and trade. World market prices of agricultural products and inputs (e.g., fertilizers) have been unstable. It is true that the world price events associated with World War I, the Great Depression, World War II, and the recent worldwide inflation, compounded by monopoly oil prices and the price effects of short crops, caused a great deal of economic instability. Much is also made of the secular decline in the terms of trade of agricultural crops, but this decline in large measure reflects the relative decline in real

costs of producing farm crops. In the United States, for example, the
relative prices of "all crops" declined by 40% between 1910 and 1972.
Despite government price supports and complementary farm programs
to raise crop prices, the production effects of the decline in real costs
could not be stayed. D. Gale Johnson analyzes this issue more fully in
this volume and also the issue pertaining to the losses and gains from
trade during the recent very high world prices of agricultural products
and fertilizers. Contrary to the widely held view, he shows that for
most of the low-income countries the gains exceeded the losses.

Currently, various arguments are advanced on behalf of welfare considerations with the implication that economic efficiency in agricultural
production is at many points inconsistent with the welfare of the population. This concept of welfare has also been "imported" from high-
income countries. It is characterized by progressive income taxes, with
a substantial part of the income from them allocated to low-income
people as income transfers. What these high-income countries do in
collecting public revenue and making income transfers is a far cry from
the procurement of food grains from farmers to supply urban "fair-
price shops" and by this means subsidizing consumers at the expense
of agriculture.

Moreover, the adoption and efficient use of new high-yielding seed
varieties is not necessarily inconsistent with gains in the welfare of
small farmers. Barker and Anden (1975) show that between 1966 and
1972 small farmers were about as prompt as large farmers in adopting
modern rice varieties in various parts of Asia and in profiting from the
adoption. Their sample consists of twenty-seven villages throughout
Southeast Asia. Except for one village (Pedapulleru, India), the rates
of adoption by large and small farms were very similar. The percent of
farmers reporting increases in profit from the better rice varieties was
remarkably similar for small and large farms, except in Pedapulleru
(Barker and Anden, Table 14). The presumed trade-off between efficiency in production and the welfare gains of small farmers in modernizing agriculture is therefore subject to serious doubts.

The most compelling reason why government interventions adverse
to agriculture become more serious over time arises out of the fact that
the economic effects of any major intervention call for additional interventions. Thus the process of expanding the political market is self-
generating. One control leads to more controls and as a consequence
governments become increasingly enmeshed in administering the
economic affairs of agriculture. As a rule, this process begins on the
convenient premise that a market-oriented economy is inherently inefficient in achieving economic growth. The presumption is that the mar-

ket is most inefficient in providing the necessary inducements for rapid domestic industrialization. The curtailment of imports of industrial products protects the infant industries. The import substitution that this entails, however, increases internal prices, including those that farm people pay for industrial goods. The growth of infant industries is also affected by the level of wages, and real wages in turn are strongly affected by the price of food. In the short run cheap food can be had by reducing the internal prices that are paid to farmers, and by importing, as many countries did in the late fifties and sixties, large quantities of P.L. 480 cheap food grains from the United States.

Further enmeshment of governments in agriculture becomes the order of the day. The market is deemed to be inefficient in producing and distributing the new seeds of the high-yielding varieties of crops and the government proceeds to nationalize this activity. The established private agricultural marketing system is viewed as the cause of regional and of specific urban food shortages; again, as occurred in India, the solution chosen is to nationalize these markets. Elsewhere, additional state marketing boards have been established to replace the private agricultural markets, as in Kenya (see Heyer et al. 1976). When it becomes evident that farmers are curtailing their use of fertilizer for lack of incentives, governments, instead of allowing the prices received by farmers to rise, resort to subsidizing fertilizers and thereby become even more enmeshed in administering agricultural prices.

PRODUCTION CONSEQUENCES OF UNDERVALUING AGRICULTURE

The effects of weather aside, the normal annual, peacetime production of the world's agriculture is remarkably stable. It is much more stable than industry, with its business cycles, its abrupt declines in plant utilization and the associated unemployment. This secular stability of agriculture is a clue to the fact that large, quick increases in *total* agricultural productivity are not possible. Even under the best of circumstances, it takes more than a year or two to complete particular types of capacity-increasing investments. These simply cannot be had on short notice. Annual purchases of fertilizer and of other currently acquired inputs will not suffice to enlarge the aggregate productive capacity of agriculture. Shifts among crops in response to a marked increase in the price of a particular agricultural product relative to other products that are close substitutes in production are often large in one or two years. But agricultural production as a whole cannot be increased that quickly.

Substantial additional agricultural capacity requires two important time-consuming steps. There will be lags on the part of farmers in deciding that the improvement in incentives is not transitory. Sufficient confidence to undertake the required investment may not come readily in many low-income countries once policy is changed for the better because of bad past experiences. The next step consists of undertaking and completing various intermediate and long-term investments that will enhance the capacity of agriculture. These steps are both necessary in the modernization of agriculture. There are no short cuts. Quick modernization is a will-o'-the-wisp. Optimum incentives for a couple of years will not suffice.

It is no secret in economics that there is an important difference between the behavior over time of the demand for food and of the supply of agricultural products. As economic growth and agricultural modernization occur over time, the demand curve shifts to the right (increases) mainly because of rising family income and population growth. The demand for food in low-income countries is a good deal more elastic than that in high-income countries. The supply curve, however, is more complex. During any short period *it is highly inelastic*. But economic history tells us clearly that over time as modernization takes place, the supply curve *shifts to the right and down*. The real price of most farm products declines as a consequence of reductions in the costs of production. A considerable part of the real welfare gains over time is accounted for by reductions in costs of agricultural production. Herein lies the prospect for substantial welfare gains in low-income countries during the next several decades.

The chain of actions and interactions to improvements in incentives is long and complex. It includes: (1) activities of agricultural research enterprises; (2) response of farmers in adopting the worthwhile output of that research; (3) price of capital and its efficient allocation in increasing the physical and biological capacity of agriculture; (4) quality of the stock of human capital, mainly schooling and health of farm people; (5) efficient markets for agricultural products and for the inputs that farmers purchase; and (6) use of public funds to subsidize the food grains that are made available to those in the population who are deemed to be too poor to pay open-market prices. Currently, however, this agricultural chain is not in good shape.

The distortion of agricultural prices affects the adoption of the research output and this in turn affects the research agenda. Price distortion, therefore, tends to misguide agricultural research. Overvalued products receive unwarranted attention and all too few resources are allocated to research of the undervalued products. National agricultural research is more directly subject to the implied misallocation of research resources than that at international research centers but even the latter are not immune (see Evenson's analysis of this issue in this volume). Moreover, it is noteworthy that governments that undervalue agriculture have a propensity to treat agricultural scientists as high-class clerks.

Sugar beets are vastly overvalued in the high-income countries that have temperate climates, as already noted. As a consequence, far too much research is devoted to sugar beets. The main economic aspect of this problem turns on the differences between research costs and social returns to the research. When the agricultural product is overpriced, research workers are misled on the social value of their contributions to that product. Research on improving wheat varieties suitable to Mexico was in part induced by the overpricing of wheat within Mexico. But the social contribution of the new high-yielding varieties was less than the price that farmers received. In India also, during the early years of the rapid increases in wheat production, wheat was overpriced. The social returns to rice research in Japan are much less than the private returns that are garnered by farmers as a consequence of the very high rice price supports (see Otsuka 1977).

In terms of the food supply over much of the world, the general undervaluing of agricultural products reduces the potential returns to agricultural research. The resulting adverse effects on the relevant research enterprises are not to be dismissed lightly. All too little research has been undertaken on high-yielding wheat varieties in the Argentine as a consequence of distortion of wheat and fertilizer prices. I have noted elsewhere (1977) that in Thailand the Bangkok prices of corn and rice have been approximately equal per ton although in the open world market the price of rice tends to be more than twice that of corn. Wong (1976) has estimated the adverse effect of Thailand's export tax on rice production and on related research. In the case of corn, much of which is exported by Thailand to Japan at world prices, the favorable price has induced research to develop hybrid varieties suitable to Thailand. It should be noted that, in the context of my analysis, corn in Thailand is neither over- nor underpriced. Hertford et al. (1977) show that research on wheat in Colombia started early and new local varieties did even better than Mexican wheats. Nevertheless, the acreage devoted to wheat fell sharply from 1953 to 1973, in large part because of the importation of cheap P.L. 480 wheat; the resources allocated to wheat research, in 1972 prices, were cut by half between 1967 and 1973.

Incentives to produce rice, the principal food crop throughout much of South Asia, are low because it is much underpriced by many governments. At the same time, fertilizer is overpriced. The adverse effects on national rice research strongly support the argument here advanced. India is a prime case in point. Between 1948–52 and 1972 wheat production in India increased more than fourfold, whereas the rate of increase in rice production was half that of wheat. The 1976 *Asian Agricultural Survey* (Asian Development Bank 1977, Appendix I, Tables 4.4 and 8.6) shows that the farm prices of paddy at three locations in India for June–July, 1976, were among the lowest in the eleven countries listed, excepting only Bangladesh and Burma. The high Indian farm price of fertilizer relative to that of paddy was exceeded only in China and Thailand. The Indian yields per hectare are the lowest. These 1976 prices and yields are consistent with the study by Timmer and Falcon (1975) based on 1970 farm prices and yields.

The prices of wheat and rice in India in relation to world prices for each year between 1961 and 1972 are estimated by Sukhatme (1976). The official exchange rates show wheat substantially overpriced, especially after 1963. By the free market exchange rates for rupees, wheat in India, during most of these years, was somewhat underpriced. Rice, however, was seriously underpriced by both exchange rate tests. Applying the official exchange rate, rice was underpriced between 10 and 50% over the period 1961 to 1971, except in 1963. Adjusting these prices for the overvalued rupee, the open market exchange rates for the rupee show that rice was underpriced by 50% and more, except in 1963, when it was underpriced by 31%. (See Tables A-1 and A-2 of my Appendix A, in which I consider in detail rice and wheat prices in India.) No wonder that the profitability of growing rice has been much impaired.

Although rice research in India has been going on for decades, fertilizer-responsive varieties were long neglected, as Evenson (1977) has shown. The prevailing overpriced fertilizer and the underpriced paddy continue to confront the rice research enterprises with discouraging price signals.

Agricultural research endeavors throughout much of Central Africa are even more disoriented than in Asia by the economic disarray of agriculture. The prospects are dim, even for the agricultural research that has been organized and supported by foundations and by funds from foreign governments. Many African farmers, because incentives are lacking, are not adopting the available improved plants and techniques.

The process of increasing the productive capacity of agriculture requires not only the inputs that embody the output of research but also various forms of complementary capital. Many excellent studies are now available on the adoption by farmers of new and more productive inputs resulting from research. I shall deal all too briefly with the economics of adoption. Unfortunately, studies of the functioning of the capital markets that serve farmers in low income countries are at best mainly descriptive. Rice, among the annual crops, and tree crops require more complementary forms of capital than most other crops before it becomes profitable for farmers to adopt the superior varieties presently available. The underpricing of farm products seriously thwarts both the optimum use of capital and the adoption rate. It stands repeating: when intermediate and long-term investments are required, it takes considerable time before the adoptions will yield returns. Moreover, the time pattern of costs, the time it takes to obtain the additional productivity, and the risks over time all vary from crop to crop and from country to country.

One thing, however, is clear. Wherever the farm product is underpriced, even though superior varieties are at hand, the adoption is at best only partial. The British palm research center in Nigeria developed varieties of palms that are much more productive than the native palms. But few Nigerian farmers could afford to plant and bring the better varieties to fruition, mainly because the state marketing board seriously reduced the price that producers receive for palm fruits. The benefits from the research of the Nigerian palm research center were realized, however, in West Malaysia where the producers of palm fruits were not exploited by a government monopoly vested in a marketing board.[4]

Policy makers and some agricultural experts make the mistake of generalizing the adoption process that occurs under exceptional circumstances. When the cost of adoption is small relative to the value of the gains in productivity, when the gains can be had during the course of a crop year, and when the additional risks are minimal, adoption occurs rapidly even though the price of the product is low. But this combination of costs, returns, and risk is very much the exception. It is true that the adoption of hybrid corn in the heart of the Corn Belt in the United States during the thirties took place rapidly at a time when the price of corn in retrospect is viewed as having been low. The patterns of adoption, the difference in them between the Corn Belt and the South, and the reasons for this difference are set forth by Griliches (1960). The rapid adoption of Mexican wheat in the Punjab is another case in point. Although it was a more costly innovation than hybrid corn in the United States because of the difference in fertilizer requirements, wheat at that time was overpriced in India in relation to its international price (see Appendix, Table A-2). These two cases, however, are exceptional because at the time and place of the adoption no large investment in complementary forms of capital was required.

Irrigation and related investment to control and to improve the utilization of water are especially important in rice production. Tube wells and on-farm ditches to distribute the water are investments that farmers can and do undertake when the costs are warranted relative to the returns. But there are some irrigation facilities that are beyond the ability of individual farmers even though they were to act collectively. C. H. Hanumantha Rao (1975) has argued convincingly that the government of India has been allocating all too few public funds to irrigation. Randolph Barker in his paper in this volume agrees and he examines in some detail the unsolved problems pertaining to the investment in irrigation.

But in undertaking this form and also other types of investment to increase the capacity of agriculture, the government and the farmers of India are at best responding to price signals that are badly distorted. The underpriced rice is by all odds the wrong signal in allocating capital efficiently to and within agriculture.

The elimination of the segmentation of farm-product markets is one step in correcting a part of price distortions. Another important step would be to stop all types of grain procurement. The protection that is given to the fertilizer industry in India is costly to the economy (M. S. Rao 1972). The freeing of internal fertilizer prices is yet another step in reducing agricultural price distortions. Import restrictions on all manner of industrial products are also contributing to the price distortions in which India is enmeshed. Last but not least would be to use public revenue to buy the food grains for the "fair-price shops," instead of acquiring these grains at the expense of farmers.

CONCLUDING REMARKS

When the political market suppresses the entrepreneurial role of farmers, countries cannot succeed in modernizing agriculture efficiently. Political prices cut two ways. In a goodly number of high-income countries farm products are overpriced and food is dear. In many low-income countries food is kept cheap at the expense of farmers and there are food shortages and such pricing forecloses the production of food more cheaply over time. In such low-income countries more and cheaper food will only be forthcoming provided that it is profitable for farmers to modernize agriculture.

But the profitability and success of agriculture in many low-income countries are much impaired by governments. When internal markets are segmented by government the advantages of the full extent of the market are lost. When exports and imports are restricted, agricultural prices call forth uneconomic production. When state marketing boards are granted a monopoly, the prospects for agriculture become dim. When governments authorize the procurement of food grains from farmers, the incentives to invest and to adopt superior varieties and techniques are impaired. When the welfare costs of "fair-price shops" are not financed by the government but are borne by agriculture, the full welfare gains from agricultural modernization are not to be had. Lastly, when ministers of agriculture treat agricultural scientists as clerks, the agricultural research enterprises become stagnant.

Incentives do matter. The potential large increases in agricultural production in many low-income countries cannot be realized as long as farm entrepreneurs are confronted by wrong incentives.

NOTES

1. EEC importers in late 1977 were paying import levies of $127 a ton for wheat and $42 a ton for corn, nearly double the levies of a year earlier. U.S.D.A. *World Agricultural Situation*, July, 1977, p.6.

2. I examined this issue somewhat more fully in my Elmhirst Lecture, "On Economics, Agriculture, and the Political Economy," International Conference of Agricultural Economists, July 26–August 4, 1976, Nairobi, Kenya. See forthcoming *Proceedings, 16th International Conference of Agricultural Economists, Nairobi, Kenya, 1976.*

3. This concise view of styles is from Harry G. Johnson [1975].

4. Nigerian exports of palm oil have declined sharply to the point that only 50 metric tons were exported in 1973 and none in 1974, whereas the exports from West Malaysia rose almost fivefold from 180,000 metric tons in 1967 to 872,000 in 1974.

REFERENCES

Asian Development Bank. 1977. *Asian Agricultural Survey 1976. Rural Asia: Challenge and Opportunity.* Manila, Philippines.

Barker, Randolph, and Anden, Teresa. 1975. "Factors Influencing the Use of Modern Rice Technology in the Study Areas." In *Changes in Rice Farming in Selected Areas in Asia*, pp.17–40. Los Baños, Philippines: International Rice Research Institute.

Evenson, Robert E. 1977. "Cycles in Research Productivity in Sugarcane, Wheat, and Rice." In *Resource Allocation and Productivity in National and International Agricultural Research*, ed. Thomas M. Arndt et al., pp.209–36. Minneapolis: University of Minnesota Press.

Food and Agriculture Organization. 1965. "Inter-Relationships of Grains and Rice in International Trade," *Commodity Bulletin*, 39:74–75.

Griliches, Zvi. 1960. "Hybrid Corn and the Economics of Innovation." *Science* 132 (July 29):275–80.

Hertford, Reed; Ardila, Jorge; Rocha, Andres; and Trujillo, Carlos. 1977. "Productivity of Agricultural Research in Colombia." In *Resource Allocation and Productivity in National and International Agricultural Research*, ed. Thomas M. Arndt et al., pp.86–123. Minneapolis: University of Minnesota Press.

Heyer, Judith; Maitha, J. K.; and Senga, W. M. 1976. *Agricultural Development in Kenya: An Economic Analysis*. Lusaka Dar Es Salaam Addis Ababa: Oxford University Press.

Johnson, D. Gale. 1977. "Food Production Potentials in Developing Countries: Will They Be Realized?" Occasional paper no. 1: St. Paul, Minn.: Bureau of Economic Studies, Macalester College.

Johnson, Harry G. 1975. "Learning and Libraries: Academic Economics as a Profession: Its Bearing on the Organisation and Retrieval of Economic Knowledge." *Minerva* 13 (Winter):621–32.

National Academy of Sciences. 1977. *World Food and Nutrition Study*. Washington, D.C.

Otsuka, Keijiro. 1977. "Economic Diagnosis of Rice Policy in Japan Since World War II." Preliminary draft of Ph.D. research. University of Chicago.

Rao, C. H. Hanumantha. 1975. *Technological Change and the Distribution of Gains in Indian Agriculture*. Delhi: Macmillan Company of India.

Rao, Musunuru S. 1972. "Protection to Fertilizer Industry and Its Impact on Indian Agriculture." Ph.D. dissertation, University of Chicago.

Schultz, Theodore W. 1964. *Transforming Traditional Agriculture*. New Haven: Yale University Press (Reprint edition, New York: Arno Press, 1976).

————. 1970. "Agricultural Modernization Altering the World Food and Feed Grain Competition." In *Proceedings of the International Conference on Mechanized Dryland Farming*, ed. W. C. Burrow et al., pp.220–35. Moline, Ill.: Deere & Company.

————. 1975. "The Value of the Ability to Deal with Disequilibria." *Journal of Economic Literature* 13(September):827–46.

————. 1977. "Uneven Prospects for Gains from Agricultural Research Related to Economic Policy." In *Resource Allocation and Productivity in National and International Agricultural Research*, ed. Thomas M. Arndt et al., pp.578–89. Minneapolis: University of Minnesota Press.

————. Forthcoming. "On Economics, Agriculture, and the Political Economy." Elmhirst Lecture. In *Proceedings, 16th International Conference of Agricultural Economists, Nairobi, Kenya, 1976*.

Sukhatme, Vasant A. 1976. "The Utilization of High Yielding Rice and Wheat Varieties in India: An Economic Assessment." Ph.D. dissertation, University of Chicago.

Timmer, C. Peter, and Falcon, Walter P. 1975. "The Political Economy of Rice Production and Trade in Asia." In *Agriculture in Development Theory*, ed. Lloyd G. Reynolds, pp.373–408. New Haven: Yale University Press.

U.S. Department of Agriculture. 1977. *World Agricultural Situation* (July).

Wong, Chung Ming. 1976. "A Model of the Rice Economy of Thailand." Ph.D. dissertation, University of Chicago.

Appendix A

On Rice and Wheat Prices

1. The ruling world market price of wheat is far less than that of rice. Historically, however, on the British market prior to 1911–1915, the wholesale price of American wheat per ton was more costly than a ton of Rangoon rice. As of 1867–77, the price of wheat exceeded that of rice by 30%. By 1947–62, wheat was selling at about three-fifths of the price of rice. FAO *Commodity Bulletin* No. 39 (1965) gives the following price relationships:

	Wheat price as a percent of rice price
1867–77	130
1886–90	118
1896–1900	110
1911–15	100
1921–29	83
1930–39	79
1947–62	59

Since then, using the Indian market price of rice and wheat imports, the price of imported wheat was 54% of that of rice in 1970, 63% in 1972 and 45% during the first five months of 1977.

2. Difficult as it is to determine the comparability of domestic and imported rice, there is little room for doubt, even so, that the annual wholesale prices of milled rice at Sambalpur, India, have been far below the approximate c.i.f. price of rice imports. At the official exchange rates, except for 1963, the internal price was as much as 42% below the import price (col. 4, Table A-1). Adjusting for the overvaluation of the rupee, the internal price of rice, except for 1963, tended to be in the neighborhood of one-half the international price of rice imports, as shown in col. 5, Table A-1.

Table A-1

Wholesale Price of Rice at Official Exchange Rate and at Shadow (Open-Market) Exchange Rate, Sambalpur, India, and the Market Price of Rice Imports, 1961 to 1972

	Wholesale Price at Sambalpur, Orissa, Using Official Rate of Exchange	*Wholesale Price at Sambalpur, Orissa, Using Market Rate of Exchange*	*Price of Rice Imports*	*Two Measures of the Underpricing of Rice*	
				Official Exchange Rate (1) *percent of* (3)	*Market Exchange Rate* (2) *percent of* (3)
Year	(1)	(2)	(3)	(4)	(5)
	(U.S. dollars per metric ton)				
1961	82.00	54.66	114.34	72	48
1962	100.00	64.99	118.54	84	55
1963	131.00	90.99	117.51	111	77
1964	119.00	72.86	143.15	83	51
1965	124.00	66.62	172.53	72	39
1966	146.00	79.79	159.62	91	50
1967	116.00	80.65	199.58	58	40
1968	136.00	100.39	179.08	76	56
1969	131.00	90.95	184.42	71	49
1970	135.00	80.74	138.16	98	58
1971	131.00	76.62	156.31	84	49
1972	151.00	107.55	218.94	69	49

Source: Cols. (1), (2), and (3) are from Vasant A. Sukhatme, 1976, "The Utilization of High Yielding Rice and Wheat Varieties in India: An Economic Assessment," Ph.D. Dissertation, University of Chicago, Table 18, p.76.

3. The annual wholesale prices of wheat in the Punjab, at the official exchange rate, 1961 to 1963, were 15 to 29% above the import price. For the years 1964 to 1972, the internal price tended to be about 50% higher than the import price (col. 4, Table A-2). When adjustments are made for the overvalued rupee, the internal wheat price ranges from 77 to 116% of the import price, tending to approximate the import price after 1967 (col. 5, Table A-2).

4. In the procurement of wheat in the Punjab the government paid close to the market price during 1968–69 to 1970–71. But in the procurement of rice in Andhra Pradesh the price paid by the government was 20% below the market price (C. H. Hanumantha Rao, 1975, Tables 7-4).

5. In India the farm harvest prices of rice and wheat have been repeatedly fragmented by procurement policies that are enforced by zonal systems that cordon off the movement of rice between areas. This price of rice in rupees per quintal in Andhra Pradesh, between 1960–61

Table A-2

Wholesale Price of Wheat at Official Exchange Rate and at Shadow (Open-Market) Exchange Rate, Moga, Punjab, India, and Market Price of Wheat Imports, 1961 to 1972

Year	Wholesale Price at Moga, Punjab, Using Official Rate of Exchange (1)	Wholesale Price at Moga, Punjab, Using Market Rate of Exchange (2)	Price of Wheat Imports (3)	Two Measures of the Over- and Underpricing of Wheat	
				Official Exchange Rate (1) percent of (3) (4)	Market Exchange Rate (2) percent of (3) (5)
	(U.S. dollars per metric ton)				
1961	92.00	61.39	79.75	115	77
1962	98.00	63.09	80.66	121	78
1963	96.00	66.78	74.52	129	90
1964	117.00	71.19	79.61	147	89
1965	125.00	67.18	73.09	171	92
1966	116.00	65.19	78.22	148	83
1967	119.00	82.78	80.33	148	103
1968	114.00	83.94	79.21	144	106
1969	124.00	86.40	79.61	156	109
1970	125.00	74.62	74.40	168	100
1971	124.00	72.63	82.07	151	88
1972	128.00	91.63	79.29	161	116

Source: Cols. (1), (2), and (3) are from Vasant A. Sukhatme, 1976, "The Utilization of High Yielding Rice and Wheat Varieties in India: An Economic Assessment," Ph.D. Dissertation, University of Chicago, Table 19, p.77.

and 1965–66, on the average was about 6% higher than the price of rice in Tamilnadu. In 1966–67 the price difference between these two "zones" was 28%; and in 1968–69, it increased to 34%. Then in 1969–70, the farm harvest price of rice in Andhra Pradesh was 13% below that in Tamilnadu (C. H. Hanumantha Rao, already cited, Table 7.3).

The Changing Patterns of Constraints on Food Production in the Third World

SIR CHARLES PEREIRA

The apparent 1977 glut of food grains in the high-production areas of North America emphasizes the lack of storage provision for a world reserve. Ever since the World Food Conference in Rome in 1974, governments and international organizations have argued about the funding of storage operations, with little success. The U. S. government, faced with an immediate problem, decided to reduce the acreage to be planted. This sudden surplus, which even now is barely adequate as a world reserve, emphasizes the world problem of maldistribution of food production, which already involves hunger on a massive scale. The first report of the International Food Policy Research Institute (1976) calculated that the current rate of progress in food production was not enough to avoid a world food crisis in ten years' time. The Institute's second report (1977) reminded us that despite the dramatic recovery of grain supplies in the past two years, the per capita production in two-thirds of the low-income countries categorized by the United Nations as "most severely affected" was still below the level of the beginning of the 1970s. Food aid has not been enough to prevent a similar fall in the per capita consumption in most of them.

Figure 1 illustrates the world problem. Both high-income and developing countries have increased their food supplies at similar rates but that of the less-developed countries has barely succeeded in matching their population growth. As a result, on the left-hand side of the graph the problem is of fluctuation of supplies and markets, while on the right the problem is the present hunger of the undernourished, which the United Nations now estimates to total 450 millions. Table 1 indicates the increase of this problem over the next two decades. Estimates vary, but their overall message is consistent; they conceal, of course, wide variations both within each group of countries and even wider inequalities within many countries. Hunger is thus already a world problem which, without strong international action, could be-

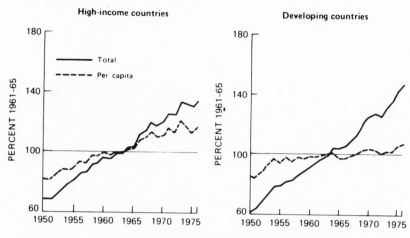

Figure 1. Growth of Food Production

Source: National Academy of Sciences. 1977. *World Food and Nutrition Study.* Washington, D.C.

Note: Food production has been increasing equally fast in both groups, but population growth has cancelled gains in supplies per capita in the less-developed countries.

come rapidly and tragically worse. I want to discuss two theses on the strategy and one on the tactics of the campaign to rid the world of hunger.

THE DOMINANT CONSTRAINTS

The first of my theses is that agricultural technologies have already been developed to the stage at which the historical dominance of biological and physical constraints on production has now given place to political, social, and economic constraints. Although many scientific and technical problems remain to be solved, their scale is now minor in comparison with that of the "social engineering" required.

In the simplest terms, the political interest of the less-developed countries in their own rural problems has not yet reached the level of sustained national priority, however often such priority may be declared at times of urgent food shortages. Largely as a result of the lack of interest by the educated minority, management is the critical missing factor in the agricultural production of the poorer countries.

A further constraint is the acceptance among the donor countries that the development of all countries must follow the same historical path,

Table 1

Food Production Needed to Sustain World Population Growth

Population (millions)

Year	High-Income Countries (mainly in temperate zones)	Less-Developed Countries (mainly in tropics and subtropics)	World Production of Food Grains (million tons)
1977	1200	2800	1200
A.D. 2000	1700	4800	2000 (minimum)
			3000 (full supply)

Source: National Academy of Sciences. 1976. *Science, Technology, and Society: A Prospective Look.* Summary and Conclusions of the Bellagio Conference, June 20–27, 1976, Bellagio, Italy. Washington, D.C.

and that full urban development with priority for higher education must precede attention to the unexciting details of rural areas. As a result the World Food Conference in 1974 was told that only 10% of international aid funds for the last three decades had gone into agriculture. This has produced an unnecessary lag in agricultural development.

An overriding constraint is the time scale. British agriculture was neglected, for trading-policy reasons, until 1939. Wartime expansion secured the maximum area of cropping in our small islands. Wartime lessons were well learned and from 1950 a substantial effort was made to improve output from the limited land available. Major inputs of fertilizers, capital, research and development, technical advice and agricultural education, with a literate population of farmers under a competent administration, achieved a 75% increase of output in the quarter century from 1950 to 1975. Yet, with none of these technical advantages, the poorer tropical countries must achieve an even greater expansion of food production in the same time span, as outlined in Table 1.

The constraint of time scale is rendered more acute by a factor of fundamental importance which has been largely ignored in the voluminous discussions on the world food situation. This factor is the geographical, and hence climatic, redistribution of the world population. Over 80% of the 2,500 million increase to A.D. 2000 will become dependent on agriculture in the Inter-Tropical Convergence Zone, where the hazards of drought and of flood are inescapably greater than in the temperate zones. The incidence of large-scale famines must thus be expected to increase more rapidly than an extrapolation of past experience would indicate.

That this constraint of time scale is itself changing, that it is becoming more acute, is implicit in the accelerating nature of human population growth, as Malthus foresaw in 1798. He was then concerned with predictions for a distant future. We now labor under the immediate constraint that the problem is already with us, as indicated by the United Nations assessment of some 450 million people now seriously short of food in southeast Asia, Africa, Latin America, and the Middle East. Immediate short-term relief can be won only by the mass transfer of food over large distances. This is, both logically and economically, no solution to the main problems although it distracts attention and resources from them.

THE PHYSICAL AND BIOLOGICAL CONSTRAINTS

The constraints which I have outlined now replace those physical and biological constraints which have dominated agricultural history, but I want to look briefly at the main technical fields in which success has been essential for progress in food production in less-developed countries. Throughout most of their history the developing countries have responded to increased demands for food by expanding the areas planted. Only a few still have that option, and much of the land remaining unused has limitations of potable water supply, soil, climate, topography, and communications. The major increase must come from the production of existing farmlands and ranches. Intensification involves both the removal of limitations of nutrition and of pests and diseases in order to realize the yield potential of local varieties or breeds best adapted to the environment, and also the selection of improved genetic material capable of greater response to inputs. The very effective output of the system of international centers, which are maintained by the Consultative Group for International Agricultural Research, has extended the collection, assessment, and use of the germ plasm of food crops worldwide; although response to fertilizers is critically important for major increases in food production, there are many independent improvements. By selection for rapid growth and for better plant geometry it has proved possible to improve both yield and reliability. The International Rice Research Institute in the Philippines has shown, for instance, that new rice varieties grown without fertilizer have consistently outyielded traditional varieties at four experimental stations (De Datta et al. 1974) but in practice they are grown for their profitable response to inputs.

Intensification of cropping, which is essential if the vast and growing urban populations of the less-developed countries are to be fed, makes increased inputs inevitable. By greatly increasing the return per man-hour of labor, per millimeter of rain, per cubic meter of irrigation water, and above all, per hectare of land, the increased nutrient inputs make both economic and social sense. Organizations to manufacture and distribute the fertilizers and to supply the credit to enable the farmer to use them are well-established techniques already fairly successful in some less-developed countries. That inputs and credit can be organized rapidly with determined government support and sound international advice is already demonstrated in the "M 99" program of rice production in the Philippines.

All such improved production depends critically on a measure of government control in the use and conservation of the basic resources of soil and water. This applies in all climates from the semiarid to the humid, and from extensive ranches to paddy fields. We can rightly claim to have the technology to feed the world only if we do not destroy the agricultural environment in doing so. Soils that have accumulated over geological time can be washed away and dispersed irrecoverably in a few seasons of misuse. I have already noted that the intensification of population growth toward the equator is concentrating the food production problem into areas of unstable climate. The temperature limitations of the growing season are indeed reduced or eliminated, but the greater variability of rain seasons, the heavier and more destructive rainstorms, and the higher evaporation rates all combine to accelerate soil erosion.

Communities have responded to such physical limitations of their environment with a degree of success that varies with the level of social organization, some achieving highly productive and stable systems, others perpetrating destructive misuse, erosion, and poverty. History demonstrates both effects on a large scale in Mesopotamia, where imaginative and successful engineering in 2400 B.C. established productive irrigation, fed from the Tigris and drained by the Euphrates, and sustained it for 4,000 years (Willcocks 1911). Over that long period the success of the irrigation waxed and waned. Jacobson (1958), describing the varying efficiency of the irrigation system from 2400 B.C. to A.D. 1600, concluded that "a particularly close relationship exists between the flourishing of irrigation agriculture and the existence of a stable and vigorous central government." Discipline in the use of land, however, must extend to the headwaters of river basins as well as to the irrigation schemes in their floodplains. Overgrazing in semiarid country is the most widespread cause of deterioration of the river flows into muddy torrents. Failure to clear increasingly heavy silt loads blocking the irrigation channels led the Tigris to breach its banks and to change its course. Ruins of cities now stand in the desert while the land mis-use in the headwaters continues. West (1958) calculated that the floods of 1953 on the Tigris carried 14 million tons of soil and rock debris past Baghdad in one day.

Organization of agriculture to avoid the hazards of soil erosion, or the even more insidious hazards of waterlogging and salinity from irri-gation with inadequate drainage, must be on a watershed basis and must often be done on a large scale, whatever the size of the farming units. The scales are determined by the gradients of valleys, the areas of flood plains, the depths of soil, and capacities of waterbearing strata under large stream-source areas. This need not rule out the small farmer, as many smallholder schemes with sound soil conservation measures have demonstrated, but soil and water resources cannot be developed by the random decisions of a multitude of individual farmers with limited knowledge and resources.

Semiarid lands are particularly vulnerable to misuse by human pop-ulations which depend almost entirely on cattle, sheep, goats, and camels. These ruminants which can digest the sparse herbage need do little damage if the numbers are restrained. Now that the herds are no longer decimated by diseases, the result in all countries has been over-stocking. Science has been successfully applied to the improvement of pastures by sowing of drought-resistant legumes and deep-rooted pe-rennial grasses, as in Australia, and correction of mineral deficiencies has often given big increases in forage production. Wide year-to-year variations in rainfall, however, can halve the carrying capacity without notice. This tests the skills and resources of the most advanced agricul-tural managements (Pereira 1977). The recent African tragedy of the Sahel was not a blind stroke of climatic mischance but the inevitable result of the overloading of a fragile ecology. Earlier droughts had been known and statistical analysis shows no deterioration of the rainfall regime (Bunting et al. 1976). Here science and technology can guide regulation of stock numbers, but only governments can impose land-use discipline (Pereira 1973).

The more successful the agriculture, the greater is the help which farmers need from the veterinarians and from crop-protection scien-tists. The establishment of large numbers of adjacent crop plants of the same species is inescapable for efficient production, but it gives formidable opportunities for the large-scale development of pests and diseases. Plant breeders have made great progress in the assembly of germ plasm collections from which to select genes for resistance to pests and diseases and they have developed skillful techniques for incorporation of selected genes into improved varieties. The Inter-

national Board for Plant Genetic Resources, one of the initiatives of
the Consultative Group for International Agricultural Research, is organizing and extending this work for food-crop plants on a worldwide
scale. Wild relatives of crop plants and primitive varieties selected in
the past for survival are vitally important sources of resistance. The
latest high-yielding varieties of rice issued by the International Rice
Research Institute show resistance to five major diseases and to two
major pests. This is of very great importance for world food supplies,
but genetic resistance alone can rarely succeed for long in crop
protection since minor pests and diseases develop to replace those
defeated by the plant breeder. Biological control must often be supple-
mented at short notice by protective chemicals in a continuously shifting battlefront where active technical support is needed for all scales
of agricultural production. This is a field where close support from
research, development, and advisory services will remain necessary,
but one in which successful techniques are well established. It is a battle in which agricultural science can hold the line, but will suffer many
temporary local defeats by the biologically versatile attackers.

Close technical support is a basic form of input to highly productive
agriculture. As agricultural development brings new crops or new
varieties of familiar crops onto a wide range of soils with acidity, alkalinity, mineral deficiencies, and toxicities, the need for skilled diagnostic advice in the field, with close support from laboratory services,
will increase. Those who yearn for the simple agricultural life, free
from such technical complexities, must face the facts of population
growth and the insistent need for more food.

My thesis that physical and biological factors are now secondary
constraints does not imply that science has not a great deal more to
offer. There are basic advances still to be made, such as the replacement of industrial nitrogen fixation by those bacterial activities in
soils and legumes which are already capable of maintaining natural
ecologies. An increase in the efficiency of photosynthesis and a decrease in apparently wasteful respiration losses will, I believe, eventually secure major increases in plant yields, but the practical effects
of such research are not likely to be felt in time to affect the problems
outlined in Table 1.

THE CONFUSION OF OBJECTIVES AND MEANS

My second thesis is that, having set up elaborate United Nations
structures for agriculture, health, and meteorology (the FAO, WHO,
and WMO) to help national governments of developing countries,

and having reinforced these by the international agricultural research centers as highly active growing points for tropical food production technology, we are witnessing an increasing confusion of the objectives. In the councils of the donor nations there is a growing recognition of the extent to which poverty impedes the distribution of food in the poorer tropical countries. Emotional political movements are increasingly demanding that science be used not only to increase agricultural productivity but also to correct the maldistribution of wealth in the poorer nations. Under the slogan of "priority for the poor farmer" there lies a deep and serious misconception of what science can do. Any improvement to the productivity and disease resistance of crop plants or livestock that can be of help to the small-scale farmer is likely to be used even more effectively at higher standards of agricultural management and resources. Table 1 and the United Nations' estimates of malnutrition show that the food situation in the poorer countries is urgent. There is a serious danger of losing the race to produce food supplies for the fast-growing numbers of people being born, while trying to maneuver science to achieve social reform. Both food and social justice are indeed urgently needed, but failure to produce enough food causes inescapable suffering while that due to social inequality can be avoided by social measures. Millions of the world's poorest citizens live in the vast cities of the developing countries and they must be fed. Some of the small-farmer practices, such as intercropping of maize with groundnuts or with climbing beans, should indeed be studied and improved, but I believe that to divert the energies of research centers away from the major scale-neutral techniques of productivity and to limit them to the devising of programs that can help only the small-scale farmer is to revert to the philosophy of the Luddites.

To anyone familiar with exhausted tropical soils, the economic attractions of "low-input technology" imply serious hazards. Careful and skillful conservation of all wastes and the inculcation of those tenets of good husbandry well known to western gardeners, as Albert Howard taught in India a century ago, has very real advantages for the small farmer, and in the absence of purchased fertilizers these will win for him rather better crops than he is now getting. But this will not produce the quantum jump in productivity that will lift him the first stages above poverty and give him the surpluses with which to feed the cities. The drive to concentrate on "low-input technology" must be used with moderation. Crop varieties capable of gleaning the last traces of phosphate from a poor soil may succeed for three or four seasons but then reduce the soil to nutritional sterility. I have seen large stretches of

soil in Africa completely worked out by overcropping and finally abandoned. A few deep-rooted trees survived but no weeds or grasses volun-
teered on the bare soil. It is important that politicians should not set
the scientifically impossible task of continuous farm output without
replacement of soil nutrients.

As an agricultural scientist I have to convince the economists and
the sociologists that crops will not accept a plea of poverty in place of
the supply of nutrients. The increasing food deficit will not be made
good without a great increase of farm inputs in the countries where
the food is needed. These farmers are poor and their countries are poor
largely because the agricultural output of their land is a miserably
small fraction of its potential yield. They need help in modernizing
their agriculture rather than in making minor improvements to traditional subsistence methods. Better crop varieties, adequate fertilizers,
more help with crop protection, better guidance on difficult soils, and
better use of irrigation are all involved. This brings me to the tactical
level of methods of implementation.

EXPLOITING SUCCESS:
A SUGGESTION FOR INITIATIVE

Traditional methods of agricultural extension, working against the
inertia of poverty among those too close to the boundary conditions of
survival to risk new practices, are too slow to meet the essential targets
of food supply; even the backing of first-class research and development skills is not enough, as we have seen in the Puebla Project to extend new maize technology in Mexico, and in scores of bilateral aid
programs. The educated and able young men and women in the poorer
countries congregate in the cities because there are no attractive outlets in a subsistence farming countryside for their enterprise and initiative.

The exceptions where such opportunities do occur are to be found
primarily in the tropical plantation industries by which tea, coffee, oil
palm, sugar, citrus, bananas, and other export crops are produced.
These industries employ full-scale modern technologies, but until a
decade or more ago their boundaries with surrounding subsistence agriculture often showed stark contrasts between good farming practice
and the soil erosion and meager output of primitive traditions. But
there is now a real pattern of success to be seen in the use of these
productive centers as nuclei for substantial numbers of smallholders.
The Commonwealth Development Corporation (1977) announced the
commissioning in 1976 of four new tea factories in Kenya, bringing the

total in productive operation to nineteen. Six more are in preparation. About half are run by the Kenya Tea Authority, which provides supply, maintenance, and marketing services to more than 100,000 small farms. The scheme has grown on sound commercial principles and the factories are repaying their capital loans. Somewhat similar Commonwealth Development Corporation schemes for smallholders produce sugar in Swaziland and Zambia, tea in Malawi, bananas in Dominica, and palm oil in three Pacific islands. The model has been extended also to the cereal crops: production of urgently needed wheat and maize in Tanzania is being undertaken on the same basis of a large nucleus estate (converted from a tanning-bark enterprise), which organizes supplies of seed throughout the country to many small farmers, using the improved varieties supplied by the International Maize and Wheat Improvement Center in Mexico. Such a pattern of organization offers challenging and exciting opportunities for the educated, able, and ambitious, and brings into the rural areas the secondary clerical and artisan skills essential to intensive production. At the same time, it accomplishes advances in two very different time scales, the immediate and urgently needed quantum jump in the production of food and the slower building up of modern agricultural practice among the traditional subsistence farmers. While these schemes have leaned heavily on expatriate management skills in the past, they have proved excellent training grounds for local managers who are rapidly taking up these responsibilities.

The opportunities to organize efficient seed supply, storage, and transport, and to reduce the costs of fertilizers by bulk transport and local storage are impressive. Modern heavy transport vehicles are able to use quite primitive dry-season tracks in the tropics, if bulk storage is available to receive the loads. This combination has been used with success in Swaziland where the fertilizer stores also accommodate the harvest and provide return loads in the dry season. The availability, on the spot, of effective clerical services can play a critical part in the success of credit schemes for small farmers. These are all details from experience but they serve to illustrate the principle of stimulating the subsistence area with centers of production which will attract the enterprising from the cities. There are many variations. Most of us consider that China has chosen an unacceptably hard way, although with impressive success. Israel has achieved high production from marginal lands by her kibbutzim. Brazil has recently undertaken an outstanding initiative to upgrade the careers and resources of rural agricultural research and development services and to attract able young graduates into the rural areas.

The organization of such nucleus production centers and attached smallholder schemes is definitely not a task for the international centers of the Consultative Group, but the technical support of improved crop varieties and "packages" of production agronomy from the international centers can be a critical factor in arming the national services with the means for success. In many countries the civil services in the rural areas are not flexible enough either to cope with such new patterns or to attract the enterprising and ambitious staff essential for success; para-state organizations drawing on commercial expertise, as the Commonwealth Development Corporation has demonstrated, offer successful alternatives. One basic lesson which civil life can learn from the military arts in the worldwide struggle with poverty is to exploit success.

REFERENCES

Bunting, A. H.; Dennett, M. D.; Elstone, J.; and Milford, J. R.   1976. "Rainfall Trends in the West African Sahel." *Quarterly Journal of the Royal Meteorological Society* 102:59–64.

Commonwealth Development Corporation.   1977.   *Annual Report and Accounts for 1976*. London.

De Datta, S. K.; Saladaga, F. A.; Obcemea, W. N.; and Yoshida, T.   1974. *Proceedings FAI-FAO Seminar on Optimising Agricultural Production under Limited Availability of Fertilisers*, pp.265–88. New Delhi.

International Food Policy Research Institute.   1976.   *Meeting Food Needs in the Developing World*. Research Report no. 1. Washington, D.C.

———.   1977.   *Recent and Prospective Developments in Food Consumption: Some Policy Issues*. Research Report no. 2. Washington, D.C.

Jacobson, T.   1958.   *Salinity and Irrigation: Agriculture in Antiquity*. Dyala Basin Archaeological Report, 1957–58. Baghdad: Ministry of Irrigation.

National Academy of Sciences.   1976.   *Science, Technology, and Society: A Prospective Look*. Summary and Conclusions of the Bellagio Conference, June 20–27, 1976. Washington, D.C.

———.   1977.   *World Food and Nutrition Study*. Washington, D.C.

Pereira, H. C.   1973.   *Land Use and Water Resources*. Cambridge: Cambridge University Press.

———.   1977.   "Land Use in Semi-Arid Southern Africa." *Philosophical Transactions of the Royal Society of London* B 278:555–63.

West, B. G.   1958.   "The Soils of Iraq and Their Management." *Prospects of Iraq Biology* I, 15. Baghdad: Biological Society of Iraq.

Willcocks, Sir William.   1911.   *Irrigation of Mesopotamia*. London: Spon.

COMMENT

P. A. Oram

Sir Charles Pereira raises a number of pertinent issues and has shown characteristic modesty (and even restraint) in addressing those of broad interest to social as well as biological and physical scientists. Indeed I am not sure he may not have gone too far in his first, and perhaps his central thesis, in respect of defining the scientific and technical problems as being on a minor scale in comparison to the "social engineering" required to lift the constraints on production.

Professor Steppler's paper (in this volume) offers some further food for thought on this issue, as does Evenson's, which, if it does not exactly run contrary to Pereira's, at least implies that for a number of commodities and agroclimatic regions, we lack an adequate base of technology.

In view of these doubts an important question is in what respects the range of technology we *do* have available for crops in the tropics and subtropics (this varies from good for wheat to very poor for roots, pulses, and many vegetables) is adequate to push food production along at least in line with population growth, while the research base which Evenson argues is still largely lacking is created. In the case of wheat and shallow-water paddy rice, it is clear from studies by staff of the International Maize and Wheat Improvement Center and the International Rice Research Institute that substantial progress could be made to increase yield merely by proper use of existing good agricultural techniques and well-adapted varieties (Perrin and Winkelmann 1976, Herdt and Barker 1977). But for how many other crops (and livestock) is this true?

If it *is* broadly true then Pereira's thesis is correct. This is not to say that research could be "put on a back burner," but at least the pressures to develop technology-potential capability in many countries which currently do not have it would be somewhat less.[1]

A constraint on developing more sophisticated research capabilities in poor countries which is perhaps not sufficiently recognized at present is the extremely uncoordinated and fragmented nature of technical assistance to research, education, and training (Oram 1977). This is because of a very poor information base from which to plan, and also due to inexperience on the part of many aid donors (as Dalrymple [1977] points out in a recent U.S. Agency for International Development working paper). Pereira rightly draws attention to the contract-

Table 1

Comparative Estimates of Potential
for Expanding Cultivated Area

	1974 Actual Arable Area	Calculated Potential Arable Land (Mill ha)				
		FAO (IWP) (1)	Club of Rome (2)	Alan Strout (3)	U.S.A. (4)	Wagen-ingen (5)
Latin America	127	570	429	586	680	692
Africa Sub-Sahara	186	304	423	470	733	658
N. Africa/Near East	80	80	86	80	NA	122
Asia—Market Economy	274	296	278	330	627	360
Asia—Centrally Planned	132	NA	122	201	—	388
Developing Countries	799	1250	1338	1667	2040	2220
North America	235	—	392	347	466	533
Oceania	46	—	150	70	154	275
Europe—Market Economy	116	—	163	137	174	164
Europe—Centrally Planned	278	—	382	280	356	491
Industrialized Countries	673	NA	1087	834	1150	1463
World	1472	NA	2425	2501	3190	3683

	1974 Actual Arable Area	1974 Arable Area as a Proportion of Potential Arable Land (%)				
		FAO (IWP) (1)	Club of Rome (2)	Alan Strout (3)	U.S.A. (4)	Wagen-ingen (5)
Latin America	127	22	30	22	19	18
Africa Sub-Sahara	186	61	44	39	25	28
N. Africa/Near East	80	100	93	100	NA	66
Asia—Market Economy	274	93	99	83	65	76
Asia—Centrally Planned	132	NA	100	66		34
Developing Countries	799	53	60	48	39	36
North America	235	—	60	68	50	44
Oceania	46	—	31	66	30	17
Europe—Market Economy	116	—	71	85	67	71
Europe—Centrally Planned	278	—	73	99	78	57
Industrialized Countries	673	NA	62	81	58	46
World	1472	NA	61	59	46	40

ing time scale; if, as was suggested at the recent meeting of the Consultative Group on International Agricultural Research (Drilon 1977), it takes seven to ten years to build a sound national research organization and twenty-five years to develop a fully fledged college of agriculture capable of turning out graduates of respectable quality, some difficult decisions as to where the priorities should be and what type of institution to support may have to be made. I do not think, on the whole, that the international community is yet geared up to offer the right kind of help to those developing countries seeking it in this field of agricultural planning.

Nor do I believe that there is yet a sufficient base of knowledge of the physical resources available for agriculture to permit their rational management; this lack is exemplified by the gross discrepancies in global and regional estimates of the potential cultivable area which are shown in Table 1. The figures quoted by Steppler support this argument; Pereira's statement that only a few countries still have the option to extend cultivation to new areas conflicts with the optimistic forecasts Steppler quotes for Latin America and Africa, and further reinforces my point. At the Food and Agriculture Organization Traveling Seminar on Rainfed Agriculture in Monsoon Asia (FAO 1975b) the need for a better understanding of crop/soil/climate relationships was repeatedly stressed as being fundamental to improving productivity in rain-fed areas.[2] As a follow-up meeting in Canberra demonstrated, we are still far from having this knowledge or an agreed methodology to produce it.

The approach to defining research and development priorities on an agroclimatic zone basis, which would greatly facilitate both the design

---

Notes:

1974 Arable Area: Taken from FAO *Production Yearbook* Table 1, Vol. 28-1 (FAO,1974a). Includes Permanent Crops. Data Mostly 1970 or later.

Col. 1: FAO estimates for Indicative World Plan (FAO, 1970) (Ch. 2. Tables 6-8). Data for Asia Expanded to include countries omitted from IWP.

Col. 2: Calculations by Mesarovic and Pestel (1974). *Second Report to the Club of Rome* (Table III A-2).

Col. 3: Calculations by Strout (1975). Resources for the Future. Unpublished Study (Annex Table III).

Col. 4: U.S., President's Science Advisory Committee (1967). *The World Food Problem* (Vol. II. Adapted from Tables 7-6 to 7-9).

Col. 5: Buringh, van Heemst, and Staring, Agricultural University, Wageningen (1975). *Computation of the Absolute Maximum Food Production of the World* (Table 15).

As these five sources have different base-years and also vary in their estimates of "Actual" arable area in the base-year they are all compared here to the same base-year taken from the 1974 FAO *Production Yearbook* (1974a).

Table 2

Distribution of Land by Major
Classes of Use and Region, 1975

Region	Total[1] Area (1)	Arable Area[2]		Permanent Pasture	
		mill-ha	% of (1)	mill-ha	% of (1)
World	13,400	1,507	11.3	3,044	22.7
Developed Countries	3,276	413	12.6	867	26.5
N. America	1,934	250	12.9	245	13.0
W. Europe	385	97	25.2	72	18.7
Oceania	795	46	5.8	467	58.6
Centrally Planned Countries	3,486	414	11.8	745	21.3
Europe (Mainly USSR)	2,342	279	11.9	390	16.6
Asia (Mainly China)	1,145	135	11.8	354	30.9
Developing Countries	6,630	680	10.3	1,432	21.6
Africa	2,384	190	8.0	680	28.5
Latin America	2,065	140	6.8	530	25.6
Near East	1,204	81	6.7	188	15.6
Far East	893	267	30.0	37	4.0

Region	Total[1] Area (1)	Forests		Remainder[3]	
		mill-ha	% of (1)	mill-ha	% of (1)
World	13,400	4,052	30.3	4,797	35.7
Developed Countries	3,276	821	25.0	1,174	35.9
N. America	1,934	627	32.5	811	41.7
W. Europe	385	120	31.1	96	24.9
Oceania	795	45	5.7	238	29.9
Centrally Planned Countries	3,486	1,127	32.4	1,200	34.5
Europe (Mainly USSR)	2,342	948	40.5	724	31.0
Asia (Mainly China)	1,145	180	15.7	477	41.6
Developing Countries	6,630	2,104	31.7	2,520	36.4
Africa	2,384	550	23.0	964	40.5
Latin America	2,065	1,031	50.0	364	17.6
Near East	1,204	140	11.7	795	66.0
Far East	893	347	40.0	242	27.0

Notes:

[1] Includes inland water areas.

[2] Includes land under permanent crops.

[3] Includes some unused but potentially productive land.

Source: FAO *Production Yearbook.* Vol. 29, 1975.

of technology to meet the needs of environmental niches and the identification of investment opportunities, is therefore frustrated by the absence of a generally accepted system of agroclimatic classification.
However, even if this existed, national agricultural statistics are always
collected on some administrative basis (district, block, prefecture, for
instance) and these invariably cut across ecological zones. A new and
more rational approach to gathering and analyzing land use and crop
production data is urgently needed.

Any system that relates population distribution more closely to production potential would help to define the extent to which a country
is in a land-surplus rather than a labor-surplus environment, where the
opportunities for land expansion still exist, and what the real costs of
their exploitation might be under sound management. Here I would
like to draw attention to the misleading nature of some recent studies
on land availability which seem to suggest that much new land could
be brought into production in the tropics at low cost.[3] As Table 2
shows, this would generally have to come from land now under pasture
or forest, both of which are shrinking and often overexploited resources
(Bene, Beall, and Côté 1977). The environmental and social costs of
this could be very great unless the transition to cultivation is carefully
controlled, and both Pereira's and Steppler's papers emphasize the
need for more discipline in future land use, as did the World Food
Conference (FAO 1974b).

However, past experience of trying to enforce discipline on nomadic
graziers, shifting cultivators, or wood gatherers, for example, has not
been too happy; and this may well be because the attempts were made
in a vacuum of knowledge as to the pressures they were under and
there was a lack of any alternatives to offer them as a means of improving their lot if they accepted such discipline (Tribe and Pratt 1975).

It seems to me that in many of the apparently land-surplus areas of
the developing world, especially in Africa, there are constraints on
developing new land that are very imperfectly understood. These
vary from local problems of land tenure and lack of draft power to
widespread limitations imposed by remoteness, poor soils, or diseases
such as river blindness or sleeping sickness. Inadequate understanding
of the type, location, magnitude, and costs of alleviating these constraints is in itself a major constraint on agricultural production; and,
as a recent World Bank report (1977b) points out, has been an important cause of failure in land-settlement projects.

I therefore believe that in addition to discussing the needs of intensification in the *Asian* monsoon environment (which is generally rather
well researched and documented), some consideration of the ap-

proaches required elsewhere in the world would be timely. Although the great weight of attention devoted to Asia is understandable because of the absolute magnitudes of the population and potential food deficits there, in relative terms a number of other countries, particularly in Africa, face equally severe or perhaps even more critical problems of poverty and malnutrition.

Whether we are considering Asia, Africa, or Latin America, the issue of what to do about the poor farmer and agricultural laborer will inevitably arise. As you will see from Pereira's paper, this is a burning issue about which there are strong feelings. I sense in many statements, particularly in the press, an implication that population pressure is necessarily evil: it has been argued, however, (for example by Boserup [1965], Clark and Haswell [1966] and Hayami et al. [1976]) that it can act as a spur to innovation in agriculture and to the adoption of new technology.[4] Table 3 lends support to this contention.

Moreover, people are a resource in themselves. Until recently in several Asian countries, labor was the main factor contributing to increased output from the land; and it can be shown that variations in cropping intensity in several Asian countries are highly correlated with the intensity of labor and draft power per unit of land resource.

Whether we like it or not, a multitude of people in many developing countries have to find employment as well as food from agriculture; lack of purchasing power is often as serious a cause of malnutrition as low agricultural productivity. In this light a narrowly food-oriented development strategy has inherent dangers.[5] Until the growth of population can be reduced, this situation will not improve; indeed in absolute terms the land may have to support more people at least to the end of the century. Short of revolutionary land reform, farm structure is therefore likely to grow more fragmented. While it may not be practicable, let alone scientifically pure, to attempt to design technology solely for the smaller or poorer farmers, it makes sense to give priority to measures which will not aggravate their lot, where the situation is one of predominantly small farms and surplus labor.[6]

This, as Pereira rightly points out, also implies some drastic rethinking of institutional approaches; and if (as Barker argues in his paper) existing institutions were often designed in a land-surplus situation, which no longer persists in many countries, this may be a major reason for their failure. A pertinent question is whether farmers are not getting the right technology package because the right package does not exist, or because the institutions responsible for transmitting knowledge and skills to them are somehow inadequate. The answer to this may tell us whether it is research, or delivery systems (including extension), that should receive the weight of investment.[7]

Table 3

Regional Differences in Land-Use Intensity (1974)
(Based on Averages of 10 Countries per Region)

Indicators	Asia	Near East	East Africa	West Africa
Total Population Sq Km Arable Area[*]	593	392	305	135
Agricultural/Population Sq Km Arable Area[*]	138	57	117	40
Ha. per Animal Unit [*]Arable/Pasture	1.3	5.2	6.3	8.0
Irrigated Area as % Arable Area	29.8	29.2	3.1	1.2
Fertilizer, Units NPK/ Ha. Arable	67.9	45.3	5.1	3.4
Tractor Units per 1000 Ha. Arable	3.0	4.9	0.8	0.4
Cropping Intensity (Percent)	90	67	69	57

[*] Includes permanent crops.

Source: All data taken from FAO *Production Yearbook*, Vol. 29, 1975 for 1974 base year, except agricultural population (base 1970).

Lines 1 & 2: Arable land includes permanent crops and temporary pasture but not permanent pasture. Also includes fallow. Agricultural population is defined as all persons depending for their livelihood on agriculture (including nonworking). It is debatable whether this or total population is a better measure of pressure on land. The latter is misleading for industrialized countries or those with larger food imports. It greatly inflates the figure for all countries, but particularly for the more densely populated Asian and Near East countries.

Line 3: Arable as defined above plus permanent pasture. Animal units ≡ Camels 1.1, Buffalo 1.0; Cattle 0.8, Sheep and Goats 0.1.

Line 4: Irrigated equipped area as percent net arable area *not* including permanent crops or pasture unless otherwise stated.

Line 5: Arable as defined under 3. Fertilizer expressed as units NPK.

Line 6: Arable as defined under 3. Tractors include 4 wheeled and motor-cultivators .5 m.c.'s = 1 × 40 H.P. tractor.

Line 7: Cropping intensity $= \dfrac{\text{Total Harvested Area}}{\text{Total Arable Area (as defined under 1)}} \times 100.$

This brings me to my final point. As I was writing this comment everything seemed to point to agricultural development, as well as the practice of agriculture itself, becoming increasingly expensive. Physical projects, settlement and infrastructure, the generation of knowledge, technology delivery systems and other institutions, manpower training and support, and the growing need to farm more intensively—all are becoming more costly in real terms.[8]

Pereira concludes that capital is likely to be less of a constraint in

Table 4

Comparison of Average Capital Aid to Agriculture for the 36 Low-Income Food-Deficit Countries (Grouped by GNP per Capita)

Quartile	GNP per Capita US $	Total Aid Mill US $	Aid per Capita US $	Aid/Ha US $	Share of Agriculture in GDP %
Group I	92.4	251.8	1.89	5.68	53.6
Group II	125.0	489.2	1.24	4.00	40.31
Group III	187.7	503.0	2.61	9.88	42.58
Group IV	287.9	317.6	3.00	7.69	35.41
Total		1561.6			

Source: Consultative Group on Food Production and Investment, 1977.

the future. Despite the recent increases in lending to agriculture I am not sure of this; an ongoing study by the International Food Policy Research Institute indicates that capital inflows to the thirty-six low-income food-deficit countries as well as domestic expenditures on agriculture may have to be more than doubled by 1985 if the widening gaps between food production and projected demand referred to in Pereira's paper are to be reduced.[9] Where will all the capital come from? Will aid continue to go, as Table 4 suggests is happening at present, to the more advanced rather than the poorest of the developing countries? Does poverty compound poverty because more money cannot be utilized effectively in the poorest countries due to lack of local skills?

Whether capital will continue to flow to agriculture in increasing quantities seems likely to depend largely on whether it is used more efficiently, and in turn helps to increase the efficiency of farming so as to reduce costs per unit of production. This seems to bring us back once more to the question of how best to combine the vast human and technical resources at our disposal through "social engineering," which I regard as the key issue of Pereira's paper.

NOTES

1. The magnitude of this task should not be underrated; six years of thought and discussion by the Consultative Group on International Agricultural Research and its Technical Advisory Committee have not yet resulted in agreement as to how best to help strengthen national research capabilities.

Serious consideration is now being given by the Consultative Group to establishing an International Service for National Agricultural Research.

2. Studies undertaken by the International Maize and Wheat Improvement Center (Perrin and Winkelmann 1976) and the International Rice Research Institute (Herdt and Barker 1977) emphasize the crucial role played by agroclimatic factors in relation to the adoption by farmers of the research output of the international agricultural research centers.

3. For example, a recent report presented to the Consultative Group on Food Production and Investment (1977) states, "It is clear that in virtually all parts of the world actual production is only a small fraction of potential levels. This is particularly true for the developing countries where not only yields per hectare are low but also the scope for expanding arable land is considerable. The largest concentration of attractive agricultural development potentials exists in Africa; not only is 60 percent of total potential agricultural land relatively cheap to bring to production and/or to high yields, but that continent also contains 30 percent of the world's most attractive lands."

4. The elasticity is not infinite, of course, and some ecosystems are more fragile than others. A low population density does not necessarily mean that an area is underutilized in relation to the carrying capacity of the land for people and animals. The weak point lies in our current inability to identify the point at which this capacity is overstrained in the light of available agricultural technology.

5. While food production is clearly of the highest priority, there are dangers in an obsession with food self-sufficiency per se. This may obscure comparative advantages for the production of other agricultural commodities which could permit countries to finance the import of food, inputs to grow more food, or other essentials (Valdés and Huddleston 1977). The production and processing of a number of those commodities is also more labor intensive than that of food crops (Tropical Products Institute 1975).

6. On the other hand, science should not be expected to remedy gross social inequalities. It is unlikely to be rewarding to devote large scientific resources to devising measures to alleviate the condition of the "poorest of the poor." Such problems need to be attacked by other means. Nor can science be expected to provide something for nothing. It would benefit all farmers to be able to control pests and provide nitrogen to plants by biological means or to develop more efficient fertilizer formulations, and these are scientifically valid objectives. However, too much should not be expected from "low-input" technology; it is unlikely that a 3.5% annual growth of food production will be feasible without substantial use of purchased inputs. Pereira is right in calling attention to the danger of falling between two stools in expecting science both to increase productivity and to correct the maldistribution of wealth.

7. Pereira suggests an ingenious approach to combining rapid agricultural growth, through centralized modern management, with the longer-term task

of upgrading the production techniques of traditional farmers. This is only one of many systems which have been tried without a consistent overall record of success. There are difficult methodological problems facing planners in evaluating and comparing institutional performance and in trying to identify the approach most likely to succeed in a given environment. A recent World Bank (1977*a*) study shows that capital:output ratios vary widely both across project types and regions and concludes that the diversity of results permits no easy generalization.

8. Irrigation and land development costs are likely to rise because the best sites and soils have already been developed, and those remaining are either more difficult to develop or in more remote areas with high infrastructure transport and settlement costs (World Bank, 1977*a*, 1977*b*). Both to develop and manage the physical resources more efficiently, and to facilitate the intensification of agriculture which most development strategies see as the quickest means of increasing food production (Mellor 1976, Hayami et al. 1976) will require a training program of unprecedented magnitudes from the grass roots up. Recent estimates by the Food and Agriculture Organization (1977) of personnel required for water resources' development, and by Oram (1977) of graduate research and extension workers suggest education and training costs by 1985 several times those today, and consistent with the Indicative World Plan calculations (FAO 1970, Chap. 2) of a cumulative "human-resource" investment of over $2.5 billion over a fifteen-year period.

9. It should be stressed that this Institute's food gap calculations (1976, 1977) to which Pereira refers are projections of what *may* happen if current trends in production are not accelerated, and while valuable in highlighting the stark possibilities of a food/population confrontation they are not a prediction of what *will* happen.

REFERENCES

Bene, J. G.; Beall, H. W.; and Côté, A.   1977.   *Trees, Food and People: Land Management in the Tropics.* Publication IDRC-084e. Ottawa: International Development Research Centre.

Boserup, E.   1965.   *The Conditions of Agricultural Growth: The Economics of Agrarian Change under Population Pressure.* Chicago: Aldine.

Buringh, P.; van Heemst, H. D. J.; and Staring, G. J.   1975.   *Computation of the Absolute Maximum Food Production of the World.* Wageningen, The Netherlands: Agricultural University.

Clark, Colin, and Haswell, M.   1966.   *The Economics of Subsistence Agriculture.* London: Macmillan & Co.

Consultative Group on Food Production and Investment.   1977.   Progress report on research project, "Food for a Doubling World Population. Identification of Countries with Potential for Rapid Expansion of Food Production." Study coordinated by the Free University, Amsterdam. Mimeographed. Washington, D.C.

Dalrymple, Dana G. 1977. "Development and Diffusion of New Agricultural Technology Institutional Aspects." Mimeographed. Washington, D.C.: U.S. Agency for International Development.

Drilon, J. D. 1977. "High Level Agricultural Manpower in Indonesia and the Philippines." Mimeographed. Paper presented at Centers Week, Consultative Group on International Agricultural Research, Washington, D.C.

Food and Agriculture Organization.' 1970. *Indicative World Plan for Agricultural Development*, Vol. 1. Rome.

————. 1974a. *Production Yearbook*. Vol. 28-1. Rome.

————. 1974b. *The World Food Problem: Proposals for National and International Action*. Agenda item 9, U.N. World Food Conference, Rome.

————. 1975a. *Production Yearbook*. Vol. 29. Rome.

————. 1975b. *Report of the FAO/UNDP Expert Consultation on the Use of Improved Technology for Food Production in Rainfed Areas of Tropical Asia*. Rome.

————. 1977. "Water for Agriculture." Paper prepared for the U.N. Water Conference, Mar del Plata, Argentina.

Hayami, Yujiro; David, Cristina C.; Flores, Piedad; and Kikuchi, Masao. 1976. "Agricultural Growth against a Land Resource Constraint: The Philippine Experience." *Australian Journal of Agricultural Economics* 20, no. 3 (December):144-59.

Herdt, Robert W., and Barker, Randolph. 1977. "Multi-site Tests, Environments, and Breeding Strategies for New Rice Technology." Research paper series no. 7. Los Baños, Philippines: International Rice Research Institute.

International Food Policy Research Institute. 1976. *Meeting Food Needs in the Developing World*. Research report no. 1. Washington, D.C.

————. 1977. *Recent and Prospective Developments in Food Consumption: Some Policy Issues*. Research report no. 2. Washington, D.C.

Mellor, John W. 1976. *The New Economics of Growth: A Strategy for India and the Developing World*. Ithaca: Cornell University Press.

Mesarovic, M., and Pestel, E. 1974. *Mankind at the Turning Point: The Second Report to the Club of Rome*. New York: E. P. Dutton.

Oram, P. A. 1977. "Training Requirements for Research and Its Application." Mimeographed. Paper presented at Centers' Week, Consultative Group on International Agricultural Research, World Bank, Washington, D.C.

Perrin, R., and Winkelmann, D. 1976. *Impediments to Technical Progress on Small versus Large Farms*. El Batán, Mexico: International Maize and Wheat Improvement Center.

Strout, Alan. 1975. "World Agricultural Potential: Evidence from the Recent Past." Discussion draft. Mimeographed. MIT Energy Laboratory and Resources for the Future, Inc.

Tribe, D. E., and Pratt, D. J. 1975. "Animal Production in Relation to Conservation and Recreation." In *Proceedings of the III World Conference* on *Animal Production,* ed. R. L. Reid. Sydney, Australia: Sydney University Press.

Tropical Products Institute.   1975.   *Research Needs and Priorities in Relation to Certain Agricultural Commodities.* Vol. 1. London.

U.S., President's Science Advisory Committee.   1967.   *The World Food Problem.* Washington, D.C.: The White House.

Valdés, Alberto, and Huddleston, B.   1977.   *Potential of Agricultural Exports to Finance Increased Food Imports in Selected Developing Countries.* Occasional paper no. 2. Washington, D.C.: International Food Policy Research Institute.

World Bank.   1977*a*.   "A Perspective on the Foodgrain Situation in the Poorest Countries." World Bank Staff Working Paper no. 251. Washington, D.C.

———.   1977*b*.   "The Settlement of Agricultural Lands: An Issues Paper." World Bank Report no. 1670. Washington, D.C.

PART II

RESOURCES AND ENVIRONMENT

Natural Resources and
Unsolved Environmental Problems

Civilization would have been impossible without agriculture
—H. G. Baker (1965)

HOWARD A. STEPPLER

In considering world agricultural production, it seems only rational to assume that the natural resources are those most directly concerned with agriculture and that the environmental problems relate to those natural resources.

The natural resources are an integral part of the agricultural production system. Thus this paper will briefly examine the components of the system and their relative importance to production. Then it will consider the constraints to more effective utilization of those resources, and finally will examine the nature of these constraints and comment on probable strategies of research. I have deliberately referred to the agricultural production system rather than farming systems. The latter implies that the farmer is to be considered as a part of the system. I do not deny that he is a vital part of the total system (and that he is a natural resource), but others in this volume treat of him.

Further, I have avoided the use of the term "food production system," which suggests processing and other infrastructural dimensions devolved from the primary production. Again, I recognize the validity of concern, but would suggest that basic to those activities is a sound primary production system.

All agricultural production systems have three basic components:

(1) the climatic component, with temperature, rainfall, and day length being most important;[1]

(2) the edaphic component, where the major physical characteristics are texture, depth, stoniness, and topography, while chemical and biological factors revolve around the nutrient-supply capacity, the pH/alkalinity/salinity complex, and the biological activity of the soil;

(3) the biological component, which is the green plant together with its associated array of diseases, insects, pests, and weeds. This

factor may have an additional dimension, namely the animal, which, irrespective of its feeding habits as a herbivore or carnivore, is totally dependent on the green plant, and will, in addition, have its associated complex of diseases and pests.

Of these three components, the key is the growing green plant. Only it, through photosynthesis, can utilize solar energy to combine the elements of the atmosphere and nutrients of the soil to form, say, storable carbohydrates or protein which then can be used as food for man and animals.[2] The avenue to increased productivity is through providing an "improved" environment for the plant so that its efficiency can be enhanced.

The components and their various factors need to be considered both in terms of resource base and in terms of constraints in use. I shall consider first the resource base.

Temperature, both its diurnal variation and its seasonal variation, is the major determinant of the distribution of crops. The sun is the resource base and, as such, is constant. The variation is primarily a function of location on the earth's surface and movement of the weather systems. Since solar energy drives the photosynthetic process, anything that interferes with that source of energy or affects its flow to the plant will affect the productivity of the system.

According to Hare (1968), the total vapor content of the atmosphere is equivalent to only 22 millimeters of precipitation in July. Further, the expected residence time in the atmosphere is approximately 10 days, during which the vapor may travel as much as 10,000 kilometers. Since individual daily rainfalls can frequently exceed 22 millimeters by a factor of two or more, it is obvious that there is little relation between rainfall and precipitable water. The global content of vapor is relatively stable, but as the degrees of convergence may vary widely, the amount of rainfall in a particular area can likewise vary. It is safe to say that if one area of the earth is wetter than normal, some other area will be drier than normal. The resource base of moisture in the atmosphere is constant and renewable. However, the rainfall in a given area and for a given time can be quite variable, and hence gives the impression of a fluctuating resource.

In the absence of a restricting (normally below freezing) temperature, seasonal variation in rainfall will determine the length of the growing season for agricultural production. Rainfall can be as effective as temperature in restricting an agricultural system, operating under natural conditions, to seasonal production.

Photoperiod or day length is a function of latitude and time of year, and is nonvariable. As a factor in the climatic package, however, it operates as a determinant of flowering response in plants and may influence physiological cycles in animals and pests.

The edaphic factors seem more tangible and easier to conceptualize. Of these, undoubtedly land per se is most obvious. As our knowledge of world soils improves, so does our estimate of potentially arable land. Kellogg and Orvedal (1969), using 28 soil groups, estimated the area of potentially arable soils as 3,182 million hectares, of which approximately 1,400 million hectares are currently in cultivation. Mesarovic and Pestel (1974), using ten land masses, estimated the potentially arable land at 2,425 million hectares, again with 1,425 million in cultivation. Buringh, van Heemst, and Staring (1975), using 222 broad soil groups and the new world soil maps published by the Food and Agriculture Organization, estimate the potentially arable area at 3,419 million hectares with 1,406 million currently used. They further estimate that some 470 million hectares of the total area could be irrigated (currently 201 million are irrigated).

While the estimates vary by as much as 1,000 million hectares, one fact does emerge: there is still unused land which could be brought into agriculture.[3] Buringh, van Heemst, and Staring (1975) have estimated a cereal production potential—using a C_3 cereal such as wheat or rice—of 49,830 million tons per year using all the land, or 32,390 million tons using 65% of cultivated land (the present proportion) for cereal. These estimates take into consideration potential irrigation and limitations due to soil and climate, and are forty and thirty times current production. Further, they believe that Latin America and Africa south of the Sahara are the most promising areas, and Australia is the least promising, while Mesarovic and Pestel favor North America and Australia as the most promising. (I personally feel that Buringh, van Heemst, and Staring present much more valid estimates of area, although their estimates of potential productivity seem overly optimistic.)

Along with land as a physical resource, one must consider the "quality" of that land in its ability to support plant growth. Essential and nonreplaceable are those plant nutrients necessary for plant growth, particularly nitrogen, phosphorus, and potassium; there can be no substitute for these. Without them, and this means essentially any nutrient, all growth ceases. The productivity of land, and hence of an agricultural production system, is inseparably linked to the nutrient supply as well as to those other climatic factors—light, moisture, and temperature.

There are basically two aspects to the plant nutrient[4] resource base. One concerns the nutrient status naturally occurring in soils—this refers to both the available supply and the release rate from unavailable forms in the soil. The other concerns the reserve in various areas of the world of nutrients, such as those found as minerals which may be used to supplement the natural nutrient supply. Buringh, van Heemst, and Staring (1975) considered the natural nutrient supply in arriving at their projection of world cereal production. To illustrate, natural nutrient status varies from near zero (e.g., 2 parts per million) of phosphorus (P_2O_5) in many savanna soils (oxisols and ultisols) of Latin America, to over 140 parts per million in many temperate-region soils which have high release capacity.

Many estimates have been made of the nutrient resource base of the second type (e.g., nutrients found as mineral) and of the three macro nutrients, nitrogen (N), phosphorus (P_2O_5), and potassium (K_2O).[5] Nitrogen is usually supplied in the form of nitrates, ammonia, or urea, and in such forms it is largely synthesized from atmospheric nitrogen. The problem is not one of the resource base of N_2 but rather of the energy required in the synthetic process. Of all plant nutrients N_2 is the only one which can readily recycle to its basic form. Further, unlike the other macronutrients, N can be fixed by biological processes associated with certain plants[6] and hence the process becomes the resource base.

Pinstrup-Anderson (1976) indicates that world phosphate-rock resources are sufficient for about 700 years at current rates of consumption; of that supply, 16 billion tons, equal to 150 years' supply, is recoverable at current costs. He further states that world potash resources are estimated at 79 billion tons of which 10 billion are readily recoverable and equal to about 450 years' supply at current consumption rates. The resource base of either of these nutrients appears adequate for the immediate future, but this must be tempered by the fact that (a) in the case of phosphorus, the phosphoric rocks are of an increasingly lower grade, hence more costly to process, and (b) neither phosphorus nor potassium once applied to the soil will recycle in the same time frame as N—they are more likely to require upwards of 10,000 years before recovery.

The acidity/alkalinity/salinity characteristic of the soil can very markedly determine the productivity of a system on that soil. Thus, the land resource base is affected in quality, while the resource base associated with the factor itself is the material necessary to reduce the impact of that factor on production. In the case of acidity, we are concerned with supplies of limestone; in alkalinity it may be sulphur or some compound to neutralize the bases; in salinity we are likely to be concerned with adequate water to leach soluble salts. All three factors are naturally occurring characteristics of soils which may be worsened by mismanagement, salinity being an ever-present problem in irrigation agriculture.

As previously mentioned, the green plant is the key component in the production system whether the end product is a plant material or an animal product. While the plant kingdom is large—upwards of 300,000 species—the number of "economic" species is very small. If one uses a very broad definition such as any plant used for food, fiber, medicinal, or ornamental purposes anywhere in the world, then the number may reach into the thousands. However, if your definition is more rigorous, then the number drops dramatically to a very small number, probably less than a hundred, and down to ten or below if you consider the major food crops of the world.

At issue is the evidence that we are dependent on a very few plant species to supply our major food requirements. Plant exploration over the past fifty years has not added any new species to our list of major food crops. A recent study published by the National Academy of Sciences (1976) lists thirty-six underexploited tropical species of which four are seed crops and three roots and tubers. Burton (1968) says, ". . . more potential food for man lies hidden in the germ plasm of our major food crops and their related species than in exotic food crops yet to be discovered." Strong evidence supports that statement. Sorghum has been changed from a tall forage crop to a short-statured grain producer through plant breeding. Triticale, again the product of breeding by crossing wheat and rye, has emerged as the only "new" cereal crop in this century.

The resource base of the plant kingdom appears large, but the resource base of the major food crops is startlingly small. Further, when one considers the plant resource base for a particular ecological region, then the germ plasm available becomes even more restricted by reason of climatic constraints. Many of our crops have reached their significance outside of their centers of origin. Thus, when new germ plasm is needed for plant improvement, the search must generally be made in the center of origin—the center of greatest diversity—not the area of economic importance (Table 1).

The other major factors in the plant component are the pests that limit the performance of the plant below its genetic potential or may destroy plants outright. Unfortunately these seem to have an unlimited resource base and, like plants themselves, they are dynamic. Many pests, particularly diseases, can mutate to overcome resistance which the plant breeder has built into his variety, while many insects can evolve genotypes resistant to chemical controls. Further, pests do not

Table 1

The Centers of Origin of Some World Crops
and Their Centers of Major Production

Crop	Center of Origin	Center of Major Production
wheat	Near East	North America
		Argentina
		Australia
potato	Peru	Europe
sorghum	Ethiopia	southern United States
coffee	Ethiopia	Brazil

respect national boundaries. They can migrate on their own as have wheat rust in North America and locusts in North Africa, or they may be inadvertently transported by man.

There are essentially three avenues open to agriculture to overcome the pest: (1) develop resistance to it; (2) develop a means to destroy it; and (3) develop a means to live with it. Each implies a different resource base. In the first instance the resource base of the economic plant and related species is most critical. In the second case the means to destroy might come from another biological organism as in biological control, or it might be a direct product of research and search for chemical control. In the third situation, control is likely to arise from the practice of good management (destruction of alternate hosts, timely operations). Most pest-control systems will be integrated, containing elements of the three approaches.

The plant resource base is thus critical, not only in providing a means to enhance productivity per se, but also as a source of germ plasm which will protect the plant from pests and provide adaptative genotypes to new environments. Every effort must be made to protect that base from further erosion. An expansion of the base into new exotic species should not take precedence over expansion and preservation of the germ plasm critical to our present major food crops.

The unsolved environmental problems are those which are the major constraints to the production system. Since the three components are always present and in many combinations of their various factors, a problem is to conceptualize the working system and to develop the strategic approach. One can too easily become mired in the minutiae of research tactics and lose sight of the strategy, let alone the problem. One such approach to conceptualization is to develop a typology which classifies on a strategic rather than tactical basis. To this end, three sets of bipolar descriptors are used for the typology and will be applied in turn to the climatic, edaphic, and biological components.

The descriptors used are:

(1) Stability or constancy.

The factor is described as stable or nonstable. These are not mutually exclusive and definitive categories, but rather subjective value judgments. Thus a factor can be stable at point A but different yet again stable at point B, and this could also read as time A versus time B. Likewise, a nonstable factor implies that it is subject to considerable variation, generally appearing to be at random. Rainfall is one example. The classification thus carries with it the suggestion of predictability when stable and nonpredictability when nonstable.

(2) The ability to modify/manipulate the factor.

The factor is classified as either capable of manipulation by man or not capable of manipulation; the judgment is based on present knowledge and economic rationale. Thus, total rainfall cannot be manipulated because of the massive energy required to increase water-vapor load in the atmosphere. Some may argue that cloud seeding does manipulate rainfall, but I would suggest that this is tinkering with the local weather. Again, soil texture cannot rationally be modified, while plant nutrient status can be altered in many ways. The ability to manipulate a factor identifies a point in the system where change can be made.

(3) The transportability of the factor.

The factor is classified as transportable or nontransportable, that is, it can be moved from area to area with distance nonlimiting. Thus, temperature is not transportable; soil pH is not transportable. On the other hand, plants are highly transportable: One can move them to any region of the world, provided the conditions in the recipient region are suitable. Transportability of a factor provides yet another point at which a system can be changed.

This classification yields eight major groupings. They throw light on the nature of a constraint and provide some insight into the strategic approach to a solution without commenting on the complexity of the problem or the tactics to be used. Thus, a factor which is classified as "stable, cannot be manipulated, cannot be transported," requires that solutions must be developed *in situ*. Further, the solution to "remove" the constraint will not be found in the factor per se, but rather in the manipulation of other components of the production system.

The application of these descriptors to the climatic, edaphic, and biological components is shown in Tables 2, 3, and 4. The highest degree of flexibility in achieving solutions rests with the biological factors. A lesser flexibility in developing solutions rests with the edaphic factors; while they are nontransportable, nonetheless many can be

Table 2

A Classification of Climatic Factors

Descriptor	Rainfall	Temperature	Day Length
Stable			√
Unstable	√	√	
Can be manipulated			
Cannot be manipulated	√	√	√
Transferable			
Nontransferable	√	√	√

manipulated *in situ*. Further, as indicated, the resource base for plant nutrients has two components and one of these—added nutrients—is transportable.

The most intractable component is the climatic, where factors can neither be transported nor manipulated. As the taxonomy would suggest, the major unsolved problems should be those associated with climate. This is amply supported by such events as the recent shortfalls in cereal production, the Sahelian drought, the unprecedented rainfall of Tunisia of 1969, and the drought in England in 1976.

Since it is not feasible, given the present and foreseeable level of technology, to modify the factors of climate, two major strategies remain to a solution of the problems. One strategy is to modify the other components of the system to better fit the climatic regime of the area. This means a combination of management of the edaphic factors to reduce the adverse impact of the climate and simultaneous modification of the plant to respond optimally to the new management and associated climate. Inherent in this, however, is the assumption that the system is designed for one climatic regime. If any component of that regime changes, then one would expect less than optimal performance.

Table 3

A Classification of Edaphic Factors (*in situ*)

Descriptor	Nutrient Status	pH Salinity	Toxic Compounds	Texture	Drainage	Topog- raphy
Stable	√	√	√	√	√	√
Unstable						
Can be manipulated	√	√	√		√	
Cannot be manipulated				√		√
Transferable						
Nontransferable	√	√	√	√	√	√

Table 4

A Classification of Biological Factors Associated with Plants

Descriptor	Maturity	Hardi-ness[1]	Reaction to			Nutri-tional Quality	Yield
			Disease	Insects	Pests		
Stable	$\sqrt{}$[2]	$\sqrt{}$[2]	$\sqrt{}$[2]	$\sqrt{}$[2]	$\sqrt{}$[2]	$\sqrt{}$[2]	
Unstable							$\sqrt{}$[3]
Can be manipulated	$\sqrt{}$	$\sqrt{}$	$\sqrt{}$	$\sqrt{}$	$\sqrt{}$	$\sqrt{}$	$\sqrt{}$
Cannot be manipulated							
Transferable	$\sqrt{}$	$\sqrt{}$	$\sqrt{}$	$\sqrt{}$	$\sqrt{}$	$\sqrt{}$	$\sqrt{}$
Nontransferable							

[1] The ability to survive in a particular environment but not including disease, etc.

[2] This does not imply nonvariability within a genus or species, but rather constancy for a particular genotype.

[3] This arises from the fact that the plant is part of the system and hence subject to variation in other components.

The second strategy is to improve the forecasting of weather change, both in terms of accuracy and, most importantly, in extending the time range of forecasting for more adequate warning. To produce a forecast which could cover perhaps six months, of which the central period is the growing season for a crop, would give an opportunity to prepare for and use a system appropriate for that predicted weather pattern; the longer the forecast period, the better from the standpoint of the agricultural production scientist. The same would apply to improved prediction of long-term climatic change. This second approach would be coupled with the technology for production systems appropriate to each anticipated climate pattern.

Irrigation, land drainage, water storage, and water movement control are variables in management which can be used, generally in combination, to reduce the impact of the precipitation factor. The use of plant cover similarly may become a management practice in adjusting to climatic impact.

The taxonomy shows that the edaphic factors are more amenable than the climatic. They are stable in space and are nontransportable, but they can be manipulated. The factors capable of manipulation are mainly those associated with chemical and/or biological characteristics. One approach used by many agronomists is to develop technology which will maximize production under natural nutrient status. The danger in this approach lies in developing a technology which is more efficient in removing nutrients from the soil. A very real possibility exists, therefore, of worsening the situation, particularly in soils with a very limited reserve of nutrient and release capacity. Even in soils with high natural nutrient status, the problem arises, albeit delayed. For example, the grassland soils of western Canada are now showing responses to applied nutrients after upwards of seventy-five years of cropping. This is not to deny the need to improve the efficiency of nutrient use and recovery from the soil by the agricultural systems, but rather to recognize the drain on soil nutrients by plant growth.

The alternative approach is to improve the quality status by the addition of appropriate nutrients to supplement the natural supply and to meet the needs of the growing crop. The same reasoning applies to the problems of pH, alkalinity, and salinity. Some manipulation may be effected in the production system which will yield higher productivity, but as a rule a much higher level of production will be achieved by modifying the constraining factor. Implicit in both of these approaches is the location-specific nature of the problem and the need to transport to the area quantities of the nutrients and/or the soil amendment. These materials must, in addition, be supplied on a regular basis.

One immutable fact must be recognized: growing crops require nutrients obtainable only from the soil. If all of the plant material is returned to the soil on which it was grown, then there is effectively no nutrient loss but also very little food to sustain man; it is essentially a closed system. If, on the other hand, the edible portion of the crop is transported from the site of production, the nutrient supply will be steadily depleted and ultimately productivity will drop unless the removed nutrients are replaced from some external source.[7] Unfortunately, the source is frequently a considerable distance from the area of need; for instance, about 85% of the world's currently known potash reserves are found in western Canada. Morocco accounts for about one-third of world exports of phosphoric rock.

In comparison with the other components, the biological factors offer the greatest opportunity for solutions to constraints in the production system. The taxonomy would clearly suggest that the biological component be examined critically in every system in conjunction with the other components that may appear to be the major constraint. Thus, the nutrient status is extremely low in the *llanos* (oxisols and ultisols) and *campo cerrado* of Latin America. The need to correct this deficiency and overcome the toxicity is self-evident, but the need also to seek more efficient plant systems must proceed at the same time.

The capacity to manipulate the plant component can only be retained if we conserve the germ plasm in our economic species and their related species and genera. New developments in the area of wide crosses (somatic cell fusion, tissue culture) will widen the horizon from which genetic resources may be used. The urge is thus to conserve from broader areas rather than narrower.

The animal sector of the biological component has much the same taxonomy as that of the plant sector. It has, however, the added dimension that the feed supply is plant material, and hence is subject to all of the problems inherent in the plant system. More time is required to produce significant change in the animal system than is normal in the plant system. Animals can be transferred, but not on the same scale as plants. The entire animal-production (particularly the large animal) system, in fact, has not been subject to the same rigor in research as evident with plants, for example, breeding for improved efficiency of conversion of roughage. Most research has been concerned with manipulation of the environment of the animal, including feed and disease, rather than the animal itself.

One ineluctable fact emerges from a study of the classification. The agricultural production system is location-specific. While much basic work on the transportable and manipulatable factors can be done in a centralized location, the development of the technology package for the agricultural production system must be done in the zone of ultimate use.[8] If zones of similar characteristics could be confidently identified, then theoretically one could use the same production system in each zone. While this can be done on a very broad base, experience to date points to the need to do considerable adjustment research even when systems are transferred to areas that appear similar.

The constraints to production are primarily an integral part of the natural production system. Man-induced constraints tend to be localized and in most cases arise from mismanagement (e.g., accelerated water erosion or unbalanced nutrient application). On the other hand, as has been previously suggested, the major international or continental constraints are natural phenomena and present the greatest challenge in unsolved problems.

Returning to the earlier discussion of natural resources, an alternate interpretation of the question would be to consider major world ecosystems as the resource and examine the constraints to that system. In this approach the discussion will devolve to an examination of the same three basic components of the agricultural production system but with more clearly defined component parameters. I shall briefly refer to two such ecosystems: (a) the mountain environment and (b) the great area of oxisols and ultisols, the *llanos* and *campo cerrado* which cover much of South America.

In December 1974 a workshop was held in Munich to discuss the problems of the mountain environment and an interdisciplinary approach for a future strategy.[9] The workshop clearly emphasized the dimensions of the problem as exemplified by the statement that "about 10% of the world's populations live in mountain regions, mostly in developing countries . . . another 30–40% live in the adjacent lowlands." The lowland areas are much affected by, although physically removed from, the activities in the mountain regions; for example, the mountain areas recharge lowland water. Admittedly the regions vary, but they have some features in common: slope and altitude which in our taxonomy would be stable, nonmanipulated, and nontransferable. Solutions must be sought in the areas themselves, not only for the sake of better utilization of the zone per se but, of equal and probably greater importance, because of the impact on agricultural production areas removed from the site of the mountain.

Probably more than in any other ecological zone, the human element is inextricably entangled with the mountain environment. The aesthetic, recreational, and "quality-of-life" characteristics excite many to decry the destruction of the mountain; the obvious industrial resource that exists in terms of water power excites the pragmatic business interests; while the unrelenting pressure of population forces increasing use of the mountain for production of its food and fuel. A great challenge is there to develop systems of management and use which meet the needs of all groups and at the same time impart stability into the system.

It is estimated that there are 1,660 million hectares of tropical oxisols and ultisols, of which 822 million hectares are potentially arable. The largest continuous block, some 760 million hectares, is found in tropical America, mainly South America. Here it occurs as approximately one-third savanna and two-thirds forest. The soils are characterized by low natural plant-nutrient supply, high acidity, aluminum and in some cases manganese toxicity; in many clayey-textured soils there is a high phosphorus fixation. Temperature is not limiting, but the area is subject to seasonal drought which may be as long as six months. Clearly our taxonomy indicates research *in situ* to seek solutions.

The deceptively luxuriant tropical forests of these areas conceal a nearly closed cycle with all nutrients locked into the vegetation. Break the cycle by removing the tree cover and the soils rapidly (in some cases in as little as two years*) drop to zero productivity. The savanna areas—*llanos* of Colombia and *cerrado* of Brazil—are grass- and galleria forest-covered, with current use a very extensive beef animal-grazing

---

* P. Sanchez 1977: personal communication.

system which has a low level of production. Population pressure to use both the savanna and the forested areas urgently demands the development of an appropriate agricultural system technology. The unplanned removal of forest could result in nearly irreparable damage. Systems that minimize erosion (ideally, in fact, stop erosion), that make most efficient use of both natural and applied nutrients, that accommodate the toxicity and pH/acidity, and that present nutritionally acceptable and economically viable production, are urgently needed. The Food and Agriculture Organization's Proposals for Action estimates that 75% of the colonization in these areas could be spontaneous. Such development takes place without the benefit of planning for land use and unfortunately sound information on best use of the area is lacking. One of the largest land resources still available for agricultural production could be irretrievably damaged unless immediate action is taken. The research must embrace all three components of the production system, including the animals, since effectively, a new area requires development of technology rather than modifications in existing technology.[10]

A theme which is common to the two areas deals with the interface between agriculture and forestry. The exactions on forested areas in large measure come from agriculture and man's need for fuel. The rational production system in these two zones must consider optimal land use and balance agriculture and forest use both to stabilize the zone and meet the needs. A recent study by the International Development Research Centre, Ottawa, (Bene, Beall, and Côté 1977) has focused attention on these problems and has identified research needs. It is obvious that solutions to the environment-*cum*-agricultural production problems of either of these zones will encompass elements of "agroforestry."

SUMMARY

No attempt has been made to discuss the many exciting avenues of research that are being followed at present, or to suggest directions which research might take in the future. In the context of this paper I consider these to be tactics. Several recent reviews are listed in the Appendix. My concern here has been with the strategy of approach to constraints.

A set of strategies emerges from the study of the resource base, the constraints, and the typology. They indicate that we would be well advised to:

(1) Develop systems of agricultural production, including cultivars, which are better adapted to variable climatic conditions.

(2) Develop higher-confidence (i.e., lower-error) weather forecasting, particularly for the long range and of climate trends.

(3) Develop systems of agricultural production which are most efficient in using the large underutilized land masses, particularly the savanna soils and tropical forest soils and mountain areas which impinge on lowland agriculture.

(4) Maintain and increase the momentum of research on the biological component, including both plants and animals.

(5) Develop agricultural production systems which make more efficient use of plant nutrients per se and of those nutrients, transported in agricultural products, which can be recycled.

An additional strategy concerns research itself. Planners and those associated with the financing of research must realize the inescapable need for research at all levels, from basic to applied. The final "simple" improved technology used at the farm level has probably evolved from highly sophisticated basic research in what, to some, might seem to be such exotic disciplines as studies on photorespiration in cell cultures or *Endogne* species in the mycorrhiza. A balanced rational approach must be used in support of research activities, not only with respect to basic versus applied research, but also in relation to the ecological areas. Finally, it should be clear that man as such does not enter the production system as an input. He is the manager of the system. Concern, however, with the social and cultural problems of society, laudable and important as they are, will *not* supplant the need for water control or additional plant nutrients or a disease-resistant crop cultivar. Only attention to agricultural research can accomplish this.

NOTES

1. Wind, while obviously a component of climate, is much more elusive when viewed as a factor in an agricultural production system. There is no resource base as such but as a factor it can operate most decisively as a constraint. Wind erosion can be a most destructive force. Wind can transport foreign pollen so as to make pure-seed production nearly impossible, and can transport disease organisms over great distances, e.g., wheat rust spores from Texas to Saskatchewan. Wind patterns, for example the monsoon, are, of course, intimately involved in weather system movements.

2. "Man the Provider," the agricultural-theme pavilion at Expo 67, the World's Fair in Montreal, referred to this as "Nature's Basic Cycle" and developed the pavilion presentation around it.

3. A most important point stressed by the authors cited is that the "good" land is already under cultivation. What remains, and this is certainly true of the tropics which contain upwards of 50 percent of the unused potential, has

massive problems to be solved in order to bring it into significant production.

4. I have deliberately avoided the use of the word "fertilizer" in this paper. One might say that there are in fact myths associated with fertilizer, but not with plant nutrients. Plant nutrients are needed. They are added to overcome deficiencies in the natural system and/or to provide the nutrient basis for increased productivity. They are not an unnecessary frill (as is sometimes suggested with regard to fertilizer) used at the whim of the agriculturists. Even scientists contribute unwittingly to this misunderstanding, e.g., Pinstrup-Anderson (1976) states that "fertilizer plays a major role in certain other crops, such as sugarcane, cotton, coffee, banana, and potatoes in developing countries," implying that fertilizer "plant nutrient" is not important in many crops. Such an implication is clearly false and misleads the public on the indispensable role of fertilizer plant nutrients.

5. Plant nutrients are normally divided into macronutrients, those required in large amounts (generally upwards of 25 kg/hectare), generally nitrogen, phosphorus, and potassium; and micro, those required in small amounts (generally less than 5 kg and frequently less than 1 kg per hectare), such as iron, boron, sulphur, zinc, manganese, magnesium, copper, and molybdenum. Upwards of 60 elements have been found in plants but their essential role is not established. Division into macro and micro does not imply importance, since a microelement, for example zinc in many soils, may be critical to plant growth. There are, in addition, elements which may be essential for animal health, but not needed for plant growth. Cobalt is such an element, while selenium deficiency can cause physiological problems in animals and an excess of it in plants can be toxic to animals. Thus, in animal production systems, the nutrient requirements of both the plant and the animal must be considered.

6. Much progress has been made in recent years in improving the efficiency of N-fixation in legumes and in identifying similar processes in other crop species. For more detailed information, see:

American Society of Agronomy. 1976. Biological N Fixation in Forage-Livestock Systems. Amer. Soc. Agron. Special Publ. No. 28. Madison, Wisconsin.

Hardy, W. F., and A. H. Gibson (eds.). 1976. A Treatise on Dinitrogen Fixation. Wiley-Interscience, New York.

7. Nutrients removed in kg per metric ton of grain (not including that in roots, stems, leaves, and chaff) for three major food crops are:

	N	P_2O_5	K_2O
corn	16.00	6.28	4.74
wheat	20.82	10.41	6.24
rice	10.41	4.16	2.08

When this is extrapolated to the nutrients in the grain of these three crops for the quantity which enters world trade (not total world production), one obtains the following estimates:

Grain and Nutrients[1] Moving in World Trade—1973

Commodity	World Production	World Trade	Nutrients in Trade Portion		
			N	P_2O_5	K_2O
corn	311.78	49.68	.795	.312	.235
wheat	375.24	81.14	1.689	.844	.506
rice	208.48	9.24	.009	.038	.019
Total			2.493	1.194	.760

[1] Million metric tons.

Nutrients in Grain in Export as Percentage of Total Consumption[1]

	Total Consumption	World Export	Contents in 3 Grains	Percentage of Export
N	38.80	8.09	2.49	30.7
P_2O_5	22.78	4.38	1.19	27.1
K_2O	19.94	12.98	0.76	5.9

[1] Million metric tons.

These data lead to three observations: (1) there is a heavy demand on plant nutrient supplies to maintain production; (2) the total amount of nutrient which is moving in international trade is much higher than that reflected in fertilizer statistics; and (3) the recipients of exported grain—and these include many developing countries—should develop systems of recovery and use of these nutrients in their own production.

8. There are many who believe that the only valid and useful agricultural research is done on the farm. A new cultivar which has reduced photorespiration and potentially higher yield will be the result of very complex physiological, biochemical, and genetical research carried out under laboratory conditions and ultimately tested in the field. The myth that the only valid agricultural research is done on the farm should and must be exposed and exploded. The farm is of course the final proving ground.

9. The German Foundation for International Development sponsored this interdisciplinary workshop to discuss and formulate a strategy for mountain development. Some forty people drawn from various disciplines, ranging from agronomy to glaciology to tourism, and representing fourteen countries and agencies attended. The recommendations, working papers, and the "Munich Mountain Environment Manifest" were published by the German Foundation (DOK 799B/a., Dr. Müller-Hohenstein, editor.) While the recommendations call for action on the international scene, unfortunately little evidence of this has been seen to date.

10. A recent study completed by the National Academy of Sciences (*World Food and Nutrition Study: The Potential Contributions of Research*, National Academy of Sciences, Washington, D.C., 1977) has recognized the urgency to develop better soil and water management on the oxisols and

ultisols. Out of over 100 priority research areas this was one of the 22 finally selected for highest priority.

REFERENCES

Baker, H. G. 1965. *Plants and Civilization*. Fundamentals of Botany Series. Belmont, Calif.: Wadsworth Publishing Co.

Bene, J. G.; Beall, H. W.; and Côté, A. 1977. *Trees, Food and People: Land Management in the Tropics*. Publication IDRC-084e. Ottawa: International Development Research Centre.

Buringh, P.; van Heemst, H. D. J.; and Staring, G. J. 1975. *Computation of the Absolute Maximum Food Production of the World*. Wageningen, The Netherlands: Agricultural University.

Burton, G. W. 1968. "Food Resources in the Plant Kingdom." In *The Food Resources of Mankind*, ed. H. A. Steppler, pp.67–80. Montreal: Agri World Press.

Hare, F. K. 1968. "Land, Water and Climate as Parameters of Food Production." In *The Food Resources of Mankind*, ed. H. A. Steppler, pp.32–51. Montreal: Agri World Press.

Kellogg, C. E., and Orvedal, A. C. 1969. "Potentially Arable Soils of the World and Critical Measures for Their Use." *Advances in Agronomy* 21: 109–70.

Mesarovic, M., and Pestel, E. 1974. *Mankind at the Turning Point: The Second Report to the Club of Rome*. New York: E. P. Dutton.

National Academy of Sciences. 1976. *Underexploited Tropical Plants with Promising Economic Value*. Washington, D.C.

Pinstrup-Anderson, P. 1976. "The Role of Fertilizer in Meeting Developing Countries' Food Needs." Paper presented at 12th Annual Conference, Missouri Valley Economic Association. Mimeographed. Florence, Ala.: International Fertilizer Development Center.

Appendix

Suggestions for Further Reading

American Society of Agronomy. 1976. *Multiple Cropping*. ASA Special Publication no. 27. Madison, Wis.

Bassham, J. A. 1977. "Increasing Crop Production through more Controlled Photosynthesis." *Science* 197 (August):630–38.

Centro Internacional de Agricultura Tropical. 1973. *Potentials of Field Beans and other Food Legumes in Latin America*. Series Seminars no. 2E. Cali, Colombia.

————. 1975. *Potential to Increase Beef Production in Tropical America.* Series CE—no. 10. Cali, Colombia.

Duckham, A. N., and Masefield, G. B. 1971. *Farming Systems of the World.* London: Chatto & Windus.

Eckholm, E. P. 1976. *Losing Ground: Environmental Stress and World Food Prospects.* New York: W. W. Norton & Co.

Engelstad, O. P., and Russel, D. A. 1975. "Fertilizers for Use under Tropical Conditions." *Advances in Agronomy* 27:175–208.

Leach, G. 1976. *Energy and Food Production.* Guilford, England: IPC Science and Technology Press.

Pirie, N. W. 1976. "The World Food Supply: Physical Limitations." *Futures* 8(December):509–16.

Schechter, J. 1977. "Desertification Processes and the Search for Solution." *Interdisciplinary Science Reviews* 2(March):36–54.

Spedding, C. R. W. 1975. *The Biology of Agricultural Systems.* London: Academic Press.

Wareing, P. F., and Cooper, J. P., editors. 1971. *Potential Crop Production.* London: Heinemann Educational Books.

PART III

DISTORTION OF INCENTIVES

Distortions of Agricultural Development Resulting from Government Prohibitions

W. DAVID HOPPER

The 1966 precursor of summer's heat arrived in Delhi by mid-March. The prevailing wind had backed from northwest to southwest, from carrying the cool breezes of the plateaus of Turkestan to pushing before it the warm winds of Arabia and the Indian Ocean. The ceiling fans at the Delhi School of Economics spun wildly in an effort to cool the bodies, if not the tempers, of those participating in a seminar on the possible and probable consequences to India of a massive introduction of high-yielding seeds of dwarf wheat and rice varieties. The seminar participants were government bureaucrats, scholars from agricultural and general universities, a sprinkling of foreign advisors and expatriate technical assistants, and a few political leaders, including, when time permitted, India's minister of agriculture.

Within the first few hours of a three-day meeting, the discussion focused on a call by many participants for government prohibition of further imports of high-yielding seeds and for government efforts to ban the spread to farmers of the genetic stocks of dwarf materials then available on the research stations of the nation. Despite the protests of the few, the meeting carried a clear consensus for prohibiting the entry and use of the new varieties. Fortunately for the nation's hungry masses, the politicians ignored the consensus. The high-yielding, dwarf genes were imported from Mexico and the Philippines. Some 18,000 tons of dwarf wheat seed arrived in Bombay from Mexico in late spring of 1966, the largest seed transfer in world history. By 1970, India's wheat production had doubled the previous record of 1965.

There were many factors at play behind the call for prohibition of the elements that would generate a spectacular rise in India's food output. No one at the seminar was under any illusion about the nature of the recommendation, that the government use the coercive power of the state to prevent farmers from adopting practices that promised to raise their yields.

There were no illusions about the desperate nature of the food crisis facing the nation. In 1966 food production had plummeted to almost 10% below the best previous year. To recommend such a prohibition under these circumstances was not done lightly. For many, especially the most influential of the academics at the seminar, the issue centered on the question of production expansion versus social and distributive equity. Even the most ardent supporter of the use of the new plant materials recognized that farmers without access to secure irrigation sources would not gain from the use of the dwarf varieties because of limited moisture availability. They would be economically disadvantaged in the future by a disproportionate rise in output from the irrigated areas of the country. The new production technology would benefit only some of the nation's wheat and rice farmers. The result would foster inequality among rural people, an outcome clearly at odds with the Indian constitution which has as a central theme the creation of an egalitarian society.

The arguments were, of course, more elaborate. Some participants questioned whether the new varieties would raise yields. And because they might not, farmers should not be encouraged to invest in them. Others argued that if production did increase, the inelastic demand for cereals would reduce overall farm income, leaving cultivators worse off than before the introduction of the output-improving techniques. Still others expressed concern about the large amounts of fertilizer the country would have to import if the production potential were to be achieved and the consequent large drain on foreign exchange reserves. And the fertilizer argument was extended: It was claimed that India's domestic supplies of plant nutrients could only be increased by proprietary technologies presently held by large multinational corporations, technologies that would not be provided without the participation of these corporations in the Indian industrial economy. This participation should be avoided because of fears of foreign economic exploitation. Further, there were those who insisted that no technological advance should be introduced before land, credit, and other institutional and social reforms were carried out. In their view, a prosperous farm community would make reforms more expensive to the state (by raising the compensation to be paid for expropriated land, for example) and politically more difficult because kulak farmers would have greater political power. Perhaps strangest of all were those who believed that the introduction of high-yielding varieties was a plot of Western nations to undermine traditional Indian culture and society by setting the peasant on an irreversible course to capitalistic, industrially intensive farming. Finally, there was a small group who argued most strenuously that prohibition was needed to prevent the destruction of Indian peasant self-sufficiency: The use of fertilizer, purchased seed, large amounts of irrigation water, insecticides, and so on, would force the peasant into the market economy, a consequence that should be avoided even at the cost of state coercion and reduced food availability.

But it was the small group who claimed that technological innovation was the only hope for feeding India's population that ultimately influenced the politicians. The most massive change in Indian food-production techniques was launched.

Intellectual crosscurrents of the Delhi seminar still surface in one form or another in debates over agricultural and rural development around the world. The recourse to direct prohibition of some element of technical advance is practiced by virtually all countries. Until a few years ago, Canadian plant breeders held an unshakable attachment to the 60-pound bushel of wheat. The release to farmers for cultivation of any variety, no matter how well it yielded, which did not pass the 60-pound test weight was strongly resisted. The dwarf wheat varieties developed in Mexico that test weigh at 54 to 56 pounds per bushel were unacceptable for release even though they yielded 20 to 30% more total grain weight per acre. While this position has been modified now, high-yielding varieties are still discriminated against if they cannot be easily identified and separated from other approved marketable grain.

Interventions by government to prevent or penalize the use of particular farm production factors or to guide the course of agricultural or economic development can be by direct or indirect means.

The most familiar example of a direct intervention is the banning of certain, long-lasting insecticides that may have side effects harmful to other flora or fauna of the environment. The most celebrated of these insecticides is DDT. The evidence for its deleterious environmental effects seems strong although many doubters remain. But it seems also that in using the coercive power of the state to prevent the use of DDT, very little consideration was given to comparing the benefits of its application in agriculture and in the control of human-disease vectors, such as the mosquito, with the costs to the environment of its further application. It is true that there was, and is, a fear that the continued and likely increased use of DDT worldwide might trigger irreversible changes in the global environment that would threaten the stability of the entire biological world. Such fears are not easily disproven. Yet, in the debate over DDT use there seems to have been less concern with rational scientific fact than with fear, a fear that rapidly spawned appeals and pressures for political intervention.

The banning of DES as a feed supplement for cattle is another case in point. The possibility of carcinogenic links between DES and test animals was enough to generate a legal prohibition and the benefits of lower-priced beef were foregone. Similar prohibitions seem to be in preparation against the use of many herbicides in general farming and antibiotics in poultry and hog production. Again, the evidence for each prohibition seems to rest less on scientific assessments and economic appraisals of costs and returns than on the emotions generated by fears of the unknown or the apprehensions of the "unnatural."

When scientific evidence clearly indicates a serious risk of deleterious effects from the use of a particular product, society has an unquestioned right to protect itself from these effects, but the balancing of scientific findings against emotion-based argument is always difficult. The discussion most typically forces the politician to legislate what he interprets to be the truth. His ultimate justification for the legislation is that truth is determined by a majority of the voters, not by the test of the laws of proof. That is probably the reason why few scientists make good politicians, and why few politicians feel at home with scientists.

The debates over direct prohibitions that find their justification in social objectives are easier for the politicians to understand and handle. Such prohibitions, however, suppress production advances no less than those that arise from a failure to adequately assess scientific evidence.

A classic example of prohibitions that limit agricultural advance for social reasons are those against the use of agricultural machinery. Nearly every developing country has one or more laws or regulations banning the importation or the use of tractors, harvesters, intertillage machines, or some other mechanically-powered farm implement. The theory supporting these actions is simple: Large rural populations have a surplus of labor; modern, powered farm implements substitute for labor, ergo, they should not be permitted because they will reduce the useful employment of rural people.

The argument is specious. The main source of rural poverty is the low productivity of rural labor. This low productivity is inherent in the traditional agricultural technologies based on muscle energy. Productivity will not be altered appreciably without expanding the capacity of individual farmers to cultivate their landholdings more intensively. Intensive cultivation can only be accomplished by a radical change in the tools used in the production process. There is much evidence that better tillage machines open opportunities for the multiple cropping of tropical soils previously closed because of the impossibility of rapidly preparing the land between crop seasons. The better control over the timing and the precision with which farm operations can be carried out using mechanically-powered implements leads to other significant savings, for example, in controlling seed rate, applying water, or accurately placing fertilizer for more efficient use by the plant. Yet the myth persists that modern machinery is deleterious to the well-being of traditional rural peasants and should be proscribed in the name of economic equity and social advancement.

China's recent decision to mechanize all its farms by 1985 may cause some nations to reappraise their prohibitions against mechanical farm implements. The Chinese cite three reasons for their mechanization policy: it will facilitate multiple cropping and make more effective use of crop inputs by enabling farm practices to be conducted with better timing and operating precision; it will permit farmers to expand their land and their food and cash crops significantly by reducing the present large acreage that must be allotted to pasture and fodder for draft animals; and it will reduce the physical tedium of farm labor while increasing its productivity. All these are sound, valid reasons that may be recognized as such by other nations.

Prohibitions on agricultural implements or on other productive factors such as the use of large tube wells for irrigation can deny farmers the advantages of scale economies. Withholding external sources of efficiencies from low-income farmers likely will hold them within the static bounds of their traditional technologies. The gains from expanding size of operation are often considerable, and not the least of these gains is the opening of new opportunity for the release of peasant entrepreneurship, initiative, and innovation.

Direct prohibitions aimed at nearly all nontraditional farm inputs can be found in one country or another. In many countries there is a fear that cash-crop production will reduce local food supplies; therefore, the use farmers make of their land is controlled. In others, farmers are permitted to divert only small parts of their acreage from export cash crops to commodities for the domestic market. In many nations, the infrastructure of modern farm services has not been extended to all farmers because some of them are ethnically different from the dominant society; to preserve indigenous and tribal heritages some farmers are deliberately left outside the main effort of nation building. In still other countries, farmers in the watersheds behind recently constructed modern dams are restricted to following cultivation and cropping practices that supposedly will prevent undue silting of the reservoir. When dams are built to generate electric power and provide water for irrigation, the irrigation purpose is most often given a much lower priority claim on the reservoir's stored water. Often the need for tax revenue to pay the costs of an irrigation project results in prohibitions on the

private exploitation of groundwater sources in the command area even
when such water is plentiful (replenished from massive canal seepage)
and its use would clearly repay the costs of exploitation with higher
farm yields.

The catalogue of examples of prohibitions is large. Many prohibitions are simply foolish. An example is the requirement in some South
Asian countries that all grain be sold in jute bags when bulk handling
is cheaper and more efficient but is opposed by the jute lobby. Other
prohibitions are instituted for bureaucratic convenience. Such a one
is the requirement that all animals must be slaughtered at abattoirs
located in only a few major urban centers. The savings in bureaucratic
procedures and inspection costs are lost many times over in the transportation of live animals from producing areas and in the shipment of
dressed meat to outlying consumers. But some prohibitions are based
on sound scientific principles, and these include the attempts in parts
of Africa and Latin America to control animal numbers on common
rangeland to prevent overgrazing and erosion of the grasslands.

Added to the list of direct prohibitions must be those which governments enact or promulgate against the transfer of advanced technologies which they have developed or acquired to other societies. Malaysia, for example, has strong controls on the release to other countries
of seed of its high-yielding oil palms and the clones of its high-yielding
rubber varieties. Several countries restrict export of the parent lines
of hybrid seed and even the international movement of animal semen.
But restrictions of this sort are less frequently governmental than they
are proprietary. Private seed producers carefully control access to their
seed lines. Hatcheries have patented hybrid poultry strains that are
available only under license or through partnership arrangements.
Technologies of manufacture and of product design are most often
proprietary matters held as company secrets or under patent laws. The
use of these technologies or designs involves some form of purchase or
of joint venture. Patent-protection laws are being extended to include
more of the world's countries; and they are being expanded to embrace
more products, for example, seed and animal lines, and industrial manufacturing technologies, especially in the chemical and pharmaceutical
industries. The extension of proprietary patent protection will further
impede the free flow of new, more efficient production techniques, and
deny to those who do not have the purchasing power to buy, or the
investment potential to bargain on joint venture arrangements, the economic advantages inherent in the use of modern production techniques.

Indirect prohibitions—those exclusions which arise as the result of
government actions designed to accomplish other purposes are perhaps
more important than direct interventions in limiting increased farm

production. A notable example is found in the mechanisms governments use to escape the attendant social and human problems of scale
economies in agriculture by legislating against farm-size growth. Limitations on farm size carry major long-term implications for the structure of rural society; these implications are likely to generate problems
as great as those that would arise from the unhampered play of a free
land market. Because the economic and social dislocations produced
by a legislated maximum farm size are evident mainly in the long term,
they are ignored by politicians with a short-term perspective as they
strive to avoid grappling with the immediate problem of too many
people for too little land. But limiting farm size has an impact on the
rate of innovation and agricultural modernization. Modern farm technology is often lumpy in its adoption and application; that is, the use
of new techniques, and particularly investments in land improvement
and new implements, become economic only if they can be spread
over holdings of a minimum size. A small irrigation pump may require
a command area of many acres more than the legal maximum farm
size to be economic. A tractor of the size demanded by local soil conditions may be too powerful to till a small acreage efficiently. Effective
use of plant-protection measures may depend on their application to
block acreages that are greater than the maximum prescribed farm
size. These are but a few examples.

Other indirect policies of government can also depress agricultural
output and slow rural progress. Some act to distort product and factor
prices and reduce the incentives to cultivators to produce more. Import
restrictions on machinery, fertilizers, pesticides and other agricultural
chemicals, improved livestock, or better seed, for example, are direct
interventions. But tariffs and other import duties often have a devastating effect on the growth of output. In like manner, government controls
over foreign exchange can and often do effectively keep many high-
productivity inputs from local farmers.

Less obvious are the indirect effects of public policies that divert
national resources to nonagricultural uses. In many Third World nations, large expenditures are made on defense, leaving too few resources for domestic civil development. What resources are available
are too often used for urban development at the expense of farm and
rural investment. Too frequently governments assume that the investment elasticity of supply in agriculture is zero; that is, they assume
agriculture will continue to produce and grow with little or no allocation of national capital resources to nurture it. This is an incorrect assumption that has had a ruinous short-term impact on the advance of
farm production throughout the Third World.

The priority that governments give to social objectives over economic growth is another important source of an indirect depression of farm-output growth. The extreme case is Tanzania. Government efforts to bring about a social transformation by building large cooperative villages have been responsible for a major decline in national food output. The uprooting and resettlement of rural people, often far from their traditional lands, has caused farm production to drop to a point where the nation must import large quantities of food. In this case, the ideology of social reform has fully replaced any drive for economic growth. As long as food aid (or long-term loans for food purchases) is supplied to Tanzania by the industrial nations, the social experiment will continue.

While the Tanzanian example is an extreme one, determination to build a "new" rural society has resulted in programs and administrative practices that have severely constrained or destroyed farmer incentives in many countries. Mexico's *ejido* program is another example. The *ejido* is a large cooperative society farming a substantial area of land. Each member of the society has his own private plot and receives the produce of that plot. But each year the plots are redistributed among the members in a manner designed to ensure that the member who had a low-yielding plot one year receives a high-yielding plot the next, and vice versa. This egalitarian pattern of land redistribution eliminates any private incentive to members to invest in long-term land improvement. The *ejido* system prohibits long-term private ownership of land; this prohibition is rooted in a social ideology designed to ensure that all members of the cooperative enjoy the same income opportunities from land. The economic effect is to hold production to the level set by the least-competent farmer.

Political policies that favor particular groups or private interests at the expense of the rural population of the nation are also sources of constraint to higher agricultural production. An instance is the elaborate structure of protective networks of licenses, quotas, or market allocations that governments build around and for their domestic industries to protect manufactures from outside competition and, too often, from internal competition. These interventions sap competition and suppress the vitality of industry, destroying its ability to generate the strong support needed for agricultural modernization. Such protective networks are seldom provided for the farm industry. Indeed, with food aid available on concessional terms and a strong political concern in many Third World countries to provide cheap food to urban consumers, domestic farm economies are most often left open to the full force of world competition and subsidized giveaway programs.

One prohibition that looms large in agricultural progress is that imposed by governments in the name of plant and animal quarantine. Thousands of tons of grain can enter virtually any country on commercial account without more than a glance at samples taken to assess delivered quality against contract promise. Yet when a small packet of grain is labeled as being seed or for use in plant breeding or research, if it is admitted at all it is often subjected to such a rigorous examination for pathogens that its usefulness as a viable source of new genes is destroyed. While every society has a right to protect itself against the introduction of unwanted pests and diseases, the right must be exercised with a recognition that the risks of disease introduction must be measured against the potential for increased agricultural output that will accrue from research founded upon a larger diversity of genetic plant and animal materials than is available locally. There can be no dispute about the need for quarantine protection. Should cassava mosaic disease move from Africa to Latin America in a careless transfer of biological material, the results would be devastating, perhaps equivalent to the consequences experienced in Ireland when the potato blight entered that country in the mid-nineteenth century. Quarantine protection must be given a most careful examination by all biological scientists and by their governments. But there should be a more careful assessment than now seems to be the rule of the risks that are acceptable and unacceptable. It is the scientific community who set quarantine standards, and there is little evidence that a careful rationality determines what the standards should be. Emotion, conviction, and disciplinary interests of pathologist and breeder and geneticist seem to guide the debate and determine its outcome. In the absence of rational assessment, some nations undertake great risks; others use legal prohibitions to avoid the risks and thereby sacrifice the benefits. It is a most serious matter. Modern agriculture rests upon continued varietal and breed improvement. Without a large pool of diverse genetic material, the modern animal or plant breeder is unable to break from the yield limitations inherent in the genes carried in the traditional biological resources of his nation. Such a limitation can stifle research and smother farm progress in all but the very large countries.

Observations from many nations reveal a multitude of direct prohibitions, sanctions, and powerful government interventions that influence, suppress, or distort the progress that can be made towards a more fruitful world agriculture. All prohibitions, whether sound or foolish, are direct constraints on production; all close to cultivators significant opportunities for technological innovation; and all should be more carefully assessed than they appear to be at the present time for their impact on reducing the benefits and increasing the costs of agricultural advance.

In the years ahead, however, it seems likely that few of these prohibitions will be removed. If anything, the current trend in most countries is to more, not less, interdiction and proscription in national economies. The desires of politicians, especially in the Third World, to engineer fully and in detail the social, economic, and political transformation of their societies suggest that rural people will face a living and working environment that is increasingly subject to control by techniques of state intervention. The likely result of this control is already evident. Unless the interventions are as comprehensive as they have become in totalitarian China (where the communes are essentially capitalistic corporations with an assured and docile labor force), developing countries will do little more than replicate the history of the past three decades of inadequate farm progress. At worst, they will repeat the experience of Tanzania—farm output will drop and there will be a greater national dependency on the charity of others. It is not a pleasant prospect.

But this prognosis is likely to be only a short-run phenomenon. The longer term can be viewed more optimistically. A stagnant farm sector in Third World countries will mean widespread food shortages. And these shortages, compounded by other social and economic difficulties engendered by low agricultural and rural growth, will force a new view of how development can best be achieved. The lessons from the few countries, such as Brazil and South Korea, where fewer rural-development prohibitions are found and where farm-output growth has been high under essentially market conditions, will be learned and emulated. It is from these lessons that the new view will be derived.

COMMENT

Keith W. Finlay

W. David Hopper's wide variety of examples has tellingly illustrated how government intervention by direct or indirect methods can adversely affect the utilization of technological innovation in increasing agricultural production.

As a member of the staff of an international agricultural research institute devoted to the development of new agricultural technology and to assisting the strengthening of national maize and wheat research and production programs, let me further illustrate how government intervention directly affects the adoption of new technology.

One of the most important aspects of assistance in strengthening national programs in developing countries is the training of research, production, and administration personnel. International centers such as the International Maize and Wheat Improvement Center with which I am associated are involved in various aspects of training, particularly those associated with the development of production-oriented skills enabling scientists to utilize their academic training to produce or adapt technology of value to their nation.

Most of the scientists that receive this type of training have bachelor's degrees, although in a number of developing countries where there are very few university graduates, young male graduates of agricultural high schools are accepted for training. Following this "in-service" training, those scientists with obvious leadership potential and unexploited ability for further academic training are provided with graduate fellowships to train as future research and production leaders in their national crop programs.

Government policy with regard to the employment of the trained young scientists can have a very serious implication on the development of this national expertise. A number of countries have policies which preclude agricultural high school graduates without college degrees from ever being able to assume leadership positions, no matter how outstanding their abilities and experiences. An even worse impediment is the lack of recognition of graduate degrees from certain countries. For example, in the francophile countries of North Africa, master of science and doctoral degrees obtained in North America and Britain are not recognized in comparison with those earned in France. This means that some of the most outstanding young scientists with the highest level of training are given inferior posts and are not able to contribute effectively to their nation's development.

Another common government policy, not limited to developing countries, is the system of promotion by seniority. This procedure is particularly unfavorable in developing countries where assistance agencies try to help build a cadre of young scientists and administrators, trained in modern technology, who can move up and strengthen the whole national structure. The seniority system often forms a major barrier to the development of a logical pattern of well-trained staff.

Dr. Hopper has mentioned in his paper the impediment to free movement of improved plant materials caused by plant-quarantine regulations. There is of course the danger of introducing devastating pests and diseases by the free movement of plants from one country to another, thus endangering an agricultural industry based on susceptible plants. However, the principal problem is not the existence of quarantine regulations but rather the validity of the criteria on which any existing regulations and laws are based. Many countries have been so overzealous in adopting quarantine regulation that importation of superior germ plasm is virtually impossible.

Not uncommonly, seeds of improved new varieties are sent to countries urgently needing them to increase food production. There the seed is subjected to such severe physical and chemical treatment that all seed viability is destroyed. In many instances the time taken within a bureaucratic system to test these seeds in quarantine is excessive and they reach the scientist far too late to be of any value in his breeding and production programs. The responsibility for quarantine does and must continue to reside with the importing nation. However, there is a need to ensure that any existing regulations are sensible and suitable for the particular stage of development of the national program.

Often associated with plant quarantine are the seed laws of the nation. Two aspects of these seed laws in many countries have adversely affected the rate of adoption of new technology and improved varieties. The first of these concerns the development of a seed industry to provide pure seed of improved varieties for farmers. There is a real need for an efficient seed industry in many countries. However, in the developing world the responsibility for this function is generally placed with a government bureaucratic organization. Very few of these organizations have been successful. They tend to introduce a range of restrictions rather than an effective and efficient organization and structure to provide good seed for the farmers. Those countries which have allowed private industry to operate a seed industry have, in general, been more effective.

With respect to the creation of a seed industry in developing countries, there is another form of intervention which is worth mentioning. International agencies, such as the World Bank and the Food and Agriculture Organization of the United Nations, have very actively supported development of seed industries. The basis for this support is well founded. However, these agencies often have been unrealistic in advising developing countries to adopt seed laws far too complex for their stage of development. Many of the regulations are based on the highly sophisticated agriculture of Europe and North America and therefore impose a wide range of restrictions and procedures that only serve to limit the multiplication and availability of improved seeds to the farmers.

The status of the international agencies is such that the governments of developing countries accept much of their advice on face value, especially if it is tied to financial support. This example highlights the need for assistance agencies of all types to be aware of all aspects of the local agricultural industry. Often with the best of intentions, the agencies' advice can be counterproductive, inducing the recipient government to intervene with laws and regulation which slow down rather than speed up its rate of progress.

Other aspects of the breeding, multiplication, and release of new varieties are adversely affected by government policies. For example, it is common practice in many developing countries to require a plant breeder to test his potential new varieties for five to seven years or more in a number of environments before the varieties can enter the seed-multiplication process for release to farmers. This long testing process can be very expensive in loss of income to the farmers and total production to the nation, especially if the variety has improved yield or is disease and pest resistant.

The problem of lengthy testing procedures is compounded if the breeder is endeavoring to overcome a highly variable and virulent disease problem that is affecting production. Under these conditions it is common for new varieties to have an effective life in farm production of as little as three to four years. This means that many potentially useful selections will become susceptible to new races of the pathogen, even before they can enter commercial production, if the testing time is unduly long.

In recent years, particularly in industrialized countries, governments have been introducing legislation to protect breeders' rights in new crop plants. By this procedure, a breeder may register a new variety and have it patented so that he, or his sponsoring company, receives financial recompense for all seed sold into commercial channels. This relatively new form of legislation has some very serious implications to the rapid spread of superior varieties, especially to developing countries.

Until recently, with very few exceptions, all improved genetic materials of major crop plants have moved freely from government to government, and from research organization to research organization. This has enabled countries to make maximum use of new and improved germ plasm, either within their own breeding programs, or directly into commercial production. If there is a widespread adoption of breeders' rights the free flow of improved germ plasm will be impeded.

The international agricultural research centers associated with the Consultative Group on International Agricultural Research have become a major source of improved germ plasm of crop plants. As yet they have been unaffected by breeders' rights legislation. They are adopting policies which will preclude their genetic materials being locked into a system of legislation which would slow down or reduce the effectiveness of their impact in developing countries.

The basic features of policies of the international centers are:

(1) The centers are producing genetic variability and do not release finished commercial varieties.

(2) This material as it is produced is freely available to legitimate users worldwide. For example, the International Maize and Wheat Improvement Center has a priority system. The top priority is for the release of new maize and wheat germ plasm to governments of developing nations; secondly, to national universities and research organizations of developed countries that can make use of the material in their research and breeding programs; and finally, to legitimate private seed companies. However, in this last case, only material at the early stages in its genetic development is released. By this technique, private seed companies, a number of which are extremely important in speeding up the development of agricultural production in developing countries, have access to genetic variability, but at a stage where their own breeders will carry out the selections and breeding procedure to take the material to the finished-variety stage. In all cases the international centers require that the collaborating agencies provide an exchange of valuable genetic materials and data resulting from testing all genetic materials supplied by the centers.

Another important impediment which has been introduced by the breeders' rights legislation is the need to test the proposed new variety in an extremely detailed manner to establish not only level of performance and adaptability but its originality, from the patenting point of view, by recording a large number of characteristics under a wide range of environmental conditions. This stage of identifying the uniqueness of the new variety has literally doubled the time necessary to produce and release it.

All of these examples indicate some of the ways in which government policies and interventions can influence the introduction and adoption of new technology.

Reciprocal aid-type trade agreements between developing countries and other nations have been another major source of frustration to agricultural scientists attempting to upgrade national production. Often, inappropriate types of fertilizer and farm machinery are provided to the farmers as a result of these trade agreements. Mixed fertilizers, with high proportions of phosphorus and potash, are often sold to developing nations when all local research indicates farmers can obtain optimum crop returns by utilizing nitrogen only.

Because of the large capital expenditures often involved, the trade exchange of inappropriate farm machinery also can be a costly policy decision. Some cultivation equipment often lasts less than one season in the soils with poor structure found in many parts of the developing world.

Recent experiments in Algeria by the Food and Agriculture Organization and our Center demonstrated that Australian and Canadian cultivator-drills were able to increase yields of wheat by up to 50 percent in some regions by controlling wild oats at the time of seeding. European drills were ineffective in weed control and could not withstand even a single season of use. Even so, Algeria recently built a local factory to produce European-type drills. This is likely to be an expensive policy decision.

It is obvious from the above examples that a major gap exists between the national scientists and the policy makers. The agricultural economist could do much to help fill this gap by becoming a "dirty hands" member of the research and production team. Economists from ministries of agriculture and planning, working with agricultural scientists at the farm and village market level, could help design field experiments to better answer relevant production questions. They could also become the information link between the farmers, the scientists, and the decision makers to ensure that relevant information is available at the time that important policy decisions must be made.

The International Maize and Wheat Improvement Center's economists in several parts of the world are encouraging and assisting national economists to undertake these roles. The response is very encouraging.

Agricultural Pricing Policies
in Developing Countries

GILBERT T. BROWN

Most developing countries for the last quarter century have had policies designed to lower the prices of food and other agricultural goods and to increase the prices of manufactured goods.[1] Trade and foreign-exchange practices have been major instruments of these policies, along with tax, direct price, and other market-control measures. The conventional wisdom supporting this twisting of the terms of trade against agriculture has had four main pillars, based on the assumptions:

(1) that aggregate agricultural production is not very responsive to price changes;

(2) that the chief beneficiaries of higher prices would be the larger-size farmers;

(3) that higher food and other agriculture-related prices such as clothing would most adversely affect low-income consumers; and

(4) that manufacturing provides a more rapid means of growth, and that achieving that growth depends upon large transfers of income (profits) and foreign exchange from agriculture to manufacturing. Thus, policies that depress agricultural prices and increase manufacturing prices will result both in more rapid economic growth and in a more equal distribution of income.

Lagging agricultural production and overall economic growth in many developing countries that have followed such policies, however, have led to increasing concern about measures that reduce farm incomes and incentives. Argentina, Egypt, Kenya, the Ivory Coast, Pakistan, Peru, the Philippines, Thailand, and Uruguay are among the countries which have acted to significantly increase agricultural relative to nonagricultural prices in the last several years (Appendix A). Greater emphasis in the development literature on employment-led and rural-development strategies, and on strategies to meet basic needs and to benefit persons in the lowest 40% of the income distribution, has also provided new intellectual support for price policies more favorable to agriculture, including lessened subsidies for capital goods, less overvalued exchange rates and protection for industry, and increased production of foodstuffs and other wage goods.

In contrast to those of the developing countries, price policies in the industrialized countries during this period have been distorted in favor of rather than against the farmer, and the typical problem has been overproduction rather underproduction of agricultural commodities. Moreover, as pointed out by D. Gale Johnson (1977), greater agricultural productivity per hectare in industrialized than in developing countries is a phenomenon that has occurred largely since the 1930s, and within the period of differential price policies. In the period 1934–38, grain yields averaged 1.15 tons per hectare in industrial countries, and 1.14 tons (i.e., the same level) in developing countries. By 1975, however, grain yields in industrial countries were more than double those in developing countries, 3.0 tons versus 1.4 tons per hectare. This is not to argue, of course, that the more rapid growth in agricultural yields and production in the industrialized countries is due solely to differences in price policies. A plausible hypothesis is that both the more favorable farm prices and the more rapid growth of farm yields in industrial countries reflect efforts to support farm incomes and increase agricultural productivity, while developing countries have generally been much more concerned about increasing industrial incentives and production, and urban incomes.

The focus of this paper is not on the factors that explain the differences in growth rates between developed and developing countries, however, but on the effects of recent pricing policies in today's developing countries. My hypothesis is that agricultural production, income distribution, and economic growth would all benefit from reduction or elimination of distortions that reduce agriculture's domestic terms of trade. The relation of agriculture's domestic terms of trade to income distribution and economic growth particularly are problems whose complexities outrun our capacity to measure by formal models, but they are also problems that are too important to neglect.

Several general problems of terminology or analysis should be briefly mentioned. First, references to "free-market" prices are to those that would exist in absence of specific controls and policies that now distort the relation of agricultural to nonagricultural prices, including those relationships that magnify differences between domestic and world-market prices. This is not to imply that world-market prices are "free," or that policy should aim to equate domestic and world-market prices or price relatives at all times. Neither is it to imply that shadow free-market prices can be known with exactitude, or to ignore that we are dealing with neither a first- nor even a second-best world. Rather, the comparison to probable prices "in the absence of controls" reflects only a judgment about approximate price relationships. Second, references to changes in prices are to changes from existing distorted price relations, not from the traditional equilibrium-price starting point of economic theory. Usually the discussion concerns what would happen if the distortion between existing prices and free-market or "equilibrium" (using that term loosely) prices were reduced. Thirdly, prices are an incomplete measure of incentives. If agriculture's relative productivity is increasing, it is possible for agricultural incomes and incentives to be growing at the same time that agricultural prices are declining. Fourthly, a fundamental distinction must be made between measures such as price controls, taxes, and subsidies that artificially lower food and agricultural prices and measures such as on-farm investment, technological advances, and rural infrastructure development (e.g., roads, electricity, and water), that lower prices by lowering the real costs of production. Reductions in real resource costs of production (i.e., increases in input yields) may benefit urban dwellers, farmers, and rural laborers alike.

PRICING POLICIES AND AGRICULTURAL PRODUCTION

Efficient Use of Resources

Higher prices may stimulate agricultural production by (1) causing producers to move closer to their production-possibility frontier by better use of resources, (2) encouraging use of more labor and other variable resource inputs to reach higher production-function and output levels, or (3) inducing investment and the discovery and adoption of new agricultural technologies that result in new, lower-cost production functions.

The usual empirical basis of arguments that agricultural production is not very responsive to price changes rests upon multiple-correlation analysis of the acreage or output of a particular crop in relation either to the relative prices of that crop versus others, or to several presumably independent variables, such as output price and use of fertilizer, labor, and water.[2] The price elasticity of aggregate agricultural production is less than for individual crops, of course, since substitution between crops may account for an important part of the response of a single crop to changes in its relative prices.[3] This multiple-correlation methodology can be faulted on several grounds, including the lack of independence between prices on one hand and the level of use of fertilizer and other inputs.[4] The use of acreage rather than output in most such studies underestimates the price elasticity of production by not taking account of changes in yields, which have been accounting for an increasingly large part (now more than half) of the annual growth in world food-grain production.[5] Also, it is doubtful that yearly fluctuations in prices are an adequate proxy for changes in the income expectations that determine rates of investment in agriculture and its supporting infrastructure, labor inputs, and the adoption of new techniques. These decisions appear to depend more upon whether expected profitability is above or below a "threshold" level of acceptability, and may be little affected by yearly price fluctuations unless these cause longer-run expectations of profitability to change. Moreover, incentives are a function of net income and not just prices, and therefore a new technology may importantly change the incentive effect of a given set of prices, as happened during the Green Revolution in wheat and rice.[6]

Price incentives may cause farmers to use improved seeds, along with more fertilizer, pesticides, and other purchased inputs, to adopt improved cultural practices, and to apply more family or hired labor. All of these ways of increasing the efficiency of resource use may occur at once, for example, if a small farmer decides to reduce or give up his off-farm employment—or a son does not migrate to the city—in order to adopt the more labor-intensive techniques required to reap the benefits of new varieties. Generalities about most small farmers as "subsistence" farmers unaffected by agricultural prices are at best misleading.

Timmer and Falcon (1975) have found a close rank correlation between unhulled rice (paddy) prices and rice yields among Asian countries. For 1970, they found that rice yields varied from 5.64 and 4.55 metric tons per hectare in Japan and Korea to 2.1 to 1.7 tons per hectare in Indonesia, Thailand, the Philippines, and Burma. At the same time, the ratio of the price of a kilogram of rice to the price of a kilogram of fertilizer nutrients showed a similar wide variation, from 1.43 and .96 in Japan and Korea to 0.4 to 0.1 in Indonesia, Thailand, the Philippines, and Burma. This pattern of inter-country relationships between prices and yields cannot be explained as short-term elasticity response, but may well be indicative of the long-run responsiveness of production to incentives. While the price data used in this study were only for one year, the differences in national prices are very substantial, and reflect long-standing differences in price policies among these countries. It is noteworthy that the three countries with the highest yields—Japan, South Korea, and Taiwan—have some of the poorest soils among the nine countries studied. The high prices to farmers in these countries appear necessary to cover the costs of achieving these yields under the given climatic, soil, and other conditions, even though the decisions to pay such high prices may have been primarily political (Hayami 1975). It is interesting to speculate to what levels rice yields and production would fall in Japan if farmers there received the same price as Thai farmers, or conversely the levels to which rice yields and production would climb in Thailand within a few years if Thai farmers faced the same rice and fertilizer prices as Japanese farmers.[7]

Shifts in the Production Function

The most important long-run effects of price incentives on production may be through price-induced shifts in the production function, rather than through greater efficiency of resource use with existing production functions. These long-run effects depend upon the extent to which the incentive structure has an important effect upon technological change (both on research and on adoption of new techniques by farmers), on public and private investment related to agriculture, and on institutional change affecting agricultural output (land reform, extension services, marketing, and distribution facilities).

Clear links have been demonstrated between pricing policy and both the discovery and nature of new technological discoveries, and the adoption of these techniques by farmers. The relationship between relative prices of land and labor in Japan and in the United States, and the very different directions of technological change in these two countries in the last century, has been well documented (Hayami and Ruttan 1971; Yamada and Ruttan 1975). The late-1973 jump in oil prices has also presented ample evidence of the link between prices and research. Much of the agricultural research initiated since then is "energy saving," with heavy emphasis on reducing fertilizer requirements, for example, through nitrogen fixation, seed treatment, and placing a small amount of fertilizer close to the seed or seedling roots.

The link between price incentives and private investment in chemical inputs, labor, land leveling, irrigation, and other measures to increase farm output is almost axiomatic. Studies of diffusion of new techniques and of new investment in developing countries indicate that where profitability of adopting a new technique or investing, say, in a tube well is very high, that the new techniques will be rapidly adopted and the new investment quickly made (Yasin 1965; Eckert 1974). At the margin at least there are wealthy individuals who make choices between agricultural and nonfarm investments. A large proportion of upper- and even middle-class individuals in South Asia reside in cities and have a profession, a business, or a government job, but own substantial farmland operated by a hired manager or tenant (sometimes a relative). For these individuals, as for the small farmer deciding how to divide his time between his own farm and other employment, the choice between farm and nonfarm investment (and employment) is a recurring one. Higher returns to farming certainly attract more labor and more investment (*ceteris paribus*) into farming. Moreover, the higher returns generate more income and saving, and, therefore, the ability to finance more investment in agriculture. Nearly all studies show high marginal saving rates among even poor farmers (e.g., Adams 1976). Thus, an important part of the additional income accruing to farmers through higher prices is likely to result in greater savings and investment. In countries where farm yields are low and returns to additional investment in agriculture are high (e.g., where fertilizer use is well below optimal levels because farmers lack financial resources, as is true in much of South Asia and other food-deficit low-income countries) an important part of that saving is likely to be invested in farming.

Public investment and institutional changes may also be importantly affected by prices, but research on these topics is in its infancy. Evidence has been presented that public investment in irrigation in the Philippines has been closely correlated with the import price of rice (Hayami and Kikuchi 1978). There has certainly been a tendency for some officials to think of nonagricultural development as somehow more important than progress in agriculture. Higher prices for agricultural products will make at least the nonshadow-priced value of agricultural output greater, and the nominal or financial rate of return to agricultural projects more attractive. The more attractive financial return may induce highly productive institutional development, such as more effective agricultural research and extension systems, and input distribution and output-marketing systems (Arndt, Dalrymple, and Ruttan 1977).

INCOME DISTRIBUTION

Low food and other agricultural prices are politically popular on the grounds that they increase real incomes and employment of the urban poor, and that the only losers are large farmers. There is a high cost attached to such low prices, however, if their effect is to retard cost-reducing investment and innovation in agriculture. Competition between farmers and traders assures that most of the decline in unit costs will be passed on to consumers in lower prices, though per capita farm income will also rise as output rises. Moreover, studies of the effects of price distortions and controls in specific countries usually conclude that it is the upper- and middle-income urban groups (including employers) and large farmers who are the chief beneficiaries.

Arguments that higher food prices hurt low-income (particularly urban) consumers who have to buy most of their foodstuffs are usually based on the short-term income effects of higher food prices on the assumption of unchanged incomes (i.e., higher relative prices).[8] These studies tend to ignore even relatively short-run adjustment processes that reduce the income loss, such as shifts in consumer demand toward substitute foodstuffs, and the fact that in low-income countries urban wages usually respond fairly quickly to the cost of basic foodstuffs (Appendix B).[9]

Given the relationship between wages and food prices, it seems probable that food prices may have more effect on urban profits than upon real incomes of urban labor. The logic of the common argument in developing countries that food prices must be kept low in order to assure the competitiveness of manufactured exports rests entirely on this assumption.[10] The benefit to employers of below-market agricultural prices is even clearer in the case of nonfoodstuffs. Cotton yarn and textile manufacturers in Pakistan, for example, for many years have been able to buy cotton from farmers (many of whom are quite poor) at no more than two-thirds and sometimes half of world market prices because of foreign exchange and export tax controls, but they sell much of their output at world market prices.

Price and production controls nominally intended to provide low-cost food to poor urban groups also tend to divert production away from those crops. In Peru, low official prices have greatly reduced production of *frijol canario*, a popular bean which has been a major source of protein for low-income urban consumers, and the limited output is being channeled through black markets at prices about 60% above the official control prices.[11] In Egypt, farmers have increasingly diverted land, fertilizer, and other inputs from growing wheat, maize, rice, and cotton—for which they are given quotas to sell to the government at low, controlled prices—to growing fruits, vegetables, and livestock, which are not price controlled. This diversion helps assure supply of these latter foods for middle- and upper-income urbanites, though at a high cost in terms of the balance of payments (lower export earnings from cotton and rising wheat import costs), and in massive budget subsidies to lower the retail price of imported wheat.

Food price controls also frequently benefit middle- and upper-income urban groups at the expense of lower-income rural producers. In Kenya, for example, price controls on meat and maize transfer income from low-income herdsmen and farmers for the benefit of middle- and upper-income urban dwellers.[12] In Peru, middle- and upper-income urban groups are the major beneficiaries of large government expenditures to subsidize the retail prices of imported wheat and meat. This subsidized import of wheat has also lowered the incomes of the nation's poorest farmers—those in the high-altitude Sierra region—who have thereby lost most of their cash markets for wheat and wheat substitutes such as quinua and potatoes.

The fact that national food subsidy schemes funnel food largely into urban areas hurts the often-poorest large segment of society, namely landless laborers in food-deficit areas. Movement of significant amounts of grain in Kenya, and until very recently in India, for example, have required a government permit. The result has been to depress prices in surplus food-grain production areas but to raise them in deficit rural areas. The grain collected in surplus areas is sold in Nairobi, Delhi, and other centers at controlled prices, with significant portions going to government employees and other relatively well-to-do groups (access to the ration system for the very poor and the illiterate is often difficult). Because of the official preemption at harvest time of most rail and other freight facilities for the transport of grain into urban areas, grain prices in chronically deficit areas of Kenya and India, even at peak marketing seasons, have not uncommonly been as much as twice the government procurement price. Consequently, landless laborers and other net purchasers of food in these generally lowest-income rural deficit areas must pay much more for their food than the higher-income urban purchasers of government-subsidized food grains, or the relatively higher-income landless laborers in surplus production areas such as the Punjab.

Such sharp regional price variations also adversely affect national production. While farmers can get high prices for expanding production of the food grain in which their area is deficit, these are normally high-cost and inefficient areas for such additional production. Indian farmers in Hyderabad, for example, try to grow wheat for which they have inadequate rainfall and must use irrigation water that (either at the national procurement price for wheat or at world market prices) could be more profitably used for other crops.

Marketing Controls

Most developing-country controls on price margins and marketing between farmers and consumers are supposed to protect consumers against "monopolistic" traders. The few significant studies of such controls, however, suggest that such interventions frequently have very adverse effects on efficiency, production, and income distribution. The most comprehensive Indian study concluded that the private grain market was highly competitive, that traders operated efficiently within government-imposed technological and policy constraints, and that government's efforts, rather than being expended in market controls, could have been much more fruitfully directed toward helping to improve the competitive environment, including improved farm-to-market transportation facilities, standardization of weights and measures, grading of produce, dissemination of market price and stock information, and managing national support price and buffer stock programs (Lele 1971, esp. p.220 ff.). Periodic threats by the Indian government during the prior twenty-five years to nationalize all trade in grains, and the issuing of new rice-milling licenses primarily to cooperatives and public-sector firms, however, had resulted in very little private investment to improve either storage or milling facilities (Lele 1971, p.223). Furthermore, government-agency marketing costs are several times as high as those of private traders, who flourish despite government policies.

A study in Peru concluded that marketing measures initiated to eliminate abuses by middlemen represented one of the major constraints limiting agricultural production, and might lead to destruction of the pool of private marketing talent with no comparable gain in public-sector expertise.[13] Because of stringent laws and penalties against speculation and monopolization, there is little private investment in storage facilities in Peru. This lack of storage facilities results in periodic gluts, scarcities, and excessive price fluctuations as wholesale truckers move products between consumption centers on a day-to-day basis to attempt to take advantage of spatial price differences. Lack of accurate market information is another problem in Peru. A large proportion of transactions takes place on the black market, but only official prices are reported for Lima, and wholesalers in other towns are reluctant to provide accurate price information for fear of fines and jail sentences for price violations.

Input Subsidies and Income Distribution

Farm subsidies also benefit primarily middle- and upper-income farmers in low-income countries. Large-scale farmers buy most subsidized inputs. Poorer farmers usually lack the money to buy adequate amounts of fertilizer and pesticides, and are commonly unable to get credit except at near-prohibitive private rates of often 60 to 100% per year. Even in countries with subsidized bank credit for agriculture, rich farmers get most of the credit because of legal or administrative restrictions and/or through open or disguised bribery. Credit and subsidy programs for tractors, tube wells, and other fixed investments also go mostly to the largest and richest farmers. Data from Kenya indicate that about 80% of fertilizer, which has been subsidized for many years, has gone to large farmers. Also, farmers with less than forty acres spend no more than one-fifth as much on tractor cultivation as do the least mechanized of the large farmers. This serves to skew the farm-income distribution by reducing agricultural employment and concentrating farm income. Yet, despite the high foreign exchange and government-budget cost of large-scale mechanized agriculture, Kenyans farming less than ten acres produce substantially more maize and they employ much more labor per acre than large farmers.[14] While comparable figures are not available for most other poor countries, observation supports the same kind of skewdness in the use of purchased inputs, with similar consequences.

Water is also a subsidized input, provided at less than its costs to the government, in most countries with large public irrigation systems. The farmers who receive this subsidized water generally have substantially higher incomes (because of the water) than farmers without access to public irrigation. Thus, claims that water should be subsidized to help small farmers misses the point that most farmers with irrigation have higher incomes than those who do not. Also, larger farmers often obtain more than their normal entitlement by bribes to the local authorities.

Nutrition and Poverty

Studies of nutrition needs in developing countries point to the importance of a special mechanism (e.g., food stamps and direct feeding programs) to provide food to malnourished low-income groups. The need of the very poorest is an income problem that cannot be solved solely by increased production. It is estimated that about 2.5% of present food-grain supplies, properly distributed, could eliminated serious malnutrition (Reutlinger and Selowsky 1976). General price subsidies in urban areas are a grossly inefficient mechanism for getting the moderate amounts of additional food required to malnourished people. There is a need to focus on how to relieve poverty-induced malnourishment without distorting food and agriculture prices and production on a national scale.

DEVELOPMENT STRATEGY AND AGRICULTURAL PRICING

The ultimate question about agricultural-pricing policies is their effect on economic development, including income distribution and social consequences. We are unable at the present stage of development of our profession to model and quantify adequately an entire economy in a way that measures its complete response to particular variations in the infinite array of relative prices. We can progress toward that goal, however, by examining the effects of agricultural-pricing policies on government budgets, national saving and investment, and the balance of payments.

Government Budgets

Government budget receipts' and expenditures' data (1) shed further light on the effect of government actions on farmer incentives and income distribution, (2) provide information relevant to cost-benefit analysis of certain tax, subsidy, and government expenditure programs, and (3) constitute an important element in national saving and investment. At the same time, those receipts and expenditures that flow through the government budget are only a part of the total income-transfer effects of government interventions.

Tables C1 through C3 (Appendix C) present calculations of the transfers of resources between producers, consumers, and the government due to the effect of government budget and nonbudget measures on the prices received by farmers and the prices paid by consumers for wheat in Pakistan in various years, and distinguish between those transfers included and excluded from the government budget.[15] These tables show a large transfer of income from wheat producers to consumers through lower than world market prices for marketed domestic wheat, including that procured by the government. These transfers are estimated at 348 million rupees in 1966 and 1,540 million rupees in 1976, and they equalled 62% of the income received by farmers from marketed wheat in the former year and 52% in the latter (i.e., farmers received about 62% of the world market price for their marketed wheat in 1966, and 66% in 1976). At the same time, farmers received budgeted government subsidies on inputs used in producing wheat equal to about 7% of the domestic value of marketed wheat at domestic prices in 1966 and 10% in 1976.[16] Consumers received transfers from less than world prices for their purchases in the private market, and from sales through officially controlled ration shops, of both domestic and imported wheat at substantially less than the government purchase price plus handling and administrative costs. The net result of these transactions, as summarized in Table C3, has been a large income transfer from producers (1,237 million rupees in 1976) equal to 41% of the value of marketed wheat at domestic prices, and a large income transfer to consumers (3,280 million rupees in 1976) equal to somewhat more than the total payment to domestic farmers for their entire crop of marketed (including government-procured) wheat.

Benefit-Cost Relations. One of the important questions is whether the benefits of these subsidies (in providing lower-cost wheat to consumers) are as great as their costs, as reflected in the first instance in the economic and social costs of increases either in taxes and/or government borrowing, or of decreases in other government expenditures, or perhaps a combination of these. All consumers are beneficiaries of the system, whether they buy government-rationed and price-controlled wheat or make their purchases in private markets. The cost of these subsidies weighs heavily on small "subsistence-level" farmers. In Pakistan, such farmers sell more than 30% of all marketed wheat (Pakistan 1963, Vol. II) but receive only a small fraction of the fertilizer, pesticide, tube well, tractor, and other subsidies.[17] Also, the average real income or standard of living of these small farmers is considerably below the average urban income.

As for cost effectiveness in reaching really poor urban and nonfarm rural consumers, the facts that many of those in the lowest 40% of the income distribution are farmers or rural workers who would benefit from higher farm prices, and that some of the poorest urban dwellers would have stayed on or returned to farms if farm prices and incomes had been higher, suggest that low food prices penalize rather than help many of the poor. As noted earlier, it has been estimated that, worldwide, about 2.5% of present grain supplies, properly redistributed, could eliminate serious malnutrition. For Pakistan this figure would be considerably higher, but the 2 billion rupees of government budget subsidies to lower wheat prices in 1976 amounted to one-half the value of all marketed wheat (including sales of imported wheat at domestic prices). Thus, on budgetary grounds alone (ignoring production and other indirect effects), this is an extremely expensive way to provide low-priced wheat to those who are in real poverty; it could be done at much less expense through a direct food subsidy or other income-supplement program.

A typical and in no way exceptional example of the relation of the cost of these budget subsidies to expenditures on agricultural extension, research, education, and statistics is available from Pakistan budget data. For fiscal year 1975, the latest year for which these data are available, subsidies to consumers for wheat and to farmers for purchased inputs at the provincial and national government levels were budgeted to equal about 60% of all other current and capital expenditures on agriculture, irrigation, and water development projects of both the central and provincial governments (see Appendix D).[18] The cost of subsidies was drastically underestimated, however, and actual subsidy payments amounted to about 90% of the budgeted level of other current and capital expenditures on agriculture, irrigation, and water. For one other comparison, actual wheat subsidies in Pakistan in fiscal 1975 were forty-four times as great as budgeted capital and current expenditures on extension services, and fifteen times as great as total budgeted expenditures on agricultural extension, research, education, and statistics. It seems unlikely that the benefits of wheat subsidies were as great as would have been a near doubling of the real budgeted resources devoted to all agriculture and water development programs. It also seems reasonable to suggest that increased expenditures on these latter categories would likely have done far more than the subsidies to lower food prices, though with a time lag for the benefits of these expenditures to be translated into increased output, lower production costs, and lower consumer prices.[19]

The benefit-cost relations of input subsidies to farmers are less subject to comparisons than are those to consumers. Input subsidies are usually defended on one or more of three grounds: (1) that they encourage the adoption of more productive techniques using the subsidized resources, thereby increasing national production and income; (2) that they help maintain low food (and raw-material) prices; and (3) that they help low-income farmers. Input subsidies to lower food and raw-material prices are primarily a cost of other policies that depress agricultural prices, and are intended to reduce the adverse production effects of low farm prices. As already noted, input subsidies benefit primarily upper-income rather than lower-income farmers. Subsidies to encourage the adoption of more productive inputs, such as fertilizer, have positive benefits during at least their initial introduction. Once the benefits and technique of using the input are widely known, however, the continuation of such subsidies serves largely to increase the benefit-cost ratio of using the input, and a judgment must be made if this is better done by the subsidy or by increasing the price of the output (assuming its price is artificially depressed below free-market levels). While the answer to this question may vary depending upon particular circumstances, the use of the subsidy may be the less efficient solution for two reasons. One is that the subsidy only affects the cost of the subsidized inputs, but does not encourage the use of labor or other nonsubsidized inputs. Such subsidies may encourage the use of imported tractors, for example, but not the increase of output through more use of labor per unit of capital. The second disadvantage is that low prices of certain inputs, particularly water, are often associated with widespread waste and inefficient use of the resource.

If input subsidies do not step up agricultural production at the same rate as would higher output prices, however, such subsidies will result in both lower output (income) levels and higher long-run food and raw-material prices than would higher present-output prices.[20] Minimum support prices, while having some of the characteristics of a subsidy, have several advantages over input subsidies. One is that they reduce the price risk faced by farmers, which is that of a sharp drop in crop prices. Thus a support price has some of the effect of a price increase (by raising the average expected price to farmers) while only occasionally raising the actual price above free-market levels. The cost of a support program for storable commodities such as grains may also be less than significant subsidies on fertilizer and other inputs.

Taxation. There is a substantial literature on the economic advantages of direct rather than indirect taxation of agriculture, since land and income taxes do not directly affect either relative product prices, cropping patterns, input/output price ratios, or the output levels from which farmers will realize the maximum levels of income (profits) (Bird 1974). High levels of land taxation were very successfully used both to stimulate agricultural output and to transfer resources to the government and to industry during the modernization of agriculture in Japan and in colonial India. However, the lack of significant levels of such taxation in most developing countries today, and the presumed administrative as well as political difficulties in their imposition, are often cited as reasons for focusing on indirect taxation of agricultural commodities, and particularly on taxation of exports. Changes in taxation will be a budgetary requirement of price and subsidy changes in many countries. A package combining higher output prices with reduced subsidies and increased land taxation could work to everyone's interest, and be more politically acceptable than a change only in prices and subsidies.

Saving and Investment

The effects of pricing policies on national saving are obviously very complex. Budget subsidies to consumers during the high grain-price era of the 1970s rose to roughly one-fourth of total government expenditures in some food-deficit countries such as Egypt and Pakistan, and to as much as 5% of gross domestic products. These were exceptional years, but such subsidies are typically still a significant drain on saving and hence on resources available to finance investment.

Substantial savings may also be lost through income transfers from agriculture to the rest of the economy through price distortions. Studies of private saving rates among rural and urban groups show higher marginal saving rates in rural than in urban areas. Furthermore, small-farmer marginal saving rates appear to be almost as high as those of large farmers (Adams 1976). Farm saving rates might have been further increased if pricing policies had made investment in agriculture more attractive. Thus, the distortion of input and product prices in order to funnel income away from farmers and toward industry may have significantly reduced national rates of saving and, therefore, of investment. Rates of overall economic growth may hence have suffered from lower rates of saving and investment as well as from misallocation of budget and investment funds. This is just the opposite effect, of course, from that predicted by many economists who argued in the 1950s and 1960s, from inadequate empirical data, that marginal saving rates of the urban sector and/or industrialists were higher than those of farmers.

Moreover, observation of the industrial sector in many developing countries suggests that relatively little productive investment may result from the involuntary transfer of income from agriculture to industry. Rates of utilization of physical capital are extremely low in these countries (Winston 1971). Moreover, much of the income transferred may not even result in physical, productive investment, but rather may be frittered away in inefficiency and increased consumption, such as in wage increases to already relatively high-income (compared to small farmers) industrial workers, to additional and unneeded employment of workers (especially in public-sector industry), increased consumption by managers, and general failure to aggressively seek to reduce costs and/or increase quality in protected industries.

The effect of price policy on investment will consist both of its effect on saving and on the allocation of that saving between alternative investments. How price incentives may affect the distribution of investment between agriculture and industry has already been discussed.

Balance of Payments

While the totality of potential effects of relative changes in agricultural prices upon the balance of payments is very complex, spectacular balance of payments' changes appear feasible in some countries by reducing price distortions against agriculture. Kenya's move in early 1975 toward world-market prices for both agricultural products and inputs has virtually eliminated previous large expenditures for wheat and sugar imports, both by increasing domestic production of these crops and by cutting demand for each by about 20% through substitution of alternative domestic foodstuffs. Reduction of subsidies on imported farm equipment that have mostly benefited rich farmers and encouraged capital-intensive and import-intensive agricultural production techniques seems to be simultaneously strengthening the balance of payments, increasing wheat production and lowering its cost, and improving incomes and employment among relatively poorer sections of Kenya's rural population.

Declines in rice exports from Burma and in agricultural exports from Pakistan and Egypt are only a few examples of the sometimes very substantial declines in export earnings that have resulted from paying farmers much less than the market value of their crops.

Higher (closer to market level) agricultural prices might also significantly reduce nonfood imports by changing the distribution of income and hence the composition of demand. If less discrimination against agricultural prices shifted income distribution in favor of farmers, there would be changes in the composition as well as the level of demand for both consumption and investment goods. Research indicates that such shifts would tend to increase demand for labor-intensive domestic products and reduce demand for capital-intensive and imported products (Soligo 1974; Cline 1972).[21] In addition to improving the balance of payments, such a shift in income distribution and the composition of demand might have other benefits from increased employment opportunities, wages, and profits in both industry and agriculture, from greater development of light manufacturing, marketing, and construction, and from relatively greater growth of small cities and regional market centers.

CONCLUSIONS

Analysis and research on the significance of price policy in general and agricultural price policy in particular have not kept up either with practical experience concerning policies affecting prices in developing countries or with changes in development-strategy theories. The designing of research work to answer the many relevant questions is a formidable project.[22] However, there are several types of studies that might be especially useful. First, detailed case studies of the decision making of individual farmers are badly needed. Much of our "conventional wisdom" about farm-level response to changes in agricultural prices, for instance, is based upon aggregative data rather than detailed studies of farmer decision making. Detailed studies have only recently begun on how developing-country farmers of different income levels spend their time and earn their incomes, including time spent working and maintaining or improving their own farms, on related marketing and other activities, and on other income-generating activities.

Second, detailed case studies of the effect of particular price policies in individual countries are needed. Evidence from various sources has been presented in this paper about some of the consequences of particular price policies and mechanisms in particular countries. Such material needs to be much more systematically examined and incorporated into the knowledge of development specialists and policy makers. Relatively little serious research is focused on this topic, and what information is available is mostly regarded as interesting anecdotal case material. The substantial manpower cost of detailed case studies is one barrier; the inadequacy of our present data and analytical tools to deal with all the complexities of pricing-policy issues is another. The problem is too important to neglect, however, and in the process of seeing what can be accomplished with current tools of analysis new analytical breakthroughs are likely.

Third, it is important that the overall structure of price policies be studied as well as the place of price policy in overall economic policy. Such studies have generally not been undertaken because they are "unwieldy," "vague," and generally thought to be too big to be productive. Nevertheless, the examples cited here of the relative neglect of agricultural pricing issues suggests that these issues are also too important not to be the subject of some direct work, rather than always working with the pieces. These studies will necessarily be national studies initially. Studies of the effects of major changes in policy structure in individual countries also have the value of indicating the effect of alternative policies in countries with the same culture (except for changes over time), natural resources, geographical location, and other elements which cast doubt upon international comparisons between different countries. In time, however, it would also be useful to look at comparative policy structure and growth experiences in different developing countries since perhaps 1950. For example, what were the characteristics of price policy and/or overall economic policy of countries with rapid overall growth (Japan, Taiwan, Korea, Yugoslavia, Pakistan prior to 1970), and how did these policies compare with those of countries which experienced difficulties during all or most of that period (India, Tunisia, Ghana)?

Fourth, the role which developed countries could play in helping to overcome agricultural pricing policy problems in developing countries should be examined. For instance, could foreign aid donors play a valuable role by helping to finance a phased adjustment in urban food prices over several years, both to avoid sharp short-term income effects from higher prices and to cover the period between the undertaking of farm-level price increases and rural investment-institutional development programs and the actual achievement of increased and cheaper food-grain supplies? Foreign aid for institution-building purposes in agriculture should also be reconsidered. To some extent this type of aid has fallen into disrepute because of poor results from aid, for example, to agricultural credit institutions and extension services. These experiences should be reexamined to consider the extent to which a more comprehensive approach, including improved pricing policies as well as institutional reform and investment, might succeed in achieving important breakthroughs in both institutional performance and agricultural productivity. Developed countries could also make an important contribution by managing their own agricultural production and import and export programs so as to minimize disruptions to world markets (Johnson 1975, pp.33–34, and 1977). Developing countries are both reluctant to rely on world markets for their own food needs because of uncertainty about the availability of supplies and market prices, and hesitant to invest substantial resources to increase their own production for export.

NOTES

The views expressed are those of the author and not necessarily those of the World Bank.

1. One of the best quantified analyses of these price distortions for a particular country is by Pursell, Monson, and Stryker (1975). They concluded that in the 1967–72 period, price and profit incentives in the Ivory Coast (1) favored relatively capital-intensive agricultural techniques; (2) discouraged agricultural output; (3) caused new industrial activity to diverge substantially from social profitability; (4) favored production for domestic and West African Economic Community (CEAO) markets and discouraged exports to Europe and non-CEAO markets; (5) resulted in negative value added in the processing of agricultural exports by some of the Ivory Coast's largest firms; (6) favored the use of imported rather than domestic machinery and equipment in agriculture; and (7) created industrial monopolies. This price structure seems fairly typical of those observed in many developing countries.

2. See Behrman (1968) for a summary of such studies and a detailed analysis of the difficulties in making and interpreting such measurements. Such studies have tended to show price elasticities ranging from about 0.1 to 0.5 or 0.6 for major food grains and 0.5 to 1.1 for nonfood crops.

3. Very few estimates of the price elasticity of aggregate agricultural production have been made. For one example, see Herdt (1970).

4. Some studies have incorrectly assumed that irrigation and fertilizer use, for example, are independent both of each other and of price, though each of these assumptions is false. They then reach the statistically and logically questionable conclusion that fertilizer and irrigation are more important than price in determining farm output.

5. The growth of yields reflects shifts in production functions as well as price elasticity, strictly defined as that of a particular function. However, the shift towards greater use of yield-increasing inputs such as improved seed and chemical fertilizers, whose use in developing countries twenty years ago was inconsequential, has greatly increased the potential price responsiveness of yields and output.

6. Likewise, input price changes affect profitability and these may not always be picked up by measures of relative prices in particular studies. Use of profitability rather than prices as an independent variable is limited by data availability.

7. Thai prices to rice farmers have recently moved much closer to world prices as the export tax on rice was greatly reduced in 1976. Fertilizer prices have also been lowered by more liberal import policies. The consequences of these changes on Thai rice and total agricultural production will be an important test case of the significance of farm prices.

8. For a comprehensive presentation of the short-run income effects of higher prices on low-income consumers, see Mellor (1975).

9. Annual data on food-grain prices and wages in Pakistan over an eighteen-year period, for example, show declines in real wages in years when food prices rose sharply, but more or less full recovery by the following year. See Appendix B.

10. Adjustment of the exchange rate is a much more appropriate instrument to assure export competitiveness, and is one that would encourage efficiency of resource use and greater food and nonfood domestic production.

11. Unpublished report on conditions in late 1974.

12. However, meat in particular is often sold at black-market prices. Meat price controls have recently been relaxed, and those for the more expensive grades eliminated.

13. Unpublished report on conditions in late 1974.

14. A study by the Kenyan Central Bureau of Statistics and the Ministry of Agriculture (1972) concluded that farms of less than ten acres produced nearly three times as much maize and employed nine times as much labor per acre, compared with the large mechanized farms. A private sample survey in 1975 also found higher yields on small farms, but by substantially smaller margins (Hesselmark 1976).

15. Adopted from the technique used by T. Josling in several studies (see Josling 1969 and FAO 1975).

16. Fertilizer and pesticides accounted for more than 90 percent of budgeted farmer subsidies. The wheat crop subsidy was estimated to equal 50 percent of the total subsidy on fertilizer, on the basis of irrigated and rainfed wheat acreage (Pakistan 1975) and application of fertilizer per acre between major crops in irrigated and rain-fed areas (National Fertilizer Corporation of Pakistan 1977).

17. A subsistence farmer is traditionally defined in Pakistan as one with no more than 12.5 acres, which is regarded as the minimum farm size at which

a farmer can support himself and his family, though this naturally varies with the productivity of the land, his capital investment, and cropping pattern.

18. Mostly fertilizer and pesticides, and excluding the implicit subsidy in below-cost provision of irrigation water.

19. This comparison must be tempered by awareness of administrative and other limitations on the short-run "absorptive capacity" of research and extension services in many countries.

20. Barker and Hayami (1976) estimated that the social return per unit of government expenditure on a fertilizer subsidy would be greater than on expenditure supporting the price of rice above its import price. The assumptions and scope of this static analysis are so restrictive, however, as to be inconclusive as a guide to policy.

21. Cline estimates the amount of import saving that could be achieved by income redistribution in Brazil and Mexico as no more than 2 to 3%. This is because "the truly large changes in gross output after income distribution are the increases in agricultural production and processed foodstuffs." While the import component of agricultural production is relatively low, the absolute size of these import increases almost offsets the decline in imports for production of much more import-intensive goods. Brazil also imports large amounts of wheat. Cline's estimates are static and therefore may underestimate import savings over time. Also, they do not take into account potential growth of exports as the result of increased agricultural production.

22. Aspects of price policy about which more information is needed include: the relationship of agricultural prices to technical innovation and diffusion, public and private investment in agriculture, crop yields and aggregate production, farm mechanization, and the structure of consumer and investment demand; the income-distribution effect of specific price policies and mechanisms on specific income groups, regions, and other groups of consumers and producers in urban and rural areas, hence on regional as well as national welfare and development; the costs and benefits of alternative price and market-control mechanisms; the feasibility of replacing large-scale food subsidy schemes with programs targeted to the low-income malnourished; the relationships between food prices and urban wage rates; the interdependence of agricultural and industrial growth, including income-distribution consequences; the effect of price policies on the budget, inflation, saving, investment, and balance of payments. To these might be added research on the existing structure of agricultural prices in different nations and groups of nations and the significance of this structure both for world market prices and for development, and on problems of stabilizing world market prices and facilitating price and output adjustments in individual countries.

REFERENCES

Adams, Dale W. 1976. "Mobilizing Household Savings through Rural Financial Markets." Occasional paper no. 256. Mimeographed. Department of Agricultural Economics and Rural Sociology, Ohio State University, Columbus.

Arndt, Thomas M.; Dalrymple, Dana G.; and Ruttan, Vernon W., eds. 1977. *Resource Allocation and Productivity in National and International Agricultural Research*. Minneapolis: University of Minnesota Press.

Barker, Randolph, and Hayami, Yujiro. 1976. "Price Support versus Input Subsidy for Food Self-Sufficiency in Developing Countries." *American Journal of Agricultural Economics* 58:Part I (November):617–28.

Behrman, Jere R. 1968. *Supply Response in Underdeveloped Agriculture*. Amsterdam: North-Holland.

Bird, Richard M. 1974. *Taxing Agricultural Land in Developing Countries*. Cambridge, Mass.: Harvard University Press.

Cline, William R. 1972. *Potential Effects of Income Redistribution on Economic Growth*. New York, Washington, and London: Praeger Publishers.

Eckert, Jerry B. 1974. "Private Tubewell Numbers in Pakistan: A Synthesis." *The Pakistan Development Review* 13, no. 1 (Spring): 94–105.

Food and Agriculture Organization. 1975. "Agricultural Protection and Stabilization Policies: A Framework of Measurement in the Context of Agricultural Adjustment." C 75/LIM/2. Item 9.2 of the Provisional Agenda. 18th Session. Rome.

Hayami, Yujiro. 1975. "Japan's Rice Policy in Historical Perspective." *Food Research Institute Studies* 14, no. 4:359–80.

Hayami, Yujiro, and Kikuchi, Masao. 1978. "Investment Inducements to Public Infrastructure: Irrigation in the Philippines." *Review of Economics and Statistics* 60, no. 1 (February), pp.70–77.

Hayami, Yujiro, and Ruttan, Vernon W. 1971. *Agricultural Development: An International Perspective*. Baltimore: Johns Hopkins Press.

Herdt, Robert W. 1970. "A Disaggregate Approach to Aggregate Supply." *American Journal of Agricultural Economics* 52, no. 4 (November): 512–20.

Hesselmark, O. 1976. "Maize Yields in Kenya, 1975." Unpublished paper. Nairobi.

Johnson, D. Gale. 1975. *World Food Problems and Prospects*. Washington, D.C.: American Enterprise Institute for Public Policy Research.

———. 1977. "Food Production Potentials in Developing Countries: Will They Be Realized?" Occasional paper no. 1, St. Paul, Minn.: Bureau of Economic Studies, Macalester College.

Josling, T. 1969. "A Formal Approach to Agricultural Policy." *Journal of Agricultural Economics* 20, no. 2 (May):175–95.

Kenya, Central Bureau of Statistics and the Ministry of Agriculture. 1972. "A Comparison of the Intensity of Cultivation in Large and Small Farms in Kenya." *Kenya Statistical Digest* 10, no. 1 (March):4–9.

Lele, Uma J. 1971. *Foodgrain Marketing in India*. Ithaca and London: Cornell University Press.

Mellor, John W. 1975. "Agricultural Price Policy and Income Distribution in Low-Income Nations." World Bank Staff Working Paper no. 214. Washington, D.C.

National Fertilizer Corporation of Pakistan, Ltd. 1977. *Distribution and Use of Fertilizer in Pakistan: General Farmers Investigation Survey.* Lahore.

Pakistan, Agricultural Census Organization, Ministry of Agriculture and Works. 1963. *1960 Census of Agriculture, Vol. 2, West Pakistan.* Karachi.

Pakistan, Central Statistics Office. 1972. *25 Years of Pakistan in Statistics, 1947–72.* Karachi.

Pakistan, Ministry of Food, Agriculture Cooperatives, Under Developed Areas and Land Reforms. 1975. *Agricultural Statistics of Pakistan 1975.* Islamabad.

Pursell, Garry; Monson, Terry; and Stryker, J. Dirck. 1975. "Incentives and Resource Costs in Industry and Agriculture in the Ivory Coast." Mimeographed. Washington, D.C.: World Bank.

Reutlinger, Shlomo, and Selowsky, Marcelo. 1976. *Malnutrition and Poverty: Magnitude and Policy Options.* World Bank Staff Occasional Papers no. 23. Baltimore and London: Johns Hopkins Press.

Soligo, Ronald. 1974. "Consumption Patterns, Factor Usage and the Distribution of Income: A Review of Some Findings." Presented at the Southern Economic Association meeting, Atlanta, Georgia, November 1974. Mimeographed. Rice University, Dallas, Texas.

Timmer, C. Peter, and Falcon, Walter P. 1975. "The Political Economy of Rice Production and Trade in Asia." In *Agriculture in Development Theory,* ed. Lloyd G. Reynolds, pp.373–408. New Haven: Yale University Press.

Winston, Gordon C. 1971. "Capital Utilisation in Economic Development." *Economic Journal* 81 (March):36–60.

Yamada, Saburo, and Ruttan, Vernon W. 1975. "International Comparisons of Productivity in Agriculture." Paper presented at National Bureau of Economic Research Conference on Productivity Measurement, Williamsburg, Virginia, November 13–14, 1975.

Yasin, M. Ghulam. 1965. *The Economics of Tubewell Irrigation.* Publication no. 133. Lahore, Punjab: [Pakistan Govt.] Board of Economic Inquiry.

Appendix A

Some Recent Changes in Agricultural Price Policies

Among the most dramatic changes in price policy have been those in Uruguay and Kenya. From 1975 Uruguay has substantially raised prices paid to farmers so that these are much closer to world market prices, and has made some progress in reducing high rates of protection to domestic manufacturing. Kenya in January, 1975, moved to adopt world market prices for most agricultural commodities, including food grains, though basic agricultural prices are still controlled at geographically and seasonally uniform prices, and extensive controls at farm gate, wholesale, and retail levels still remain. Peru has also moved in the same direction as Kenya, though on a more gradual commodity-by-commodity basis. As of October 1976, domestic rice prices in Peru had been raised to about 10% above world market levels in an attempt to generate exports by increasing production and reducing domestic consumption. The Ivory Coast raised the domestic price of rice (a small-farmer crop) substantially above world market levels and moved from a production deficit to surplus position. The Ivory Coast is providing both incentive prices and a package of productivity-increasing inputs to producers of other than coffee and cocoa. The price of rice to farmers and consumers in the Philippines was increased in early 1976 after an extended period of concern that rising costs were squeezing production incentives. Egypt has been moving to relax very extensive price and production controls as part of its overall effort to liberalize its economy. Pakistan has substantially raised farm gate wheat, rice, and cotton prices since 1974, though all are still significantly below world market levels, and has lifted a previous ban on exports of other foodstuffs.

Table B-1

Average Daily Employment and Wages, West Pakistan, 1952–69

	1952	1953	1954	1955	1956	1957	1958	1959	1960
1 Average daily number of factory workers	123,726	159,526	168,450	76,494	140,011	175,111	151,966	196,244	95,448
2a Total wages paid (Rs 000)	93,511	128,691	141,954	81,098	153,086	182,278	166,665	204,843	236,800
2b Rupees/worker/year	756	807	843	1,060	1,093	1,041	1,097	1,044	1,212
3a Price of wheat per maund, F.A.Q. Karachi (Rs)	11.19	11.56	13.37	12.00	12.00	12.56	13.25	13.25	13.25
3b Maunds wheat/worker/year	67.6	69.8	63.1	88.3	91.1	82.9	82.8	78.8	91.5
4a Price of rice (Kangni) per maund, F.A.Q. Karachi (Rs)	12.37	14.06	14.50	11.44	12.87	18.37	22.19	20.12	20.12
4b Maunds rice/worker/year	61.1	57.4	58.1	92.7	84.9	56.7	49.4	51.9	60.2
5 Wages/worker (1961 = 100.0)	66.20	70.67	73.82	92.82	95.71	91.16	96.06	91.42	106.13
6 Consumers food price index for industrial workers in Karachi (1961 = 100.0)	74.23	78.87	80.28	78.21	78.69	86.20	95.94	90.97	97.34
7a Real wages (2b ÷ 6)	1,018	1,023	1,050	1,355	1,389	1,208	1,143	1,148	1,245
7b CPI for industrial workers	78.35	84.02	87.34	84.32	83.72	89.08	96.68	92.93	98.21
8 Real wages (2b ÷ 7b)	965	960	965	1,257	1,306	1,169	1,135	1,123	1,234
9 Wheat production (000 tons) W.P.	2,961	2,367	3,587	3,136	3,317	3,581	3,508	3,845	3,847

Table B-1 continued

	1961	1962	1963	1964	1965	1966	1967	1968	1969
1 Average daily number of factory workers	215,438	207,101	276,011	243,034	292,124	253,660	291,420	231,727	974,652
2a Total wages paid (Rs 000)	246,125	336,725	354,180	372,234	421,853	397,882	422,700	379,704	1,836,610
2b Rupees/worker/year	1,142	1,626	1,283	1,532	1,444	1,569	1,450	1,639	1,884
3a Price of wheat per maund, F.A.Q. Karachi (Rs)	18.10	18.66	17.04	17.34	18.21	17.36	24.82	23.07	18.05
3b Maunds wheat/worker/year	63.1	87.1	75.3	88.4	79.3	90.4	58.4	71.0	104.4
4a Price of rice (Kangni) per maund, F.A.Q. Karachi (Rs)	20.12	20.10	20.10	20.10	20.10	20.10	31.35	41.29	20.75
4b Maunds rice/worker/year	56.8	80.9	63.8	76.2	71.8	78.1	46.3	39.7	90.8
5 Wages/worker (1961 = 100.0)	100.00	142.38	112.35	134.15	126.44	137.39	126.97	143.52	164.97
6 Consumers food price index for industrial workers in Karachi (1961 = 100.0)	100.00	102.34	100.04	104.85	114.55	120.88	131.93	134.76	135.14
7a Real wages (2b ÷ 6)	1,142	1,589	1,282	1,461	1,261	1,298	1,099	1,216	1,394
7b CPI for industrial workers	100.00	101.25	99.92	103.08	109.34	114.87	125.01	127.83	129.71
8 Real wages (2b ÷ 7b)	1,142	1,666	1,284	1,486	1,321	1,366	1,160	1,282	1,452
9 Wheat production (000 tons) W.P.	3,754	3,963	4,104	4,096	4,518	3,854	4,266	6,317	6,513

Source: *25 Years of Pakistan in Statistics, 1947–1972* (Pakistan 1972).
1: p.36; 2: p.36; 3: p.322; 4: p.322;
6: pp.343 & 346; 7a: pp.343 & 346; 9: p.86.

Appendix C

Subsidy Data for Pakistan

Table C-1

Producer Subsidy Equivalents—Wheat, Pakistan, for Selected Years from 1966 to 1976

	1966	1970	1972	1973
Domestic Production (000 tons)	3,854	7,179	6,782	7,325
Marketed Production (000 tons)[1]	1,310	2,440	2,306	2,490
Govt. Procurement	21	1,001	205	1,321
Wholesale Markets	1,289	1,439	2,101	1,169
Prices (Rs per maund)				
Govt. Procurement	13.5	17.0	17.0	22.5[a]
Wholesale Markets (Lyallpur)	15.7	17.6	20.5	21.5
Marketed Production Value (million Rs)[2]	559	1,152	1,267	1,493
Govt. Procurement	7.7	463	95	809
Wholesale Market Sales[3]	551	689	1,172	684
Policy transfers to producers (million Rs)				
Marketed Production at world market prices	907	1,862	1,596	1,940
Price Protection[4]	−348	−710	−329	−447
Direct Subsidies[5]	38	59	40	104
Total Producer Subsidy	−310	−651	−289	−343
Proportional Subsidy (%)[6]	−55	−57	−23	−23
Domestic price as % of world market price	62	62	79	77

	1974	1975	1976
Domestic Production (000 tons)	7,508	7,552	8,700[e]
Marketed Production (000 tons)[1]	2,553	2,568	2,958
Govt. Procurement	1,234	1,217	2,340
Wholesale Markets	1,319	1,351	618
Prices (Rs per maund)			
Govt. Procurement	25.5	37.0	37.0
Wholesale Markets (Lyallpur)	27.5	42.2	37.4
Marketed Production Value (million Rs)[2]	1,844	2,778	2,986
Govt. Procurement	857	1,226	2,357
Wholesale Market Sales[3]	987	1,552	629
Policy transfers to producers (million Rs)			
Marketed Production at world market prices	3,339	4,866	4,526
Price Protection[4]	−1,495	−2,088	−1,540
Direct Subsidies[5]	139	163	303
Total Producer Subsidy	−1,356	−1,925	−1,237
Proportional Subsidy (%)[6]	−74	−69	−41
Domestic price as % of world market price	55	57	66

Notes to Table C-1 on p. 110.

NOTES TO TABLE C-1

[1] Marketed production estimated as 34% of total production. The 1960 Pakistan Census of Agriculture estimated 34.5% of production was marketed rather than used for payments in kind, self-service or seeds.

[2] Marketed production value equals price in rupees per maund times 27.22 maunds per long ton times the marketed production.

[3] Calculated at average wholesale market prices in Lyallpur, April through June.

[4] Difference between value of marketed production on basis of government procurement and Lyallpur wholesale market prices and value at average import price paid. Import prices in dollars have been converted to rupees at Rs 9.9 per dollar, a shadow exchange rate that may moderately under-value the rupee for years prior to February 1973, when it became the official exchange rate.

[5] Data on budget subsidies as supplied by the Ministry of Finance, Planning and Economic Affairs. The direct subsidy to wheat growers is estimated as one-half the total subsidy on fertilizer (see text footnote 16 for derivation of this estimate). Subsidies on fertilizer and on the cost of plant protection (spraying) accounted for more than 90% of total direct subsidies each year. The balance went for subsidies on the installation of private tubewells and on improved seeds.

[6] Subsidy calculated as a percent of the value at domestic prices of marketed wheat.

[e] estimate

[a] Announced in September 1972 as Rs 17 per maund, but increased to Rs 22.5 at spring harvest time.

Table C-2

Consumer Subsidy Equivalents—Wheat, Pakistan, for Selected Years from 1966 to 1976

	1966	1970	1972	1973
Off-farm Consumption (ooo tons)[1]	2,054	2,667	2,996	3,828
ooo tons Government Domestic Procurement	21	1,001	205	1,321
ooo tons Imports	744	227	690	1,338
Privately Marketed Domestic Wheat	1,289	1,439	2,101	1,169
Domestic prices (Rs ton)				
Govt. Procurement price	367.5	462.8	462.8	612.5
Domestic wholesale price[2]	427.4	479.1	558.1	585.3
World Market Price (Rs ton)[4]	692	763	692	779
Value of consumption at domestic prices (Rs million)	832	1,257	1,587	2,313
Government procured, including imports[3]	281	568	414	1,629
Wholesale market purchases	551	689	1,173	684
Value of consumption at World Mkt. prices (Rs million)	1,421	2,035	2,073	2,982
Policy Transfers to Consumers[5]	651	895	583	1,053
Price protection[6]	348	710	328	446
Direct subsidies[7]	303	185	255	607
Proportional Subsidy (%)[8]	78	71	37	46

Table C-2 *continued*

	1974	1975	1976
Off-farm Consumption (000 tons)[1]	3,735	3,732	4,125
000 tons Government Domestic Procurement	1,234	1,217	2,340
000 tons Imports	1,182	1,164	1,167
Privately Marketed Domestic Wheat	1,319	1,351	618
Domestic prices (Rs ton)			
Govt. Procurement price	694.2	1,007.2	1,007.2
Domestic wholesale price[2]	748.6	1,148.8	1,018.1
World Market Price (Rs ton)[4]	1,308	1,895	1,530
Value of consumption at domestic prices			
(Rs million)	2,664	3,950	4,161
Government procured, including imports [3]	1,677	2,398	3,532
Wholesale market purchases	987	1,552	629
Value of consumption at World Mkt. prices			
(Rs million)	4,885	7,072	6,311
Policy Transfers to Consumers[5]	2,750	3,780	3,280
Price protection[6]	1,495	2,089	1,540
Direct subsidies[7]	1,255	1,691	1,740
Proportional Subsidy (%)[8]	103	96	79

[1] Sum of privately marketed production and government procurement plus imports on a fiscal year basis, since end of year stock data not available. A substantial portion of domestic production is consumed in the following fiscal year.

[2] Average April–June wholesale market price in Lyallpur.

[3] Domestic wheat purchased by the government and imported wheat are both valued at the government procurement price, since the two are intermingled and sold at the same price for milling and through government-licensed ration shops at official prices. Thus, subsequent milling and marketing margins are the same.

[4] Import prices in dollars have been converted to rupees at Rs 9.9 per dollar, which may moderately undervalue the rupee for years prior to February 1973, when it became the official exchange rate.

[5] Calculation as sum of difference between domestic and world prices of privately marketed and government procured domestic grain plus budget subsidies to wheat consumers, calculated on basis of difference between government purchase and sale prices plus handling, storage, and related costs borne by government.

[6] Difference between value received by farmers and world market value of marketed domestic grain, including that procured by government.

[7] This estimate of government budget cost of consumer subsidies is based on the difference between the premilled equivalent of the price at which the government sells flour to the ration shops and the price at which the government buys the wheat, i.e., the c.i.f. value of imported wheat and the procurement price of domestic wheat. To the extent that the wheat is imported under grants, or loans, the actual budgeted expenditures in these years are correspondingly reduced.

[8] Subsidy calculated as the policy transfer to consumers as a percent of the value of consumption at domestic prices.

Table C-3

Subsidy Transfers between Sectors, Pakistan, for Selected Years from 1966 to 1976
(million rupees)

	1966	1970	1972	1973	1974	1975	1976
Producer Subsidy							
Value	−310	−651	−289	−343	−1,356	−1,925	−1,237
from consumers	−348	−710	−329	−447	−1,495	−2,088	−1,540
from Government	38	59	40	104	139	163	303
Consumer Subsidy							
Value	651	895	584	1,054	2,750	3,779	3,280
from producers	348	710	329	447	1,495	2,088	1,540
from Government	303	185	255	607	1,255	1,691	1,740
Government Budget							
Cost	341	244	295	711	1,394	1,854	2,043
to producers	38	59	40	104	139	163	303
to consumers	303	185	255	607	1,255	1,691	1,740

Appendix D

Table D-1

Allocation of Resources to Agriculture and Water Development, Nondevelopmental Revenue Expenditure, and Annual Development Program, 1974/75 Estimated Budgets, All Pakistan[1]

	Nondevelopmental Budget (millions of rupees)	As a % of Total Nondevelopment	Annual Development Program (millions of rupees)	As a % of Total ADP	Total Nondevelopmental and Developmental Budget (millions of rupees)	As a % of Total
AGRICULTURE						
Input Subsidies						
Fertilizer, Pesticides, and Seeds	—	—	588	23.1	588	16.1
Mechanization, agricultural engineering	49	4.4	35	1.4	84	2.3
Agriculture Services						
Extension	40	3.6	6	0.2	46	1.3
Research	19	1.7	52	2.0	71	1.9
Education	3	0.3	13	0.5	16	0.4
Statistics	—	—	1	neg	1	neg
Marketing	2	0.2	2	0.1	4	0.1
Integrated Rural Development Program	—	—	49	1.9	49	1.3
Subtotal, Agriculture Services	64	5.8	123	4.8	187	5.1

Table D-1 *continued*

Other Agriculture Program[2]	13	1.2	224	8.8	237	6.5
Administration	31	2.8	—	—	31	0.9
Wheat Subsidies	689	61.9	—	—	689	18.8
Subtotal, Agriculture	846	75.9	970	38.1	1,816	49.6
WATER DEVELOPMENT						
Water and Power						
Development Authority	—		486	19.1	486	13.3
Irrigation[3]	268	24.1	406	16.0	674	18.4
Indus Basin—Tarbela	—		682	26.8	682	18.6
Subtotal, Water	268	24.1	1,574	61.9	1,842	50.4
TOTAL, Agriculture and						
Water	1,114	100.0	2,544	100.0	3,658	100.0

[1] Table should be used to assess rough orders of magnitude only. Certain items are unavoidably omitted or defy unambiguous classification. Figures are ex ante estimated budget amounts and can vary considerably from amounts actually expended. Nondevelopmental revenue expenditures are more elusive than Annual Development Plan.

[2] Provincial nondevelopmental allocations to veterinary services, fisheries and forestry are excluded to the extent they do not appear in agriculture's classification.

[3] Excludes interest payments on irrigation works, which must be substantial. Total interest payments budgeted for 1974/75 are 1,740 million rupees.

COMMENT

Roger W. Fox

Gilbert Brown has presented an excellent summary of the existing theory and relevant empirical work concerning distortions resulting from price policies that maintain the terms of trade "against" the agricultural sector. His treatment of these distortions touches on the theoretical and empirical impacts on agricultural production, income distribution both within and between the rural and urban populations, resource transfers between producers and consumers, saving and investment, the balance of payments, and government budgets. He rightfully points out that adjusting agricultural and food prices is a poor and often expensive way to deal with externality problems and other market imperfections.

In general, I have no major disagreements with Brown's arguments or evidence. What I propose to do, however, is take a slightly different view of recent policy and program changes with respect to agricultural prices. To make the analyses more useful to policy makers, I believe that a forward perspective is necessary.

Brown presents evidence indicating that a number of developing countries "have acted to significantly increase agricultural relative to nonagricultural prices in the last several years." He cites the experiences of Egypt, Kenya, the Ivory Coast, Pakistan, Peru, the Philippines, Thailand, and Uruguay in support of this observation.[1] Having established this apparent change in policy, he proceeds to carefully analyze the impacts of pursuing the previous policy of maintaining relatively low agricultural and food prices. There are important policy issues surrounding the move to freer agricultural prices that need to be considered. These issues also relate to distortions of incentives.

One of the first questions that comes to mind is, will these countries stick to their new, "enlightened" policies? This obviously depends on the outcomes of these policies, particularly on what happens to agricultural and food prices, incomes and their distribution, and agricultural output. There is an implicit assumption in Brown's analysis that deregulating agricultural prices will automatically mean higher prices and consequently an improvement in the intersectoral distribution of income. Whether or not this is correct depends, among other things, on long- and short-run considerations and if the prices are in real or nominal terms. If we accept the results of the various gap analyses (e.g., International Food Policy Research Institute 1977), the increasing food deficits clearly imply higher nominal prices. But this does not necessarily mean higher food prices relative to nonfood items or improvement of the real incomes of the rural and urban poor. Historical data (see Johnson's paper in this volume) indicate that world market prices for many agricultural commodities have declined in real value during the past twenty-five to thirty years. To forecast changes in relative prices would require bringing both agricultural and nonagricultural prices explicitly into the forecasting models. To my knowledge no one has accomplished this.[2]

Moreover, in the short run and during the period of transition from regulated to unregulated prices, price changes may not correspond to the expected longer-run trends. To the extent that these short-run prices are substantially above or below previous prices, pressures will build for further changes in policy. The recent U.S. experience is a good example of this. U.S. farmers were perfectly happy with the free-market policy as long as this meant high prices. But as soon as prices began to fall, producers and their representatives exerted political pressure, made compromises with consumers (i.e., food stamp provisions), and obtained higher target prices, acreage set-asides, and the promise of direct payments. Similar events are likely to occur in the developing countries.

A reasonable interpretation of Brown's analysis is that nominal and real agricultural prices would increase in the short run, and that, as cost-reducing technology is adopted, competitive forces would cause real prices to fall. If this is correct, short-run changes in consumption could be quite important in determining the political acceptability of freer agricultural markets. Using Brown's data for the wheat market in Pakistan (his table C-2), one can develop a rough estimate of the impact of higher prices on consumption, production, and trade. For the seven years that he considers, the increases in wholesale domestic prices required to reach world-market price levels ranged from 24 to 75%; for five of the seven years the required increase was 50% or more. Assuming that a free internal wheat market would lead to a 40% increase in price and that the price elasticity of demand is −0.15, consumption would fall, ceteris paribus, by 6%, or 697,000 tons, based on the 1976 data.[3] The impact would presumably be more severe on lower-income consumers because of lower elasticity coefficients. Mellor (1975, Table 4a) reports a price elasticity of demand for food grains, taking into account only the income effort of the price change, of −0.59 for the bottom two expenditure-class deciles of the Indian population. However, with an assumed supply elasticity of 0.2, production would increase by 8% from the 1976 level, and Pakistan would switch from an

importer to an exporter of wheat.[4] Interestingly, the exports of wheat
(121,000 tons) fall considerably short of the reduction in domestic consumption. Since this example assumes no shifts in either supply or demand, it does not fully represent reality. However, it gives an indication of the magnitude of short-run (one to three years) changes that
might occur under freer markets. It is my view that a consumption
decrease of 5 to 10% (20 to 25% for the lower-income groups) would
not be politically acceptable, and that the Pakistan government would
quickly introduce measures to keep consumption near previous levels.

The above discussion suggests that there is a need to focus on policies and programs complementary to the objective of moving toward
"equilibrium" terms of trade between agricultural and manufactured
goods. This conclusion leads us immediately to a set of long-standing
issues such as those concerning minimum and maximum prices, buffer
stocks, forward pricing, crop insurance schemes, and food-security programs. The literature on these issues spans several decades, and it is beyond the scope of this paper to review all the arguments and evidence
supporting or refuting particular stabilization policies.[5] Most economists seem to assign a modest, supportive role to agricultural price
policies (e.g., Mellor 1970). Suffice it to say that many practical, operational issues exist concerning price and stabilization programs. Most of
these problems, such as determining the level of maximum and minimum prices, can be resolved through empirical research conducted at
the country level.

One of the crucial incentive issues concerning freer markets is the
effect of uncertainty on producer, handler, processor, and consumer
decisions. Brown gives this issue only minor attention, yet I feel that
it is extremely important in developing agricultural price policies for
low-income as well as more-developed economies. My judgment is no
doubt influenced by my experience in northeast Brazil where price and
yield uncertainty and associated producer aversion to risk have made
modernization of the agricultural sector extremely difficult. An effective program of minimum and maximum prices could be an important
part of the economic development programs for many countries. Currently we cannot say precisely how important such a program would
be because we have very little empirical knowledge about producer,
handler, processor, and consumer reactions to changes in risk and uncertainty.[6] In northeast Brazil, only in the last four or five years has
much attention been given to producer responses to and perceptions of
risk and uncertainty. Even though much more needs to be known about
specific cases, there is sufficient theoretical and empirical evidence to
suggest that preventing large increases and decreases in agricultural

prices would be beneficial for *most* countries. Obviously, the definition of "large," the ability to reduce price fluctuations, and the type of programs used will vary from country to country.

An interesting anomaly is that under certain conditions, price instability can be beneficial to consumers and/or producers, both individually and in the aggregate.[7] Considerable theoretical work exists on this issue; however, many of the models developed have not been empirically tested. Konandreas and Schmitz (1978) present an empirical estimation of the conditions which make grain-price stabilization desirable from the point of view of the United States. Although their study shows that U.S. producers and consumers taken together would benefit from feed grain price stabilization, the test was not conclusive for the wheat sector. This is a highly controversial issue, but consideration of the potential benefits of price instability may be important in setting price policy.

Given the above considerations, what are the general price policy instruments available to support the transition from administered prices to "free-market" prices? Four programs seem relevant: (1) guaranteed minimum and maximum prices bounding the expected market prices; (2) a domestic stocks program with accumulation and release triggered by the minimum and maximum prices; (3) appropriate use of international markets to reinforce the domestic stocks program; and (4) compensation programs to alleviate the consumption problems of the poor that result from the expected price increases. These programs can be pursued by individual countries taking into consideration their particular situations. Important in their decisions will be the number of commodities covered by the program, the determination of the minimum and maximum prices and regional price differences, the balance between public and private storage, administrative needs and abilities, and fiscal requirements. Food security schemes involving several countries could reduce the need for the specific country programs.[8] International food aid might be useful temporary assistance to the poorer consumers; however, this type of aid has been unreliable in the past. Clearly, the specific mix of programs will depend on conditions within a country as well as its position in the international community.

Brown concludes with a list of research needs relative to price policy. My orientation toward agricultural price policies under "equilibrium" terms-of-trade conditions suggests some additions. As argued above, I would give much more attention to the problems of risk and uncertainty in freer markets. The change in orientation also suggests that attention be given to the complementary nonprice policies that are needed to handle distribution and externality problems and to stimulate technical change. Taxation and nutrition intervention policies are examples. Since the transition to higher agricultural prices may be associated with inflation, more knowledge is needed about the interrelationships of agricultural (food) prices and inflation. Specific anti-inflationary policies may be needed during the transition; timing questions are extremely important. Research on the impacts of inflation and anti-inflationary programs on different segments of the population is needed for policy decision. Further studies of supply and demand for individual agricultural products and in the aggregate are needed. These studies should focus on elasticity estimates and appropriate shifters for different classes of producers and consumers.[9] Elasticity estimates at different levels in the production-distribution system can provide useful insights for policy making.[10]

Brown's paper and other literature on agricultural price policies make clear that a number of very complex issues are involved. The potential distortions from ill-conceived but well-meaning programs are large. Nevertheless, the arguments and evidence seem to support the need for relative price increases for agricultural commodities in many low-income countries. Continued effort should be devoted to determining the possible public and private gains from *positive* price policies for the agricultural sector and to providing workable guidelines for the implementation of such policies.

NOTES

1. As to reasons these countries changed their policies, economists might want to claim that it was in reaction to the persuasiveness of their arguments concerning the distortions caused by previous policies. I would argue that fiscal and other problems caused by the period of high grain and energy prices had a lot to do with the decisions.

2. For an interesting attempt at incorporating prices in a projection model for Southeast Asian agriculture, see Osterrieth, Verreydt, and Waelbroeck (1977).

3. Price elasticity of demand estimate is from Mellor (1975, Table 4a), considering only the income effect of the price change.

4. Supply elasticity is based on estimates of short-run response presented by Krishna (1967).

5. Some recent studies include Mellor (1975), Lele (forthcoming), the papers on grain reserves published by the U.S. Department of Agriculture and the National Science Foundation (Economic Research Service 1976) and papers from an Inter-American Development Bank seminar (1975). Mellor's report provides 23 pages of references on agricultural price policy.

6. Apparently, the potential gains are quite large. Hazell and Scandizzo (1976), using a mean-variance programming approach, conclude that "potential welfare gains to be had from optimal intervention policies are surprisingly large, in fact far greater than might be anticipated" (p.17).

7. Although not universally accepted, see the work by Waugh (1944), Oi (1961), Hueth and Schmitz (1972), and Bieri and Schmitz (1973). For a contrary theoretical view, see Samuelson (1972). For the policy arguments supporting price stabilization, see Hathaway (1976). Just (1977) contains a good review and evaluation of the welfare effects of stabilization.

8. The International Food Policy Research Institute is currently giving considerable attention to the feasibility and operation of food security schemes.

9. Mellor (1975) gives this considerable attention and presents empirical estimates for India.

10. To use a U.S. example, recent estimates of the price elasticity of demand for fresh summer lemons at the farm, wholesale, and retail levels yielded average values of -0.67, -1.20 and -1.76, respectively. The farm and retail values were significantly different from 1.0 (Nicolatus 1977). These estimates obviously have important implications for the operation of the federal marketing-order program for lemons.

REFERENCES

Bieri, Jurg, and Schmitz, Andrew. 1973. "Export Instability, Monopoly Power, and Welfare." *Journal of International Economics* 3 (November): 389–96.

Economic Research Service, U.S. Department of Agriculture, in cooperation with the National Science Foundation. 1976. *Analyses of Grain Reserves, A Proceedings.* Compiled by David J. Eaton and W. Scott Steele. Economic Research Report no. 634. Washington, D.C.

Hathaway, Dale E. 1976. "Grain Stocks and Economic Stability: A Policy Perspective." In *Analyses of Grain Reserves, A Proceedings,* compiled by David J. Eaton and W. Scott Steele, pp.1–11. Economic Research Service Report no. 634. Washington, D.C.: Economic Research Service, U.S. Department of Agriculture.

Hazell, P. B. R., and Scandizzo, P. L. 1976. "Optimal Price Intervention Policies when Production Is Risky." Paper presented at the [U.S.] Agricultural Development Council's Conference on Risk and Uncertainty in Agricultural Development, International Maize and Wheat Improvement Center, Mexico, March 1976. (Revised paper, November 1976.)

Hueth, Darrell, and Schmitz, Andrew. 1972. "International Trade in Intermediate and Final Goods: Some Welfare Implications of Destabilized Prices." *Quarterly Journal of Economics* 86 (August):351–65.

Inter-American Development Bank. 1975. *Proceedings of the Seminar on Agricultural Policy: A Limiting Factor in the Development Process.* March 17–21, 1975, Washington, D.C.

International Food Policy Research Institute. 1977. *Recent and Prospective Developments in Food Consumption: Some Policy Issues.* Research Report no. 2. Washington, D.C.

Just, Richard E. 1977. "Theoretical and Empirical Possibilities for Determining the Distribution of Welfare Gains from Stabilization." Giannini Foundation Paper no. 469. University of California, Berkeley.

Konandreas, Panos A., and Schmitz, Andrew. 1978. "Welfare Implications of Grain Price Stabilization: Some Empirical Evidence for the United States." *American Journal of Agricultural Economics* 60, no. 1 (February), pp.74–84.

Krishna, Raj. 1967. "Agricultural Price Policy and Economic Development." In *Agricultural Development and Economic Growth,* ed. Herman S. Southworth and Bruce F. Johnston, pp.497–540. Ithaca, N.Y.: Cornell University Press.

Lele, Uma J. Forthcoming. "Considerations Related to Optimum Pricing and Marketing Strategies in Rural Development." In *Proceedings, 16th International Conference of Agricultural Economists, Nairobi, Kenya, 1976.*

Mellor, John W. 1970. "The Basis for Agricultural Price Policy." *War on Hunger* 4 (October):4–10.

———. 1975. "Agricultural Price Policy and Income Distribution in Low-Income Nations." World Bank Staff Working Paper no. 214. Washington, D.C.

Nicolatus, Stephen Jon. 1977. "An Economic Analysis of the Marketing Order for Lemons and its Impact on the Domestic Consumer, 1954–1975." M.S. thesis, University of Arizona.

Oi, Walter Y. 1961. "The Desirability of Price Instability Under Perfect Competition." *Econometrica* 29 (January):58–64.

Osterrieth, Marc; Verreydt, Eric; and Waelbroeck, Jean. 1977. "Agriculture and Growth in Developing Countries: An Experimental Study of the Trade-off Between Agricultural Prices and the Agricultural Trade Balance." Paper presented at the 5th World Congress of the International Economics Association, Tokyo, Japan, August 28–September 3, 1977.

Samuelson, Paul. 1972. "The Consumer Does Benefit from Feasible Price Stability." *Quarterly Journal of Economics* 86 (August):476–93.

Waugh, Frederick V. 1944. "Does the Consumer Benefit from Price Instability?" *Quarterly Journal of Economics* 58 (August):602–14.

Government Price Policies for
Wheat, Rice, and Tractors
in Colombia

REED HERTFORD

Why have economic policies been most often adverse to agriculture in developing countries? Four frequently mentioned reasons can be cast as testable hypotheses. The first, the *bureaucratic behavior* hypothesis, claims simply that governments are prone to be clumsy and make mistakes. Further, they fail to learn from their mistakes. Another explanation is that policies adverse to agriculture have been profitable for the public sector. This *internal revenue* hypothesis asserts that certain agencies are established to keep public coffers full. A well-known example involves marketing boards with monopoly powers to buy farm products cheaply in domestic markets and to resell them at a profit abroad. A third explanation rests on the two-part proposition that the costs and benefits of national policies in developing countries favor those influential groups on which governments depend for political support and that the mass of rural people, being poorer and distant from urban decision centers, are not influential. This corresponds to the *political economy* hypothesis. A final hypothesis has its roots in history and the economic modernization bias against agriculture. It can be termed the *urban bias* hypothesis.

The first two of these hypotheses could account for the perversity of particular agricultural policies, but they would fail to explain why public sector policies have been generally adverse to agriculture. Why, for example, should public sector behavior be any more bureaucratic with respect to agriculture than industry? Or why should opportunities of governments to gain revenues be better in rural than in urban-based activities? Only the political economy and urban bias hypotheses can shed light on the reasons for and the extent of the sectoral bias of public policies. For this reason, they are more fundamental to the conception of public policies while the bureaucratic behavior and the internal revenue hypotheses relate mainly to the conduct and consequences of public policy. They help explain how agriculture is mistreated, once it has been decided to mistreat it!

The intention of this paper is to draw on materials dealing with price policies of a single developing nation, Colombia, in an attempt to illustrate the notions of policy conception, conduct, and consequences and to test the four hypotheses described above. The materials were selected because they are representative of the main types of interventions made by developing countries with respect to agricultural prices and, thus, should be of more general interest. Further, they were selected because they have either been key elements of policies administered by the responsible Colombian agency, the Institute for Agricultural Marketing (IDEMA—Instituto Nacional de Mercadeo Agropecuario), or because they have had pervasive effects on the pattern of rural change in that country.

The next section of the paper provides some background on the Marketing Institute. It is followed by three sections which (respectively) examine a policy to change the price level of an important food grain (wheat); look at a program to reduce the price variability of rice; and analyze a price-level change for a major farm input, tractors. A final section summarizes.

THE INSTITUTE FOR AGRICULTURAL MARKETING

The Colombian Institute for Agricultural Marketing is today a large, vertically integrated state food-marketing enterprise with more than 40 warehouses and 18 silos, a 350,000-ton grain storage capacity, 43 cotton gins, 101 supermarkets, 180 other retail stores, and 53 mobile food outlets. This infrastructure is administered through 8 regional and 94 local offices and supports the Institute's main function—the acquisition and resale of 23 commodities, including 13 basic foods and perishables and 10 processed commodities. The Institute's marketings as a proportion of domestic availability are largest for milk, rice, and wheat (Colombia, National Department of Planning 1975, p.1).

Roots of this enterprise go back to Law 5 of 1944 which established a predecessor agency, the National Supply Institute (INA—Instituto Nacional de Abastecimiento), to set "minimum prices" for producers of selected agricultural commodities. In the larger context of Colombian economic history, Law 5 itself was motivated by a policy of trade protection adopted to promote import substitution and self-sufficiency in most major farm and industrial products. Initially sparked by diminished sales of coffee during the Great Depression of the 1930s, import substitution was reinforced as a consequence of the Second World War during which the "high costs" and lack of dependability of external sources of supply (Berry 1974, p.328) were repeatedly demonstrated.

Available literature on the history of "minimum prices" is contradictory as regards the commodities affected by government intervention, especially in the early years. Law 5 itself speaks of beans, corn, rice, and wheat. Thirsk's (1973) price series indicates that, before 1955, barley, corn, potatoes, and wheat were included in the program; Adams et al. (1964) included barley, corn, cotton, and wheat; in a study of the rice program, price quotations and data on government purchases of rice were found going back to 1950 (Gutierrez and Hertford 1974, p.11); a recent Banco de Bogotá publication (1975) reports price data only for corn, rice, and wheat and government purchases for beans, rice, and wheat before 1960. Although the facts should be clarified, the implication of this literature is that only operations in wheat left a clear mark on history.

Several commodities of importance to national production were explicitly excluded from early price programs; their regulation has been taken over by different organizations. One such commodity was tobacco, placed in the hands of the National Tobacco Institute, a producer-based organization; another was coffee whose price regulation was assumed by a Coffee Price Committee composed of the Ministers of Agriculture and Finance and the Manager of the National Federation of Coffee Growers. The histories of cotton and sugar price regulation are complicated and unclear. It appears, however, that prices of both commodities have been more outside than inside the control of the government in practice, even though some interventions at retail by the National Superintendent of Prices, a dependency of the Ministry of Development, are reported.

Inferences of the policy to exclude prices of certain commodities from direct government intervention and the proliferation of organizations with similar price programs are important. One inference is that it would have been difficult, if not impossible, to orchestrate an internally consistent farm price policy even if the number of functions and activities of the Institute for Agricultural Marketing had not mushroomed as they have. Another is that coffee, cotton, sugar, and tobacco may have been excluded because the price programs contemplated by the Institute and its predecessor agencies—the National Supply Institute from 1944 to 1951, the Corporation for the Defense of Agricultural Products from 1951 to 1958, and the National Supply Institute again from 1958 to 1968, when the reins of commodity price legislation were passed to the Institute for Agricultural Marketing—were decidedly prourban and consumer biased. Supporting this inference is the fact that the Colombian Coffee Federation and producer organizations for cotton, sugar, and tobacco are among the country's strongest farm groups and clearly capable of defending their interests. By all odds, of course, the Coffee Federation is the most influential, rivaling any association outside agriculture.

Further supporting the inference that price programs of the Institute for Agricultural Marketing and its predecessors have been consumer biased are some data on milk and research recently completed on wheat. The information on rice, the third commodity for which the Institute's marketings are a large fraction of domestic availability, indicates that the price program followed for that commodity was not intended to alter its price level but to stabilize prices faced by producers. In fact, price stabilization appears to have been the main program of the Marketing Institute and its predecessors once milk and wheat are accounted for.

THE CASE OF WHEAT: A PROGRAM
TO REDUCE A COMMODITY PRICE

Dudley and Sandilands (1975) show that domestic wheat production declined in Colombia from an average of 140,000 metric tons annually in 1951–54 to 49,000 tons in 1971. Comparable estimates of consumption indicate almost a threefold increase—from 179,000 tons to 434,000 tons. To make up this increase in consumption, imports had to rise ten times in twenty years. The main cause of all these events was a halving of the real price received by wheat producers. This, in turn, Dudley and Sandilands attribute to two factors:

> First, the real c.i.f. price of imported wheat fell—by more than 20 percent. Second, the government agency responsible for wheat marketing . . . allowed the internal price to fall by an additional 30 percent relative to the import price, thereby putting Colombian producers at an increasing disadvantage relative to foreign producers (pp.332–33).

It can be inferred from the Dudley and Sandilands data that most of the decline in the real c.i f. import price was the effect of P.L. 480 concessional sales of cheap wheat by the United States government to Colombia. The additional 30% decline in the internal price of wheat can be shown to reflect a profit-maximizing behavior by the price-administering agencies which was constrained by a concern for the political consequences of price adjustments. This profit-maximizing behavior resulted in a price for wheat which was below the socially optimal price and thus inefficient. Its distributional consequences, already alluded to, obviously favored consumers over producers.

The data to support these inferences are presented in Figure 1, taken directly from Dudley and Sandilands. For the post-1950 period, three different prices of wheat in constant 1958 pesos are presented in the figure. The "actual" price is defined as the price received by Colombian producers. The "socially optimal" price is that price which would have minimized the cost to Colombia of satisfying domestic demand from

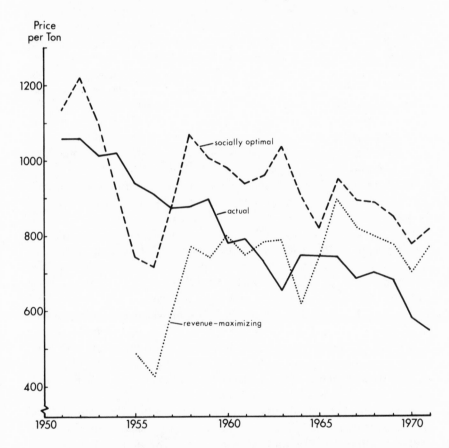

Figure 1. Actual price, socially optimal price, and government revenue-maximizing price per ton of domestic wheat, 1951–71, in 1958 pesos.

Source: Leonard Dudley and Roger J. Sandilands, "The Side Effect of Foreign Aid: The Case of Public Law 480 Wheat in Colombia." *Economic Development and Cultural Change* 23, no. 2 (January 1975), p.334.

national and international sources. This price turns out to be a weighted average of the c.i.f. peso prices of wheat imported commercially and through special sales arrangements such as those under U.S. P.L. 480. Weights equal the proportion of wheat imports affected at each price. A small upward price adjustment is made to account for the overvaluation of domestic currency. The "revenue-maximizing" price is that price which would maximize profits to the price-administering agencies from buying and selling wheat. It is slightly lower than the socially optimal price for two reasons: (1) The price administering agencies, in converting pesos to dollars, used a nominal exchange rate which was lower than the social opportunity cost of foreign exchange by reason of currency overvaluation, and (2) the price agencies failed to take full account of the costs over time of repaying loans granted by the United States to support purchases of P.L. 480 imports. This profit-maximizing price is of special interest because the Colombian government made no significant contributions to the expenditures of price-administering agencies from the time of Law 5 until the late 1960s. Without government support, we must presume that some kind of revenue-maximizing behavior was adopted by the price agencies in an attempt to cover their operating costs. If this presumption is correct, of course, a close correspondence would be observed between the actual and the revenue-maximizing prices of wheat.

This can be best examined by dividing the history of wheat pricing into three periods. In the early years of the first period, 1950–1958, prices received for wheat by Colombian farmers and socially optimal prices did not diverge widely. However, in 1954 the optimal price dropped sharply as the result of Colombia's receiving its first wheat under Title I of P.L. 480. The actual price of wheat drifted down at a much more moderate pace and then leveled off in 1958, remaining well above the revenue-maximizing price over the whole period and even above the socially optimal price until 1957. This "stickiness" of administered prices—their resistance to the sort of radical change that optimizing behavior would have required, following first shipments of cheap U.S. wheat—could have had a political origin. We know, for example, that domestic producers supplied a significant share of total wheat consumed in the mid-1950s (about 75%) and that there were still many wheat producers. A sharp drop in the prices they received might well have caused an outcry.

In the second period of pricing, 1958–1966, actual wheat prices closely approximated levels which would have maximized revenues of the price-administering agencies. This pattern tends to confirm the presumption that prices received by wheat producers maximized revenues of the price-administering agencies in the absence of contributions to their operations from the Colombian government.

In a third period, following 1966, the revenue-maximizing price for wheat rose sharply and paralleled the socially optimal price while the actual price continued its downward trend. The rise in the profit-maximizing price was consistent with a closing of the gap between the official and shadow prices of the dollar following adoption of a floating or variable rate of exchange in 1967. That domestic wheat prices did not follow the rise in profit-maximizing prices again reflects a sticky price policy induced by political concerns and sensitivities. Dudley and Sandilands explain:

> it became politically more difficult to maximize revenues since this would have required an increase in the domestic price. Concern for consumers appears to have dominated, for from 1968 to 1971 the selling price for imported wheat was frozen at 2,100 pesos per ton despite an annual rate of inflation approaching 10 percent (p.335).

In short, there is evidence overall to confirm a profit-maximizing behavior which was constrained in two of the three time periods examined. In the first, a dampening of price movements was consistent with a desire to preclude problems with producers; in the third, to avoid problems with consumers. It could be said that this behavior is symptomatic of the pricing agencies' financial independence of—but political dependence on—the Colombian government. Political constraints on price movements produced a declining long-term trend in the real price of wheat, even though the real revenue-maximizing price was practically constant after 1958; it, in fact, evidenced an upward trend if the first three years of P.L. 480 agreements are included. Finally, although P.L. 480 imports triggered and ultimately validated price patterns for Colombian wheat, they explain only a part of the observed decline in prices received by farmers. The rest is the consequence of the operation in recent years of a cheap-wheat, proconsumer pricing policy.

This latter conclusion is reinforced by picking up the story of Colombian wheat where the Dudley and Sandilands data leave off, namely 1971. The story is a simple one. In 1972, real domestic prices of wheat were permitted to edge up by about a third over 1971 and the Institute for Agricultural Marketing made money; in 1973, however, the average c.i.f. price tripled and losses went to 159 million pesos; in 1974, following further price increases in the world market, losses jumped to 940 million pesos. During the three-year period, 1972–1974, the Marketing Institute reported losses of 2.8 billion pesos on sales of 7.1 billion pesos.

Table 1

IDEMA's Losses, 1972–1974

Item		Millions of pesos
Wheat		1,082
Sorghum and soybeans		72
		1,154
Gains from other products	(392)	
Profits on cotton ginning	(52)	
		(444)
		710
Salaries, administration, and		
related expenses		1,424
Other expenses		654
Total losses		2,788

As shown in Table 1, wheat accounted for most of these operating losses.

THE CASE OF RICE: A PROGRAM TO STABILIZE A COMMODITY PRICE

Aside from wheat, market interventions by the Institute for Agricultural Marketing and its predecessors in Colombia can best be categorized as efforts to stabilize commodity prices. Of these price-stabilization activities, only those for rice have been studied in some depth (Gutierrez and Hertford 1974). For additional insights into the intentions and results of commodity-price programs, that research on rice is reviewed below.

To illustrate the workings of this price policy, reference is made to Figure 2. Farmers are taken there to have organized their production on the basis of the forecast price, P_1, well above the equilibrium price. This leads to overproduction in the amount Q_1-Q'_1. To clear the market of this oversupply, prices paid by consumers fall to P_2. On comparing these price and quantity outcomes with those of equilibrium, it can be seen that, although consumers gain a surplus equal to $b + c + d$, producers lose b of surplus $c + d + e$ of resource costs not covered by the lower price, P_2. The net results is a social loss equal to triangle e. An analogous loss, equivalent to the triangle e but positioned opposite it, results when the price forecast lies below the equilibrium price. It can be shown that the value of such triangles, as a proportion of the equilibrium values of production, is equal in any single time period to

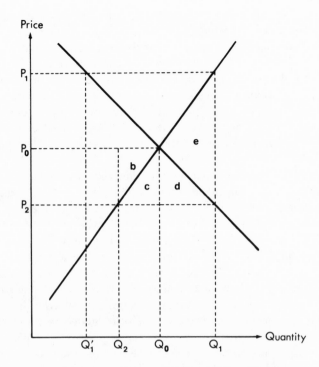

Figure 2. Costs of Price Disequilibria

$$\tfrac{1}{2}\lambda^2\left(\frac{1}{e}+\frac{1}{n}\right) \tag{1}$$

where λ is the percentage deviation of the quantity actually produced from equilibrium quantity—$(Q_1 - Q_o)/Q_o$—and e and $-n$ are, respectively, the price elasticities of supply and demand.

The role of the government has been to pinch prices such as P_1 and P_2 together so as to reduce the size of triangles like e. When the price forecast has resulted in an oversupply of rice, this would be done by buying rice at the announced "minimum price." The result, with reference to Figure 2, is a rightward shift in demand and a price higher than P_2 to consumers. Similarly, when the price forecast lies below equilibrium and a shortfall in rice supplies occurs, the government would sell from its previously accumulated "buffer stocks," effectively shift the supply curve to the right, and reduce prices paid by consumers. Note that the actual value of the expected gain from such price-stabilizing activities implied by equation (1) is smaller in any year the smaller are deviations from equilibrium and the larger are the price elasticities of demand and supply. Further, from equation (1) there is the inference that the value of this expected gain in any year may be quite small.

The following main conclusions were derived from estimates of demand and supply relations made to evaluate the stabilization program:[1]

(1) In the absence of any government intervention, the net social cost of price and quantity deviations from equilibrium would have represented on average only 0.11 percent of the value of rice production.[2] In this sense, rice may not have been the best crop to select for a stabilization program, for price instability was of rather modest proportions to begin with.

(2) The effect of government intervention was to actually increase—not decrease—the cost of price deviations. The estimated net social cost of price and quantity deviations from equilibria represented on average 0.13% of the value of rice production. Government intervention was stabilizing in only five of the twenty years examined.

Bieri and Schmitz (1974) have recently shown that a profit-maximizing price agency with monopolistic and monopsonistic powers should be expected to try to destabilize commodity prices because it pays. It thus appears possible that the profit-maximizing behavior forced on the Institute for Agricultural Marketing and its predecessor agencies in the absence of steady government financial support may explain both undesirable price outcomes described to this point—the decrease in the relative price of wheat and the increased variance of rice prices attributable to government intervention.

(3) When overhead and administrative costs were imputed to the price-stabilization program in proportion to rice's weight in the total weight of all commodities purchased by the price agencies, these costs bulked large—about 3% of the value of rice production on average, or well in excess of the proportion that the maximum possible gain from price stabilization could have represented of the value of production.

(4) Some evidence emerged that the supply curve of rice had shifted to the right when government purchases rose to a substantial share of rice production during the 1960s. This evidence, appearing in the form of a significant coefficient on a dummy variable in the supply relation, was not taken into account in the final evaluation of the rice price-stabilization program because it was felt that any number of factors could have contributed to the observed shift in supply. Additional analysis of the relation of price stability to supply would definitely be warranted.

In sum, the rice price-stabilization program was found to have increased allocative inefficiency. Because the overall impact on price of the Marketing Institute's intervention was small, investment in rice production may have been dampened only slightly. The effects of the program on the level and distribution of incomes, as a consequence, were probably minimal.

THE CASE OF TRACTORS: INTERACTIONS BETWEEN THE EXCHANGE RATE AND A RELATIVE INPUT PRICE

A higher price for foreign exchange generally improves export possibilities for all commodities. However, if the higher price is matched by higher internal prices, prospects for exports are not improved at all. So far as the exporter is concerned, the key relationship is between the value in domestic currency of a dollar's worth of exports and the cost in domestic currency of producing it, with exports becoming more profitable when the price of foreign exchange rises relative to domestic prices. Conversely, imports become more attractive when the price of foreign exchange falls relative to domestic prices. This ratio of the nominal exchange rate to the domestic price level is an "effective" rate of exchange for purposes of reckoning both the volume of exports and of imports.

Exchange-rate policies of some Latin American governments have been managed at the expense of agricultural exports, with effective exchange rates for the sector continually falling on a downward trend. This appears not to have been true in Colombia, however. From 1950 until the period of major commercial trade reforms in 1968, the nominal rate of exchange increased about seven times as the peso declined from 2.04 pesos per dollar to 15.82 pesos per dollar (International Monetary Fund), and the index of all prices received by farmers increased just five times (Atkinson 1970), implying roughly a 55% increase in the effective rate of exchange vis-à-vis agriculture. Since agriculture is, on net, decidedly an exporter of goods and services, accounting for from 60 to 80% of the value of all Colombian exports over the 1950–1968 period, the growth of agricultural exports and production should have been strengthened by this rise in the effective rate of exchange. For example, Sheahan and Clark (1967) indicated that every 10% increase in the effective rate of exchange had been associated with an increase of 9.8% in total exports of goods (excluding coffee and oils) over the 1958–1966 period.

Nonetheless, exports from agriculture did not increase over the 1950–1968 period and, in fact, evidenced on balance a modest decline.[3] Agricultural production expanded by only about 60%—just slightly in excess of the rate of population growth. And yield increases were modest. Most of the gain in output can be accounted for by area expansion. Two hypotheses concerning the causes of this modest growth can be advanced.

The first is that trends in the world price of Colombia's major export, coffee, did not favor the kinds of general increases in production and trade anticipated by trends in the effective exchange rate (Kalmanoff 1968, pp.65–75). As is well known, coffee prices, production, and exports moved up strongly through the early 1950s. After 1957, however, world prices declined; and their effects in Colombia were reinforced by a widening gap between internal and external coffee prices as transportation, hulling, and handling costs rose and as the net rates of taxation of exports increased. Available data indicate that acreage of coffee harvested stabilized shortly after the decrease in world prices began. Production continued to increase moderately but only because of the adoption of a new yield-increasing variety of coffee. That additional resources were not withdrawn in the face of downward pressures on prices was probably because there are few alternatives to the production of coffee in the cool mountain areas where it is grown.

The second hypothesis is that increases in the effective rate of exchange in 1956–57 put the brakes on imports of tractors and that, without this additional source of power, the conversion of pasture land and raw land to cropland by the commercial sector of agriculture was hampered. Production and exports thus did not grow at rates which were commensurate with evidenced trends in the effective rate of exchange.

The only part of the second hypothesis which will be studied here is that which requires establishing a relationship between exchange rates, tractor prices, and tractor stocks. A complete proof of the hypothesis obviously would also require showing that patterns of land area and production expansion coincided through time and space with patterns of change in the stock of agricultural tractors.

The necessary data are presented in Table 1. There it can be seen that available estimates of Colombia's tractor stocks point toward rapid increases in numbers until 1956–57. Although tractor stocks continued to expand thereafter, they did so at a reduced pace up until about 1962. From 1962 to 1965 or 1966, they remained practically unchanged. A slight increase was registered in 1967. These movements in tractor stocks and the data of the five related price series shown in Table 2 lead to the following observations:

1. Both relative price series for tractors, namely, prices paid in Colombia for tractors deflated (1) by a prices-received index and (2) by an index of farm wages, fell during the period that tractor stocks expanded rapidly and rose sharply around the time that the rate of increase in the stock of farm tractors diminished.[4]

Table 2

Colombian Farm Tractor Stocks and
Related Price Data, 1950–1967

	Tractor Stock (1)	Tractor Prices Paid Deflated By:		F.O.B. Peso Price of U.S. Tractors Deflated by Prices Received (4)	U.S. Tractor Price (5)	Colombian Effective Exchange Rate (6)
		Prices Received (2)	Farm Wage (3)			
Year	1,000			Index		
1950	6.5	100	100	100	94	100
1951	7.9	91	89	116	97	113
1952	8.8	90	89	115	100	108
1953	10.1	86	88	110	103	100
1954	12.2	74	81	90	101	84
1955	13.9	84	86	93	99	88
1956	15.4	89	98	87	105	78
1957	15.3	121	140	180	106	160
1958	16.3	144	165	218	114	180
1959	17.3	143	147	184	113	153
1960	18.4	136	133	178	113	148
1961	19.2	145	144	168	114	138
1962	20.1	155	143	219	114	181
1963	20.6	145	132	181	116	147
1964	20.9	203	190	147	119	116
1965	20.8	232	210	218	124	165
1966	21.3	213	197	197	128	145
1967	23.3	200	195	218	131	156

Sources:

Col. 1: Wayne R. Thirsk (1972, p. 319).

Cols. 2 and 3: The tractor prices paid in the Colombian series are from Carlos Ossa Escobar (1970, p. 50) and refer to the Cauca Valley. This valley employed about a quarter of Colombia's total stock of farm tractors over the 1950–1967 period. The prices-received series, used as a deflator of tractor prices, and the farm wage data, used to deflate tractor prices, are also taken from Ossa (1970) and refer to "hot climate" wages without meals; see, for example, Atkinson (1970, p.55).

Cols. 4 and 5: The U.S. tractor-price series, which forms the basis for the indices shown here, is taken from Fettig (1963, p.608) and corresponds to his "chained index" extrapolated through 1967, with data from the U.S. Department of Agriculture (various issues).

Col. 6: International Monetary Fund (various issues).

2. The f.o.b. peso price of U.S. tractors deflated by prices received by Colombian farmers for all crops anticipates as well or even better than

the relative prices paid for tractors by Colombian farmers the turning points and trends in tractor stocks.

3. From the last two columns of Table 1, it can be seen that trends and turning points in the relative f.o.b. peso price of U.S. tractors were largely explained by the trend through 1956 in the effective rate of exchange. The U.S. tractor-price index trended upwards rather steadily and moderately throughout the period. It registered, however, no abrupt increase around the middle and late 1950s to match the curtailment of increases in tractor stocks.

On the basis of the preceding points, it is concluded that the mechanization of Colombian agriculture was promoted by a falling relative price of tractors from 1950 to 1956–57 and substantially hampered thereafter by a rising relative price of tractors. These trends in tractor prices can be largely explained, in turn, by parallel changes in the effective rate of exchange.

It should be pointed out that the observed price-stock relationships for tractors are plausible under the regime in force for the importation of tractors. Until 1957, farm machinery imports were among items totally exempted from prior licensing or government approval. From 1957 until mid-1968, tractors and parts were subjected to refundable prior import deposits and import licensing. From 1968 on, tractors and farm machinery could be freely imported, but spare parts—produced now in Colombia—have been subject to licensing.

Previous studies of tractor use in Colombian agriculture have largely overlooked the relationship between prices and stocks and emphasized instead the encouragement given mechanization by low-interest loans from foreign lenders to purchase farm machinery. Ossa (1970), in his seminal study on mechanization, a study which concentrated on development in the highly progressive Cauca Valley, was the first to advance this hypothesis. John Sanders (1971), who began but never completed a promising study of the process of farm mechanization in Colombia, concluded from his preliminary results that "tractor financing is primarily coming from farm earnings." However, he proposed to introduce in subsequent statistical analysis a variable measuring the value of farm loans for mechanization. Wayne Thirsk (1972), following the studies of Ossa and Sanders, concluded in his doctoral dissertation on the "Economics of Colombian Farm Mechanization" that "a special feature of the Colombian situation is that the process of farm mechanization has been subsidized relative to investment in other sectors of the economy. This subsidy has been an important element in the rapid growth of farm mechanization in Colombia." While largely failing to prove either that a subsidy had been granted or that the subsidy explained the pace of farm mechanization, Thirsk did demonstrate, within a general equilibrium framework, three consequences of cheap tractor prices. These were: (1) a reduction in total labor demand caused by the relatively high capital intensity of mechanized agriculture; (2) an increase in the share of income obtained by capital, largely at the expense of labor and small-farm incomes; and (3) a diminution in the level of national income due to a more inefficient allocation of labor and capital.

The conclusion that a credit subsidy for tractor purchases launched the mechanization of Colombian agriculture rests for the most part on an impressive record of loans for that purpose. In 1949, the World Bank granted the Colombian government a $5 million (U.S.) loan at 3.5% interest just for the acquisition of farm equipment. The loan was renewed in 1954 and then repaid in 1961. Another $1.5 million (U.S.) loan was made in 1966 to a Colombian farm rental agency, INPRO-AGRO, for replacement of its equipment. In 1964 the U.S. Export-Import Bank granted Colombia a $10 million (U.S.) line of credit tied to the purchase of American-manufactured farm machinery. The Inter-American Development Bank negotiated a $12 million (U.S.) loan at 7.5% which was intended to increase the mechanization of the large-scale commercial farms. Also, special barter deals have been made with Spain, Finland, East Germany, Poland, Yugoslavia, Czechoslovakia, and Rumania to exchange farm machinery for coffee.

Although the timing of the loans did not coincide precisely with major changes in tractor stocks and tractor prices, future research should examine the possibility that the conception of these international credits was sparked by the attractiveness of selling tractors in Colombia during much of the 1950s. Many of my Colombian colleagues have asserted that there was a one-to-one relation. The most I am currently prepared to say is that the international credits may have reinforced the effects of changing tractor prices on the observed increase in tractor stocks.

CONCLUSION

This paper has examined three price policies relating to agriculture in Colombia. One affected the price level of a major crop (wheat), another altered the price stability of an important grain (rice), and a third resulted in changes in the price of a capital input (tractors). An attempt was made to unravel the consequences of these policies and to better understand their conception, conduct, and consequences in terms of the four hypotheses of political economy cited at the outset.

I think we can conclude that one consequence of government interventions was allocative inefficiency in all cases examined. All were costly to society at large. Two—the price policies for wheat and rice—also reduced incentives for farmers to produce and, they thus add support to the proposition that economic policies toward rural areas in developing countries have been prejudicial to agricultural production. One, however, was probably output-increasing. The evidence indicates that a sticky exchange rate in the 1950s made it profitable to increase imports of tractors and that these became an essential ingredient in Colombia's expansion of farmland. Tractor imports also, however, reduced the demand for labor in agriculture and probably further concentrated the distribution of incomes in rural areas by increasing capital's share of final output. This conclusion suggests that slowly adjusting exchange rates, while adversely affecting product prices, have some compensating production effects on the side of input prices. Further, where agricultural product prices are mistreated by exchange-rate policies, serious regressive consequences on income distribution, arising from the importation of agricultural inputs, may be experienced.

Support for all four hypotheses about why economic policies have been adverse to agriculture was encountered, except perhaps for the urban bias hypothesis. For example, the marketing agency responsible for administering agricultural price policies in Colombia appears to have had its roots less in a bias against agriculture than in a need to diversify agricultural exports (mostly coffee), a need which stemmed from the effects of the Great Depression on coffee prices worldwide. Yet Colombia may be an atypical case to examine by reason of the historical importance of agricultural exports in the economy. I sense that economic policies of developing nations are much less likely to be biased for historical reasons against agriculture when the exports of that sector have always mattered.

But the internal revenue hypothesis finds much support in Colombia's policies toward wheat and rice and, more generally, in her having established a marketing agency with a far-ranging mandate and no regular budget. Also, in the price stabilization policy for rice, the bureaucratic behavior hypothesis may apply. Prices were actually destabilized in that case and the only explanation other than the operational one, that destabilization may have contributed to government coffers, is that the responsible agency made mistakes in predicting price variations and setting its support levels. And, finally, the political economy hypothesis finds appeal in several quarters. For example, the government was apparently left to manage price and marketing policies only of those crops for which farmers were not powerful and well organized. Also, there is strong evidence to suggest that wheat prices failed to follow predicted patterns in certain of the periods examined, owing to the power of producer and consumer groups, especially the latter.

Nonetheless, these bits and pieces of evidence lead me to observe that we economists do not really have, as yet, a robust and thoroughgoing explanation of why agriculture is mistreated by the economic policies of developing countries.[5] We seem much better able to show, evaluate, and quantify the consequences of policies than to explain their conception and conduct. And, until we can do the latter, it seems to me that we will be poor predictors of the patterns of rural change, particularly if David Hopper's prediction (in the volume) that "rural people will face a living and working environment that is increasingly subject to control by techniques of state intervention" is borne out.

NOTES

1. Results obtained from applying the model to the rice-price stabilization program were based on the following empirically estimated demand and supply functions:

$$\text{Supply—Log } Q = 5.8 + 0.104 \, d_1 + 0.235 \, \text{Log } P^* + 0.363 \, \text{Log } H$$
$$(1.479) \quad (2.027) \quad (2.397)$$
$$+ \, 0.151 \, \text{Log } P_a \qquad R^2 = 0.96$$
$$(1.416)$$
$$\text{Demand—Log } P = 0.1 - 0.729 \, (\text{Log } Q - \text{Log Pobl.}) + 0.480 \, \text{Log } I_D$$
$$(-6.017)$$
$$R^2 = 0.67$$

where Q is rice output; d_1 is 1 for the 1960–1969 period and zero otherwise; P^* is $a_{t-1} \, P_t^g + (1 - a_{t-1}) \, P_{t-1}^d$, with P_t^g being the announced government price of rice, P_{t-1}^d the price of rice received by farmers in the prior year, and a_{t-1} the proportion of production purchased by the government last year; H is hectares harvested in rice; P_a is the wholesale price of sesame; P_t is the real price received by farmers for rice; Q is rice output predicted from the supply function equation after its estimation; Pobl. is population; and I_D is real disposable income per capita. The sesame price variable was included as an index of the (highly intercorrelated) prices of crops, such as cotton and sesame, grown in competition with or complementary to rice. Numbers in parentheses below estimated coefficients are estimated "t" statistics. Such a statistic is not reported for the coefficient on real disposable income per capita, I_D, as it was obtained from an independent study. The period of analysis was 1950–1969.

For Colombian rice, a closed economy model is consistent with facts even though rice has been occasionally traded. If a commodity is traded and tariffs

138   *Reed Hertford*

are in effect, modifications are called for in the analysis of price stabilization; these have been dealt with by Jurg Bieri and Andrew Schmitz (1974).

2. Price patterns in the absence of government intervention were simulated with the model, holding the proportion of production purchased equal to zero and going back in time before the government price-stabilization program was in effect.

3. A good summary of export developments during this period is contained in Bennett (1973).

4. It would not be expected, of course, that turning points in prices would match exactly with those of tractor stocks both because of the lagged adjustments associated with the employment of durable capital items and because of the influence of other variables on the stock of farm tractors. Nonetheless, the correspondence between the trends and turning points of tractor numbers and relative tractor prices in table 1 is quite striking.

5. A promising start on the required theory has been made by de Janvry (1977).

REFERENCES

Adams, Dale W. et al. 1964. *Public Law 480 and Colombia's Economic Development*. Medellin, Colombia: National University.

Atkinson, L. Jay. 1970. *Agricultural Productivity in Colombia*. Foreign Agricultural Report no. 66. Washington, D.C.: Economic Research Service, U.S. Department of Agriculture.

Banco de Bogotá. 1975. *Informe, segundo semestre de 1974*. Bogotá, Colombia.

Bennett, Gae A. 1973. *Agricultural Production and Trade of Colombia*. Foreign Agricultural Report no. 343. Washington, D.C.: Economic Research Service, U.S. Department of Agriculture.

Berry, Albert. 1974. "Política económica internacional de Colombia." In *Lecturas sobre desarrollo económico Colombiano*, ed. Hernando Gomez and Eduardo Wiesner. Bogotá, Colombia: Fundación para la Educación Superior y el Desarrollo.

Bieri, Jurg, and Schmitz, Andrew. 1974. "Market Intermediaries and Price Instability: Some Welfare Implications." *American Journal of Agricultural Economics* 56, no. 2 (May):280–85.

Colombia, National Department of Planning. 1975. "Situación del IDEMA." Mimeographed. Bogotá, Colombia.

de Janvry, Alain. 1977. "Inducement of Technological and Institutional Innovation: An Interpretative Framework." In *Resource Allocation and Productivity in National and International Agricultural Research*, ed. Thomas M. Arndt et al., pp.551–63. Minneapolis: University of Minnesota Press.

Dudley, Leonard, and Sandilands, Roger J. 1975. "The Side Effects of Foreign Aid: The Case of Public Law 480 Wheat in Colombia." *Economic Development and Cultural Change* 23, no. 2 (January):325–36.

Fettig, Lyle P.   1963.   "Adjusting Farm Tractor Prices for Quality Changes, 1950–1962." *Journal of Farm Economics* 45, no. 3 (August): 599–611.

Gutierrez, Nestor, and Hertford, Reed.   1974.   "Una evaluación de la intervención del gobierno en el mercado de arroz en Colombia." Folleto técnico no. 4, Centro Internacional de Agricultura Tropical. Cali, Colombia.

International Monetary Fund.   1951–1968.   *International Financial Statistics.* Washington, D.C., various issues.

Kalmanoff, George.   1968.   "The Coffee Economy of Colombia." Economics Department Working Paper no. 15, International Bank for Reconstruction and Development. Washington, D.C.

Ossa Escobar, Carlos.   1970.   *La mecanización de la agricultura en el valle del Cauca.* Serie M, no. 2. Bogotá, Colombia: CEDE, Universidad de los Andes.

Sanders, John H.   1971.   "Government Policy and the Demand for Tractors in Colombia, 1950–67." Mimeographed. Department of Agricultural Economics, University of Minnesota, Minneapolis.

Sheahan, John, and Clark, Sara.   1967.   "The Response of Colombian Exports to Variations in Effective Exchange Rates." Research Memorandum no. 11, Center for Development Economics, Williams College, Williamstown, Massachusetts.

Thirsk, Wayne R.   1972.   "The Economics of Colombian Farm Mechanization." Ph.D. dissertation, Yale University.

———.   1973.   "Income Distribution Consequences of Agricultural Price Supports in Colombia." Paper no. 43, Program of Development Studies, Rice University, Houston, Texas.

U.S. Department of Agriculture.   1950–1967.   *Agricultural Statistics.* Washington, D.C.: U.S. Government Printing Office, various issues.

Barriers to Efficient Capital Investment in Agriculture

RANDOLPH BARKER

Most developing economies lack capital for agricultural and economic development. To finance new investments, domestic savings normally are augmented by foreign borrowings. However, Schultz (1964) contends that the low productivity in traditional agriculture is not caused by a shortage of capital per se but rather by a shortage of productive investment opportunities. Introduction of new technology raises the return to capital investment and generates a demand for new forms of capital. New technology and the complementary current inputs are themselves the product of capital investments. The linkages are such that new technology may induce or be induced by new forms of capital. For example, technological advances in the fertilizer industry and the lowering of fertilizer prices encouraged the development of fertilizer-responsive varieties of cereal grains which in turn stimulated further investment in irrigation. In this chain of events, responses are molded not only by physical and human resource endowments, but also by institutions and policies which can create incentives or disincentives to further investment at any point.

In what follows I am concerned with the barriers to efficient capital investment in agriculture. I have chosen to focus on capital investment in the free-market, labor-surplus economies. I contend that capital bias exists in both private and public investment, and is due not only to market imperfections but, more importantly, to constraints arising from the organizational and institutional structure of these societies.

CAPITAL REQUIREMENTS FOR LAND- AND LABOR-SURPLUS ECONOMIES

Land-surplus economies can be distinguished from labor-surplus economies by observing the time-series relationship between the growth in the net cropped area, A, and the employment in agriculture, L, as follows:

$$A = aL^B$$

If B, the ratio of the geometric increase of A with respect to L, is equal to or greater than one, then the country is viewed as land-surplus. A "turning point" is often encountered where the opportunities for cultivating more land are extremely limited and the agricultural labor force continues to grow. It is reflected in the rising value of land relative to labor. Within a country, these turning points vary from region to region and among different crop environments. For example, in Asia the present opportunities for expanding the area of land on which lowland rice is grown are more limited than for expanding the area of upland crops. A second turning point will be reached when the agricultural labor force begins to decline because demand for labor grows and hence wage rates rise in the nonagricultural sector. In East Asia, the first turning point was reached in the late nineteenth and early twentieth centuries. In Taiwan, for example, this occurred in the mid-1920s (Lee 1971). Taiwan passed through a second turning point in the late 1960s. In a relative sense, according to my definition above, Taiwan once again became a land-surplus economy, although no one would regard the countries of East Asia as land-surplus in absolute terms.

By contrast with East Asia, South and Southeast Asia could be regarded as land-surplus for a decade or more after World War II. For example, the first turning point was reached in the Philippines about 1960 (Crisostomo and Barker 1972) and is only now being approached in Thailand and Burma. Thus, for many of the labor-surplus developing economies, the transition from land-surplus has occurred very recently. Institutions, to a large degree, have originated in a land-surplus environment.

The different technology requirements for land- versus labor-surplus economies are illustrated in Hayami and Ruttan's discussion (1971) of the Japanese versus the U.S. experience. Land-surplus economies must emphasize labor-saving technologies to increase agricultural productivity, while the focus in labor-surplus economies must be on land-saving or yield-increasing technologies. The implications of this difference for the nature and form of capital investments to augment agricultural productivity are very critical.

Growth in output per worker is generally recognized as a necessary condition for economic development. The labor-surplus economy must initially forego rapid increases in labor productivity and increase agricultural productivity through rapid increases in land productivity. Capital is also in short supply. But labor is abundant even to the point where underemployment is a serious social problem in many areas. Thus, there is a need for labor-intensive forms of technology and capital investments which increase the opportunities for productive employment of labor.

Capital in agriculture can be roughly classified into (1) private investments in power and equipment, animals, farm tools, plant propagation materials, buildings, and land, and (2) public investments in irrigation and drainage, land improvements, and farm-to-market roads. Irrigation, drainage, and land improvements will be referred to as land infrastructure.[1]

The distinction between private and public forms of investment is, of course, not clear cut. There can be private investments in irrigation and, even in a free economy, public investments in, say, power, buildings, or land. There are also other forms of capital such as human capital and research investment and working capital expenditures which are to a large extent induced by other capital investments. The above classification, however, draws attention to the critical role of public capital investment.

In the labor-surplus economies of Asia, where rice is the staple food of most of the population, investment in land infrastructure offers the greatest potential both for increasing land productivity and absorbing labor productively. By contrast, there is much debate over the social benefits of capital investment in various forms of mechanization. Does mechanization increase production or simply displace labor?

The effect of the introduction of modern varieties of rice and wheat which are suited mainly to the areas of good water control was to lower the cost per ton of cereal grain produced under irrigation, and hence, raise the marginal productivity of irrigation investment. Farmers and government officials were quick to respond. Table 1 illustrates that in the decade following the introduction of modern varieties of rice, irrigation investment and increased fertilizer use (which occurred principally on irrigated lands) were the main sources of growth in rice output. Irrigation investment has both an area and a yield effect. (The area irrigated is gross rather than net, and hence, the second crop is counted as an additional hectare). Of the countries where rice production increased at more than 2% per annum, Thailand alone achieved this growth through expanded use of traditional inputs—land and labor. There are also countries (not listed in the table), such as Burma and Bangladesh, where rice production increased less than 2%. Many of these areas of low production growth are in major river deltas where the capital requirements to control water are extremely large and where the new rice technology is unsuitable at present. More will be said about this matter subsequently.

Table 1

Estimated Proportion of Growth in Rice Output,
in Selected Asian Countries, Attributed to Components
of Area and Yield, Mid-1960s to Early 1970s

| Country | Period | Annual Rate of Production Growth (%) | Percentage Points (%) Attributed to | | | |
| | | | Area | | Yield | |
			irrigated	unirrigated	fertilizer[a]	residual[b]
Pakistan	1965–73	7.9	1.4	0	1.7	4.8
Malaysia	1965–73	5.7	3.7	0.1	1.4	0.5
Sri Lanka	1965–72	5.6	0.5	0.1	3.5	1.5
Indonesia	1965–72	4.8	2.2	−0.3	1.1	1.8
Philippines	1965–73	3.4	1.2	−0.3	1.5	1.0
India	1965–70	3.2	0.6	0.2	1.5	0.9
Thailand	1965–72	2.1	0.2	1.7	0.3	−0.1

[a] Calculated on the basis of 10 kg of yield for every 1 kg of fertilizer.

[b] Includes the contribution to yield of improved quality of land due to higher proportion of irrigated area.

Source: Robert W. Herdt, Amanda Te, and Randolph Barker. 1977. "The Prospects for Asian Rice Production." Dept. of Agricultural Economics Staff Paper no. 77-3. Mimeographed. International Rice Research Institute, Los Baños, Philippines.

BARRIERS TO THE MAXIMIZATION OF SOCIAL BENEFITS

Decisions which influence both private and public investment are made by a wide range of people with very divergent views and objectives. Although the private entrepreneur may ultimately decide whether or not to invest in a piece of equipment, government officials and foreign experts influence the type of equipment to be made available and the financial terms for purchase. Three measures of efficiency for evaluating decision criteria on investment choices are:

(1) engineering efficiency, measured as the ratio of physical output to physical input.

(2) private efficiency, measured as the rate of return to private investors at given market prices.

(3) social efficiency, measured as the rate of return to investments using shadow prices for factors and products, including the spillovers that are not captured by the investors.

The divergence from (3) toward (1) or (2) leads to a misallocation of resources. The conventional economic-development view is that the divergence from social benefits is due to market imperfections which cause private efficiency (2) to diverge from social efficiency (3). These market imperfections generally take the form of subsidized interest rates on credit, market wages above the opportunity cost for labor, and overvalued exchange rates, all of which tend to bias private investments toward more capital-intensive techniques. Taxes, subsidies, and externalities may also be sources of bias. It is further contended that lack of suitable labor-intensive technology biases the investor's decision. The recent interest in "appropriate technology" reflects this concern. One might speculate, in this connection, as to the substantial change in resource mix and technology development that would occur if international lending agencies were suddenly to declare that credit would henceforth be provided at rates in keeping with the domestic opportunity cost for capital.

Timmer (1975) and Thomas (1975) argue convincingly that when government administrators and foreign experts are involved in the choice of technology, their bias toward capital-intensive technology may be even more important than the above-mentioned factors. The foreign expert, raised in an environment of high wage rates, is familiar with projects that minimize labor input. Many of the projects are prepared by engineers who think in terms of engineering efficiency. Government officials are generally sympathetic to the views of the foreign technicians since they regard introduction of capital-intensive technology as essential to the modernization of agriculture. Organizations such as the international lending agencies and national government agencies have their own objectives, and these may conflict with or supersede development-policy objectives. For example, one objective of the government agency may be to obtain a foreign loan. One condition of the loan agreement may be to utilize equipment of a certain specification (occasionally so specific that only one firm can supply it).

The choice between capital-intensive and labor-intensive technologies is also determined by the organizational and institutional structure of society. For example, consider the impact of farm size and income distribution on demand for capital. When the farm-size distribution is highly skewed, as it is in most of the free-market economies of Asia, large farmers and landlords hold the bulk of the savings. The large farmers' preference may be for equipment that displaces labor. Labor is difficult to organize and manage. For example, as yields increase due to new technology, labor presses to obtain its share of added profits. Where labor is paid a share of harvest, it is difficult to alter the traditional sharing arrangement. The rapidly growing population adds pressure to employ more labor. Land-reform legislation is designed to transfer land to the tenants. Large farmers who mechanize to reduce their dependence on hired laborers and tenants frequently manage to avoid many of these problems. The private benefits of mechanization are considerably greater for the large farmers who have access to low-interest credit and hire laborers at the market wage rate than for the small farmers who rely more heavily on family labor.

The forms of capital bias mentioned above can be illustrated by the adoption of the tractor. Increasing evidence suggests that tractor use does not, in most cases, increase output either through changes in yield per hectare or through changes in cropping intensity (Duff 1978).[2] Benefits appear to be associated largely with reduced costs for animals and associated human labor. Tractor investment is also motivated by other less tangible benefits such as conspicuous consumption and preference for leisure or reducing the heavy work load—some of the same factors that caused U.S. farmers to "overinvest" in mechanization. The relevant question is whether or not greater social benefit can be gained by investing the capital elsewhere. The answer is almost certainly affirmative in those situations where no gain in output is achieved and the investment leads simply to a displacement of labor.

Despite the questionable social benefits of tractorization, the World Bank has loaned over half a billion dollars to Asian countries in the past decade for mechanization and has done so at well below the interest rate for investment loans from local sources. The bulk of the loans have been used for tractors and power tillers. In the Philippines, for example, two-thirds of the funds dispersed in the first two machinery loans were for four-wheel tractors (Barker et al. 1972) which indicates that the purchasing power rests with the very large farmers. Despite many alternatives, including the development of a locally manufactured small power tiller and the recommendation of an International Labour Organization report (1974) that importations of four-wheel tractors be restricted, the same pattern has prevailed in subsequent bank loans.

In summary, the adoption of tractors and power tillers in Asia has been influenced by capital bias due to (1) market imperfections, (2) preferences of decision makers, and (3) institutional structure. The development of small power tillers which could be locally manufactured and are suitable to tropical soil conditions widened the range of available choices and in some instances led to a more labor-intensive choice. However, the forces favoring the larger capital items are preponderant. Institutional changes that affect farm-size distribution are likely to occur only gradually. More farsighted lending policies on the part of international lending agencies and national governments could result in a higher level of employment without loss in economic efficiency.

LAND INFRASTRUCTURE DEVELOPMENT

The major form of capital investment to raise agricultural output in the labor-surplus economies is land-infrastructure development. I want now to concentrate on decisions about investment in that infrastructure. These investments include the development of irrigation and drainage as well as the shaping of land to improve the efficiency of water distribution. The bulk of land-infrastructure development is accomplished through public capital investment. Thus, as do the products of agricultural research, land infrastructure has many of the characteristics of a public good, such as indivisibility, externality, and jointness in supply and utilization (Hayami 1975). The analogy, however, is not complete. Irrigation systems can be developed which permit the benefits to be internalized by the private individual in accordance with his contribution to the costs. Such contributions may include not only private tube wells but small community canal irrigation facilities.

The major opportunity for substitution of private for state resources is in the community irrigation systems, where members of the community contribute their off-season labor to construct the system. To the degree that institutional and organizational factors prohibit this and necessitate an increase in state investment, social benefits are reduced. The reasons are twofold: the substitution of state resources for community labor comes at a high opportunity cost, and the state-run systems tend to be less efficient. Among government employees there is no incentive for efficiency because they share directly in neither the benefits nor the costs. Engineers constructing and operating the systems are generally unfamiliar with agricultural needs. Ineffective management in the irrigation system is coupled with a lack of communication between the managers and the end users.

The implication, of course, is that the major constraint is not a lack of labor or capital, but rather a lack of management capacity. If we take this constraint as given, the "excessive" investment in capital might be viewed as "management saving" and hence rational in maximizing social benefits, at least in the short run. I will not deal here with the underinvestment in human capital which has created this situation.

The public sector does respond to price incentives and to anticipated changes in price. Since most countries are concerned with maintaining at least some level of self-sufficiency in food-grain production, any anticipated widening of the gap in food deficits on a long-term basis would encourage investment in irrigation. Hayami and Kikuchi (1978) show, however, that in the Philippines the magnitude of new investments in irrigation tends to fluctuate, due to price fluctuations, with short-run changes in the benefit-cost ratios. Rao (1975) observes that there has been an underinvestment of public funds for irrigation in India. The same can be said for Indonesia, given the acute food deficit situation now facing that country. Even the international lending agencies have not been immune to short-run thinking about long-term investments. Given the short time horizon of policy makers, we might expect to find most countries tending to underinvest public funds in irrigation.

In what follows, the problems associated with the exploitation of ground-water resources, the development of community irrigation systems, and the development of national irrigation systems will be discussed.

Tube Wells

There is a wide range of technologies available for lifting water; these include mechanical pumps, animal-powered methods such as the Persian wheel, hand methods, and, of course, windmills. However, when water must be lifted more than a few feet, the mechanical pump normally is most efficient both from the standpoint of engineering and economics. For the installation and operation of the mechanical pump and tube well, a wide range of technologies is also available. Factors affecting the cost and degree of capital intensity include the (1) drilling technique, (2) power source and type of engine, (3) type of pump, (4) screening material used, and (5) agency installing the well (Thomas 1975).

Tube wells and low-lift pumps have been an important source of irrigation in South Asia, but are less important in Southeast Asia. Presumably this is due to differences in ground-water availability, although in many instances ground-water resources have not been properly identified and mapped. There is a high degree of variability in ground-water supply and in the proximity of the supply to the land surface. Where water can be pumped to the surface from a depth of twenty feet or less, small low-lift pumps, four inches in diameter, can be used; these cost, roughly, about as much as a power tiller.

Private tube well development had a major impact on agricultural output in West Pakistan (Mohammad 1965) and in northern India. But their proliferation down the Gangetic Plain into eastern India and Bangladesh encountered obstacles. The heavier monsoon rainfall reduces the benefits to irrigation in the wet season. Therefore, the principal benefits have come from irrigating the dry-season wheat crop. The small size of farms and fragmentation of holdings in this region further reduce the economic incentives for private tube well development. Farms and land parcels are too small for one tube well, and the sharing of wells among farms creates problems in community cooperation and organization.

In view of these constraints, one of the most interesting innovations has been the bamboo tube well developed in eastern India during the mid-1960s. The "invention" of the bamboo tube well was not a chance occurrence but part of a process of induced technical and institutional innovation (Clay 1975). In areas with sandy alluvial soils, private contractors learned that by substituting bamboo casing for steel pipe and by using simple drilling methods, they could reduce installation costs and install wells more rapidly than the government rigs. Farmers found that they could cut costs by installing several wells and using a single mobile diesel-pump set. Cost per hectare irrigated was reduced by more than 50%. While the bamboo tube well has greatly increased private investment, Clay (1975) points out that, contrary to popular opinion, the large farmer has been the major beneficiary. The bamboo tube well can be used only in a fairly limited area of high water table and porous sandy soils. The technology is not transferable, but has been designed locally to complement a very specific environmental and institutional setting.

In other areas there is no ready substitute for more costly technology. Due to the constraints resulting from fragmentation of holdings mentioned above, there has been an underinvestment in private tube wells, and public tube wells have been a major source of exploitation of ground-water resources. The sad performance of the state tube wells is well documented (see, for example, Moorti 1971). Common problems include the attempt to irrigate too large a command area and the undependability of the supply due to frequent breakdowns, lack of spare parts, equipment thefts, and diversion of water by the influential members of the community. Tube wells are also operated by local groups, but these too have encountered major problems. Inability to exploit ground-water resources fully with private capital and inefficiency in the use of public investment have substantially reduced the benefits from tube well irrigation.

The encouragement of private investment in tube wells can result in negative externalities, if excessive exploitation of the ground-water resources lowers the water table. Thus public regulatory control over private investment may be desirable in some situations.

Communal Irrigation

The resource endowments of the individual members of the farming community, who range from large farmers to landless laborers, differ widely. Hence, their absolute and relative shares in the benefits of a given project will also vary. Whether or not a communal irrigation project is undertaken depends on the ability of the community leadership to convince a sufficient number of people that it is to their mutual benefit to participate and to convince the national government that their project is worthy of support. Both are formidable tasks, and the rules of the game—persuasion, coercion, forging signatures when necessary—are not part of economic literature. Thus, for the system to work at all the benefits must be very substantial.

A recent study by Kikuchi et al. (1978) details how the development costs and benefits of a small communal irrigation system in the Philippines have been shared. The participation of individual community members depended to a large degree on their relationship with the community leaders, who, in this case, were share tenants. Even though landlords received a substantial share of the benefits, they did not contribute to the project. It cannot be expected that they would participate in a project initiated by the tenants. One of the consequences of the gradual land reform in some countries of Asia (e.g., India and the Philippines) has been to discourage the landlords from investing their savings in agriculture.

The benefit-cost ratio for the project was three to one (with the communal labor valued at the farm wage rate), and thus, there was a strong incentive to participate. The *investment-inducement coefficient*[3] or the ratio of the government fund allocated to infrastructure development to the total resource investment was 1.50. This means that two-thirds of the total investment came from the national government and one-third came from local sources, primarily in the form of low opportunity-cost communal labor supplied during the slack months of agricultural production. In theory, if the landlords had contributed in proportion to the benefits they received, this ratio could have been increased still further.

A major problem is that a leader who takes on both the formidable task of organizing his community for public works and convincing the government to contribute will benefit only marginally from the project if he is a small landholder. So only a rare individual dedicated to the community good will offer to organize a community project. On the other hand, if the leader is a large landholder, he will benefit substantially, but other members of the community will see the project as a means of promoting his interests rather than contributing to the common benefit. In this case, it would be extremely difficult to persuade the community members to contribute their labor.

Due to the lack of enlightened local leadership, we find only scattered examples of such projects which are successful. Many are failures. On the average, when the benefit-cost ratio is low, the tendency is to invest too few community resources in irrigation. It appears that governments are becoming increasingly aware of this and are attempting to assist local communities in initiating these projects. The *simple irrigation* schemes in Indonesia, which are financed by domestic and foreign capital, are one example (Booth 1977). But the problem of local leadership described above will probably impose a major constraint on the success of communal irrigation projects.

The recent experience of China and the historical development of irrigation in East Asia offer an interesting contrast to what has taken place in contemporary South and Southeast Asia. Growth in food output in China has been sustained by a major public investment in irrigation. Through the commune organization, it has been possible to mobilize labor and capital for investment in community irrigation works. The commune production team (typically about thirty families working about ten hectares of land in the high and stable yield areas) is the primary unit where decisions are made about the sharing of profits and the allocation of resources for agricultural production and for investment. Leadership in the commune is provided by the cadre of the Communist Party members who occupy most positions of responsibility down to the production-team level. Economic and non-economic incentives encourage production teams to utilize their labor for capital investment during the slack season, particularly the winter months. In the sharing of profits by the production team rather than by the family (as in the free-market economies), labor is paid not on the basis of private opportunity cost, but on the basis of community or social benefit.

A list of farm machinery from a grain-producing commune in the Yangtze River Valley provides an insight into the sequence of capital investments made by one community (Table 2). There was a continuous investment of human labor in land-infrastructure development. In 1976 labor was being utilized to straighten canal systems and to lay pipes to bury the entire conveyance network underground. Threshing machines were among the first pieces of capital equipment to be purchased to release more labor for productive investment. Irrigation pumps augmented the land-infrastructure investment, allowing complete control over irrigation and drainage. This was followed by the introduction of tractors for transport and for land preparation, which, together with an emphasis on breeding short-duration crop varieties, permitted an even more intensive use of labor. Despite the heavy investment in equipment and machinery, the labor input per hectare is comparable to that of Java and yields are about 50%

Table 2

Inventory of Agricultural Machinery in Chien Chan
Commune, Wusih Country, Kiangsa, China

	1966	1976
*Diesel engine (12 hp)	—	243
Diesel engine (25 hp)	—	11
Diesel engine (4 hp, for transplanter)	—	37
Gasoline engine (4 hp, for transplanter)	—	30
Hand tractor (12 hp)	2	171
Large 4-wheel tractor	—	1
*Seedling puller	—	4
*Transplanter	—	25
*Mower for grain	—	18
Electric motor	288	1112
Thresher (electric)	231	368
Thresher/cleaner (electric)	—	54
Power sprayer	—	54
Hand sprayer	312	802
Duster	3	177
Boat engine	—	65
Grain cleaner	—	285
Pump with motor	61	224
Crusher for water plants	—	5
Flour grinder	12	40
Rice miller, 5 FPH	24	38
1-ton trailer	—	14
Rice huller	2	2
Huller-crusher for wheat	1	2
Hand cast for 2-wheel tractor	—	124

* Indicates the machines in short supply.

Source: International Rice Research Institute. A Report on the Scientists' Visit to the Peoples Republic of China, October 1976. Los Baños, Philippines: International Rice Research Institute (forthcoming).

higher. Although the list of equipment is impressive, it might not differ greatly from that of a leading community in India.

The pieces of equipment currently felt to be in short supply are indicated by asterisks in Table 2. They include transplanters, seedling pullers, and grain mowers. The return to these investments is not likely to be large. In fact, over time, the return to investment in the form of both labor and capital has declined rapidly. It would appear that the opportunity for more productive investment lies in other poorer communes or in industry. China soon may need to reform its own institutions to strengthen the link between various segments of the economy in order to promote more rapid development.

In the terminology of recent literature, the commune production team is an "induced institutional change." Through the development of this institution, China has been able to lower the cost of the land-infrastructure development needed to foster growth in agricultural productivity under a land constraint by fully utilizing available community labor in the off-season for capital investment. It is important to emphasize that, despite the incentives, institutional changes of this kind do not occur automatically. Witness, for example, the widely acknowledged failure of Russian agriculture to achieve an efficient organizational structure.

Observers are quick to recognize that the commune system in China is not transferable to other Asian countries. But the issue is frequently left at that. The historical development of land and water resources in East Asia depended on a very different set of institutions which nonetheless were based on community leadership and action. For example, Hayami (1975) describes the institutional characteristics of Japanese agriculture in the Tokugawa period and the institutional adjustments during the Meiji Restoration that made it possible to utilize community labor in Japan for irrigation development. Because the growth in population was slower and because the population pressures developed gradually over a longer period of time, institutional adjustments were worked out gradually without social disruptions.

There are also examples in South and Southeast Asia where community resources were mobilized for land-infrastructure development over a fairly wide region. But these tend to be regions where strong population pressures were exerted for a long period of time. The *subak* systems in Bali and the irrigation societies in the Ilocos region of the Philippines are two well-known examples. The 1903 Philippine census shows that the average farm size in the Ilocos region was less than one hectare.

However, these cases are fairly rare. In most regions in Southeast Asia, as previously noted, community structures have been molded according to the traditional land-surplus economy before the first turning point. The community institutions have lagged behind the rapidly emerging need for the leadership and discipline required to mobilize communal labor for construction and maintenance of irrigation systems. Such a lag in the institutional adjustment represents a major factor underlying the underinvestment in land infrastructure at the community level.

National Systems

Government investment in land infrastructure represents, to a large extent, a substitution for community investment. This investment is required when the community lacks the capacity to invest. There are, of course, some components of large-scale irrigation systems that require outside capital. However, a potentially large portion of the national systems can be developed and managed with local resources. Two types of national systems are evident: those which range from a few thousand to 100,000 hectares and larger ones which occupy the major river deltas in Asia and sometimes cover several hundred thousand hectares. These latter schemes have a special problem which will be discussed subsequently.

In national systems, there is a potential interactive role to be played by the government and the community in both the development and the operation of facilities. In a developed society, there is normally a dialogue betwen the community and the government when the new irrigation system is proposed. Community interests have a major influence over system location, design, and construction. In the developing economies, the only dialogue is between the national irrigation authority and the lending agencies. As we observed earlier, both parties tend to have a capital bias in their view of the project.

Commonly, one observes the following progression of events in the development of national systems. The government initially may construct the primary and secondary canals in the system in anticipation that the local community will complete the tertiary canals and farm ditches. Partly because village organization and leadership are lacking, as described earlier, the local community takes no action. The farmers may lack the organizational capacity or even the simple ditching and leveling equipment and technical advice needed to complete the job. In many cases, due to poor management of water in the major laterals, there may be essentially no benefits to be gained. The farmers blame the irrigation authority who, in turn, blames the farmers. Amidst complaints that the system is not working properly, the national irrigation authority responds in the only way that it can, with more capital investment to undertake land consolidation and lay out the tertiary canals and farm ditches. The construction cost per hectare doubles (Takase and Wickham 1977).

As with construction, the major weakness in the operation and maintenance of the system seems to be institutional or organizational rather than technical. The water delivered to each farm cannot be metered. Normally everyone is charged an equal amount per hectare, usually only enough to cover operation and maintenance costs. However, those managing the system take no steps to ration the water and insure its equitable distribution. The farms at the head of the canal waste water; the farms at the end seldom have enough. The system operates with an efficiency well below that projected in the initial feasibility studies.

The choice among system designs at the national level is influenced by the thinking of the engineers who are primarily responsible for both designing and operating the system. The more "modern" the system, the better. For example, it is common to design systems on a standard that will allow water to be rotated within fifty-hectare blocks. Such a system is compatible with the level of technical skills in East Asia. But in most of South and Southeast Asia, no advantage can be obtained from this system until the water can be properly controlled and distributed in the main laterals.

In short, the design of the system fails to take into account the management constraint. This natural bias toward engineering efficiency and capital intensity is reinforced by personal experience. Those who run the system know that a more labor-intensive solution does not work because it is difficult to obtain active participation of the farmers. Thus, the existing organizational and institutional structure of the irrigation network, and the weak linkage between those delivering the water and the end-users, serve as the ultimate constraint to the maximization of social benefits in the design, operation, and maintenance of the system.

The large river-delta schemes pose a serious problem for development. The benefits from smaller projects in the system cannot be realized until an extremely large investment is made to achieve a degree of water control which would make the smaller systems feasible. The situation is illustrated in Figure 1. A substantial upward trend in rice yields occurs in northern India and Pakistan, and in southern India and Sri Lanka. But yields show no upward trend in eastern India and Bangladesh where the crop is grown mainly in the wet season. Water control is a major constraint to increased yields in this region.[4] Without adequate water control the new technology has made little progress. The alternative is either to change the environment through land-infrastructure investment or, through research, to change the plant type to suit the environment. Either alternative will require a considerable amount of time and investment before there are benefits substantial enough to encourage either private or community investment.

In closing this section on land infrastructure development, I would like to emphasize two points.

First, the three forms of irrigation development—tube wells, communal irrigation systems, and national systems—are by no means complete substitutes one for another. We have to differentiate between situations in determining which form of capital investment is better. The large river deltas, for example, clearly require significant public invest-

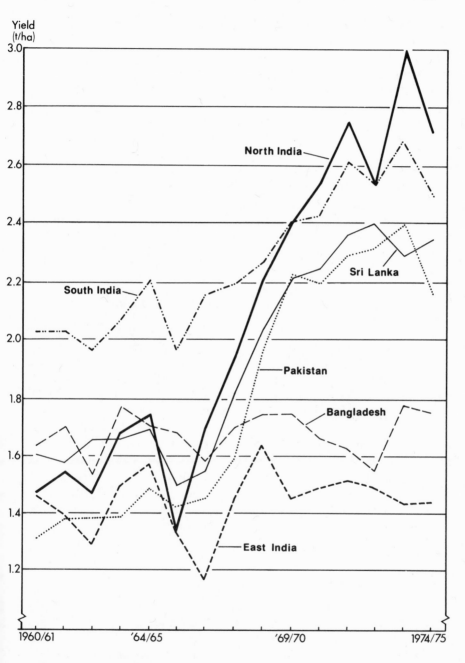

Figure 1. Rice Yield Trends in India (three regions), Bangladesh, Pakistan, and Sri Lanka, 1960/61 to 1974/75

ment before private or communal investments can become profitable. In many situations, however, it does appear that substitution of community labor for public investment could reduce the cost of irrigation development and make fuller use of existing labor. The free-market economies encounter considerable difficulty in organizing community labor for capital investment. This is a form of "market failure."

Second, the sequence of capital investments is extremely important. Land-infrastructure development paves the way not only for the use of modern inputs such as new seed and fertilizer, but also for productive investment in other forms of capital such as tractors. The historical experience of East Asia and Mainland China provides evidence of the importance of the time sequence of investments. Initial investments should raise the productivity of subsequent investments and, in the labor-surplus economies, expand employment opportunities.

THE PRESSURES FOR INDUCED
TECHNOLOGICAL AND INSTITUTIONAL CHANGE

There have been several recent attempts to determine whether future food supplies in Asia will be adequate to meet future demand (International Food Policy Research Institute 1976; International Bank for Reconstruction and Development 1976; and Asian Development Bank 1977). Despite differences in assumptions and projection techniques, these studies indicate that current trends would lead to a sizable gap between food grain production and demand in Asia by 1985, ranging from 25 million tons (International Bank for Reconstruction and Development 1976) to 40 million tons (International Food Policy Research Institute 1976). These studies are somewhat academic since, on a world basis, supply (excluding stocks) must equal demand in the target year, but they are useful to indicate the magnitude of the pressure to increase food supplies.

The studies which attempt to estimate the magnitude of the investments required to close this gap are more useful. The Trilateral Commission Report (1977), which devotes most of its attention to irrigation, estimates that food-grain production can be doubled at present levels of technology by 1990 (4.8% per annum) at an annual irrigation-investment cost of $4.5 billion (at 1975 prices) or about six times the current investment rate of $700 million. This implies an annual growth in irrigated command area of over 5% per annum compared with the current rate of 2%. Based on a more modest irrigation growth rate of 3% per annum, Herdt et al. (1977) project a growth in food production of 2.4% at current levels of technology. Thus, without further gains from technology in the next decade, this rate of growth in irrigation will be inadequate to meet a 3 to 4% growth in demand for food.

Change in output per hectare is the product of change in capital intensity (capital per hectare) and change in capital efficiency (output per unit of capital invested). As noted earlier, the introduction of modern seed-fertilizer technology has had the effect of improving the efficiency of capital investment. However, as fertilizer input approaches the optimum level on existing irrigated land, increased capital intensity will have to compensate for the declining contribution of fertilizer to output growth. Furthermore, as irrigated area continues to expand, the cost of developing new lands for irrigation will rise gradually. Kikuchi (1975) shows that the cost-income ratio rose sharply in Taiwan and Korea following the introduction of modern inputs in the 1920s. This ratio currently is rising in the Philippines and probably in most other parts of Asia.

The extraordinary growth in capital requirements for land-infrastructure development over the next decade will create a strong incentive to improve capital efficiency. The response to this incentive should take the form of increased activity in the development and introduction of technological, organizational, and institutional innovations. Technological change can be embodied in new forms of capital such as the bamboo tube well, or in modern rice varieties that perform well under poor water-control conditions. There also will be mounting pressure to improve technology for the nonirrigated regions. It can be anticipated that research in the biological sciences and in engineering will bring technological advances in these areas, although there are no major breakthroughs on the horizon at present.

In summary, it has been observed that a number of developing countries in Asia have only recently moved from a land-surplus to a labor-surplus condition. For these countries, land infrastructure is currently the most critical capital investment needed to increase agricultural production. Such an investment could be achieved most efficiently by full utilization of community labor in the development and operation of irrigation systems. However, the social structure of these economies has been molded under centuries of land-surplus condition (particularly in Southeast Asia) and under a highly skewed farm-size distribution (particularly in South Asia). This social structure erects a formidable barrier to the investment of social-overhead capital at the optimum level.

To keep pace with food demand, public capital investments needed to maintain the growth in agricultural production should increase sharply over the next decade. There will be strong incentives for institutional reforms and other measures to raise the productivity of these investments. There is a growing recognition that the "software" of land-infrastructure development has been neglected, but there is no clear understanding as to what organizational and institutional changes are needed and, under the existing social structure, what can be accomplished; social science research that comes to grip with these issues can accelerate the process of change toward a more optimum institutional structure.

NOTES

The author is indebted to Yujiro Hayami, Robert W. Herdt, and Colin Barlow for their comments and suggestions.

1. This is the term used by Hayami (1975). As used in this paper, it includes private investment in tube wells as well as public investment in canal irrigation systems, although the latter represents the major portion of investment.

2. Although the majority of farm surveys suggest that yields on mechanized farms are higher than on nonmechanized farms, the impact of tractor adoption is invariably confounded with fertilizer input and other management factors. Experiments on rice-farm fields in the Philippines using five combinations of tractor and animal power under three soil conditions showed no gain in yield for mechanization.

Personal correspondence with Binswanger (1977) in regard to a survey of the literature on mechanization in South Asia supports Duff's (1978) conclusion that output gains have not occurred in most cases.

3. A concept developed by Ishikawa (1967).

4. Not everyone would agree with this statement. There are many scientists who argue that the appropriate technology does exist, but there is a "constraint" in moving this technology from the experiment station to the farmer's field. While it is indeed wrong to suggest that all of the problems of eastern India and Bangladesh can be solved by adequate water control, I doubt that extension of existing technology is currently the dominant constraint in most areas.

REFERENCES

Asian Development Bank.   1977.   *Asian Agricultural Survey 1976. Rural Asia: Challenge and Opportunity.* Manila, Philippines.
Barker, Randolph; Meyers, William H.; Crisostomo, Cristina M.; and Duff, Bart.   1972.   "Employment and Technological Change in Philippine Ag-

riculture." *International Labour Review* 106, nos. 2–3 (August–September):111–39.

Booth, Anne. 1977. "Irrigation in Indonesia." *Bulletin of Indonesian Economic Studies* 13 [published by Australian National University, Canberra]. Part I in no. 1 (March):33–74 and Part II in no. 2 (July):45–77.

Clay, E. J. 1975. "Equity and Productivity Effects of a Package of Technical Innovations and Changes in Social Institutions: Tubewells, Tractors, and High-yielding Varieties." *Indian Journal of Agricultural Economics* 30, no. 4 (October–December):74–87.

Crisostomo, Cristina M., and Barker, Randolph. 1972. "Growth Rates of Philippine Agriculture: 1948–1969." *Philippine Economic Journal* 11, no. 1 (First Semester):88–148. (Also in *Agricultural Growth in Japan, Taiwan, Korea, and the Philippines,* edited by H. Southworth. University of Hawaii Press, forthcoming.)

Duff, Bart. 1978. "Mechanization and Use of Modern Rice Varieties." In *Proceedings of the Conference on the Economic Consequences of New Rice Technology in Asia,* ed. Yujiro Hayami and Randolph Barker. Los Baños, Philippines: International Rice Research Institute.

Hayami, Yujiro, in association with Masakatsu Akino, Masahiko Shintani, and Saburo Yamada. 1975. *A Century of Agricultural Growth in Japan—Its Relevance to Asian Development.* Tokyo: University of Tokyo Press.

Hayami, Yujiro, and Kikuchi, Masao. 1978. "Investment Inducements to Public Infrastructure: Irrigation in the Philippines." *Review of Economics and Statistics* 60, no. 1 (February), 70–77.

Hayami, Yujiro, and Ruttan, Vernon W. 1971. *Agricultural Development: An International Perspective.* Baltimore: Johns Hopkins Press.

Herdt, Robert W.; Te, Amanda; and Barker, Randolph. 1977. "The Prospects for Asian Rice Production." Dept. of Agricultural Economics Staff Paper no. 77–3. Mimeographed. Los Baños, Philippines: International Rice Research Institute.

International Bank for Reconstruction and Development. 1976. "Developing Country Food Grain Projections for 1985." Bank Staff Working Paper no. 247. Washington, D.C.

International Food Policy Research Institute. 1976. *Meeting Food Needs in the Developing World.* Research Report no. 1. Washington, D.C.

International Labour Office. 1974. *Sharing in Development—A Programme of Employment, Equity, and Growth for the Philippines.* Geneva: International Labour Organization.

International Rice Research Institute. Forthcoming. *A Report on the Scientists' Visit to the Peoples Republic of China, October 1976.* Los Baños, Philippines: International Rice Research Institute.

Ishikawa, Shigeru. 1967. *Economic Development in Asian Perspective.* Economic Research Series no. 8. Tokyo: Kinokuniya Bookstore Co.

Kikuchi, Masao. 1975. "Irrigation and Rice Technology in Agricultural Development: A Comparative History of Taiwan, Korea, and the Philippines." Ph.D. dissertation, University of Hokkaido, Japan.

Kikuchi, Masao; Dozina, Geronimo Jr.; and Hayami, Yujiro. 1978. "Economics of Community Work Programs: A Community Irrigation Project in the Philippines." *Economic Development and Cultural Change* 26, no. 2 (January):211–25.

Lee, Teng-hui. 1971. *Intersectoral Capital Flows in the Economic Development of Taiwan, 1895–1960.* Ithaca: Cornell University Press.

Mohammad, Ghulam. 1965. "Private Tubewell Development and Cropping Patterns in West Pakistan." *Pakistan Development Review* 5, no. 1 (Spring):1–53.

Moorti, T. V. 1971. *A Comparative Study of Well Irrigation in Aligarh District, India.* Cornell International Agricultural Development Bulletin 19. Ithaca: Cornell University.

Rao, C. H. Hanumantha. 1975. *Technological Change and the Distribution of Gains in Indian Agriculture.* Delhi: Macmillan Company of India.

Schultz, Theodore W. 1964. *Transforming Traditional Agriculture.* New Haven: Yale University Press (Reprint edition, New York: Arno Press, 1976).

Takase, Kunio, and Wickham, Thomas. 1977. "Irrigation Management as a Pivot of Agricultural Development in Asia." Report for *Asian Agricultural Survey 1976.* Mimeographed. Manila, Philippines: Asian Development Bank.

Thomas, John Woodward. 1975. "The Choice of Technology for Irrigation Tubewells in East Pakistan: Analysis of a Development Policy Decision." In *The Choice of Technology in Developing Countries,* pp.31–67. Harvard Studies in International Affairs no. 32. Cambridge, Mass.: Center for International Affairs, Harvard University.

Timmer, C. Peter. 1975. "The Choice of Technique in Indonesia." In *The Choice of Technology in Developing Countries,* pp.1–29. Harvard Studies in International Affairs no. 32. Cambridge, Mass.: Center for International Affairs, Harvard University.

Trilateral Commission North-South Food Task Force. 1977. "Provisional Report at North-South Food Task Force Meeting." Manila, Philippines.

COMMENT

EARL O. HEADY

Dr. Barker has prepared an interesting paper emphasizing land infrastructure investment as a means of increasing food production. Within the restricted area of land infrastructure investment, he has concentrated only on irrigation development, with emphasis delineated further around the institutional forces which cause new irrigation projects to be biased toward capital-intensive systems, to be inefficient, or not to be undertaken. He also details how institutions serve to distort the efficient use of water after projects have been completed. He has provided an interesting and useful collection of the variables, customs, and institutions which mold or restrain water use and investment in it. In one sense, this is a relevant emphasis because improved use of potentially available water is one large source of increased food production. To the extent that the Green Revolution set of inputs (seeds, fertilizer, and pesticides) has taken or will take agricultural production to a new plateau, the efficient utilization and management of water in the developing countries can take production to a second plateau. Most of these countries are located in those parts of the world with tropical climates, wet and dry seasons with surplus and deficit water supplies, respectively, and year-around growing seasons.

Yet we still do not know how much investment can be made profitably in water systems for developing countries or where it can best be made. The extension of irrigation over the developing world is only one means of increasing agricultural production. There is a wide range of other options and, if the world is serious about producing more, these investment alternatives need to be better inventoried. The major opportunities are included in:

(1) Agricultural research which will boost yields and improve investment opportunities for cultivators. A good deal of quantitative analysis has gone into measuring social and private returns to investment in research. However, the range of opportunities within this subset also is vast and little has been done in establishing priorities relative to (a) the conformance of research with the stages of development for individual countries, and (b) the relative magnitude of return among research alternatives.

(2) Land infrastructure investments to increase the supply of tillable land or the amount of water available for it. Irrigation is but one of several possible investments in land infrastructure. However, it is

more obviously profitable in selected locations of some developing countries than are other forms of land infrastructure investment.

(3) Agricultural extension and other facets of a communication system to bring knowledge of improved technologies to farming. Research which generates productive and profitable new technologies is ineffective until results can be carried to cultivators with the knowledge and capital to apply them. In earlier times, extension facilities were readied before research had been conducted to supply knowledge for communication. The stock of knowledge now is increasing to a level where more thought and systematic investment needs to be directed toward an optimal scale and organization of extension education. Robert Evenson indicates that if the estimates of the proportional value of agricultural production invested in extension were added to private investment in communication of technology, the figures might be about comparable for developed and developing countries. Considering the small size of farms in developing countries, the relative investment in extension education might need to be larger than in developed countries. Further, if, as Finis Welch indicates, individual education and extension facilities serve as substitutes, extension education may well be substituted to offset the lack of school education for farmers in developing countries. Too, the proportion of agricultural output represented by extension investment in developing countries might exceed that of developed countries where farmers are rather highly educated. Again, the optimal extent and form of extension investment is still to be estimated.

(4) The farmer's use of capital. My own search leads me to the conclusion that small farms are restrained by lack of capital, are tardy in innovating, and restrict their investment accordingly. (Further detail is provided in a later section of this paper.) They need more capital if they are to attain the frontier of their food production possibilities under a dynamic technology environment.

(5) Processing and distributing inputs. While chemicals, seeds, and other capital inputs can be imported, there are countries and locations where further investment in the fabrication of inputs could be economic and is needed to lower the real cost of inputs. We need to know more about the conditions and locations where these investments are economic in developing countries. In too many countries, these inputs are priced too high relative to the commodities they produce. Farmer investment in food production is restricted accordingly. There also are questions of where and to what extent these investments can be carried by the private sector or can be justifiably subsidized by the public sector.

I can muster no quantitative comparisons of the range over which any of the above categories will provide a higher marginal return than investment in another category. However, it seems logical that investment return in one category will not exceed that of other categories over the full range to which the former might be subjected. It is often tempting to suggest that returns on one investment opportunity (e.g., research) for developing agricultures will dominate all other categories. But this can only be speculation until effort is devoted to evaluation of other alternatives. In a few cases, investment in roads and other infrastructure items may be needed to open lands for cultivation and provide a market environment that is profitable for increased production. Also, capital is needed for community storage in some countries to prevent harvest-time price drops that discourage the use of adapted capital technologies. But again, the extent of these investment needs has not been inventoried.

SOURCES OF GREATER FOOD AVAILABILITY

A summary of potential sources of increased food production also may suggest the range in forms of capital which can play some role in greater agricultural production. These alternative sources include:

(1) Higher yields per hectare on presently cultivated lands through labor- and capital-intensive systems which include improved biological and mechanical technologies, improved water use and management, multiple cropping, intercropping, and related means. Barker's emphasis on land infrastructure development and irrigation is in this general category. The category also includes investment in research and various on-farm investments.

(2) Converting uncultivated land into production. For example, it has been estimated that only 44% of the world's potentially arable land is under cultivation (Cummings 1974). While this figure seems too low, the world evidently does have an amount of land which can still be brought into crop production. Shifting cultivation over fairly large regions such as central Africa prevails because land is available and because cultivators, restrained by capital, substitute this practice for purchased fertilizers. Conversion of more of this potential arable land to permanent production would occur under private investment if commodity prices were at sufficiently high levels over an extended period of time. The U.S. Soil Conservation Service estimated that 264 million acres, later reduced to around 110 million, of land in the United States is potentially class I and II land but is not cropped. Part of this land is now under tree cover; conversion for crops would

involve sizable capital costs. Part is in pasture with lower conversion costs. If grain prices remained at their highest levels of recent years, about $12 for soybeans and $5 for corn and wheat, a larger amount of this land would have been brought into production. Conversion of potentially arable land in other regions of the world can have capital requirements beyond the control of individual farmers. Capital requirements can be heavy for leveling tropical jungles, controlling second growth, and maintaining soil fertility for crop production on tropical soils, but if real grain prices reach and remain at high levels, due to growth in either population or income at higher rates than for food production, investment in this type of land improvement also will be needed.

(3) Saving a greater proportion of crops now produced. Estimates indicate extremely high losses due to rodents, birds, and spoilage in developing countries. Whether or not these losses are as great as speculated, they are of some importance. However, their control typically is out of reach of the individual farmer. In the sense of public goods and externalities, he can chase the birds away but they only fly elsewhere. If he poisons the rats, the supply is replenished from neighboring farms.

(4) Diverting a greater proportion of grains from livestock to human consumption. Current world food production of grains could extend over a much larger population, or provide improved diets for the existing world population, if less of it were used for meat production in the developed countries and more were traded to poor countries. It is recognized, of course, that some meat production is forthcoming from land which cannot grow food crops. Still the proportion of land which can be used for either food or feed crops is so large that great capacity exists for extending world food availability through allocation of more grain to human consumption. If per capita income in developing countries rose fast enough, this reallocation would occur through the market.

DISTORTIONS IN CAPITAL INVESTMENTS

Distortions in capital investments for the alternatives summarized above arise partly because there is little knowledge of where the return is the greatest. They also occur for reasons summarized by other authors in this book. The pricing policies for commodities and inputs serve as a restraining force in many countries. As commodity prices are kept low through export taxes, barriers to trade within a country, and other means, farmer investment is burdened. Similarly, high prices for inputs such as fertilizers due to investment in inefficient domestic plants, as compared to lower-cost sources obtainable in international markets, serve similarly. Short supplies of administrative, management, and technical manpower for efficient project implementation and biases toward industrialization have warped investments away from agriculture over the last three decades. Some of these biases have had a political base, for example, the need to develop industry to generate employment for growing city populations. Barker suggests that professional biases also alter the course of capital investment, for example, favoring investment in very large irrigation projects while tertiary canals and discharge ditches are not extended to farms. The "visibility" of these projects also may cause them to be favored over research installations and other means of agricultural improvement.

While distortions in capital investments over the past three decades may have been fairly serious, it is possible that considerable improvement will occur in the future. There still is a "long road ahead" in some newly independent countries. However, in others there has been time for a considerable accumulation in trained manpower, administrative experience, knowledge of investment alternatives, planning abilities, and understanding of agricultural and trade policy needs. I believe that the next two decades will reflect a great improvement in planning and administration of productive development investments in many developing countries. There are, of course, several recently independent countries which will still need to build up a stock of trained manpower.

If improvements are made in public investments for agriculture, decisions on investment to produce food still must be made by individual farmers in market economies to which subject I now turn.

CAPITAL RESTRAINTS FOR FARMERS

It is recognized that technologies must be available for profitable investment by farmers if they are to extend food production through use of capital- and labor-intensive systems. The generation and communication of these technologies generally must come from public capital in developing countries. But once they are available, does capital available to or demanded by the individual farmer limit their application? While large farmers may have sufficient capital available to them, there is some evidence that this is not true for the small farmers who dominate in developing countries (Schutjer and Van Der Veen 1977; Valdés, Dillon, and Scobie 1978). In Thailand, for example, which has been tardy in agricultural development, small farmers in entire regions use an extremely modest amount of capital per *rai*. Of course, pricing policies in Thailand (especially the rice premium or export tax, and historically the high fertilizer prices) have not been conducive to use of more capital.

It is somewhat typical for cooperatives or public institutions supplying credit to favor the large farmers while small farmers use the scarce traditional sources of borrowed capital. Whether or not large farmers have sufficient capital from their own savings or other private or institutional sources to adopt favorable technologies, small farmers as a group are restrained in the use of capital through its price and availability in the market. Hence, if they are to contribute fully to increased food production and gain equitably from new technology, institutional credit supplies need to be increased and directed more efficiently to small farmers. Typically, the village moneylender has always been looked upon negatively; both he and his high prices for borrowed capital are considered bad. What is bad, of course, is not the moneylender, but the supply conditions of capital. While credit supplies from institutional sources are insufficient, the moneylender performs a positive role in the village. Without him, capital supplies would be even more scarce and interest rates would be even higher. The appropriate way to drive him out of the village is not by violence but by appropriate credit programs which increase the capital supply, reduce interest rates and make it more profitable for him to go elsewhere.

An increase in the credit supply is necessary to allow all farmers to use more capital, as is generally required with new technologies directed towards greater yields per hectare. But it does not guarantee that they all will use more. Even in the presence of new technologies, some low-income farmers may decide not to borrow money. The restraint on their demand even with the availability of new technology can be explained in the context of utility maximization in selections between expected income and its variance for decisions made under uncertainty (Anderson, Dillon, and Hardaker 1977; Valdés, Dillon, and Scobie 1978). However, we will use a related but abbreviated explanation. As long as capital is supplied on an equity basis, uncertainty facing the cultivator is increased; that is, the more he borrows the more divergent can be the financial outcome, depending on yield and price realizations, and the greater the possibility that he could be forced into bankruptcy and lose his initial capital stake (Griffin 1972). The situation is illustrated in Figure 1a. It is possible that over a relevant range of investment, returns to capital might even be constant as indicated by R. However, the cultivator is projected to discount this return to line D_1, his demand for borrowed funds. The discount from R (i.e., the difference between R and D_1) is at an increasing rate because the "degree of uncertainty" increases as borrowing increases. With an initial inelastic supply, S_1, of borrowed capital available, the cultivator's equilibrium use of capital is OM_1. Now, if we drive away the moneylender by increasing the supply of credit to that indicated by S_2, capital use is increased only slightly, to OM_2, because the culti-

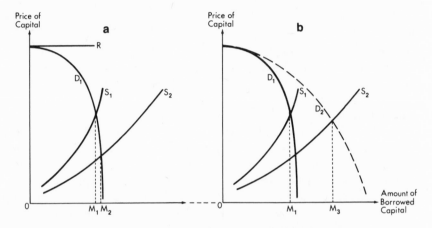

Figure 1. Equilibrium of supply and demand in capital use.

vator's demand for capital is so inelastic, since he receives borrowed funds which mortgage his own small equity. Hence, increasing the supply of capital alone is not sufficient to cause substantial increases in the use of capital by the low-income farmer with a small equity-capital base. By some means, we must increase the elasticity of his demand for capital in the manner of D_2 in figure 1b. Then, with capital supply increased by S_2, demand or use of capital increases from OM_1 to OM_3. In our case, to change the farmer's demand for borrowed capital is as important as to increase the supply of capital available to him.

However, to extend the demand from D_1 to D_2, the supplying of capital must be unmoored from the cultivator's equity. Private suppliers are unwilling to offer credit under these conditions and even the public supply in developing countries still is too often tied to equity. Of course, "risk" to the lender is increased greatly once the supply of credit is not tied to the borrower's equity. Yet there is widespread need in developing countries to make this break as a means of increasing the cultivator's demand for capital and his use of improved technology. The risk can certainly be lessened or perhaps largely eliminated if management services are provided along with the credit. In fact, management and capital are highly complementary resources in all agricultures, but especially so in developing agriculture. More of the farm-credit facilities in developing countries should combine capital supply and management services in the manner of supervised credit. The proposition that management is a more limitational resource than capital in developing countries provides another basis for this tie-in.

Supervised credit, in the sense that management services are included as part of the capital bundle, also should be tied to the items for which the credit will be used. Thus, a simple farm plan is called for from those who implement the credit-supply activity. It should, for example, indicate the bundle of practices for which the credit will be used (i.e., the variety and amount of seed, the mix and amount of fertilizer, the kind and amount of pesticides, and perhaps even the need for irrigation).

In specifying capital availability by management bundles, emphasis more nearly is given to the set of technologies which are to be encouraged. The advantage of this approach was illustrated in some newly irrigated oases of Saudi Arabia where an attempt was being made to settle nomad livestock raisers. At first, to encourage greater output and new technology, a subsidy above the market price was paid for output with the suggestion that the farmer use the favored technology. His inclination was not to do so, however, until the subsidy was tied to the inputs which he should use.

The pattern of the distribution of benefits from development is another reason for breaking the tie between equity and the supply of capital to the farmer. Without this step, those farmers with the largest equity borrow the most capital and realize the greatest gain from new technologies made available as part of the public investment in development. It is rather easy even to find credit cooperatives where the members and directors are largely the wealthier of the village while the smaller and most severely capital-limited farmers still must borrow from the traditional sources under the traditional conditions of capital supply to the individual cultivator.

If the objective were the singular one of improving technology and getting greater food output for the world, another procedure with potentials of short-run success would prevail. It would give franchises to advanced farmers of developed countries who would come into a less-developed country and set up a farming operation based on advanced technology. With the franchise limited to a definite time span, one long enough to guarantee a sufficient return to investment, and a guarantee given for purchase of unexhausted capital items, farmers from developed countries could soon have large operations underway based on advanced technology. These possibilities have been illustrated by the Dutch farm concerns which initiated successful sugar beet operations in Ethiopia, by Swiss enterprises which set up initial farming operations in irrigated oases of Saudi Arabia, Iowa farmers who have begun producing corn and soybeans in Brazil, and others. As in the case of the Swiss in Saudi Arabia, a second benefit could be simultaneously derived from such an effort: namely, teaching unskilled persons the practice of farming and new technology.

Undoubtedly, a broad movement of this kind not only could get appropriate kinds of capital and technology into use but also could bring a rapid upsurge in food production where the potentialities exist. It is not, however, a viable alternative for two major reasons: (1) A greater food supply is not the singular objective of agricultural development. Equitable distribution of the benefits is a goal which also must be given a nonzero weight. Use of the franchised expatriate would generally eliminate employment and income opportunities for local farmers. (2) The long-run need is to develop an institutional system which generates applied technology and effectively communicates it to cultivators in mesh with capital supplies through which it is implemented. Other than for demonstrational purposes, the franchised expatriate route only provides an excuse for postponing this fundamental step in development.

MISCELLANEOUS CONSIDERATIONS

A final note on capital and credit use at the cultivator level is in order and also has an institutional base. There still are tenure arrangements where the tenant pays rent in share but must pay all costs associated with implementing new technologies. As has been well documented theoretically, these conditions restrain both the amount of capital it is profitable for him to use and the supply of marketable commodities. The solution for this situation can be land reform which converts the tenant into an owner. However, as implied in new legislation being enacted in Thailand, increased incentive for capital use can be created if crop shares are modified and the landlord is required to participate in variable production costs accordingly. There are circumstances under which this procedure will encourage capital use and innovation by farmers as readily as the conversion of them into owners who have inadequate credit but are supplied with the required facilities by public agencies.

REFERENCES

Anderson, Jock R.; Dillon, John L.; and Hardaker, J. Brian. 1977. *Agricultural Decision Analysis*. Ames: Iowa State University Press.

Cummings, Ralph W., Jr. 1974. *Food Production and the Energy Dilemma*. Working Papers of the Rockefeller Foundation. New York: Rockefeller Foundation.

Griffin, Keith B. 1972. *The Green Revolution: An Economic Analysis*. Geneva: United Nations Research Institute for Social Development.

Schutjer, Wayne A., and Van Der Veen, Marlin G. 1977. *Economic Constraints on Agricultural Technology Adoption in Developing Nations*. Occasional paper no. 5. Washington, D.C.: U.S. Agency for International Development.

Valdés, Alberto: Dillon, John L.; and Scobie, Grant. 1978. *Economics and the Design of Small Farm Technology*. Ames: Iowa State University Press.

Hard Policy Choices in
Improving Incentives for Farmers

MARTIN E. ABEL

INTRODUCTION

Various options, consistent with general national political and economic objectives or goals, are open to low-income countries for reducing distortions that affect their agricultural output. In discussing them, my starting point is the growing body of literature on the type, nature, and effects on agricultural production of various actions that distort incentives in low-income countries. There is strong evidence that distorted incentives are legion in low-income countries (Saleh and Goolsby 1977), and that these distortions typically retard agricultural output. On occasion the reverse is true, that is, distortions favor agricultural production above optimum levels. However, the latter situation is more prevalent in high-income countries.

The focus of this paper is on agricultural production. I do not discuss the relationship between economic distortions and the distribution of income and wealth although it is a very important topic.

My task is both factually and conceptually difficult. It is factually difficult because low-income countries represent a wide array of economic systems, stages of development, governmental structures, and political ideologies. All of these have some bearing on the extent and direction of distortions affecting agriculture. In such a heterogeneous world, it is difficult to generalize about the practicability of recommendations to reduce distortions. There are also numerous conceptual difficulties. One centers around the issue of moderating distortions. When distortions exist, eliminating or reducing some but not others does not necessarily lead to a higher level of social welfare. Another conceptual difficulty centers on what one takes as given and what one treats as variable. For example, do we accept political objectives and development priorities as given, even if they lead to the neglect of agriculture? Or, do we assume that development priorities can be influenced by people and institutions other than those concerned with directing the development process?

In this paper, I suggest broad approaches with the understanding that their validity with respect to welfare improvement must be verified both theoretically and empirically. Also, I take as given national objectives, even though one might disagree with them. However, national objectives can be modified by events and occasionally by strong evidence supporting change, as I will discuss later in this paper.

What governments of low-income countries can do about distortions must be related to the prevailing political and economic realities. These realities include, among other things, the political distribution of power and the economic distribution of wealth among and within sectors; the budgetary capacity of a country to finance development; the extent to which foreign exchange is a serious constraint to development; and the capacity of governments to bridge the gap between the short and long run, that is, the ability to deal with problems in the short run in ways that are consistent with desirable longer-term resolution of these problems.

WHAT ARE THE DISTORTIONS?

A commonplace distortion is the effort to keep the price of food to urban consumers low and, in the process, depress producer prices below reasonable alternative levels (Schultz 1964). Many food-importing countries distribute imports at subsidized (below world market) prices, whether these imports are purchased commerically or received as food aid. In addition, some countries forcibly procure food domestically at below-market prices. The problem is not that governments want to subsidize food for certain segments of the population, but that in the process of doing so they depress producer prices. India in the 1950s and 1960s and Indonesia are examples. Some food-exporting countries employ export taxes that depress domestic consumer and producer prices below world market levels. (Export taxes may also be used to raise revenue, because they are easy to collect.) The cases of rice in Thailand and groundnut and palm oil in certain West African countries fit this situation.

We should not forget that there are also countries that support food and agricultural prices at high levels and that this action also represents a distortion. In this case, agriculture receives too high an incentive from a social welfare point of view: too many, rather than too few, resources are employed in the agricultural sector. The high support price situation is common in the higher-income countries where governments can afford to support farm income or achieve self-sufficiency in selected agricultural products through high price support levels. However, one can also find instances of high price supports in low-income countries.

Timmer and Falcon (1975) have done an excellent study on how rice and fertilizer prices influence rice production and trade in Asian countries. Their analysis shows how unfavorable price relationships retard rice production.

Another major distortion centers around input prices. It is not unusual for domestic input industries in low-income countries to be protected against foreign competition through a variety of mechanisms. Such protection may be motivated by a desire to insulate inefficient domestic industries from foreign competition, by a desire to foster domestic production and, therefore, employment, or by a combination of both. Whatever the objectives, the result is to increase input prices and to discourage input use (see Rao 1972). When high input prices are combined with low output prices, the depressing effect on output is very significant. This has been the case in Argentina and Thailand.

We should note, however, that there are also low-income countries that subsidize some important agricultural inputs in order to encourage their use and to stimulate agricultural output. Subsidies can generate as much distortion as do some forms of tax on inputs. However, temporary subsidies on inputs might have some merit where farmers have not used these inputs before and the objective is to stimulate their adoption.

Subsidized agricultural credit is another form of distortion typical in low-income countries. Credit is provided at low, and sometimes negative, real rates of interest. In many countries, a large part of the subsidized credit goes to the relatively large farms and stimulates capital intensity in agricultural production. Evidence in Asia, for example, shows that per-acre productivity is lower on large farms employing capital-intensive means of production than on small farms that are more labor-intensive. As a consequence, subsidized credit distributed primarily to large farms can depress agricultural output. Additionally, problems of employment or underemployment in the rural sector are aggravated. Brazil and numerous other countries are examples.

Public investments in social and physical infrastructure can also discriminate against agricultural production and development. It is evident that most low-income countries provide many fewer social services per capita in rural than in urban areas. Underinvestment in education and health, for example, tends to retard growth in agricultural productivity. Underinvestment in rural roads, storage facilities, power, and irrigation can depress per-acre productivity growth as well as the development of new land resources (see Easter, Abel, and Norton 1977; and Spriggs 1977).

Finally, we come to the problem of overvalued exchange rates, common to most low-income countries. This problem has many effects on the agricultural sector. First, it reduces the profitability of producing for export. Domestic producer prices are unduly low in relation to world prices when measured in terms of foreign currency. If efforts are made to increase domestic producer prices, the products will be overpriced in terms of foreign currency and export sales will be reduced. For food-importing countries, imports are made cheaper by overvalued currency and contribute to maintaining cheap food prices at home. Second, overvalued exchange rates lead to a variety of administrative controls to allocate scarce foreign exchange. These controls operate on both imports and exports. To the extent that political and administrative processes are biased toward nonagricultural development, agriculture will suffer in the administrative allocation process (Little, Scitovsky, and Scott 1970).

The political leadership in low-income countries faces hard choices in trying to promote agricultural growth and development. In analyzing these choices, I will consider the major categories of distortions discussed briefly above. In certain circumstances it may be more feasible to deal with combinations of distortions rather than with each category separately because they are interrelated.

WHY DISTORTIONS PERSIST

Why have so many low-income countries ignored agriculture and distorted the economic environment in which it operates? The answer is not simple and straightforward. Yet, several hypotheses which seem to be supported by historical experience can be suggested.

It has been common for the political leadership in many low-income countries to view agriculture as a traditional, technologically static sector which offers no real hope for growth beyond meeting subsistence needs. If one has such a perception, it is only logical to look to other sectors to lead the process of modernization. This perception of agriculture is not hard to understand when one looks at the historical experience of most less-developed countries. And even in the current setting, large segments of the population in low-income countries are still engaged in basically subsistence-type agriculture with only a limited market orientation.

Added to this relatively hopeless view of agriculture is the inordinate complexity of dealing with millions of small economic units in settings where product and factor markets and public institutions are far from adequately developed. It is much easier to deal with relatively few, large-scale activities in the industrial sector than with large numbers of stubborn (wise) peasants.

It may also be easier for vested interests to capture economic rent generated in a highly regulated economy (Krueger 1974) in the more concentrated industrial sector than in the dispersed agricultural sector.

By and large, agriculture in low-income countries has been autarkic in orientation. The role of agriculture was to provide the food and fiber needs of the population. Historically, therefore, the agricultures of low-income countries were not subject to international economic forces through trade. The exceptions are certain commercial crops and a few countries that integrated their agriculture with the economies of developed countries. As a result, the principle of comparative advantage in an international context did not exert much influence on agriculture in low-income countries and did not provide a stimulus for adjustments in resource use and for productivity gains.

A related point is the absence of a perception of resource scarcity and of a recognition of the need to economize on scarce resources. Scarcity is a relative concept. Therefore, as trade theory tell us, one needs at least two points of reference (countries) to evaluate scarcity. If agriculture in low-income countries is not viewed in an international context and if the industrial sector is small, it is difficult to develop meaningful concepts of relative factor scarcity. Agriculture is thus deprived of important forces to drive resource allocation, capital accumulation, and growth.

Finally, we cannot ignore the strong desire in developing countries to imitate what the developed countries do, instead of what they have done. Some of the models adopted are post-World War II Japan, twentieth-century North America and Europe, and the U.S.S.R. One cannot be too critical of impatience, especially since the process by which developed countries evolved from agrarian societies is only now being understood, and our understanding is far from complete.

SOME HARD CHOICES

The issue of hard policy choices with respect to distortions arises from the inherent difficulty of reconciling short-run economic and political interests with long-run objectives. In all nations there are short-run economic interests which are not consistent with long-term economic goals. The more immediate concerns of influential groups in society put strong pressures on the political leadership, making it difficult for the political process to focus on longer-term problems. Policy decisions which yield results primarily in the long term may be hard to justify, particularly in low-income countries where the daily needs of most of the population are not being adequately met. Little political mileage can be gained from talking about accomplishments and progress in the distant future when present circumstances for most of the population are very bleak.

I will argue that the process of reducing or eliminating distortion is not a smooth, continuous one; rather, governments must be prepared to act when circumstances are favorable for action. And it is difficult to predict when a favorable climate for policy change will occur. To ensure that actions have a beneficial effect, governments need a long-term plan for food and agriculture and a set of feasible policy alternatives upon which to act. The policies considered should be favorable to agricultural development. By favorable, I mean that policies should be free of serious distortions which either penalize or unduly stimulate the sector's growth and development. When the political and economic environment permits progress, the actions taken should be consistent with longer-term, economically feasible objectives. Government should try to lock in gains (prevent them from deteriorating) until such time that circumstances permit another quantum jump in policy reform.

There are times when domestic agricultural prices will rise because of poor crop conditions at home or abroad. These price increases may be beyond the control of individual governments. Even though discontent may be created among the population most adversely affected, that discontent may not be sufficient to topple governments. When higher prices result from temporarily short supplies, steps could be taken to prevent them from dropping sharply when supply conditions improve, that is, to keep them from falling to their previous low levels.

In the areas of trade and foreign exchange rate policies, conditions for reform that do not threaten the existence of governments occasionally arise. These conditions could occur through a buildup of foreign exchange large enough to permit trade and monetary liberalization, or as a result of a foreign exchange crisis in which external lenders or aid givers "force" and support policy changes. Either the internal or external forces for change can be used to advantage, particularly if the alternative of not doing anything would be more detrimental to those affected by the policy changes.

A forward-looking conception of policy directions needs to consider the whole economy, not just the agricultural sector. In this way, general foreign and domestic economic policies that affect agriculture can also be adjusted to reduce or eliminate distortions.

Having said all this, two questions come to mind. First, what does one do about political leadership that either has no interest in any longer-term economic development perspective or is strongly committed to one that is inimical to agriculture? Second, what about the situation where nations lack the trained manpower to develop feasible and constructive economic plans and policies?

I do not think there is much that can be done with respect to the first question. Nations are usually regarded as sovereign, and governments, whether ruling by consent or by force, are free to choose their policies. One can agonize over countries that treat their agriculture badly, but it is difficult for outsiders—countries, international organizations, or private individuals and institutions—to do much. Outsiders can advise governments, but they cannot run them.

The second question presents us with a much less intractable problem. It is true that almost all low-income countries are desperately short of trained people, especially those competent to study, analyze, and develop longer-term development plans and policies. The urgency of everyday business keeps what few trained people there are riveted to the short run. But this is an area where development assistance can play a role.

The need for developing a pool of trained people, particularly those capable of working in the agricultural and developmental policy areas, should be viewed in the context of policy evolution. As stated earlier, policies do not evolve smoothly and continuously. Rather, they change periodically, and it is difficult to forecast the timing and the direction of changes. However, when the environment for policy change is favorable, analysts and advisors had better be prepared to take immediate and definite advantage of the situation in order to make policy improvements. Otherwise, precious opportunities are lost and may not present themselves again for some time. Developing policy capability— in the form of people and relevant research—in the low-income countries with a view toward the long-term and episodic nature of the policy process is the only approach that makes sense to me.

Organizations concerned with development assistance can provide a variety of help to increase the longer-term economic policy analysis and planning capability in developing countries. They can help expand the supply of trained people; they can provide support for the development of teaching and research institutions with a policy and planning focus; and, in selected country situations, they can participate directly in longer-term policy analysis and development planning. They can also provide an "international" environment in which people from low-income countries can work productively and within which experiences of different countries can be exchanged.

With this as background, let me now turn to some of the specific measures low-income countries can take to reduce or eliminate distortions.

Let me first discuss the issue of price incentives for both input and product prices. There are several measures that countries can adopt to correct for unduly low producer prices and, at the same time, meet the food needs of the poorest segments of society. One method is for governments to develop and implement effective programs to provide minimum levels of producer prices. Governments should stand ready to purchase products whenever their prices are at or below minimum levels and to store the products until such time as prices have risen to more favorable levels or until shortage situations develop. The objective of price assurance programs should be to provide producers with a fair and stable price, not to support producer incomes above long-term equilibrium market levels.

Price assurance schemes can also be compatible with meeting the food needs of the poorest segments of society. Food acquired under these schemes and from other sources as well can be distributed to the poorest segments of society at subsidized prices. In this way, the price of food is kept low only for those who could not otherwise purchase it, and the remaining consumers pay the unsubsidized market price.

While India has been criticized for maintaining numerous distortions affecting agriculture, it has made progress in recent years in separating producer and low-income consumer price interest. The government of India, through the Food Corporation of India (FCI), has provided price guarantees to producers and, in good crop years, accumulated grain stocks. The grain purchased by the FCI has been distributed at subsidized prices to low-income consumers, primarily in urban areas, with other consumers paying the market-determined price. Efforts to provide grain price subsidies to low-income consumers without trying to depress producer and market prices are steps in the right direction. However, more needs to be done in India to correct price distortions, particularly in the case of rice where domestic prices have been sharply below world rice prices.

I argue for some form of price assurance or stabilization scheme for two reasons: First, the product markets in many low-income countries are sufficiently underdeveloped so that large seasonal swings in prices occur. Prices tend to be depressed after harvest and rise to seasonally high levels before the next major harvest. A price support system would reduce these large seasonal price swings. Second, in the absence of undistorted linkage with world markets and world prices, some form of domestic price correction may be called for.

Another method to maintain fair and stable producer prices is to integrate food exports or imports with domestic price programs. The timing and quantity of either imports or exports should be such as to contribute to domestic price stability and provide incentive-level prices to producers. Timely knowledge of domestic production and import requirements and rapid and efficient access to world markets are required. Most low-income countries lack the trained manpower and world market orientation needed to integrate agricultural trade and domestic price efforts. Many times, their behavior actually destabilizes and depresses domestic prices. Creating the necessary capability to operate effectively in world markets should be a high priority item.

My discussion of producer price assurance efforts should not be interpreted to mean maintaining prices above market equilibrium levels. There may be certain situations where price support operations can be justified in the short run, as can subsidies to selected inputs. At times producers might need a stimulus to adopt new products or to use new inputs. The supports or subsidies should be phased out when the producers' learning process is nearly complete; they should not become permanent fixtures.

What I have said about product price supports in domestic product markets also applies to input markets, particularly for items such as fertilizer. For any given world market situation, producers should have an adequate and timely supply of inputs at reasonable prices. In many developing countries input supplies and prices would become more favorable to producers if these nations (1) stopped protecting inefficient domestic production; (2) removed constraints on imports; and (3) eliminated constraints on domestic pricing and internal geographical distribution.

Agricultural credit programs in most low-income countries are operated in ways that generate numerous distortions affecting both output levels and income distribution. The distortions come about when credit is disbursed at low (sometimes negative) real interest rates and concentrated in the hands of the wealthy. That this happens is well known; that it is difficult to correct is equally well known.

Subsidized credit and unequal access to it have a number of undesirable consequences. Capital-intensive modes of production are adopted and productivity per acre is lower than what it would probably be in an undistorted situation. The weaker segments of agriculture have restricted access to credit and their use of inputs and their productivity suffer. Agriculture may also become the back door through which nonagricultural investments are financed, thus siphoning credit away from agriculture. And finally, savings are discouraged and resources for investment are not mobilized.

The problem of distortions in the credit system is hard to remedy because it stems from the unequal distribution of wealth and power. Therefore, its solution requires fundamental political and economic reforms. In the absence of fundamental reforms, two measures can be implemented if there is sufficient political will. One is to reduce, although not necessarily eliminate, the rate of subsidy. The other is to develop special programs which effectively allocate credit to small farmers and which foster yield-increasing activities on small and large farms alike. One must be aware, however, that there are few success stories on either front.

I turn now to distortions that arise through the development and operation of such public investments as education, irrigation, and transportation. Typically, in low-income countries public investments related to agriculture are low relative to the importance of that sector, and benefits are received by relatively few people in rural areas. As with the problems in the credit area, it is difficult to reduce distortions without a restructuring of wealth and power in society or at least without achieving a greater agricultural orientation among the existing power elite.

The distortions introduced by overvalued exchange rates and all manner of trade restrictions common in low-income countries are well known, as is the difficulty of reforming policies in these areas. Experience has shown that gradual change may be infeasible. Because foreign trade and monetary reforms affect almost all people, almost everyone opposes them. Abrupt policy changes are usually required and can be made when political and economic conditions are favorable.

Leadership in low-income countries, and in countries and institutions providing outside assistance, should be made aware of at least two things. To the extent possible, it is important to know the consequences of changes in trade and exchange rate policies and what can be done to ease the adjustments implied for various groups in society. This knowledge can be generated with changing trade and exchange rate policies. Second, under the best of circumstances, governments of countries with severely distorted trade and exchange rate policies will have to endure disagreeable circumstances as a result of policy liberalization. This is in the nature of things. It is important that those providing outside assistance support the policy reforms with sufficient resources over a long enough time to make the reforms work and to make the government concerned feel that reform is not synonymous with political suicide.

SOME EXAMPLES

As we have seen, there are many sources of distortions which affect the agricultural sector, and several of these are highly interrelated. I would like to look at some of the countries that wrestled with the problem of distortion with some success, rather than at specific distortions. In this way we get a more complete picture of some of the critical issues involved.

I will look at four countries. Two of them—Taiwan and Israel—have had long-term success with agricultural development. The other two—Korea and Brazil—have had more recent experience with policy liberalization, and the process, while reasonably far along, is far from complete.

There are striking similarities between the agricultural development of Israel and Taiwan. Both countries strongly emphasized agriculture as a source of economic growth and employment. In the case of Taiwan, the primacy of agriculture was established under Japanese rule and carried forward after World War II (Abel 1976). In Israel, agriculture was first and foremost in the minds of the early Jewish settlers from Europe and has retained its status ever since. In both cases, whether the emphasis on agriculture was imposed from outside or came from within, it was a "societal" consensus.

Careful attention has been paid to product and factor prices which provide incentives to increase production. While producers have not always received world market prices for their products, prices did not discourage production. In more recent years, domestic price regimes have moved closer to world market levels.

Both countries also recognized their relative resource endowments and invested heavily and continuously to increase the effective supply of scarce resources such as water and land. Technological advances and public investments to increase land productivity and efficiency of water use were fostered in both countries. In addition to technological advance and public investment, farmers' education levels were improved and the agricultural sector was provided with abundant input supplies.

Finally, agriculture in both countries was exposed to international market forces which imparted a significant degree of dynamism. Under Japanese rule, Taiwan was, for all practical purposes, an agricultural region of Japan producing rice and sugar. After independence, Taiwan integrated its agriculture (and the rest of the economy) with Japan, the United States, and other developed countries. The export of high-valued, labor-intensive agricultural products was a major part of this integration. A similar pattern of integration was followed for the industrial sector as well. Agricultural exports have been an important source of foreign exchange earnings and domestic savings used to develop the secondary and tertiary sectors of the economy. The case of Israel is broadly similar to that of Taiwan, with agriculture playing the role of a leading sector in economic development. Agriculture has been technologically dynamic, supplied with needed public investment, and export-oriented, especially in more recent years.

In both Israel and Taiwan, agriculture was part of a larger economic-development effort characterized by a reasonably clear picture of agriculture's relationship to the total economy. Thus, agriculture was neither autarkic in an international sense nor isolated domestically.

South Korea and Brazil represent somewhat different historical experiences. It was not until the mid-1960s that both countries embarked upon a series of economic reforms that have had a profound impact on their economic growth and development. From agriculture's point of view, several elements of the policy reforms are important.

First, liberalization of trade policies and attempts to move exchange rates toward equilibrium levels had a double-edged effect. It made agricultural imports more costly and agricultural exports more attractive. In brief, the "real" value of agricultural exports became more apparent.

Second, valuing agricultural output at something approaching international prices made producers and governments think harder about the gains to be made by increasing agricultural output and exports. Investments in agricultural research have accelerated, with attention being paid to the institutional structure within which research is done. The results have been significant. Korea, for example, went from being a major rice importer in the late 1960s to self-sufficiency in recent years. The attractiveness of agricultural exports also increased with an active and successful search for exportable items, soybeans, for example, in Brazil and mushrooms in South Korea.

Third, the demands for agricultural inputs were expanded and so were the supplies, contributing to the expansion in output. Concomitant with the economic reforms was an emphasis on rural development in terms of both physical and social infrastructure. Public investments in these supported the growth in agricultural output. The emphasis on rural development was motivated partly by economic and partly by political considerations. Whatever the cause, the effect has been to improve living conditions in rural areas.

The reduction of distortions and the process of energizing the agricultural sectors in South Korea and Brazil are far from complete. And it is too early to tell if commitments to agriculture will continue. But good starts have been made and the responsiveness of the agricultural sectors to more favorable economic climates is encouraging.

SOME FINAL REMARKS

Economists despair over the existence of distortions, politicians create and live with them, and certain groups benefit handsomely from them. It is folly to think we will ever see a country, let alone a world, free of economic distortions. What can be hoped for, however, is a situation where economic distortions do not seriously impede economic growth and development.

The issue of distortions requires constant attention. It does not go away by itself. Two aspects of the political economy of distortions need to be stressed. One is that changes in economic policies result as much from events as from ideas. The other is that the ability to respond to events favorable to policy changes when they occur is vitally important. Countries must be prepared to seize upon events when they occur to move policies in the "right" direction. A sound analytic basis for evaluating alternative economic policies and a sufficient number of professional persons of all kinds to direct policy change are required. Most low-income countries are woefully short of both. Therefore, it is of utmost importance to greatly expand investments in developing adequate professional expertise, in providing a research base relevant to the policy issues involved, and in supporting national and international institutions where people can be trained and research conducted. Some low-income countries have done a good job in establishing these preconditions for responding to opportunities to improve economic policies. But most have not, and many have not even made a serious start. Individuals and institutions concerned with aiding low-income countries should, in my opinion, give high priority to increasing policy research and advisory capabilities in these countries.

REFERENCES

Abel, Martin E.   1976.   "Irrigation Systems in Taiwan; Management of a Decentralized Public Enterprise." *Water Resources Research* 12 (June): 341–48.

Easter, K. William; Abel, Martin E.; and Norton, George.   1977.   "Regional Differences in Agricultural Productivity in Selected Areas of India." *American Journal of Agricultural Economics* 59 (May):257–65.

Krueger, Anne O.   1974.   "The Political Economy of the Rent-Seeking Society." *American Economic Review* 64 (June):291–303.

Little, Ian; Scitovsky, Tibor; and Scott, Maurice.   1970.   *Industry and Trade in Some Developing Countries: A Comparative Study.* London: Oxford University Press.

Rao, Musunuru S.   1972.   "Protection to Fertilizer Industry and Its Impact on Indian Agriculture." Ph.D. dissertation, University of Chicago.

Saleh, Abdullah A., and Goolsby, O. Halbert.   1977.   *Institutional Disincentives to Agricultural Production in Developing Countries. Foreign Agri-*

culture, Supplement, Foreign Agricultural Service, U.S. Department of Agriculture.

Schultz, Theodore W. 1964. *Transforming Traditional Agriculture*. New Haven: Yale University Press (Reprint edition, New York: Arno Press, 1976).

Spriggs, John. 1977. "Benefit-Cost Analysis of Surfaced Roads in the Eastern Rice Region of India." *American Journal of Agricultural Economics* 59 (May): 375–79.

Timmer, C. Peter, and Falcon, Walter P. 1975. "The Political Economy of Rice Production and Trade in Asia." In *Agriculture in Development Theory*, ed. Lloyd G. Reynolds, pp.373–408. New Haven: Yale University Press.

An Overview Assessment

SIR JOHN G. CRAWFORD

My approach is that of a political economist-cum-administrator with a fairly strong, but not complete, bias to the avoidance of market distortions which affect resource allocations.[1] I am not against intervention which I see as almost always necessary given strongly held national objectives. In a freely operating market system those objectives which seek to improve the incomes of the weak (both through production and welfare measures) are not likely to be achieved in adequate measure. Martin Abel gives a hint of this approach in the first sentence of his paper[2] but I wish also to try to keep in mind the stern warning indeed given by T. W. Schultz about the danger of merely accommodating governments. For when this happens "they [economists] serve only to rationalize what is being done and lose their potential as educators." Schultz rightly says that "when this occurs, and it can be readily observed, economists become 'yes-men' in the halls of political economy." Despite the risk of falling into this category I still believe government intervention is frequently justified. Nevertheless, intervention needs to be positive and clearly serving national goals with minimum distortions. This is a complex task, as I will suggest shortly when I remind you what an agricultural policy complex looks like.

But first some questions arising from Abel's paper.

Distortions from what? Even as I used "serving national goals with minimum distortions" in the sentence above, I was not sure what I meant by the word "distortions." Many of the authors herein use as their bench mark "world" prices (without very clear definition); but perhaps the price we should be concerned with is one determined by a domestic market situation under conditions of controlled imports of farm products and inputs. Neither is really satisfactory.

World price is probably the favorite candidate for economists making judgments about national policies and I found the discussion in Gilbert Brown's paper very helpful. It is unfortunate that world price is not always easily identified, nor is it a very stable affair. So then what are we talking about: price at any and every point of time, no matter how it fluctuates? Again, at what place: Chicago, or markets served by dumped surpluses from the European Economic Community? Should the ratio of wheat price to rice price necessarily be the same as at any other chosen spot—again Chicago or Los Angeles? Is it a permissible distortion to put a floor to prices as part of a continuous incentive to producers? I believe intervention by way of a floor price to sustain incentive to farmers is a justifiable policy although I fully recognize its uselessness if it is not enforceable.

Will the result of intervention necessarily be bad if the objective is to serve some target for growth in supplies of grains which recognizes, for example, need (population growth), some income elasticity, some system of direct attention to the very poor, and some imports to assist in smoothing out irregularities in supply? Regard does need to be had to relativities of grain prices and the world situation as well as lack of alternative crops in some areas. But the essential need, if trade is not a complete option, is to elicit investment which will produce the supplies of domestically grown crops needed after due allowance for affordable supplies of imports (commercial or aid).

So I do not reject close watch on world prices provided obvious distortions in them can be isolated. But I then have to decide whether translating them in terms of currency exchanges, which are not really "free market" either, will give results which will yield, say, the grain supply a country needs. Let us look again at the large stocks of grain (mostly wheat and rice) India now holds. Are these a sign that prices have been too high for the needs of the market? Possibly yes.

But to the layman this must seem nonsense since, clearly in a country with so much malnutrition and poverty, these stocks are hard to explain. The economist can explain them as the strong evidence of lack of effective market demand, associated very largely with rural and urban poverty and high unemployment. Since the domestic income distribution and market system does not dispose of the stocks it is a reasonable proposition to consider selling overseas from them, given that only, say, eight million tons out of the twenty million are adequately stored and that eight to ten million tons may well meet the needs of domestic buffer stocks policy.

If we do not sell these stocks—that is, export them—can domestic consumption be stimulated? The fair-price shops system seems inadequate to the task. On the other hand, entering world trade is not the simple decision that I think Gale Johnson rather implies in his paper. How could the government of India explain such grain sales to the world and within two or three years be again seeking major help on the food front on genuine grounds of need? There is a reasonable solution which I believe would satisfy all parties. This is to develop a domestic market for the surplus by using it as a wage fund for rural "works" to provide roads, water, and so on. We can agree that public deficit finance for such works without food backing in a situation of high income elasticity is dangerous, but this danger is considerably less now that there is a large food backing adequate for a quite significant investment program. But for how long? One can understand the hesitancy of the government of India since it reasons that it may be raising false expectations of a permanently higher level of public sector employment in rural areas. It is a hard choice, especially as the stocks will deteriorate despite efforts to turn them over if nothing is done. There is a permanent policy need for assuring supplies for a limited rural works program and this could be assured if imports could be relied upon when stocks fell. (I believe there is a real job here for the International Food Policy Research Institute to look at the role of national stocks backed by access to international market for agreed purposes. The terms could be conditional if India's balance of payments situation were to deteriorate from its very healthy state of late 1977).[3]

A GENERAL COMMENT

Now let me turn to a more general comment which tries to make specific the implications of many of the papers in this volume. I believe that the task of recognizing and reducing distortions makes more sense against a background of a national development strategy. This is often difficult to achieve but it is difficult to reform haphazard pricing and investment decisions without a view of strategy which is in turn reflected in national economic and trading policies.

Agriculture, even in India, is not the whole economy, but it is an enormous part. Let us look at its components. The list alone will remind us of the serious problems of resource allocation involved. I am not discussing planning as such, but I use the device of a five-year "plan" as the best way to bring home what agricultural policy and agricultural planning call for. (I stress food, but my remarks have general application to agriculture.)

First, a decision must be made about what *food* supply is hoped for, modified finally by what seems practicable, both for production and trade. This involves some recognition of population growth, income elasticities, and efforts to improve the nutritional status of the poor and "needy." Provision has also to be made for inputs such as fertilizer. A judgment must be made about domestic production and that proportion which can come from imports, in either a trading or aid position. (Yes, I know P.L. 480 can be bad!)

Second, since India does have advantages in production of sugar, jute, cotton, and some other nonfood crops, some judgment has to be made about the proportion of resources likely to go to these crops. And, incidentally, the normal situation does allow the ruling prices—admittedly some "administered"—to be the guide to decisions by farmers.

Then we recognize that farm production is a function of many variables, for all of which resources have to be provided—all interact with one another and no one is sufficient by itself. None is a completely independent variable. All contribute to the incentives to produce. So we consider:

Prices (as they happen or a floor to be assured?).

Storage (to cover fluctuations, support floor prices?).

Inputs for production, especially increased production, and including *water* (surface and groundwater for irrigation, wholly or partially?); *fertilizer* (we are a long way off a "no-input" situation); *pesticides; power* (for pumps and tube wells).

Improving technology by research (I should have put this first) and *improved extension systems in support* (always assuming the pricing system is functioning in incentive terms!).

Capital, both public sector and private investment (farm improvements, irrigation) and working capital. (We may note in passing the very many inefficiencies in raising capital, including the inexcusable nontaxation of larger agricultural incomes.)

Institutions (and they are not least in this panoply of requirements) which will enable all, but especially small farmers—who in India are the great majority—to obtain their share of technology and support inputs. It is one thing to have a technology neutral to scale; it is quite another to assume that all institutions stand readily adaptable to the task of supplying the wherewithal for implementation. The evidence is ample that small farmers will respond to policy incentives if the necessary institutions are available in support. Again, a reference to institutions may suggest that everything must be held up until land reform is complete. Realism dictates, however, that progress must be achieved without waiting for complete land reform to occur. This is not a remark hostile to land reform but is designed to suggest that the selection of a single factor, such as land reform, to precede all other efforts is a very bad mistake of judgment.

Political Will. Clearly all the above carries a further hard decision of Political Will. What share of total resources (including aid) will go to agricultural investment and production? There are other claimants, including export industries, social services, and especially education and health. In India's First Plan, some 37% of total Plan expenditures were on agriculture and allied programs. In the Fifth Plan, the target is 22%—almost certainly not enough. Investment in irrigation certainly has to be stepped up; but so do most of the other expenditures indicated, not least those in the research area (and, again, especially for rice).

Priorities. Priorities for agriculture will be higher in times of stress than when apparent need diminishes. This may be happening now; and yet I believe the quality of effort (and hence value for money and administrative effort) has risen. More specifically directed effort, for example, could go to the rather neglected rice bowl of northeast India—Uttar Pradesh, West Bengal, Orissa, and, one would hope, Bihar. Again, developing command areas in irrigable areas where only the dams and major distributor canals exist is likely to be highly positive in returns. That is, good money is not merely being thrown after bad, but is completing a job not properly done in the first place.

I could give many further examples (development of ground water, of credit institutions, of research and extension) which reflect an awareness that while price incentives will always elicit significant response, they are not sufficient. Institutions have to be developed in support and, of course, research and extension in agriculture depend everywhere on public sector backing and activity. In no way am I rejecting the importance of the price mechanism which in India still calls for review: I have, however, been trying to put it in perspective.

A FINAL OBSERVATION

In closing, I want to discuss briefly some functions of the International Food Policy Research Institute which John Mellor now directs. The formation of this Institute was the result of the recognition by the Technical Advisory Committee of the Consultative Group on International Agricultural Research (which built up the system of international research centers) that something more was required than the excellent work being done in some of the international centers and elsewhere on constraints limiting the adoption of new technologies (Randolph Barker's work at the International Rice Research Institute is an outstanding example of what is being accomplished). I want to cite some of those problems that were rather left up in the air, in the total research scene. These include:

(1) The real nature (disaggregated) of *the* world food policy problem, which turns out to be very different from area to area and country to country.

(2) Great questions of trade in food (these are *not* really covered in the New International Economic Order) as well as of security stocks, purpose and management, both national and international.

(3) The many questions going beyond one country's resolution. These range widely in area, nature, and magnitude. Among them are these three. Can the needs of the Sahel countries be met in regional terms? Given the very small-country characteristics of South Pacific countries, can their fisheries' resources be developed cooperatively? Finally, how can India, Pakistan, Nepal, and Bangladesh be assisted to develop the full potential of the Ganges and Brahmaputra river systems?

(4) The need to assist individual countries in developing their food policies. Here the effort must be predominantly in the area of translating technology into national policies which embrace all the categories I have stressed earlier. The International Food Policy Research Institute must interface with both the international and domestic agricultural and rural research systems on the one hand and national governments and international agencies on the other. It has already started to help in Bangladesh and I believe it will not lack opportunities for applied research.

Finally, the International Food Policy Research Institute is developing a role in feeding results of its analytical work and field research to other organizations concerned with international food problems. Here I refer to work done for the Consultative Group on Food Policy Investment, estimating requirements for increased food production, and to the potential of the Institute's service relations with the World Food Council. Mellor will have a task in keeping service under constraint in the interests of research in the areas outlined. The need is vast and resources limited.

NOTES

1. Some evidence of my bona fides in respect of the market principle is a current official assignment in Australia which is to advise ways and means of restructuring highly protected industry. The object is to give both domestic and international market forces more scope—but to do this some interven-

tionist policies in support of development of industry where comparative advantage lies may be necessary.

2. "Various options, consistent with general national political and economic objectives or goals, are open to low-income countries for reducing distortions that affect their agricultural output."

3. Incidentally, given the huge unemployment and underemployment situation in India, I find Edward Schuh's remedy (proposed in his paper herein) through training rather small comfort.

PART IV

INTERNATIONAL MARKETS

International Prices and Trade
in Reducing the Distortions
of Incentives

D. GALE JOHNSON

While international trade provides a broad range of alternatives that can assist all nations to obtain the achievable output from their resources, there has been a general reluctance in most countries most of the time to take full advantage of the opportunities. The reasons for this reluctance are numerous and vary over time and across countries.

In recent years there has been much criticism of the manner in which international trade functions and of the way in which the benefits of the trade are distributed among the numerous participants. The criticism that has come from sources representing developing countries is of most interest in the present context. If international prices and trade are to serve a useful purpose in reducing the distortions in incentives that affect agriculture within numerous countries, including the developing countries, it is important that some note be taken of this criticism.

A recent critique of the functioning of international markets in agricultural products is contained in the proposals for an "Integrated Programme for Commodities" as proposed by the United Nations Conference on Trade and Development (United Nations 1975). The nature of the critique may be found in the statement of the objectives of this Programme and in what these objectives would mean in terms of commodity arrangements. A condensation and summary of these points was prepared by my late, distinguished colleague, Harry G. Johnson (1976), and I quote from that summary:

The 'Integrated Programme for Commodities' has four general objectives:

(i) To encourage more orderly conditions in general in commodity trade, both with regard to prices and the volume of trade, in the interest of both producers and consumers;

(ii) To ensure adequate growth in the real commodity export returns of individual developing countries;

(iii) To reduce fluctuations in export earnings; and developing country exports of primary processed products.

(iv) To improve access to markets of developed countries for developing country exports of primary and processed products.

These are restated in relation to commodity arrangements as follows:

(a) Reduction of excessive fluctuations in commodity prices and supplies, taking account of the special importance of this objective in the cases of essential foodstuffs and natural products facing competition from stable-priced substitutes;

(b) Establishment and maintenance of commodity prices at levels which, in real terms, are equitable to consumers and remunerative to producers, . . .

(c) Assurance of access to supplies of primary commodities for importing countries, with particular attention to essential foodstuffs and raw materials;

(d) Assurance of access to markets, especially those of developed countries, for commodity exporting countries;

(e) Expansion of the processing of primary commodities in developing countries;

(f) Improvement of the competitiveness of natural products vis-à-vis synthetics;

(g) Improvement of the quantity and reliability of food aid to developing countries in need.

Much of the complaint about the functioning of international markets expressed in the presentation of the New International Economic Order relates to the economic and market relations between the developed and the developing countries. What is not often noted, and certainly not by the advocates of the Integrated Programme for Commodities, is that the developing countries are generally unwilling to trade agricultural products among themselves on a reasonably free and consistent basis.

Imagine an arrangement in which the developing countries permitted free trade among themselves in the cereals and held their combined net trade with the industrial countries at a fixed quantity.[1] Research at the University of Chicago on grain reserves shows that if the developing countries followed such a policy grain prices would be quite stable within the developing countries. This result follows from the estimates of the optimal carryovers of grain for such an entity. For all developing countries (excluding the Centrally Planned Economies of Asia), if there were free trade in grain, optimal carryovers of grain would exceed 2.5 million tons no more than half of the time.[2] In only one year out of twenty would optimal carry-overs be in excess of 15.0 million tons. For the Far East, which produces approximately half of the grain raised in the developing countries (excluding the Centrally Planned Economies of Asia), the sum of the optimal carry-overs for the individual countries is approximately 15 million tons at a probability of 0.5 and 33 million tons one year out of twenty.

Optimal carry-overs of grain of 2.5 million tons no more than half of the time mean that the expected price changes from year to year are likely to be little greater than the cost of storage for a year. The optimal carry-over that could be expected to occur one year out of twenty cannot be directly related to the amount of price instability, but some empirical estimates that we have made imply that it would be unlikely (a low probability of occurring) that year-to-year price variation would exceed 25 to 30% more frequently than one or two years out of twenty.[3]

It is quite clear that so far as grains—the major source of calories —are concerned, the developing countries could be much more the masters of their own fate than they are or have been. The primary obstacles to their being so are their own national policies which require that they interfere with international trade with all other countries—developing as well as developed.[4]

While, as I will argue, there is merit in the critique of how world trade in agricultural commodities functions, it is probably true that even if all of the defects alluded to were remedied (though not necessarily by the means suggested) most developing countries would be unwilling to take full advantage of the alternatives provided by international trade. At the present time only Hong Kong and Singapore take full advantage of the opportunities provided by trade. All too many developing countries have national policies and objectives that conflict with the functioning of a relatively free and open market. The explanation of the failure to take full advantage of the opportunities of trade is as simple as that. In other words, a relatively free and open market poses a threat to numerous national programs such as domestic price stability, below-market prices for the presumed benefit of consumers, a forced pace of industrialization through import substitution, or to the view that national planning of a detailed nature is required to achieve both rapid economic growth and greater equity in the distribution of income. Such measures may well be politically acceptable within some developing countries, but their acceptance should be based on the recognition that many of the potential advantages of international trade are lost as a consequence.

FUNCTIONING OF INTERNATIONAL MARKETS

The objectives of the Integrated Programme for Commodities imply several criticisms of the functioning of international markets for agricultural products. Two are particularly relevant to any discussion of the potential for use of international prices and trade to reduce distortions of incentives within the developing countries. They are (1) instability of prices and (2) the low absolute level and declining level, in real terms, of the prices of many agricultural products. There is some validity to both of these complaints or criticisms in the sense that governmental policies do increase the instability of prices in international markets and probably have the effect of lowering the level of such prices part of the time.

I have dealt with these issues elsewhere (1973, 1975) at some length and here will only summarize the major points that support the conclusions. Much of the instability of international market prices for agricultural products, particularly grains, sugar, dairy products, and beef, results from the efforts of numerous governments to achieve a high degree of price stability in their domestic markets. Consequently, when variations in either world demand or supply conditions occur, the adjustments required are forced upon only part of the world's market—international prices and the domestic prices in those countries that permit their prices to vary with the international prices. Probably the most extreme case of instability resulting from governmental policies is sugar, where only a small percentage of the sugar market is outside of the controls of both consuming and producing nations. For the grains, well over half of the production and consumption—some estimate as high as 80%[5]—occurs at prices that differ significantly from international market prices. When efforts are made—and to some degree succeed—to stabilize internal nominal prices through varying net trade, substantial price instability is created in international markets. If production declines in the world, with total demand either stable or increasing, governmental policies affecting half or more of total grain production and consumption prevent any response to the change in the supply-demand situation and all of the adjustment must occur in those nations that permit their prices to follow the international market prices. I have estimated that at least half of the rapid increase in grain prices after mid-1972 was the result of governmental policies of internal price stabilization; only half could be explained by production declines and the devaluation of the U.S. dollar. It is probably also true that a very large fraction of the grain price declines of the past year can be explained by these same policies.

The complaint of the developing countries that international market prices for many, if not most, agricultural products are highly unstable has considerable merit. Even in the absence of governmental policies that prevent international market prices from being reflected in consumer and producer markets, the relatively low short-run elasticities of supply and demand for agricultural products result in significant price instability. The governmental policies add significantly to the instability. But what the proposers of the Integrated Programme for Commodities entirely ignore is that the developing countries themselves contribute significantly to international price instability for many farm products through their own domestic policies. For example, the developing countries consume approximately 44% of all grains, including 88% of the rice and 42% of the wheat, and in most, if not all, of the developing countries domestic prices are divorced from international market prices through controls and manipulation of imports and exports.

While it is true that international market prices for many agricultural products are more unstable than they would be if governments followed different policies than they do, it is not obvious that developing countries always lose as a result of price instability. In fact, the rapid increase in prices for agricultural products that started in 1972 resulted in an increase in the net export surplus from agriculture and forestry for all developing market economies and from agriculture alone for thirty-one of the largest developing countries, excluding all OPEC countries except Indonesia.

During 1966-70 the net export surplus of all developing countries for agriculture and forestry averaged $8 billion annually. For 1972 through 1974, the export surplus for the same group of commodities was, respectively, $10 billion, $13 billion, and $13 billion (Economic Research Service, 1976). If the OPEC countries are excluded, the export surplus remained the same for 1966–70 and increased by more than $1 billion annually for 1972–74. Only a small part of the increase in the export surplus was required to purchase fertilizer; over the three years the increased cost of fertilizer was about $1 billion annually.

Table 1 presents summary data for thirty-one developing countries— the average annual value of agricultural exports and imports for 1969–71 and 1973–75 and the net change in average annual net exports for the two periods. The market developing countries included have populations of 7 million or more and are ranked from lowest to highest levels of per capita income in 1975. A plus figure in the last column means that the average annual value of agricultural exports increased

Table 1

Value of Agricultural Exports and Imports, for Developing
Market Economies, Annual Averages, 1969–71 and 1973–75

Country[a]	Value of Exports, Annual Average		Value of Imports, Annual Average		Net Change in Annual Exports Minus Imports[b]
	1969–71	1973–75	1969–71	1973–75	
		(Millions of dollars)			
Ethiopia	111	226	15	18	112
Bangladesh	198	136	228	517	−351
Burma	90	114	13	13	24
Pakistan	236	361	135	394	−134
India	644	1,367	677	1,234	166
Sri Lanka	313	398	160	306	− 61
Tanzania	191	287	30	122	4
Zaire	104	153	52	166	− 65
Indonesia	470	864	235	628	1
Madagascar	108	178	26	48	48
Kenya	162	310	57	84	121
Uganda	213	281	24	26	66
Cameroon	159	297	28	59	107
Sudan	293	427	59	148	45
Egypt	526	808	245	904	−377
Mozambique	124	198	36	48	62
Thailand	520	1,385	95	178	782
Philippines	384	1,207	160	311	672
Ghana	264	463	66	116	149
Morocco	230	373	159	572	−270
Ivory Coast	323	670	91	182	256
Subtotal[c]	(5,663)	(10,503)	(2,591)	(6,074)	(1,357)
Colombia	534	962	86	172	342
Korea	77	273	469	1,163	−498
Syria	143	219	108	289	−105
Malaysia	708	1,566	244	573	529
Chile	37	73	222	493	−235
Peru	164	304	133	267	6
Turkey	480	945	91	311	245
Brazil	1,897	4,641	309	908	2,145
Mexico	721	977	178	861	−427
Argentina	1,443	2,514	130	235	966
Subtotal[d]	(6,204)	(12,474)	(1,970)	(5,272)	(2,968)
Total	11,867	22,977	4,561	11,346	4,310

Source: Food and Agriculture Organization, *Trade Year Book*, 1974 and 1975.

[a] Countries in order of estimated 1975 per-capita national income, ranked from lowest to highest.

[b] This column shows the change in the net balance of agricultural trade (value of exports minus value of imports) between 1969–71 and 1973–75.

[c] Subtotal is for countries with per-capita incomes of less than $500.

[d] Subtotal is for developing countries with per-capita incomes $500 or more.

more than the average annual value of agricultural imports. Of the thirty-one countries, twenty-one had a larger increase in the value of exports than in the value of imports. India, the most populous of the nations included in the table, had a greater increase in the value of agricultural exports than of agricultural imports. South Korea had the largest adverse change in its balance of agricultural trade. The second largest annual loss was incurred by Mexico which shifted from being a net grain exporter in 1968–71 to a net grain importer in the later period; this shift was due not to price changes in the international markets but to the effects of domestic policies. For the thirty-one countries as a group, the net annual increase in the export surplus of agricultural products was $4.3 billion.

While I continue to accept the view that price instability imposes costs through its effects upon the allocation of resources, it is not obvious that it has been the developing countries that have lost from the income transfers brought about by the upsurge in agricultural prices after mid-1972.

The second complaint is that the prices of many, if not most, agricultural crop products are low and declining, in real terms. To some degree, low prices and declining prices are separate complaints. There are times that the first has some validity. Governmental policies that induce high-cost production can have an adverse effect upon international market prices. How serious this effect can be depends upon the elasticity of supply for the product in the rest of the world and whether actions are taken to reduce output in areas with a comparative advantage, such as occurred in North America and Australia with respect to wheat during the 1960s and early 1970s.

The complaint that the real prices of crop products have declined and are declining has considerable empirical validity. But this does not mean that such prices are inequitable or unfair or that there is any reasonable alternative course of events. In fact, if one seriously contemplated the alternative, namely, that the real prices of food crops had remained stable or risen during this century, the adverse effects upon the developing countries would have been great indeed. These adverse impacts would have been both relative and absolute. Relative to the high income of industrial countries, stable or rising real prices and costs of food crops would have been adverse to the developing countries since a much smaller fraction of the incomes of the industrial countries is expended upon food crops (including livestock feed) than is true in the developing countries. Thus the real income differences between the two groups of countries would now be even greater relatively than they are.

The much more serious effect would have been an absolute one—

a loss of real income and consumption in the developing countries—
if the real prices of food crops had not fallen during the twentieth
century and especially during the past three decades. *The real prices
of food crops have fallen because the real costs of producing food crops
have fallen.* In the past six decades the declines in real prices, based
on U.S. data, have ranged from approximately 15% for rice to about
35% for wheat and corn.[6] If the real prices of grain had remained
stable or increased, a larger percentage of the resources of the developing countries would have had to be devoted to the production of
food than is now the case and real incomes would be even lower than
they are. Some of the consequences would have been a much smaller
increase in life expectancy than has occurred and an increase in the
degree of malnutrition.

It is, unfortunately, probably true that the real costs of producing
food grains in many of the developing countries have not declined as
much as in North America, Australia, or France. Even if the decline
in real costs had been the same for each food grain, the much greater
importance of rice among the grain crops in the developing than in
the industrial countries has almost certainly meant that the developing
countries have not gained as much from productivity increases. But
this failure has nothing to do with the trading relationships between
the developing and the high-income countries. It tells us something
about how both the developing and industrial countries have allocated the resources devoted to agricultural research and investment
in agricultural resources.

A case can be made that in the decade or two prior to 1973 international prices of sugar, rice, and dairy products were reduced by the
policies followed by the industrial countries (D. Gale Johnson 1973,
Chap. 7). It is possible that wheat and cotton prices were adversely
affected at times, but not by very much. This is not said to justify
the agricultural protectionism that prevailed in the past and continues
in Europe, North America, and Australia.

Brief comments are in order concerning the other criticisms of the
functioning of international markets for agricultural products. It is
valid, in my opinion, for the developing countries to press for improved
access of their primary and processed products to the markets of developed countries. Many industrial countries have relatively high
rates of effective protection for the processing of agricultural raw materials. In the absence of such protection more of the processing of
agricultural products would be done in the production area. The developed countries have used protection to maintain or even increase
the production of farm products for which the developing countries
have a significant comparative advantage. Probably the most important

commodity in this category is sugar, with at least 40% of the world's sugar being produced in the wrong places. There are many fruits and vegetables in a similar protected situation in the developed countries.

With respect to the second of the objectives of the Integrated Programme for Commodities—ensuring adequate growth in the real export earnings of individual developing countries—I have already commented upon the impossibility and undesirability of preventing the declines in the real prices of food products. However, export earnings depend upon volume of exports as well as the prices of those exports. The proponents of the Programme have said very little about the role of the policies of the developing countries in influencing the growth of their exports. Basudeb Biswas (1976) summarizes the results of his study, "An Economic Analysis of India's Export Performance, 1950–1970," as follows:

> Taking a summary view . . . it seems fair to say that although India's exports are subject to structural handicaps in terms of unfavorable commodity composition and low growth destinations, there is sizable scope for public policy to improve the performance by raising the competitiveness of the exports and by increasing the exportable supply and containing the domestic demand for exportables. The low estimates of aggregate price elasticities of demand are not the whole story, for several export sectors would have sizable elasticities and a selective attention to those sectors, while still avoiding the general disincentives in the form of exchange overvaluation and the like, seems to offer considerable potential for improving the growth of exports substantially. The limited analysis done here for other similarly placed countries should reinforce such optimism about the relevance and impact of trade policies.

Mellor and Lele (1975, p.107) earlier came to essentially the same conclusions from a slightly different viewpoint:

> India's failure to realize the export potentials nascent in the past two decades of development trade trace primarily from the capital intensive growth strategy and secondarily from the bureaucratic restraints that were, at least initially, themselves a product of the growth strategy. The strategy reflected a compromise of the two principal areas of trade advantage upon which India might have capitalized. The one was the use of low cost labor to compete in producing labor intensive commodities for export to high wage countries, and the other, closely interacting with the first, was to use a large, growing domestic market to foster efficient manufacture of relatively labor intensive consumer goods.

It is quite evident from the experience of India and other developing countries that export earnings are not solely—probably not even primarily—exogenous consequences of the functioning of international markets but depend in a very important way upon the policies of the developing countries themselves. International markets can be made more effective instruments for the benefit of mankind but not all of the adjustments and changes are the reseponsibilities of the developed countries.

EXAMPLES OF PRICE DIFFERENCES
IN DEVELOPING COUNTRIES

It hardly seems necessary to present data here on the substantial price differences for farm products that have prevailed and now prevail in the developing countries. One needs only to glance at the price data collected by the Food and Agriculture Organization for numerous agricultural products to be convinced that large differences exist.[7]

A few examples may be given. In late 1975 the price of paddy rice in Egypt was 10.2 U.S. cents per kilogram; in Sri Lanka, 21 cents; in Thailand, 13 cents; and in the United States, about 19 cents. In the same time period the wholesale price of milled rice was 39 cents in Brazil, 12.9 cents in Egypt, 17 cents in India, 24 cents in Indonesia, 48 cents in South Korea, 21.5 cents in the Philippines, 17.5 cents in Thailand, and 37 cents in the United States. The export price for Thai rice was 34 cents.

As agriculture is modernized, input as well as output prices become important. Table 2 presents data on the price of nitrogen relative to the paddy price for nine South and Southeast Asia nations. Inspection indicates wide differences in the price ratios and thus in the profitability of using nitrogen on rice. One should not be surprised that the lowest levels of use of nitrogen per hectare of arable land are found in Burma and Thailand and that Sri Lanka has a much higher usage rate than either India or Bangladesh.

Table 3 is concerned with another point, namely, that the control of international trade is not sufficient to achieve an increase in price stability. Wholesale prices are given for five grains—barley, maize, sorghum, wheat, and rice—for India and the United States. Prices in the United States are used to reflect international market prices, which they did reasonably well most of the time involved.

In terms of the absolute levels of prices, India achieved a high degree of price stability for wheat and for rice in the market at Calcutta. The Orissa rice market exhibited significantly less stability but this was due to barriers to trade in rice within India as well as the failure to relate rice prices to international prices.

Table 2

Ratio of Nitrogen to Paddy Rice Price for
Selected Asiatic Developing Market Economies, 1965–1976

Country	1965–69	1970	1971	1972	1973	1974	1976
Bangladesh	—	1.36	1.31	1.78	1.52	1.21	1.93
Burma	8.31	5.33	4.61	—	—	—	1.81
India	1.97	1.97	1.93	1.77	1.56	2.23	—
Indonesia	—	—	—	—	—	—	2.48
Korea	1.47	1.07	0.85	0.74	0.92	0.77	1.42
Philippines	3.38	3.81	2.33	2.33	1.62	4.07	3.56
Sri Lanka	1.44	1.33	1.33	1.27	1.20	—	2.04
Republic of China	3.23	2.23	1.97	1.80	1.72	—	0.78
Thailand	—	8.10	10.30	9.44	—	9.16	4.08

Source: Asian Development Bank, Asian Agricultural Survey 1976. Rural Asia: Challenge and Opportunity. Manila, Philippines: Asian Development Bank, 1977, p.164.

The other three commodities present a rather different pattern. Maize, barley, and sorghum prices increased to higher levels than in the United States in late 1974 and early 1975. The Indian prices of maize and barley did not decline until the very good 1975 crop was harvested and then the decline was precipitous—a fall of 50% in a few months. At the end of 1975 the prices of these two grains had fallen below the U.S. prices. While the sorghum price data are less complete than the others, by the beginning of 1975 sorghum wholesale prices had gone significantly above wheat wholesale prices in India and also above U.S. wheat prices. The sorghum price in India did not fall significantly in 1975, but by December 1976 it was at 9.97 cents per kilogram compared to a U.S. price of 9.2 cents. While maize, barley, and sorghum are much less important food grains than either wheat or rice, they are grains that are produced by and eaten by some of the poorest people of India. The failure to permit international trade in these grains on a reasonably free basis resulted in relatively high prices in the last half of 1974 and the first half of 1975 and then very low prices in the latter part of 1975. The low prices persisted throughout 1976.

The primary means used to achieve price stability was through governmental purchase of grains and the storage of these grains. By the end of 1976 India had accumulated governmental grain stocks of 18 million tons. India had storage space of good quality for little more than half that amount. As a consequence, substantial quantities of the grain stored in areas inadequately protected from insects and rodents

Table 3

Wholesale Prices of Five Grains, in India and the United States, in U.S. Cents per Kilogram

Year and Month	Maize India	Maize U.S	Barley India	Barley U.S.	Wheat India	Wheat U.S.	Rice India I^a	Rice India II^b	Rice U.S.	Sorghum India	Sorghum U.S.
1970	8.9	5.7	5.9	5.6	12.5	6.1	13.5	14.5	18.8	7.6	5.3
1971	8.3	4.6	6.1	5.2	12.4	6.0	13.1	14.5	19.2	8.2	4.8
1972	10.3	7.2	9.2	6.8	12.8	9.2	15.1	14.3	19.6	6.3	6.6
1973	10.8	11.4	13.7	13.1	10.3	17.8	15.8	14.1	53.2	6.1	9.2
1974	17.1	12.8	17.0	18.6	13.9	16.2	21.0	17.9	44.4	—	13.1
1974											
VI	18.4	11.7	15.9	13.1	14.7	15.4	18.4	18.5	55.1		
VII	20.3	12.4	18.8	13.9	15.0	17.0	19.7	18.4	50.7		
VIII	20.9	14.5	19.9	13.6	14.8	17.0	24.2	18.1	48.5		
IX	18.5	14.5	18.5	15.2	14.1	17.2	25.8	17.9	43.7		
X	12.9	14.8	17.2	17.5	13.9	19.3	25.8	17.9	41.7		
XI	14.1	—	16.5	18.2	14.1	19.1	25.7	17.8	44.1		
XII	15.6	13.9	16.0	14.7	14.6	18.6	23.9	17.8	45.9		
1975											
I	17.8	15.6	17.1	14.5	15.6	16.9	25.4	19.0	45.9	19.0	11.2
II	17.9	12.3	16.6	13.2	14.7	15.8	27.5	19.1	45.9	18.9	10.6
III	16.8	11.1	16.8	11.7	14.9	14.7	27.8	19.3	45.2	18.7	10.9
IV	16.9	11.9	—	14.3	13.3	14.6	27.9	19.0	45.2	18.0	11.2
V	16.1	11.1	12.4	13.0	13.0	13.2	27.2	18.5	41.9	18.3	10.6
VI	14.4	11.4	12.0	12.6	12.6	12.6	26.9	17.9	42.5	16.8	10.9
VII	14.7	12.0	9.9	11.2	12.2	14.4	26.2	17.5	43.0	17.1	11.0
VIII	14.8	12.7	10.0	14.2	12.0	16.2	26.3	17.1	41.6	16.8	11.8
IX	12.3	11.7	9.4	14.8	11.7	16.9	—	16.7	37.3	16.4	11.3
X	9.4	10.6	8.2	14.2	11.9	16.4	17.0	17.0	36.9	16.9	11.3
XI	8.9	10.8	7.8	11.5	—	14.7	15.5	16.6	37.5	16.3	1.0
XII	8.4	10.2	—	—	14.4	14.2	15.2^c	16.7	37.4	15.1	10.7
1976											
VI	9.8	11.0	—	—	11.6	13.0	13.8	16.6	—	9.9^d	9.2^d

^{a} Orissa.

^{b} Calcutta.

^{c} January, 1976.

^{d} December, 1976.

Source: Food and Agriculture Organization, *Monthly Bulletin of Agricultural Economics and Statistics,* various issues, and *Production Yearbooks,* 1975.

and, probably, from the weather were lost. An alternative to storage that was not utilized by the government was export of the grain and the retention of the foreign exchange earnings for future grain purchases, if needed.

The data in Table 3 indicate quite clearly that India could have exported both wheat and rice during 1975 and 1976 at prices equal to or above the internal market prices. While the export market for rice is a relatively thin one, the differences between the domestic prices for rice and the U.S. wholesale price were so large that it is obvious that Indian rice, even if of low quality, could have been exported at prices substantially above the prices in India. A curious aspect of the situation, which I can only describe as anomalous, was that during 1975 and 1976 India imported almost 13 million tons of wheat and almost all was imported commerically. Thus India would not have had to export its own wheat but could have resold the wheat it purchased once it was known how large the domestic crops were going to be in the two years.

It is not obvious what benefits are expected to be derived from a pattern of relative prices that depart significantly from international market prices. This statement in no way assumes that international market prices are "fair" or "equitable" or that such prices always reflect underlying conditions of supply and demand. What international prices do reflect are, on the average, measures of the alternatives available to a nation and thus a guide for its own use of resources. If wheat sells in the world market for half or less than rice, what does India gain from maintaining the prices of the two grains at approximately the same level? Or what has Thailand gained from holding the domestic price of rice substantially below the export price, or Egypt by holding the price of cotton at low levels relative to livestock products? The evidence is that the gains are small and the costs are substantial. As noted, it is not obvious that any of these price distortions results in a more equal distribution of income and in most cases they result in additional inequities, either between rural and urban people or within agriculture.

INTERNATIONAL TRADE AND INCENTIVES

It is not possible in a single paper "to prove" that the failure of the developing countries to make reasonably full use of international markets and/or to reflect international market prices in domestic prices has had serious adverse effects upon agricultural production and incomes. Professor Schultz, in this volume, refers to several studies that document the adverse effects of low product prices and high input prices upon agricultural production in India, Thailand, and Colombia.

There is one publicly available report produced under governmental auspices that is quite remarkable for its frank critique of the agricultural price policies of a developing country. *Egypt: Major Constraints to Increasing Agricultural Productivity* (U.S. Dept. of Agriculture 1976) was produced by a joint team from the U.S. Department of Agriculture and the Egyptian Ministry of Agriculture. Some of the more striking facts and conclusions are provided by the following quotations (p.22):

> Agriculture has been assigned by the Egyptian Government the major task of providing (1) low-cost food and industrial raw materials for a rapidly increasing population, (2) foreign exchange and investment funds to permit rapid industrialization of the country, and (3) employment for a growing work force. The chief means for accomplishing the first two goals has been to establish low prices to farmers for certain controlled agricultural products, permitting (1) sale of food products through Government-operated stores at low prices to urban consumers, (2) sale to processing industries of raw materials at low prices, and (3) export by the Government of certain items at a price that in many cases exceeds the equivalent price to farmers by severalfold. Distortions caused by this pricing system in recent years have intensified because of the sharp advance in international prices for most agricultural and industrial raw materials. The third goal has been accomplished by a continuation of labor-intensive agricultural operations that in many cases have been unchanged for thousands of years. Demand for Egyptian workers from nearby oil-rich Arab countries may reduce the labor supply, so that more efficient methods will need to be introduced. To some extent this already is taking place, as tractors are increasingly used for land preparation and there is a partial shift from transplanting to direct seeding for rice.
>
> Results of price distortions are widely evident and openly discussed throughout agricultural circles in Egypt. Farmers use fertilizer allocated to cotton for vegetables, for which announced wholesale and retail ceiling prices admittedly are ineffective. Cotton planting is delayed to permit two or three cuttings of catch-crop clover instead of the one cutting that was standard until recently, thereby reducing cotton yields. Often the farmer is unable to meet his quota for seed cotton, and this may result in an inability to pay off his loan for cash inputs that were supposed to be used on that crop. Quota rice frequently finds its way into the much more lucrative free market. When too large a part of the quota is undelivered, the Government tends to raise the price to the farmers for the following year, perhaps returning 30 percent of the international market price instead of 25 percent, resulting in a 20-percent increase in farm prices, assuming no change in international price levels. But the foreign exchange to the Government from the undelivered quotas is gone forever, as is the extra rice consumed in Egypt (due to the low price to consumers) which might otherwise have been exported.

I will comment on only one of the points made in discussion of Egyptian pricing policy. It is noted in the study that the income distribution effects of low livestock prices do not result in an increase in the equality of the income distribution since these products are consumed primarily by middle and upper income groups. In most of the developing countries it is almost certainly true that low consumer *and* low producer prices result in an increase in the inequality of the income distribution. Most of the very poor people in the developing countries live on farms; urban consumers generally have higher incomes than farm people. Thus if farmers are taxed, through low prices, to provide low-priced food for all or some urban consumers it is highly likely that income is being transferred from the poor to the not-so-poor. It is seldom, if ever, recognized that this is the consequence of pricing major farm products below international market prices.

It should be noted that not all of the policies that hold producer prices below world prices are designed solely for the benefit of domestic consumers. Many developing countries impose export taxes on agricultural products. While these taxes have the effect of lowering domestic consumer as well as producer prices, in a number of cases the sole objective is to transfer resources from agriculture to the government. This is true when the product on which the export tax is imposed, such as cocoa or palm nuts in a number of African countries, is unimportant in domestic consumption. The long-standing rice premium in Thailand was first viewed primarily as a tax measure; only later was the maintenance of the premium justified in terms of the effects its elimination would have on consumer prices. It is, of course, often easier to tax products as they cross a national border than it is to obtain taxes from many other sources. However, when exports are taxed, and often very heavily, a nation is taxing the product or products in which it has a comparative advantage and is thus discouraging the expansion of farm output which it produces at relatively low cost.

DO PRICES MATTER?

The factual evidence is clear that prices do matter. There are wide discrepancies in the relative prices of the major food crops in the developing countries, and in numerous developing countries the prices received by producers for one or more important crops have been and are substantially below world market prices.

During the 1950s there were numerous public officials and economists in the developing countries (and in the high-income countries, as well) who argued that price policy was unimportant because the small peasant farmers of the developing countries did not respond to price incentives. Some even went so far as to claim—though never to substantiate the claim empirically—that price responsiveness was perverse. In other words, higher output prices resulted in smaller total output or at least smaller marketed output. These views were either abandoned or publicly suppressed as a result of the extensive research on the price responsiveness of farmers in the developing countries. These studies showed that the elasticity of supply of farm products was at least as high in the developing countries as in the industrial countries. And Professor Schultz's *Transforming Traditional Agriculture* added a strong theoretical and empirical base in support of the rationality and responsiveness of developing-country farmers.

But the importance of prices in influencing farmers' decisions is once again being questioned. The newer arguments are more subtle than the old. They rest not on the position that there is no farmer response to price but that increased production is much more dependent upon other factors than upon price, thus leaving the impression that if other conditions for output growth are met there is considerable leeway for the use of prices to meet other goals, such as income distribution, political objectives, and inflation control.

Two quotations will suffice to present the issue:

> Since *a priori* price would be expected to be a significant force in promoting the use-intensity of purchased inputs to bring about what we have christened here the pure increases in per hectare yields, we have examined the relative roles of price and technological change in accelerating the use of fertilizer—the leading input for increasing yield. While few would deny the pertinence of the crop-fertilizer price-ratio in influencing fertilizer application to areas under crops and therefore the need to maintain it within a favorable range, the crucial question here is whether having regard to the magnitude of the step-up required in fertilizer use, a major reliance can be placed on the price instrument to deliver the required increase. In this connection, it is pertinent to note that a leading factor behind the failure to achieve the targets of agricultural production in the Third and Fourth Plan periods has been the shortfall in achievement compared to the targets in respect to fertilizer use—the actual achievement having been half of the targeted increase in both the periods. Given the magnitude of the task involved in achieving such targeted increases, the moral of our finding that technological progress is an instrument of far greater consequence than the relative price of fertilizer in accelerating the use of this input becomes obvious. It underscores the fact that an over-simplistic and therefore excessive preoccupation with price can do more harm than good by distracting

attention from the harder but more important tasks which belong in the non-price world of achieving technological breakthroughs and relaxing such real constraints as stand in the way of their becoming a reality on the farmers' fields. (Narain 1976, pp.39-40).

While maintaining low prices has clearly discouraged production, it is not clear to what extent a policy of high prices *per se* has contributed to higher total foodgrains output in the region. There is an inherent difficulty in isolating the impact of product prices on aggregate foodgrains or agricultural supply from that of other measures to raise agricultural production. In the short run, a higher price accompanied by the introduction of new techology may encourage the use of fertilizer and other cash inputs and move output towards a higher production possibilities frontier. But in the long run, to what degree do higher prices encourage investment in irrigation, even more superior technology, etc., thereby including a further shift of the frontier? (Asian Development Bank 1977, p.162)

These quotes do not represent a blatant rejection of the role of price policy in agricultural development. Yet either or both of the quotations can provide justification for minimizing the role of prices and incentives in the expansion of agricultural output. It is perhaps somewhat odd that Narain, in the first quotation above, justifies minimizing the role of prices by noting that shortfalls in fertilizer supplies in India were a "leading factor behind the failure to achieve the targets of agricultural production in the Third and Fourth Plan periods." The shortfall in fertilizer supplies represented a failure of the Indian government to permit the price system to function.

Prices do matter. Prices affect decisions made by farmers—how much fertilizer to use, how to allocate their land and labor among crops, and whether it pays to invest in tube wells or in improvements of irrigation systems. But prices also matter to others who have a direct relationship to agriculture—research institutions, producers of farm inputs, credit agencies, and extension agents. Where the price of fertilizer is five to ten times the price of grain, there is little point in research institutions undertaking research on methods of applying fertilizer or on crop varieties that will give a significant response to fertilizer. Firms will be reluctant to make investments to produce farm inputs for which demand is restricted by low farm-product prices. Similarly, the supply of credit—as well as the demand for it—is affected by farm-output prices.

But I do not want to leave the impression that it is only prices that matter. There is no single policy instrument, by itself, that can make a significant difference in the rate of growth of agricultural output. This is true whether one is considering research, irrigation, fertilizer prices and supply, new seed varieties, or output prices. When I argue that prices matter, it is in the context of as many appropriate conditions as can be achieved. Output price increases will call forth greater additional output under some sets of conditions than under others.

If there is continuing investment in research resulting in a flow of new varieties, new methods of protecting plants from diseases, insects, and rodents, investments and improvements in irrigation, and readily available supplies of modern inputs at reasonable prices, an increase in prices will evoke much larger increases in output than if some or all of these conditions are not met. In fact, if these conditions are met it is almost certain that, if output prices are constant or even declining, output will grow. But this in no way implies that prices are not important.

It is not appropriate to say that prices are either "low" or "high" unless one has some bench mark for comparison. It is not obvious if what is meant by a high price is one significantly above world market prices that a nation gains as a result of a strong positive output response to such a price. The additional output results from a cost that is greater than what would be required to obtain the same output through trade. If an output price is below international prices, there is some output that could be produced domestically at a lower cost than the product could be acquired through trade.

But even if relative output prices are reasonably well aligned to relative international market prices, incentives in agriculture may be inappropriate. In numerous developing countries the official exchange rates result in a significant overvaluation of the currency. Such overvaluation acts as a tax on exports and a subsidy on imports. Since the overvaluation of the currency would mean that the value of imports would exceed the value of exports, controls are imposed on the available foreign exchange and the internal prices of imports of importance to agriculture are likely to be increased in order to restrict demand. Thus agriculture is caught in a scissors—less than real international market prices for what it produces and higher than real international prices for the modern inputs that would contribute to increased output.

CONCLUDING COMMENTS

The functioning of international markets for agricultural products leaves much to be desired. It would be possible to substantially improve these markets. Prices are more variable than they would be if both the developed and developing countries followed different domestic and trade policies. Markets are restricted and often quite capriciously closed. Yet with all these defects, the international market prices of agricultural products come much closer to reflecting the true alternative costs of various commodities than do the managed domestic prices of many, if not most, developing countries.

Data have been presented that indicated wide discrepancies in the relative and absolute prices of food crops in the developing countries. The profitability of applying fertilizer to rice varies greatly among the developing countries. In several developing countries the farm price of rice has been held significantly below international market prices. If the objective of such a policy were to increase the equality of the distribution of income, it is quite certain that it has the opposite effect. In addition, of course, the policy has had the effect of reducing rice production.

Developing countries may attempt to achieve a greater degree of price stability by the control of international trade than would result from permitting domestic prices to fluctuate with international prices. A brief analysis of price behavior of food grains in India in recent years indicates that greater price stability was achieved for wheat and rice but not for maize, barley, and sorghum, which are the food grains consumed by the poorest members of the Indian society.

Prices do matter. Farmers, like the rest of us, respond to economic incentives. Price policy is not the only policy measure that matters, but this is true of any other policy measure. Agricultural production occurs in a complex and interrelated system. If the most effective use is to be made of the resources of the developing countries, farmers must have appropriate price incentives. If these are not provided, many of the other efforts that are made to expand agricultural output will either be misdirected or will have limited effects. It is not only farmers who are affected by the prices that they receive, but it is also the numerous institutions—both public and private—that serve agriculture whose decisions are influenced by the prices of agricultural products.

NOTES

The preparation of this paper was supported, in part, by a grant from The Rockefeller Foundation to The University of Chicago. However, I accept full responsibility for the content of the paper.

1. The fixed quantity could change in response to long-run trends in production and demand for grains with the developing countries as a group but it would not vary from year to year in response to production variability within the developing countries.

2. The optimal carry-overs are carry-overs in excess of working stocks, which we assume are a constant proportion of grain production and thus vary little from year to year.

3. This analysis assumes that while there is free trade in grains among the developing countries, trade with the rest of the world is controlled and, to some degree at least, prices within the developing region are insulated against prices in the rest of the international market.

4. There are probably no other important agricultural products in which the developing countries could ignore the market provided by the industrial countries. On balance, the developing countries are large net exporters of agricultural products to the rest of the world but they are net importers of grains. Moreover, I do not want to leave the impression that I believe that it would be in the interest of the developing countries to have free trade in grain amongst themselves and tightly controlled trade with the rest of the world. The objective of presenting the example was to indicate that there exist possibilities of trading relationships among developing countries that have not been explored.

5. Art van Stolk (1976, p. 19), managing director of van Stolk's Koninklijke Commissiehandel, The Netherlands, said the following in late 1976: "The World is not one big market for grains, but a great number of distinctive separate markets tied together somewhat spasmodically in many instances by the world markets and world market prices for grains. These world prices for grains are not reflected directly on about 80 percent of the grain consumed in the world. And if you leave out the U.S., Canada, and Australia, which are the large exporting countries, more than 95 percent of the grain consumed in the world is consumed in isolation from the *direct* effect of world price."

6. The estimates of declines in real prices (and costs) are, admittedly, somewhat impressionistic and are based on U.S. farm prices in 1910–14 and in the late 1960s and early 1970s, with some adjustments for direct payments made to wheat producers during the latter period. The use of changes in real or relative prices to estimate changes in real costs almost certainly represent an underestimate of the decline in real costs since over the six decades the real price of farm land increased significantly. The real wage of farm labor also increased substantially—actually much more than the real price of land —but more importantly the returns to farm labor increased relative to the returns to labor generally in the economy.

7. Such data are published periodically by FAO in its *Monthly Bulletin of Agricultural Economics and Statistics* and *Production Yearbooks*.

REFERENCES

Asian Development Bank. 1977. *Asian Agricultural Survey 1976. Rural Asia: Challenge and Opportunity*. Manila, Philippines.

Biswas, Basudeb. 1976. "An Economic Analysis of India's Export Performance, 1950–1970." Ph.D. dissertation, University of Chicago.

Economic Research Service, U.S. Department of Agriculture. 1976. *Foreign Agricultural Trade of the United States*. Washington, D.C.

Johnson, D. Gale. 1973. *World Agriculture in Disarray*. London: Macmillan and Fontana; and New York: St. Martin's Press and New Viewpoints.

———. 1975. "World Agriculture, Commodity Policy and Price Variability." *American Journal of Agricultural Economics* 57, no. 5 (December):823–27.

Johnson, Harry G. 1976. "World Inflation, the Developing Countries, and 'An Integrated Programme for Commodities.'" *Banca Nazionale del Lavoro Quarterly Review* 119 (December):19–20.

Mellor, John W., and Lele, Uma J. 1975. "The Interaction of Growth Strategy, Agriculture and Foreign Trade: The Case of India." In *Trade, Agriculture and Development*, ed. George S. Tolley and Peter A. Zadrozny, pp.93–113. Cambridge, Mass.: Ballinger Publishing Co.

Narain, Dharm. 1976. "Growth of Productivity in Indian Agriculture." Occasional Paper No. 93. Department of Agricultural Economics, Cornell University, Ithaca, New York.

United Nations Conference on Trade and Development. 1975. "An Integrated Programme for Commodities: Specific Proposals for Decision and Action by Governments." Report by the Secretary General of UNCTAD, TD/B/C.1/193. New York City.

U.S. Department of Agriculture. 1976. *Egypt: Major Constraints to Increasing Agricultural Productivity*. Foreign Agricultural Economic Report no. 120. Prepared by a joint team from the U.S. Department of Agriculture and the Egyptian Ministry of Agriculture. Washington, D.C.

Van Stolk, Art. 1976. "World Grain Economy: Price Effect on Demand." In *Proceedings of the 1976 International Seminar on Wheat*, pp.19–26. Washington, D.C.: Great Plains Wheat, Inc.

COMMENT

JOSEPH W. WILLETT

In this paper Professor Johnson has made a number of very important points, but I believe two are the heart of his argument. First, he says that international prices of agricultural products are distorted. This both reflects and contributes to an inefficient pattern of production wherein, by economic criteria, the wrong amounts of commodities are produced in the wrong places at the wrong times. The welfare effects of this distorted pattern are often negative. His second central point is that despite their shortcomings, international prices provide opportunities, and countries, particularly developing countries, should take advantage of the opportunities. They should make greater use of international prices as guides for allocation of their agricultural resources.

Put in that sequence, the second point seems a little surprising. On the face of it, it may seem questionable to argue that international prices do not reflect a desirable international pattern of production, and at the same time advise developing countries to use them as guides for allocating their resources. But this is not a contradiction. And Professor Johnson gives a number of examples to support his argument that, however bad they may be, international prices do provide opportunities for developing countries to improve their economic situations.

The point is especially important because, as Johnson points out, there is a rising level of criticism, particularly by the developing countries, of international prices and the world trading system. In the United Nations Conference on Trade and Development, developing countries have proposed a major restructuring of the pricing and trade system and this would involve negotiated prices for a number of commodities.

While I agree with most of what Professor Johnson has said in his paper, it seems to me that there is something of a chicken-and-egg problem here, and in particular I do not find his admonitions to the developing countries completely convincing with respect to their problems with unstable prices. Wildly fluctuating agricultural prices can have bad effects, and prices have been fluctuating greatly in recent

---

The opinions expressed in this paper are the responsibility of the author, and are not necessarily consistent with official policy of the U.S. Department of Agriculture.

years. It seems to me quite understandable for a country to want to try to protect itself against such fluctuations imposed from outside. Johnson gives examples and concludes that the control of international trade by a number of countries has not been sufficient to achieve an increase in price stability, and further argues that the developing countries do not always lose as a result of international price instability. But this does not seem to me to make entirely convincing the argument that they should not try to lessen instability of some domestic prices. And if a country, acting unilaterally, is going to try to stabilize its prices to a greater degree than those in international markets to which its domestic prices have been tied, it is going to have to interfere with trade to some degree. It might engage in stockpiling, but it would still have to interfere with trade.

Professor Johnson has argued very effectively, especially in other papers, that when governments set policies which insulate their domestic markets from international markets these policies, to a large extent, cause the instability of international prices of agricultural commodities. That is, if commodities were allowed to flow freely, in response to the incentives of prices in the international markets, those prices would not be nearly as unstable as they are. Fluctuations in supply due to variations in the weather and other factors, and fluctuations in demand due to variations in disposable income would cause prices to vary but not nearly so much. This I think to be well established, and we at the U.S. Department of Agriculture have made the same point. But most governments do interfere with agricultural trade, and the resulting unstable system presents an individual country, and particularly a small and weak developing country, with the problem of preventing the instability from imposing unacceptable burdens on its domestic affairs. This leads me to conclude that international negotiations are essential in trying to improve the working of the agricultural trade system. It may be that countries will not take down those barriers intended, at least in part, to protect them from instability until they are convinced that the instability will be corrected (Hathaway 1978). However, I think I must add here that most of the barriers were erected during a period of relatively stable prices. Johnson has recognized the significance of unstable food prices for less-developed countries in other papers, and has made a specific proposal for a grain-insurance scheme, which could relieve the poor countries of many problems arising from fluctuating grain supplies and prices (Johnson 1978).

As far as international negotiations are concerned, we are approaching a critical stage in the Multilateral Trade Negotiations and other discussions of grain reserves and here we have a great potential for significant progress toward solution of the problems of fluctuating supplies and prices. Unfortunately the outlook does not seem promising because of positions governments have already taken.

Here I would like to add a parenthetical comment that I think there is some danger of misunderstanding arising from the way that Johnson has organized his discussion of the UN Trade and Development commodity proposals. His arguments center especially on grains, which are not included in the proposals.

The ten "core" commodities proposed in February, 1975, for inclusion in an Integrated Commodity Program were coffee, cocoa, tea, sugar, cotton, rubber, jute, hard fibers, copper, and tin.

Despite my minor misgivings about some arguments stated by Johnson in his particular paper herein, I agree with his main thesis, which I understand to be that governments' manipulation of agricultural commodity prices are usually ineffective with regard to their objectives and often end up doing more harm than good. There is much evidence supporting this thesis.

I do not think it would be realistic to expect that in the future governments will do a much better job of manipulating agricultural commodity markets than they have in the past. The problems are too complicated. The world food and fiber system is enormously complex. Hundreds of millions of people are engaged in farming, transporting, storing, and processing agricultural products. Every one of us interacts with the system daily and most of us at least three times a day. The precise timing of many of the operations involved is critical. Technology in many of the systems is extremely dynamic, requiring rapid adjustments in inputs and in the methods of combining inputs, and forcing major adjustments in production patterns and specific techniques. Also the role of agriculture is essential to solution of the problems of economic development. Within the agricultural sector major adjustments of resources must be made, and the traumatic changes related to population movements from farms and rural areas to industrial jobs and urban locations must take place. And, as has been emphasized in the last few years, the system is becoming increasingly internationalized, with complex trade patterns being developed.

Johnson and others in this volume refer to the main reasons governments almost universally have tried to manipulate agricultural markets. Desires to obtain government resources from taxes, welfare considerations, questions of justice or equity in returns to resources, desires to transfer resources to poor countries for development investments, international politics, and the attempt to respond to interest groups' political pressures, whether they be those of commodity producers in the developed countries or of city consumers in the developing countries, have all given impetus to the criticisms of the price system cited by Johnson and to the manipulations of it attempted by governments around the world.

Implementation of the UN Trade and Development proposal would very likely make the system work worse, not better. It is aimed at raising and stabilizing prices of exports from poorer countries. If it raises prices, that would amount to a transfer of resources similar to the effects of aid programs, but hidden under another name and other formulas. The transfer would have no necessary relation to real needs nor to other aid or welfare considerations; the benefits would be proportional to the amount of production. Some recent studies indicate that implementation of the UN Conference proposals would have little benefit for the poorest countries.

These proposals were stimulated by the Organization of Petroleum Exporting Countries' success, but many of the commodities in the proposal already have serious competition from substitutes, and none has all the characteristics that underlay the petroleum producers' success. Agricultural products also differ from petroleum in that a crop not produced is lost forever, and there are substantial storage costs not relevant to petroleum left in the ground. Elaborate rules and bureaucracies are required to control agricultural production when it is overpriced—as U.S. crop-control programs have demonstrated. Also the benefits tend to be capitalized into land values, and thus to go primarily to landowners. In addition, stabilizing prices of exports from developing countries may destabilize gross returns and income and may tend to destabilize prices of unregulated commodities.

I think economists can and should say to the policy makers: "This is a very important and very delicate system which you are trying to manipulate. If you do not change your approaches you are unlikely to be able to accomplish the goals which you profess to seek, and you are very likely to do serious mischief in other directions." As Johnson says, "Prices do matter." They are not the only elements that must be used well to make the world agricultural·system serve society's needs, but they provide critical information and incentives for hundreds of millions of decisions every day. And the record of governments in setting them at the appropriate levels to perform those essential functions is very bad.

But will the policy makers hear us and attend to us? Our experience reflects widespread frustration. It is possible, I suppose, that we are somewhat arrogant or overambitious in expecting politicians to run the world as we advise, rather than taking our economic analyses into account as one relevant piece of information. But I think one reason we are often ignored is that we fail to analyze major aspects of the problems facing policy makers.

The idea of uncoupling one set of issues from another, suggested by Schuh, follows naturally from the economists' method of analysis, but to do it in real life is not easy, and interest groups and policy makers know it. Therein lies a fundamental dilemma of economic policy. Prices can allocate resources, but they also distribute income and affect other policy objectives. If we want to prescribe policy, and expect the medicine to be taken, we must be prepared to consider the possible side effects and their interrelations, which have become very complex. For example, U.S. agricultural trade has grown so rapidly since the Korean War, and particularly in the last few years, that it is now large enough to significantly affect a number of important U.S. government objectives. Our agricultural trade can raise farm income, contribute to a healthy balance of payments, reduce the burden on taxpayers, improve world food security, and help to stabilize prices; it can help to combat malnutrition in the world, contribute to development of poor countries, and improve international relations. However, these goals are sometimes inconsistent with each other, and agricultural trade policy issues usually revolve around balancing the conflicts that arise between the various objectives. Economists prescribing policy changes must be prepared to evaluate the trade-offs.

REFERENCES

Hathaway, Dale. 1978. "The Relationship between Trade and World Food Security." In *International Food Policy Issues, A Proceedings*. Foreign Agricultural Economic Report No. 143, Washington, D.C.: Economics, Statistics, and Cooperatives Services, U.S. Department of Agriculture.

Johnson, D. Gale. 1978. "International Food Security: Issues and Alternatives." In *International Food Policy Issues, A Proceedings*. Foreign Agricultural Economic Report No. 143, Washington, D.C.: Economics, Statistics, and Cooperatives Services, U.S. Department of Agriculture.

PART V

AGRICULTURAL RESEARCH, EDUCATION,
AND NEW INSTITUTIONS

The Organization of Research
to Improve Crops and Animals
in Low-Income Countries

ROBERT E. EVENSON

Public and private research to improve crops and livestock has long
been an important activity in most of today's developed high-income
nations. The United States has nearly a century of experience in
building agricultural productivity gains which are in substantial part
the direct consequence of such research programs. A number of European countries have an even longer record in this regard and most
other modern agricultural nations, including Japan, have also invested
significantly in agricultural research programs over many years. The
record of research programs to improve crops and livestock in the contemporary developing countries contrasts sharply with that of most
developed countries. With the exception of research programs on
sugarcane, tea, coffee, rubber, and, to a very limited extent, on rice,
virtually no long-term sustained research programs have been undertaken in developing countries. Even today, after more than twenty-
five years of development efforts, many commodities of major economic
significance are receiving virtually no research attention. The development of research institutions has been slow and difficult and it is
probably fair to say that no really first-rate national agricultural research institutions are in place in a developing country today.

Nonetheless, the post-World War II period has seen substantial
development in this area. A large number of new research institutions
have been established in many countries and the total research effort
has expanded significantly. Tables 1 and 2 summarize the available
data on investment in agricultural research and extension for regions,
and level of development. While too aggregative for some purposes,
they do serve to illustrate the major features of agricultural research investment. Table 2 shows rather clearly that the developing countries
have placed greatest relative emphasis on extension programs as opposed to research programs. If we were to add investment in rural development projects which has been especially important in recent

years, the emphasis on programs designed to implement existing technology, rather than to produce new agricultural technology, would be even further accentuated.

Table 1 also reflects the slowdown which occurred soon after 1969 in the rate of expansion of the agricultural research system. While I lack explicit data after 1974, it would appear that, with the exception of the higher-income developing countries, particularly Brazil, national agricultural research-program development has slowed substantially in this decade, both quantitatively and qualitatively. This

Table 1

Expenditures on Agricultural Research by Region 1951–74

Region	*Total Annual Expenditures in Millions of 1971 constant U.S. dollars*				
	1951	*1959*	*1965*	*1971*	*1974*
Western Europe	130.0	172.3	407.4	671.0	733.4
Eastern Europe and USSR	132.2	365.2	626.8	818.0	860.5
North America and Oceania	365.7	540.0	805.9	1203.4	1289.4
Latin America	29.7	39.2	73.0	146.4	170.3
Africa	41.3	58.0	113.5	138.5	141.1
Asia	70.0	131.0	356.4	610.2	646.0
World Total	768.9	1305.7	2383.0	3587.5	3840.7
	Percentage of Total Expenditures in Industrial Sector Research				
Western Europe	12.6	12.4	11.7	10.8	10.8
Eastern Europe and USSR	7.5	7.4	8.1	8.3	8.3
North America and Oceania	28.0	28.3	26.9	24.9	25.4
Latin America	3.3	3.6	3.6	3.2	5.1
Africa	2.9	3.5	3.5	2.9	2.9
Asia	2.8	2.5	2.4	2.2	2.2
World Total	17.4	15.9	13.9	12.9	13.1
	Percentage of Total Expenditures in "Agriculturally Related" Scientific Research				
Western Europe	19.8	19.5	24.8	27.6	27.6
Eastern Europe and USSR	27.0	26.4	19.0	17.2	17.2
North America and Oceania	11.7	11.7	12.2	16.3	16.4
Latin America	9.2	9.2	11.5	14.1	14.0
Africa	6.7	5.8	6.9	9.2	9.2
Asia	19.8	18.9	23.3	25.9	25.9
World Total	11.3	17.2	13.3	19.9	20.5

Source: James Boyce and Robert E. Evenson. 1975. *Agricultural Research and Development Programs*. New York: Agricultural Development Council.

Table 2

Expenditures on Research and Extension as a
Percentage of the Value of Agricultural Product
by Per Capita Income Group, 1951–74

Income Group (1971 U.S. dollars)	A. Percentage Expended for Agricultural Research				
	1951	1959	1965	1971	1974
I (> 1750)	1.21	1.26	1.80	2.48	2.55
II (1001–1750)	.83	1.19	1.95	2.34	2.34
III (401–1000)	.40	.57	.85	1.13	1.16
IV (150–400)	.36	.37	.62	.84	1.01
V (< 150)	.22	.28	.47	.70	.67
	B. Percentage Expended for Agricultural Extension				
I (> 1750)	—	.45	.52	.61	.60
II (1001–1750)*	—	.17	.22	.33	.31
III (401–1000)*	—	.26	.40	.46	.40
IV (150–400)	—	.67	.99	1.44	1.59
V (< 150)	—	.57	1.04	1.76	1.82

*Excluding Eastern Europe and U.S.S.R.

Source: James Boyce and Robert E. Evenson. 1975. *Agricultural Research and Development Programs.* New York: Agricultural Development Council.

has occurred despite prospective food-shortage warnings sounded at the 1974 World Food Conference of the Food and Agriculture Organization in Rome and the crisis atmosphere associated with the high foodgrain prices which prevailed from 1972 to 1975. It is a measure of the superficial nature of many national and international policy-making processes that the crisis atmosphere of the 1970s spawned so little in the way of long-term investment in measures to improve food-producing capabilities.

The establishment of the system of international agricultural research centers over recent years has clearly been a significant factor in the developing countries. The contributions of the International Rice Research Institute in the Philippines and the International Maize and Wheat Improvement Center in Mexico are substantial and well documented. The addition of these centers and several newer ones to the developing-country setting has been qualitatively and quantitatively important.

It is, of course, impossible to know the level of technical and entrepreneurial support which might have been made available to national research programs had the international centers not been built. Supporters of the centers argue vigorously that most bilateral and multilateral aid agencies would not have provided funding to national research program development in the absence of the development of the centers. A study James Boyce and I made (1975) estimated that annual bilateral and multilateral aid to national agricultural research programs in the developing countries was approximately $55 million (1971 price level) in 1959 and increased to a level of from $80 to $100 million by 1965. By 1971 this level had declined by $20 to $30 million. In the early 1970s the Food and Agriculture Organization increased its support of research programs and the level rose somewhat.

Boyce and I noted that the late 1960s and early 1970s were years of general retrenchment of institution building and technical assistance programs. We concluded that the international centers diverted in the early 1970s perhaps $20 million a year from support of national programs. The Consultative Group for International Agricultural Research has, in building the system of international research centers, achieved a net increase in agricultural research funding since the centers' funding is now approaching $100 million per year.

The decline in technical and entrepreneurial assistance to national program development has been substantial since the late 1960s. Part of this has been due to retrenchment related to political factors in developing countries. It is difficult to say how much real diversion of scientists from national to international programs took place but it is fair to note that many scientists and administrators now at international centers were once actively assisting national programs.

The question of the state of development of national programs, it could be argued, was not so serious during the period of rapid expansion of activities at the international centers. But now the system of international centers has reached a plateau. No substantial further development is envisaged over the next decade. Does this mean that bilateral and multilateral aid to agricultural research will no longer be expanded? The Consultative Group virtually acquired property rights to funding for agricultural research during the centers' expansion period. Will it now be content to husband these rights to maintain the centers at their present levels? If no institutional arrangements are available to induce an expansion of aid support to national program development the future development of agricultural research programs will rest with the developing countries themselves.

Below, I discuss some of the organization problems of further developing national agricultural research programs, given the conditions that many developing countries face. I do not deal directly with research management issues nor do I attempt to develop a detailed research-planning scheme. I concentrate on four organizational dimensions: (1) research allocation by commodity, (2) environmental

orientation or targeting of research programs, (3) the commodity-ver-
sus-discipline focus, and (4) scale and other relationships among research organizations. I attempt to discuss the problems created by the
skills' market in many developing countries.

National programs will, of course, be at different stages of development and, accordingly, the appropriate strategy for expansion will
differ by country. A set of common problems and issues, however,
enables a fairly general discussion. In the discussion of the major organizational issues set out above, the following factors are assumed
to be essentially given in the short run although later I will also discuss
these issues as being subject to change through policy:

(1) Most national policy makers will continue to opt for the quick
payoff project and will continue to overestimate the ease with which
agricultural technology can be transferred across producing environments. Research programs will continue to be under pressure to produce quick results and will more or less have to be organized within
this policy environment.

(2) Research program expansion will have to be undertaken under
severe skill supply conditions. The availability of graduate student
fellowships from the traditional granting agencies will not increase
substantially and may, in fact, decrease. A few countries will use
World Bank loan funds to support graduate study in the United States
by their students. The progress toward indigenous capacity in developing countries to train scientists will be substantial at the master-of-
science level but very slow at the level of the doctorate.

(3) Scientists will be subject to a fragmented market in most
countries. Basic university or government salaries for scientists will
be low and relatively sticky because of social pressures to keep them
in line with the salaries of lower-ranking personnel. However, the
demand by national and international agencies for the services of most
highly skilled scientists will be high. International agencies, in particular, will continue to be willing to pay international salaries for
short-term consulting services by agricultural scientists. In many cases,
the demand for these services will be largely political in the sense that
representation from poor countries will be valued. This will present a
continuing problem for the national research manager and entrepreneur in terms of achieving an environment in which scientists are able
to devote principal energies to the research task and have an incentive to maintain research skills and to acquire new research skills.

(4) Development of the international centers will reach a plateau.
Few or no new centers are likely to emerge in the next ten years.
Existing centers will continue to have only peripheral linkages to na-

tional programs but will continue to serve as important training centers and, perhaps more importantly, as sources of genetic materials and scientific information of value to national programs.

A NOTE ON THE LITERATURE ON
RESEARCH PRODUCTIVITY

I will not review at length the literature on the impact of research on productivity. It, for the most part, does not address organizational questions directly and is summarized in a number of places, particularly in the Airlie House papers now published by the University of Minnesota Press (Arndt, Dalrymple, and Ruttan 1977). The issues of scale and interrelationships among research organizations are not examined in most of the empirical work on the topic. Some papers, particularly those by Moseman and Hayami (in Arndt, Dalrymple, and Ruttan 1977) are relevant, however, for they do show the importance of regionally coordinating research programs. The question of scale economies is a very complex one and involves not only the question of size of a single research institution, but of the relationships among institutions as well. My study (1968) did measure scale economies of state agricultural experiment stations in the United States in the 1950s. My extension of this study to a later period, however, casts some doubts on whether scale economies did exist (Evenson and Welch 1974).

The literature does tend to show that a number of different types of research institutions have been highly productive. The early U.S. experiment-station system was productive for a period but then was subject to exhaustion of technology and appeared to be unproductive. Similarly, many of the early developing-country experiment systems appear to have been productive even though they were small, isolated from other scientific institutions, and relied on relatively low-level skills. Again, after a period of high productivity they appear in many cases to have slipped into low productivity.

The distinction between simply exploiting technology potential through adaptive research and both creating and exploiting technology potential is one that I find critical here. It appears that where a real technology potential exists a number of alternative institutional arrangements can exploit it. Thus, if technology potential is in some sense produced and delivered to dependent research institutions we may not have to be too concerned about the sophistication of the organization of the dependent institutions.

However, when we are dealing with research institutions which have some degree of independent capacity to produce technology potential (and to both exploit and export this potential to dependent institutions) we do have complex organizational questions. These involve communication between scientists and issues of disciplinary organization. There are substantial scale economies that may emerge but a number of related issues also become important. The establishment of identifiable "frontiers" both in technology and of related science and the utilization of high-level scientific skills becomes important.

To date, the economic literature has little to say about these complex issues. The *ex post* studies have tended to be based on short historical periods and have not always attempted to control for the levels of technology potential in judging the productivity of research. *Ex ante* studies, on the other hand, have tended to evolve strictly as simple project- and program-evaluation techniques. They presuppose that the research system has developed imaginative proposals and thus miss a critical part of the research process.

RESEARCH ALLOCATION BY COMMODITY

Perhaps the most tangible dimension of agricultural research allocation and organization is its commodity orientation. An optimal allocation of research effort does not necessarily lead to a distribution of research resources among commodities proportional to the economic importance of the commodities. There are, however, reasons to expect that in the long run such an allocation rule might be a reasonable approximation to an optimizing rule. Suppose that nature were "plastic" in yielding her secrets, in the sense that the expected discovery function (showing the probability of discovering crop or livestock improvements as a function of research effort) was the same for each commodity (or commodity subgroup). Under this condition, resources would be optimally allocated if the same proportion of the economic value of each commodity were devoted to research.

Before turning to an examination of factors which produce a nonplastic nature, let us consider the summary data in Table 3 on the allocation of research, by commodities, in the developing countries. This allocation is far from optimal. Several commodities of major economic importance are receiving only minimal research attention. The root crops, in particular, are getting very little. In general, the commodities given the most research attention are also the commodities on which research has proceeded for the longest period.

One of the reasons for nonplasticity may be that research programs

Table 3

Estimated Percentages of Product Value Expended on Research for Major Agricultural Commodities Produced in the Developing Countries of Asia 1959 and 1975

Commodity	Approximate Share of Total Commodities in 1974	Percent of Product Value Expended on Research by National Programs in South, Southeast, and East Asia (excluding Japan and China)	
		1959	1974
1. Rice	23.1	.05	.12
Upland	(3.7)	.02	.03
Shallow Depth	(8.5)	.06	.15
Intermediate Depth	(9.0)	.04	.06
Deep Water	(1.9)	.02	.03
2. Livestock and Products	20.5	.06	.11
Dairy	(12.0)	.04	.08
Others	(8.5)	.08	.25
3. Pulses	5.6	.02	.06
4. Sugarcane	4.5	.10	.24
5. Roots and tubers	4.4	.01	.03
6. Millets and Sorghum	4.4	.04	.11
7. Wheat	3.9	.08	.23
8. Groundnuts	3.1	.02	.04
9. Oilseeds	2.7	.02	.04
10. Cotton	2.7	.43	.58
11. Tobacco	2.0	.04	.06
12. Maize	1.7	.06	.12
13. Vegetables	1.6	.05	.10
14. Rubber	1.4	.40	.57
15. Tea	1.4	.10	.15
16. Bananas	1.2	.01	.02
17. Coconuts	1.1	.01	.03
18. Jute	1.1	.04	.08
19. Coffee	1.0	.05	.10
20. Spices (pepper, etc.)	1.0	.10	.15

Source: Robert E. Evenson. 1977. "Cycles in Research Productivity in Sugarcane, Wheat, and Rice," p.221. In *Resource Allocation and Productivity in National and International Agricultural Research,* edited by Thomas M. Arndt, Dana G. Dalrymple, and Vernon W. Ruttan. Minneapolis: University of Minnesota Press.

on neglected commodities have relatively low productivities in their early years. It may take several years to collect and classify germ plasm and to make physiological and pathological studies to develop the basis for a productive breeding program. The time lag between investment and payoff will thus be longer for the neglected commodities than for those crops on which research has been in progress for many years. It is not necessarily true, however, that the "internal rate of return" realized to investment in research on neglected crops in the early stages is lower than it is on more established crops. The longer gestation period combined with a high policy-discount rate (i.e., valuing short-term gains most highly), however, does provide an explanation for the tendency to invest relatively little in the neglected crops.

It is likely then that the short-term expected-discovery function will differ among commodities which have and have not gone through the "groundwork" stage. It will also differ according to the degree of "exhaustion" of what we might term the distribution of potential discoveries. This distribution is determined by the groundwork or basic research. In the early stages of work on a commodity, groundwork research is required to create potential. At later stages in commodity research, this potential will become exhausted by plant breeding and agronomic research. The capacity to create *new potential* then becomes critical. Indeed, this capacity is the key to the development of a first-rate research system. And where this capacity exists, nature tends to be plastic. Technology potential will tend to be maintained in all commodities, creating an expected technology discovery function which may be quite similar in each commodity.

A mature, fully developed research system then must allocate research effort both to technology discovery in each commodity and to the creation of technology potential. For the most part, the national research programs in most developing countries have not emphasized the creation of technology potential either of the initial type or of the continuing type. Nor, for that matter, have the international agricultural research centers, although they have made some contributions here. The developing countries are at a particular disadvantage in building capacity to create technology potential because of their limited supply of highly trained skills and because of the nature of the market for such skills. The international centers, however, are not subject to these limitations and have a clear comparative advantage in the creation of technology potential. I will return to this point later.

Given the limited skills and other problems, the same kind of resource allocation among commodities in the developing and developed countries would not be expected. This is borne out by Table 4 which reports a congruity index showing the association between research expenditures and commodity importance.[1] The index shows a closer association between commodities and research emphasis in the more-developed countries. It also shows a closer matching over time. This

Table 4

Commodity Research Congruence
by Per Capita Income Group

Income group (1971 U.S. dollars)	1959	1965	1971
I (> 1750)	.832	.810	.905
II (1001–1750)	.680	.827	.850
III (401–1000)	.769	.830	.833
IV (150–400)	.734	.830	.819
V (< 150)	.627	.705	.748

Source: James Boyce and Robert E. Evenson. 1975. *Agricultural Research and Development Programs*. New York: Agricultural Development Council.

suggests a general consistency of national government policy with conditions in developing countries. It does not, however, imply optimal policy making by national programs and especially not by international programs. The failure to establish technology potential in the neglected crops appears to be the most serious flaw in research-system development from the commodity-orientation perspective.

RESOURCE ALLOCATION BY
ENVIRONMENTAL REGION

The previous commodity-orientation discussion is incomplete in major respects. First, each crop is grown in a range of producing environments. Rice environments vary greatly from upland conditions to deep-water conditions. Sugarcane-producing environments are much less variable. The environments vary not only by location but also over time in the same location. Second, agricultural technology for all commodities has some degree of sensitivity to some or all environmental components. The agronomy literature generally refers to these as genotype environmental interactions. They differ in strength by commodity. A genotype (variety) is said to be *stable* if it has a low degree of sensitivity to changes in environment over time in the same location. It is said to be *adaptable* if it has a low degree of sensitivity to environmental differences across locations.

One of the factors in the development of the modern wheat varieties at the International Maize and Wheat Improvement Center in Mexico and, to a much lesser extent, the modern rice varieties has been the selection for adaptability or for low sensitivity to environmental differences. The maize programs of the Center in Mexico have failed to produce widely adopted new varieties largely because of the inherently limited scope for selecting for adaptability in maize.

Natural biological selection processes over the centuries produced an immense variety of plant and animal species, each having a comparative advantage in an environmental "niche." This is due, of course, to genotype environment interactions. Man's efforts to improve commercial crop and animal species have only partially overcome the problems created by these interactions. Selecting for adaptability has its price, in the sense that some other traits of economic value have to be sacrificed to obtain more adaptability. Consequently, agricultural research programs have long been organized around "target" environments. A research program designed to produce improvements for only one target environment or a set of closely related environments, even if quite successful, will produce improvements which may be transferable only to nearby or similar environments. If technology-environment interactions are strong it is quite possible for steady improvements in maize technology suited to the U.S. Corn Belt, for example, to have no value at all for maize producers in the tropics.

I will not attempt to model the optimal targeting principles in this paper. They have not been fully developed in any case. However, certain intuitive statements can be put forth:

(1) The higher the degree of technology-environment interaction in the commodity, the more target environments there will be.

(2) The higher the degree of scale economies to research organizations, the fewer the number of targets and the more stress on adaptability there will be. Conversely, if there are few economies of scientist association and the cost of pursuing multiple target programs within an experiment station is relatively low, many targets will be adopted.

(3) The more variable are producing environments over time, the fewer the targets and the more valuable will adaptability be, provided that the traits of stability and adaptability are highly positively correlated.

(4) From an international perspective, it will, in general, not be wise to totally neglect any producing environments unless they are very small. An international center attempting to produce technology for regions where national programs are weak will stress adaptability and concentrate on fewer targets.

There is little doubt that even within commodities the allocation of research funding by environmental region is far from optimal. Some dimensions of this can be seen in Table 5 which shows research-investment levels by geo-climate region. The international centers, particularly the one in Mexico, have attempted to respond to the failure of national programs to cover major environmental zones, but as a practical matter they cannot be expected to fully accomplish this task. Indeed, the problem in rice research is sufficiently important that

Table 5

Agricultural Research Investment by Geo-Climate Zone

Geo-climate Zone	Expenditures (millions 1971 $)			Number of Sub-regions	Expenditures (thousand 1971 $) per Geo-climate Sub-region		
	1959	1965	1971		1959	1965	1971
Tropical	62.6	135.2	217.0	65.37	977	2068	3319
Tropical Highlands	19.0	38.4	33.7	8.72	2176	4408	3806
Desert	13.7	27.3	35.0	23.94	571	1141	1464
Subtropical	67.0	147.8	244.0	24.18	2772	6114	10089
Pampean	48.7	90.8	145.4	45.30	10757	20044	32008
Mediterranean	100.8	159.4	265.3	75.74	1331	2110	3503
Marine	353.4	665.5	092.6	38.52	9174	17276	23431
Humid Continental	332.2	649.7	985.9	21.78	15250	29830	45266
Steepe	348.5	557.5	794.0	24.54	14201	22718	32359

	Scientist Man-Years per Geo-climate Sub-region			Standard Publications per Geo-climate Sub-region			
	1959	1965	1971	1951	1959	1965	1971
Tropical	52.6	100.0	180.2	9.0	12.4	18.4	21.6
Tropical Highlands	103.7	193.7	259.7	15.7	14.8	23.2	31.1
Desert	43.1	87.9	122.6	4.6	6.7	10.2	14.6
Subtropical	146.4	268.0	442.2	31.3	35.8	45.9	48.7
Pampean	370.2	595.1	947.9	92.9	100.0	106.6	81.7
Mediterranean	58.2	92.3	130.7	8.1	10.1	13.8	15.9
Marine	501.6	850.0	1133.2	45.1	62.2	92.6	111.5
Humid Continental	912.2	1558.7	2134.9	62.1	92.4	133.4	150.8
Steppe	581.6	1000.3	1307.9	51.8	88.0	129.1	153.5

Source: James Boyce and Robert E. Evenson. 1975. *Agricultural Research and Development Programs.* New York: Agricultural Development Council.

there is a justification for perhaps one or two more international centers. The differences between upland, shallow-water, and deep-water environments are so significant that these types of rice can be regarded as different commodities (see Table 3). It is unrealistic to expect one institution to function effectively in dealing with this much complexity.

SINGLE COMMODITY, MULTIPLE COMMODITY,
AND DISCIPLINE ORIENTATION

Two matters pertinent to the question of organizing research institutions along single commodity, multiple commodity, or mixed commodity discipline lines have been discussed briefly. The first was the choice between investing simply in technology-producing research programs and investing in more complex programs which seek both to discover technology and to create technology potential. The second was the environmental scope of the research institution. A third is the complementarity between production of scientific skills and research.

It is sensible for a national agricultural research program in its earliest developmental stage to concentrate its resources on projects having the highest payoff. Given the scarcity of high-level scientific skills, it is natural that research programs be oriented to the exploitation of existing technology potential. In this early stage, no substantial capacity to create new technology potential exists and the system might be termed a *simple adaptive* system.

As resources are expanded and experience is gained in the management of research programs, the development of the capacity to create technology potential becomes feasible. The incentive structures facing most less-developed countries, however, have retarded the development of a technology-potential capability and have led instead to an expansion of the simple adaptive system. The adverse effects have been due to:

(1) The heavy reliance of national research programs on international aid and developed-country institutions for scientific-skill production.

(2) The policy milieu supported by international agencies which admonishes the national programs to concentrate on simple adaptive research—and, correspondingly, has not aggressively supported the building of research institutions capable of creating technology potential.

(3) The role of the international centers in providing technology potential to the national programs.

(4) The disrupted skills' markets which make the building of technology-potential capacity difficult.

In the simple adaptive stage, there are relatively few economies of association across commodities, but such economies are potentially important across disciplines. At the same time there are good reasons to pursue a fairly large number of environmental targets in simple adaptive systems. These incentives lead to a system with small single-commodity experiment stations. Provided that technology potential is maintained, these simple adaptive systems can be productive and can make good use of low-level skills.

This model of research-system development is fairly prevalent in many poor countries. India, for example, had developed more than 500 experiment stations by about 1960. The major problem with simple adaptive programs is that some means of delivering technology potential to them must be available to make them productive. The failure of many national programs to build the capacity to deliver technology potential has reduced the productivity of these simple adaptive systems. The international agricultural research centers have delivered technology potential to these systems in rice and wheat and possibly maize but one should recognize their limitations in this respect.

At the international-center level, the single-commodity model also makes sense, given the complexity of dealing with the broad range of producing environments and the concern both with producing technology for them and delivering technology potential to them (this latter concern has not been stressed enough, however). Given these objectives, it makes sense to stress the economies of association across disciplines.

Investment in systems capable of producing technology potential leads generally to a hierarchy of central and branch experiment stations. The central experiment stations concentrate on the technology potential and, generally, find the disciplinary focus most productive. The critical aspect of organization to produce technology potential is the juxtaposition of commodity-oriented research programs and scientific-discipline orientation. The history of technology in many fields indicates that technology search conducted in isolation from organized scientific disciplines is subject to exhaustion. It also indicates that scientific research conducted in isolation from technology search is unproductive in that its "products" are often not valuable in terms of creating technology potential.

The federal-state agricultural experiment station research organizations in the United States represent one model of integration of technology research and scientific disciplinary research. This model suggests that the central experiment stations will find that a multicommodity focus with a disciplinary organization will be most productive. These experiment stations will also be subject to economies of scale. But the overriding factor in the productivity of such stations will probably be the extent to which a genuine scientific and technological frontier exists and is maintained by the scientists in the system.

It may be argued that it is unrealistic to develop these sophisticated agricultural research programs in low-income countries. Such systems are costly and demand skilled personnel. Many efforts to develop sophisticated research programs have failed because of the difficulty of maintaining skills. However, the case for investment in building such systems becomes quite feasible when the costs of importing skills via graduate training abroad and the complementarities between graduate training and scientific research are considered. The development of first-rate research and graduate-training centers in the developing countries is costly, to be sure, but the strategy of importing these skills is probably even more so.

NATIONAL AND INTERNATIONAL CENTER RELATIONSHIPS

The current advantages of the international centers are derived partly from the limitations of national systems and in part from the comparative advantages of these centers. In a setting where national research programs have not developed the capacity to pursue adaptive research, an international center will be able to produce technology suited to some of the neglected environments. For wheat and rice, the international centers in Mexico and the Philippines have, by reason of their genetic resources and systematic breeding programs, exploited technology potential developed partially in temperate-zone conditions, and they have been able to provide new technology of great economic value to some of the producing regions of the developing world.

One of the lessons to be derived from the wheat and rice experience surely is that a concentrated program of crop improvement by highly qualified scientists can quickly exploit scientific potential. But other lessons are there as well. The creation by the international centers in Mexico and the Philippines of technology potential for a number of national research programs has been a very important part of their total contribution. Most of the modern varieties of wheat and rice are what might be called joint products of the two international centers and national programs, for genetic material from the former was used in national breeding programs to produce location-specific varieties.

The role of the international centers is to some degree illustrated in Table 6 which reports measures of research-induced shifts in Asian rice-supply functions associated with rice research. The table portrays the extraordinary gains associated with the Green Revolution after 1966. It also shows that the poorly organized national research programs were producing some supply shifts prior to 1966. These supply shifts were of sufficient size to yield an internal rate of return to national rice-program investment of 39% in the pre-1966 period.

The really significant aspect evident in the table is not, however, that the investment in the International Rice Research Institute produced a major impact (84% internal rate of return), but rather that it made the national programs in rice more productive. The internal

Table 6

Estimated Annual Supply Function Shifts
Attributable to Rice Research Programs
(annual shifts expressed in percentage units)

	1959–60	1961–65	1966–71	1972–75
Attributable to national plant breeding and agronomy research	.093	.151	.461	.284
Attributable to national related agricultural science research	.137	.212	.459	.423
Attributable to high-yield varieties developed at International Rice Research Institute	—	—	.419	.387
Attributable to high-yield varieties developed independently in national programs	—	—	.066	.182
Attributable to high-yield varieties developed in national programs, but having one parent from the International Rice Research Institute	—	—	.122	.161
Total shift due to research*	.157	.319	1.528	1.430

Source: Adapted from the "low" estimates reported in table 9 of "Costs and Returns to Rice Research," by Robert E. Evenson, P. M. Flores, and Yujiro Hayami. Resource Paper no. 11 for the Conference on Economic Consequences of New Rice Technology in Asia. Los Baños, Philippines: International Rice Research Institute, 1977.

* The contribution of research occurs partly in countries other than the country doing the research. Hence, the total supply shift is not the sum of the parts.

rate of return to national program investment rose to 74% in the 1965–75 period and national programs contributed the bulk of the Green Revolution shifts.

In my judgment the programming of most of the centers is somewhat misplaced at present. The opportunity to repeat the wheat and rice experience is just not there for most other crops. The experience with maize demonstrates the powerful limits placed on international programs by genotype environment interactions. For few other commodities is there available a backlog of research work such as existed in developed countries for wheat and rice (sorghum and barley are, however, possible candidates). For the most part, other major commodities of concern to the centers and to national programs are what I have termed "neglected" commodities. The root crops, pulses, and other tropical crops have generally not gone through the groundwork stage of germ plasm collection and classification and physiology and pathology studies.

I would argue that, for the short term, the most important comparative advantage of the international agricultural research centers is in the explicit pursuit of groundwork research on neglected crops. This is, of course, being done in a number of them. What I am suggesting here is that groundwork research be more clearly and explicitly taken as an objective of the international centers. Furthermore, I would argue that the international system should carefully examine the options for initiating work on more commodities and that their staffing and programming should be organized accordingly. For some of the neglected commodities I would also urge explorations of ways to design research programs which can be undertaken by the strongest national research programs.

This groundwork research is part of the more general comparative advantage that the international research centers have in producing technology potential. This comparative advantage also extends to the production of technology potential in the more mature research fields. Here we see little aggressive action by the international centers. It may be that a single-commodity institution with "worldwide" concerns is not capable of either doing or inducing the basic work to create new technology potential. More complex organizations may be required. Nonetheless, the international centers could provide substantially more guidance in terms of inducing work in other institutions than they do at present. The history of the U.S. agricultural experiment stations would indicate, however, that it is not until a substantial period of exhaustion has set in that institutional change in the form of efforts to develop technology potential takes place. It would be very useful if the policy makers in the international system were able to short-cut this historical process.

It now is quite clear that there are further comparative advantages to an international center in terms of the collection and classification of genetic resources and their systematic dissemination. This extends to other forms of knowledge as well. These centers can perform a valuable service in facilitating exchange of relevant scientific materials. They are also emerging as centers for crossing, screening, and testing of plant materials for different environmental targets.

The international agricultural research center then has a place in the scheme of things even as national programs develop more highly. One area where such centers can make a major contribution in terms of contributing to the efficient design of commodity-research programs is in the development of a systematic classification of producing environments, by commodity. Such a classification, with an appropriate mapping, would enable the identification of neglected environments and neglected commodities with more clarity. It would also allow for more systematic environmental targeting of international genetic material.

PROSPECTS FOR MORE AGGRESSIVE RESEARCH-PROGRAM DEVELOPMENT

The study Boyce and I made, and to which I have referred at several points in this paper, is the only source of comprehensive data on international agricultural research investment. The fact that no international agency has seen fit to compile more complete and systematic data reflects the low priority given to research program development. In the introduction to this paper I indicated that the prognosis for aggressive support for building more effective research programs in most of the developing countries was not good. I also raised the possibility that international aid funding would not be utilized to aid major national program development but would instead be utilized to maintain the present system of international centers. I will discuss these matters more fully in my concluding section.

For purposes of this discussion, it will be useful to characterize alternative research program-development sequences. These sequences have a fair amount of historical validity and permit distinctions between different groups of countries.

The "Pioneering" Stage of Institution Development

In the earliest stage of developing research institutions very few well-trained scientists are available to the system. Those that are available are often burdened with administrative and organizational tasks. Scientific skills are quickly lost as the incentives and opportunities for maintaining them do not exist. National governments are seldom willing to commit scarce resources to experiment-station development in this stage and certainly do not commit resources to support graduate study. It is quite critical that international aid agencies support this pioneering phase and enable the beginnings of scientific professional development so that an awareness of the contribution that research programs can make emerges within the public decision-making process.

At the beginning of the post-World War II development period, only a handful of the contemporary developing countries had passed through this phase. The Boyce-Evenson data suggest that in Latin America Brazil, Colombia, Mexico, and possibly Venezuela had done so. In Africa only the United Arab Republic and possibly Nigeria had emerged from the pioneering stage; in Asia, Turkey, India, and possibly Malaysia, the Philippines, Taiwan, and South Korea had come through it. Many of today's developing countries have now done so and most have had substantial aid funding and aid stimulus which has enabled them to do so. But the record is far from good. Even today Paraguay and Bolivia in South America, several countries in Central America, most of the newer African nations, and Afghanistan, Nepal, Burma, and much of Indochina are probably still in this early stage.

The Simple Adaptive System Stage

In the simple adaptive stage a systematic building of simple adaptive research institutions takes place. Developing countries depend heavily on aid resources for buildings and equipment and for advanced graduate training. In the later phases of this stage some capacity for graduate training may exist, but virtually all training at the doctoral level takes place in developed countries and is supported by international aid. Research stations begin to emerge and proliferate in this stage as a serious effort is made to expand the system under the constraint of low skill levels among scientists. Many of the scientists with advanced training are, however, able to make very significant contributions at this time and even though many of the research stations are isolated and weak from a scientific point of view, they can be highly productive by exploiting some locally available technology potential.

The Advanced Adaptive System Stage

In the advanced adaptive stage a few research institutions emerge as main research stations with a responsibility for feeding technology potential to "branch" stations which are in the simple adaptive stage. The main stations have a limited capacity to aid dependent stations because the development of technology-potential capacity is extremely demanding. Developing such potential requires not only financial and technical aid but also very strong indigenous entrepreneurship and national financial support. During this stage a host of problems centering on the nature of the market for skills tends to emerge. These problems, along with basic limitations in aid support mechanisms, make it extremely difficult for countries to move into the next stage.

The Technology-Potential Capacity Stage

The technology-potential capacity stage is relatively advanced and for practical purposes no developing country has yet achieved it. Some formerly poor countries (Israel, South Korea, Taiwan, and Brazil) have probably reached the early phases of this stage, but one has to be impressed with the apparent difficulties of moving beyond the simple and the advanced adaptive stages. This technology-potential stage requires the development of genuine research frontiers and strong professional orientation of scientists, as well as an administrative and organizational structure to orient the scientists toward the solution of real problems. In practice it is associated with the development of capacity to provide strong graduate training at the doctoral level.

The Boyce-Evenson data, as noted, indicate that a number of countries have not yet moved beyond the pioneering stage in their development. Since aid agencies play a dominant role in this early stage there is substantial cause for critical comment here. Surely there is strong economic justification for aggressive support to bring virtually every country in the world through at least this developmental stage. International agencies have had much valuable experience in aiding other developing countries to achieve this stage and should not find it difficult to support the remaining countries so they can attain it.

It is difficult to say how many developing countries have managed to move beyond the simple adaptive stage into the advanced adaptive stage. It would appear that Mexico and Colombia and possibly Chile and Venezuela have reached the advanced adaptive stage in Latin America. In Africa, Kenya, Nigeria, and the United Arab Republic have probably also reached this stage. In Asia, Taiwan and South Korea and to a somewhat lesser extent, Malaysia, the Philippines, and Thailand have made progress. India and Pakistan have also developed relatively advanced research systems.

It is, of course, true that aid agencies have contributed in a major way to the progress made in most of these developing countries. If I am critical of international agencies for not developing more aggressive support mechanisms, I am implicitly criticizing national governments as well. I do not, however, find the overall record of support by international agencies to be consistent with the very substantial evidence that has emerged measuring research productivity. Surely the extraordinarily high rates of return indicated for research investment, even if discounted heavily, have called for far more aggressive programs in this area than have actually been undertaken.

As I have already noted, the supporters of the international centers argue that aid agencies have a very limited interest in funding research programs and that the flow of funds to the building of the international centers represented no significant diversion from funding of national programs. I believe it reasonable to conclude that some diversion of funding and entrepreneurship did occur. However, this diversion, even if quite substantial, does not fully explain the failure to develop more aggressive programs. One has to turn to two other factors for further insight into this question. The first is the relationship between the supply of scientific skills and research institution development. The second is the skill requirements for effective support.

National governments have relied so heavily on international aid for support of graduate training that they have lagged in developing indigenous capacity to produce scientific skills. The development of an advanced research program requires, for most larger countries, substantial numbers of trained scientists. In addition to the demand from the scientific system itself there is often a demand for scientists to serve in administrative and planning roles. As the costs of importing skills via graduate studies abroad rise the constraints on institution building become more severe. This problem is then further exacerbated by a phasing out of international support for graduate study.

To some extent this problem is part of the more general problem of achieving or inducing a transition from international aid support to a strictly indigenous institutional program. This is not an easy transition but it is, in the end, one that must be made. Many institutions in the developing countries have been so dependent on a donor agency that they have not developed indigenous leadership and entrepreneurship or a capacity for self-determination.

The matter of the capacity of international agencies to provide real technical support in the more advanced institutional-development stages is also a real one. The achievement of outstanding research institutions in developed countries requires strong influential and leadership abilities. Many of the institution-building programs of the 1950s and 1960s in developing countries were frustrated by problems associated with the lack of strong local entrepreneurial capacity. Today, however, it appears that in a set of selected institutions throughout the developing world a significant entrepreneurial capacity exists. The external support of national programs relying on indigenous entrepreneurship now represents a very realistic approach on the part of donor agencies. The World Bank in its operations has already substantially funded development of agricultural research programs in a number of countries and these efforts to date appear to have been quite successful. Other development agencies could well begin to introduce loans for building and equipping laboratories.

Recent expansion of general international programs directed toward agricultural development has been significant even though it has had little direct impact on research-system development (Kriesberg 1977). The recent World Food and Nutrition Study (National Academy of Sciences 1977) reports a well-reasoned set of recommendations calling for the United States to support research more aggressively. As these initiatives are developed further we may see significant new programs for research support. I have not been encouraged by developments to date but do not wish to be heavily pessimistic.

A number of institution-support programs modeled somewhat after the institution-building efforts of the U.S. Agency for International Development in the 1950s and early 1960s will probably be undertaken (Committee on Institutional Cooperation 1968). They will serve to bring many more institutions and systems into the simple adaptive stage and will enable others to move into the advanced adaptive stage. Such programs will generally have relatively high payoffs and should be pursued aggressively. I would argue, however, that a specific program designed to enable a few agricultural research and graduate teaching centers to develop as strong graduate teaching centers would have a very high payoff. More importantly, it would allow more rapid and effective development of adaptive systems.

NOTE

1. The index is constructed as: $I = 1 - \sum_i (C_i - R_i)^2$ where C_i and R_i are the shares of the ith commodity in total agricultural product and total agricultural research, respectively. Thus an index of one means a perfect association between the research mix and the commodity mix.

REFERENCES

Arndt, Thomas M.; Dalrymple, Dana G.; and Ruttan, Vernon W., Eds. 1977. *Resource Allocation and Productivity in National and International Agricultural Research.* Minneapolis: University of Minnesota Press.

Boyce, James, and Evenson, Robert E. 1975. *Agricultural Research and Development Programs.* New York: Agricultural Development Council.

Committee on Institutional Cooperation. 1968. *Building Institutions to Serve Agriculture: A Summary Report of the C.I.C.–AID Rural Development Research Project.* Lafayette, Indiana: Purdue University.

Evenson, Robert E. 1968. "The Contribution of Agricultural Research and Extension to Agricultural Production." Ph.D. dissertation, University of Chicago.

——. 1977. "Cycles in Research Productivity in Sugarcane, Wheat, and Rice." In *Resource Allocation and Productivity in National and International Agricultural Research*, ed. Thomas M. Arndt et al., pp.209–36. Minneapolis: University of Minnesota Press.

Evenson, Robert E.; Flores, P. M.; and Hayami, Yujiro. 1977. "Costs and Returns to Rice Research." Resource Paper no. 11 for the Conference on Economic Consequences of New Rice Technology. Los Baños, Philippines: International Rice Research Institute.

Evenson, Robert E., and Welch, Finis. 1974. "Research, Information and Agricultural Productivity." Preliminary draft of book manuscript, 1974.

Kriesberg, Martin. 1977. *International Organizations and Agricultural Development* FAER no. 131. Washington, D.C.: Economic Research Service, U.S. Department of Agriculture.

National Academy of Sciences. 1977. *World Food and Nutrition Study*. Washington, D.C.

COMMENT

VERNON W. RUTTAN

In this note I comment on three issues on which economists have made only marginal contributions and on which decision making is burdened both by thick clouds of obscurity and by the strong winds of political interest.

I start this inquiry with an assumption that the major differences in grain yield among countries and regions today are the result of investments in inputs whose productivity has been enhanced by advances in knowledge that are embodied in investment in physical and institutional infrastructures, new and more productive material inputs, and in the formal and nonformal education of rural people. A hundred years ago there were few places in the world where grain yields were significantly greater than one metric ton per hectare. Since that time, differences in output per hectare and output per worker in agriculture have widened (Yamada and Ruttan 1975). These differences have not been due to changes in physical resource endowments. Rather they are due to the technical and institutional innovations and the investments that have improved the capacity of land and labor to respond to the technical and institutional opportunities that became available.

Yet, we possess little formal knowledge with respect to the economics of location, scale, and organization in agricultural research that is helpful in decision making at the individual experiment station or research-center level or at the national or international research-system level.

THE LOCATION OF AGRICULTURAL
RESEARCH STATIONS

The literature on the location of agricultural research stations is extremely limited. Little attempt has been made to distinguish those location elements which contribute to efficiency in the supply of knowledge or technology and those which operate on the demand side to enhance the impact of new knowledge and technology on production.

A *supply-side argument* for the location of agricultural research facilities has been made by Peter Jennings in two seminal articles. He has argued that the optimum location for genetic evaluation and

246

utilization research is at or near the geographic center of origin of each particular crop (Jennings 1974; Jennings and Cock, in press). Jennings and Cock argue that the coevolution of biological restraints with the particular crop in the area of origin implies that in crop improvement work it is important to subject the improved varieties to the biological stress that exists in such locations to assure that they will exhibit minimal inherent weakness in their response to biological or biochemical stress. Jennings and Cock also argue that a technology that is productive in the center of origin can then be more successfully introduced where there is less biological stress on the new cultivar. If, on the other hand, an institute is located outside the center of origin, local development may be very rapid, but the transferability of the technology will be limited. Jennings and Cock contend that incomplete technological packages developed at the center of origin may have a much more dramatic impact on crop yields outside the center than in or near the center of origin. They point to the dramatic differences in the impact of the new rice varieties in Colombia and in Southeast Asia as an example. Although they do not explicitly mention considerations of soil quality, temperature, and related factors, I assume they would view these as micro-location factors within the area of origin.

We also have a somewhat different supply-side argument from Theodore W. Schultz to the effect that "the comparative advantage of an agricultural experiment station associated with a major research oriented university is clearly large" (Schultz 1971, p.114). The insistence by Schultz on a symbiotic relationship between research and training is related to my own observations on the "natural history" of research institutes. A new institute is often able to bring together a team of leading scientific talents that tends to experience a period of high productivity, often lasting for several decades. However, there is a tendency, after an initial period of creativity, for an institute to settle down to filling in the gaps in the literature. One protection against this process of natural aging is an environment which facilitates interaction with both trainees or graduate students and colleagues in related disciplines.

A somewhat similar argument has been made by Albert H. Moseman (1970) with respect to the location of genetic-resources centers. Moseman insists that if genetic-resources centers are to make productive contributions to the development of biological technology they must be institutionalized in locations which are conducting strong plant-breeding and genetics-research programs. Financial commitments to the maintenance of genetics-resource "archives" will face continuous erosion unless the archives are seen as contributing in a very direct way to biological technology-development programs. Moseman also cautions against an uncritical acceptance of the center-of-origin location model. He insists that "while it is important to consider the biological stresses that exist in such centers of origin, the major part of the research must be conducted in the different regions where the crop is to be produced—where the diseases, insects, temperature, soil, water, and other environmental factors affect the plant characteristics required."[*]

A *demand-side location argument* is implicit in the early work by Zvi Griliches (1957) on the diffusion of hybrid corn. Following the initial basic research, both public and private research and development efforts in the United States were most heavily concentrated in those areas where the size and density of the hybrid-seed market were greatest. The location of research effort by both the state agricultural experiment stations and the private seed companies appeared to be explained by a model in which the cost of research, development, and marketing per unit of hybrid seed sold would be minimized. In many countries public intervention in the seed-marketing system has distorted the impact of demand on the location and investment in seed improvement by the private sector genetic-supply industry.

When one considers both the supply-side and the demand-side factors bearing on the location of agricultural research institutions one seems driven toward the development of a system of international, national, and private-sector research centers in which a major internationally supported research institute located at a crop's center of origin plays a key role in the production of generalized genetic technology. This international center needs to have effective linkages for the transfer of knowledge and materials with environmentally specific and market- or demand-oriented systems of public-sector national research centers and with the private-sector genetic-supply industry.

One issue that this formulation does not deal with effectively is the location and intensity of research efforts in areas where neither the supply-side nor the demand-side criteria appear operative. The location of forage-improvement efforts by the International Center for Tropical Agriculture in the Colombian *llanos* represents a case in point. The problem soils of the *llanos* are characteristic of an area of perhaps 300 million hectares of low-density forage and livestock production and human population in the South American tropics. What criteria can one employ in deciding the location or intensity of research to improve the potential productivity under such circumstances?

---

[*] Albert H. Moseman 1977: personal communication.

The actual decision-making process with respect to the location of agricultural research institutions typically bears little relationship to the answers that would be turned up by a simultaneous solution to the demand and supply relationships suggested above. Not more than half of the new international centers are optimally located. Within national systems, nonagricultural considerations associated with employment and income generation at politically sensitive locations in the district or in the home state of a strategic member of the legislature or of the administration in power, for example, are often of dominant importance. To effectively counter such impulses, it is clear that more attention must be given to the development of a body of knowledge with respect to the location of individual units in national and international research systems.

SCALE AND PRODUCTIVITY
IN AGRICULTURAL RESEARCH

We have even less solid evidence on the relationship between scale (or size) and productivity in agricultural research than on the issue of location. And what we do have, even in the way of casual observation, often lacks precision with respect to whether the size–output relationship being referred to is that of the individual research unit (team, laboratory, department), the individual research institution (center, institute, faculty), or the national or international research system. The view that small is better was advanced with considerable heat, but with relatively little precision in concept or definition and with little empirical evidence, by some of the participants at a University of Minnesota conference on "Transforming Knowledge into Food in a World-Wide Context" in April, 1977.

The optimum scale of the research is affected by factors both external and internal to the research process. The optimum scale of a commodity-research program is, as noted earlier in the discussion of hybrid corn and as demonstrated more rigorously by Binswanger (1978), positively related to the area planted to the commodity. Determining the optimum scale of a research unit or program therefore involves balancing the increasing returns associated with the area devoted to the commodity (or problem) on which the research is being conducted against the possible internal diseconomies of scale of the research process or system. In this section I consider primarily the issue of internal factors which affect scale economies and size of the research unit or system.

In the field of industrial research and development we do have the evidence assembled and summarized by Schmookler (1966) and by

Kamien and Schwartz (1975) which indicates that industrial research and development productivity, measured in terms of patents per engineering or scientific worker, is lower in the large laboratories of the largest firms than in smaller firms in the same industry. Similar evidence has been presented by Pound and Waggoner (1972) for agricultural research. There are also case studies which suggest very high rates of return to individual public, philanthropic, and private-sector research units often having fewer than twenty scientific or technical staff per unit (Evenson 1977; Sehgal 1977). Many of the smaller "free-standing" agricultural research units are, however, engaged primarily in "genetic engineering" or in technology screening, adaptation, and transfer activities which depend only minimally on in-house capacity in such supporting areas as physiology, pathology, chemistry, or even modern genetics.

Evenson has also pointed out that during the early stages in the development of national research systems, experiment stations tend to be widely diffused; to utilize primarily technical and engineering skills, and to be commodity-oriented (1977, pp.240–44). He also points to a trend toward hierarchical organization and to consolidation into a smaller number of larger units at later stages in the development of agricultural research systems. These trends are apparently in part motivated to take advantage of mission-oriented inputs of knowledge by the basic and supporting sciences and from scale-related services in communications and facilities.

The implication is that it is not sufficient to focus attention on the economies of scale in the individual free-standing research station or laboratory or on the individual units of hierarchically integrated or horizontally interrelated systems. Nor is it adequate to focus on economies of scale within individual national systems. Evenson has also shown that the capacity of a national agricultural research system to borrow effectively from research conducted elsewhere is related to its own capacity in the supporting and basic sciences as well as in applied science.

It seems apparent that very little can be said about scale economies or optimum size of individual research units in the absence of a more adequate understanding of the effects of the size, structure, organization, and administration of the national and international research systems to which the individual unit is related.

THE ORGANIZATION AND STRUCTURE
OF AGRICULTURAL RESEARCH

The appropriate organization and structure of single experiment stations or of national and international agricultural research systems is another area in which formal knowledge is in short supply, in contrast to folklore and insight arising out of administrative experience.

Almost all university-based agricultural research and much of the work in national agricultural research systems is organized within discipline-based units. This is, however, a relatively recent development. During the period when research in agriculture was struggling to establish its legitimacy as a field of scientific inquiry, departments or faculties of agriculture were typically organized as multidisciplinary administrative units. Even the initial administrative decentralization typically involved organization in multidisciplinary units (field crops, horticulture, animal husbandry, agronomy, farm management). In the U.S. Department of Agriculture the emergence of a viable pattern of organization toward the end of the nineteenth century involved the organization of scientific bureaus focusing on a particular set of problems or commodities. For example, as Dupree (1957) concluded, "The Bureau of Animal Industry thus had most of the attributes of the new scientific agency at its birth—an organic act—a set of problems, outside groups pressing for its interests, and extensive regulatory powers" (p.165). In the United States both the U.S. Department of Agriculture's national research system and the university-based state systems evolved a structure that includes some units that tend to be single discipline (agricultural economics, plant pathology, soil science) and others which retain a broader multidisciplinary base (agronomy, animal science, horticulture).

In the university-based state systems this structure had become established by the 1920s. Very little change in structure has occurred since that time except a tendency in the 1960s for mergers of departments devoted to particular animal sciences or crop sciences. Once this structure had become established there was very little resource reallocation among the disciplinary and commodity groups (Peterson 1969). The U.S.D.A. research system has gone through a number of reorganizations since the establishment of the research-bureau pattern of organization. I am not aware of any definitive study of trends in the allocation of resources by disciplines or commodities but it would not seem unreasonable to hypothesize that the allocation of resources to the major commodities and disciplines has been relatively stable. It also seems reasonable to hypothesize that the greatest opportunities for research-resource reallocation have been within the disciplinary or commodity units. I have in mind, for example, the greater concern in recent years by soils units with nitrogen pollution and entomology units with integrated pest control, the renewed emphasis in agronomy departments on nitrogen fixation, and the shift of resources in agricultural economics departments to work in resource economics and on rural development problems. It is hard to escape a conclusion: The concept of parity is the dominant principal employed in research-resource allocation.

The aging process at the new international system does not yet appear to have imposed the same degree of structural rigidity that one observes in the U.S. and perhaps in other more mature national systems. The original institutes were organized as multidisciplinary crop research institutes (wheat, maize, rice). In recent years the resources devoted to research on animals, relative to crops, have increased. Within the crops area, research on cropping or farming systems has risen relative to research on individual commodities. (Consultative Group on International Agricultural Research Secretariat 1977a, 1977b). Within several of the international agricultural research institutes, the International Rice Research Institute for example, a dual system of organization employing both disciplinary and problem orientation has been introduced in a deliberate effort to resist the hardening of arteries around particular disciplinary or problem sets.

In both national and international systems, growth appears to have been a major factor which has supplied the lubrication necessary to avoid declining productivity of the older national systems. There are some indications that rates of return in at least some mature systems are beginning to decline (Peterson and Fitzharris 1977). As yet we do not know whether such apparent declining marginal productivity reflects an approaching exhaustion of technological potential or is a function of the structural deficiencies of mature research systems.

REFERENCES

Binswanger, Hans P. 1978. "The Microeconomics of Induced Technical Change." Chapter 4 of *Induced Innovation: Technology, Institutions and Development*, by Hans P. Binswanger and Vernon W. Ruttan. Baltimore: Johns Hopkins Press.

Consultative Group on International Agricultural Research Secretariat. 1977a. "The Consultative Group and the International Agricultural Research System: An Integrative Report." Washington, D.C.: World Bank.

————. 1977b. "Statistics on Expenditure by International Agricultural Research Centers, 1960–1980." Washington, D.C.: World Bank.

Dupree, A. Hunter. 1957. *Science in the Federal Government: A History of Policies and Activities to 1940*. Cambridge: Harvard University Press.

Evenson, Robert E. 1977. "Comparative Evidence on Returns to Investment in National and International Research Institutions." In *Resource Allocation and Productivity in National and International Agricultural Research*, edited by Thomas M. Arndt et al., pp. 237–64. Minneapolis: University of Minnesota Press.

Griliches, Zvi. 1957. "Hybrid Corn: An Exploration in the Economics of Technological Change." *Econometrica* 25 (October):501–22.

Jennings, Peter R. 1974. "Rice Breeding and World Food Production." *Science* 186 (December 20):1085–88.

Jennings, Peter R., and Cock, James H. In press. "Centers of Origin of Crops and their Productivity." *Economic Botany.*

Kamien, Morton I., and Schwartz, Nancy L. 1975. "Market Structure and Innovation: A Survey." *Journal of Economic Literature* 13 (March):1–37.

Moseman, Albert H. 1970. *Building Agricultural Research Systems in the Developing Nations.* New York: The Agricultural Development Council, Inc.

Peterson, Willis. 1969. "The Allocation of Research, Teaching and Extension Personnel in U.S. Colleges of Agriculture." *American Journal of Agricultural Economics* 51 (February):41–56.

Peterson, Willis, and Fitzharris, Joseph C. 1977. "Organization and Productivity of the Federal-State Research System in the United States." In *Resource Allocation and Productivity in National and International Agricultural Research,* ed. Thomas M. Arndt et al., pp.60–85. Minneapolis: University of Minnesota Press.

Pound, G. S., and Waggoner, Paul E. 1972. "Comparative Efficiency, as Measured by Publication Performance of USDA and SAES Entomologists and Plant Pathologists." In *Report of the Committee on Research Advisory to the U.S. Department of Agriculture,* G. S. Pound et al., pp. 145–70. Washington, D.C.: National Academy of Sciences.

Schmookler, Jacob. 1966. *Invention and Economic Growth.* Cambridge: Harvard University Press.

Schultz, Theodore W. 1971. "The Allocation of Resources to Research." In *Resource Allocation in Agricultural Research,* ed. Walter L. Fishel, pp.90–120. Minneapolis: University of Minnesota Press.

Sehgal, S. M. 1977. "Private Sector International Agricultural Research: The Genetic Supply Industry." In *Resource Allocation and Productivity in National and International Agricultural Research,* ed. Thomas M. Arndt et al., pp.404–15. Minneapolis: University of Minnesota Press.

Yamada, Saburo, and Ruttan, Vernon W. 1975. "International Comparisons of Productivity in Agriculture." Paper presented at National Bureau of Economic Research Conference on Productivity Measurement, Williamsburg, Virginia, November 13–14, 1975.

COMMENT

PAUL E. WAGGONER

"Where are you stationed?" asked an employee of a research organization with offices in fifty states. He questioned me at a scientific meeting a quarter century after my discharge from the Army, and his transitive use of "stationed," with me as the object, told me all I needed to know about large-scale research organizations. Nevertheless, I shall speak more of scale and even go on to incentives.

Is bigger better? Saying, as I do, that a bigger is not a better research organization swims against the American stream, particularly after an army of managers and engineers put a man on the moon on schedule. Since my thesis concerns research for discovery, however, and not engineering, let us look at data on discovery from agricultural research.

First, I must admit that a laboratory for discovery can be too small. Pound and Waggoner (1972) counted in the *Annual Review of Entomology* the citations to research by 167 entomologists at state agricultural experiment stations, by 23 at branches of the state stations, by 40 at the main Beltsville [Maryland] Laboratory of the Agricultural Research Service, and by 69 at their Service's branch stations. The scientists both at the main state stations and at the main station in Beltsville garnered about seven citations each whereas the scientists at the branches of both garnered only two to three. Clearly the branch stations are too small for advancing the frontiers of science.

More important, however, is whether the size of the organization or laboratory staff, in a range of 30 to 600, affects the output and impact of agricultural scientists. I have examined output by tabulating the publications, manpower, and budgets of 53 state agricultural experiment stations, as reported in 1976 by the Cooperative State Research Service. The number of scientists ranges from the 14 at the Alaska station to 528 at the Illinois station. Three stations published nothing, and one published 1,720 articles and bulletins in 1976.

Since scientists work to provide theories, methods, data, or insight, their output can be measured as articles that they feel might merit publication for all to read. When I attempted to relate the number of publications per scientist to the number of scientists working at each station, that is, its scale, I found the remarkably low correlation coefficient of .01. Undaunted, I related the cost of a publication to the number of scientists at each station and found a larger but still insignificant r of 0.16. My evidence that size did not increase output was not surprising since it confirmed a similar study of 1966–70 at the state stations (Horsfall et al. 1975). So much for sheer output.

Impact is the reason research is supported by society. Growth of knowledge is worthwhile, and I measured the impact of scientists' work by the frequency of its acknowledged use by other scientists as shown in *Science Citation Index* 1976.

A sample of scientists was drawn from a directory of soil scientists employed at the state experiment stations (U.S. Dept. of Agriculture, Cooperative State Research Service 1977). I selected a single discipline because the frequency of citation may vary among disciplines, and I selected soil science because, outside of the large Agricultural Research Service, American soil scientists are largely in the state stations. For a still more homogeneous sample I drew from "full" professors or the equivalent, omitting staff of adjunct, emeritus, and other modified status. One name was drawn at random from the appropriate department of each of the forty-six state agricultural stations in the continental United States that have professors of soil science.

The size of the department was the number of people of all ranks in the departments, excluding people with addresses outside the main location. The number of professors included emeriti since they presumably can provide counsel to a scientist. The number of teaching staff at the entire institution (usually a university) was obtained for 1970–71 (American Council of Education 1973).

The correlation coefficients for citations as a function of the variables were department size, .32; number of professors, .35; teaching staff at the entire institution, .07.

Although two correlation coefficients are statistically significant, the closest correlation explains only 12% of the variability in citations. The significant correlations are produced by one effective scientist in a large agronomy department. Transforming the observations to logarithms did not increase the correlation. I conclude that among the state agricultural stations group size scarcely affects the impact of a soil scientist's work.

Scale fails to affect impact in another field. Important therapeutic advances per dollar are not related to the size of the 4 to 16 million dollar budgets of laboratories of the pharmaceutical industry (Koenig and Gans 1975).

The lack of economies of scale in the lonely vocation of discovery is understandable. In a *New York Times* story, "Think Tanks Have Sprung a Leak," Holsendolph (1977) wrote: "The . . . mistake is allowing work groups to get too large. 'Big is bad.' The spirit of the small group is better, and the work is harder." And in an *Encyclopaedia Britannica* article on applied psychology, available to every high school student, Viteles (1965) wrote of the experiments at a factory in Hawthorne, Illinois, 1927–32: "Of particular significance is the influence . . . of a small informal organization which develops spontaneously as a function of the work situation." That brings me to incentives.

How to hold the carrot. Although curiosity is a powerful incentive and some scientists will work without a patron, money is a carrot of incentive, too. Curiosity belongs to the scientist while the money belongs to the patron. Nowadays the taxpayer is the usual patron, and congressmen, administrators, and curious scientists each want to be surrogate patrons. How will each surrogate hold the carrot?

The U.S. Congress may believe that an agricultural problem can be mitigated by research. Although their belief may be warmed by a scientist, the heat upon the legislature probably comes from society in general and without much regard for the researchability of the problem. The legislature then "earmarks" money for just that problem, be it marketing, pesticides, or cotton.

An immediate administrator of an institution for research, like a director of a state agricultural experiment station, may have a foundling problem dumped upon his doorstep. Since he is a scientist and has other scientists at hand, he can consider the researchability of the problem, and he will also consider the talents of his staff and his ability to cajole them into enthusiasm. But he can't forget the crying at the door of his organization. If the foundling seems promising, the administrator will then devote some of the organization's "hard" money to it. This is surely the source of many of the projects at stations.

An individual scientist may perceive a problem where a discovery is likely to reward his efforts. Although he reads the newspapers and knows society's needs, his ideas likely come from the proceedings of his professional society which evoke his enthusiasm. Since he will generally be on a payroll, he may turn to his employer for patronage for the pursuit of his problem. Some station projects arise this way. Since many of his ideas do come from the proceedings of his profession, however, he will be eager to turn to a panel of his professional peers, asking for a grant. The peers judge the proposal upon its researchability or professional merits, and the individual may win cash that will be *his*, both a recognition by his profession and a means to pursue his idea. Grants of the National Science Foundation sort are popular with individual scientists.

What is the outcome of these three ways of holding the financial incentive? Earmarking creates a seller's market, and I was not surprised, for example, to find funds earmarked for forestry at state experiment stations were less productive of published output at those stations than nonearmarked funds for studying forest pathology (Waggoner 1972).

Since administering the money within an institution provides a patient and persistent patron of research, I am not surprised that an experiment station could employ a distinguished geneticist steadily on a practical problem, from before his invention of double-cross hybrid corn in 1917, through his period as a protagonist for the new way of plant breeding and beyond his invention about 1950 of a way to produce seed of hybrid corn without the labor of detasseling the female parent. "There is a message of sorts in this simple fact . . . Donald Jones bulldozed hybrid corn into being with the clearness and strength of the young. He moved fertility restoration in corn on stage with the careful, deliberate steps of the experienced man who realizes the limitations of his strength" (Becker 1976). Jones's patron stuck with him all the way, and he found carrots in both science and practice.

Foundation grants awarded by peer panels provide different incentives. "Scientific progress [is] viewed as a surrogate for achieving practical results." Accountability is "largely left to those chosen to determine scientific merit," and "judges and the judged [represent] the same community." Consequently, "while research in the past [has] contributed to an array of technological benefits which could be equated with the promotion if not satisfaction of national goals, the more recent and increasingly costly scientific undertakings appear to yield ambivalent results" (Stein 1973).

The carrots held by peer panels changed the problems investigated by scientists. Where the panels held the carrots is shown by the following: in 1968 87% of the chemists reporting in the *Journal of Biological Chemistry* had grants, while only 3% of the pathologists publishing in the *Plant Disease Reporter* had a grant. It's not surprising that as grantsmanship grew in the 1950s and 1960s fewer and fewer pathologists worked outdoors where real plants grow. The frequency of reports of research outdoors fell (Horsfall 1969).

What to do? I conclude with answers to questions Schultz (1977) has asked. Both output and impact show there is no need for ever-more complex organization for decisions nor for larger scale. The flight from field research shows that market incentives such as grants do guide research entrepreneurs. We only need to hold the carrot in the right place for mankind's good. And I suggest steady patronage for science in medium-sized institutions that sense social heat via the politics of their region and sense researchability via the personal relations with the twenty to one hundred scientists who work together daily.

That way no one will be "stationed."

REFERENCES

American Council of Education. 1973. *American Universities & Colleges.* 11th ed. Washington, D.C.: American Council of Education.

Becker, S. L. 1976. *Agricultural Innovators and Innovations. Donald F. Jones and Hybrid Corn.* Conn. Agr. Exp. Station Bulletin 763. New Haven.

Holsendolph, E. 1977. "Think Tanks Have Sprung a Leak." *New York Times* (Jan. 9, 1977) III, 38.

Horsfall, J. G. 1969. "Relevance: Are We Smart Outside?" *Phytopath News* 3 (12):5–9.

Horsfall, J. G. et al. 1975. *Agricultural Production Efficiency.* Washington, D.C.: National Academy of Sciences.

Koenig, M. E. D., and Gans, D. U. 1975. "The Productivity of Research Effort in the U.S. Pharmaceutical Industry: A Statistical Approach." *Research Policy* 4:330–49.

Pound, G. S., and Waggoner, Paul E. 1972. "Comparative Efficiency, as Measured by Publication Performance of USDA and SAES Entomologists and Plant Pathologists." In *Report of the Committee on Research Advisory to the U.S. Department of Agriculture,* G. S. Pound et al., pp.145–70. Washington, D.C.: National Academy of Sciences.

Schultz, Theodore W. 1977. "Uneven Prospects for Gains from Agricultural Research Related to Economic Policy." In *Resource Allocation and Productivity in National and International Agricultural Research,* ed. Thomas M. Arndt et al., pp.578–89. Minneapolis: University of Minnesota Press.

Stein, E. R. 1973. "Public Accountability and the Project-Grant Mechanism." *Research Policy* 2:2–16.

U.S. Department of Agriculture, Cooperative State Research Service. 1977. *Professional Workers in State Agricultural Experiment Stations and other Cooperating Institutions.* Agr. Handbook 305. Washington, D.C.

Viteles, M. S. 1965. "Industrial Psychology." *Encyclopaedia Brittanica* 18, p.690. Chicago: Encyclopaedia Brittanica, Inc.

Waggoner, Paul E. 1972. "Research in Forest Pathology." In *Report of the Committee on Research Advisory to the U.S. Department of Agriculture,* G. S. Pound et al., pp.171–81. Washington, D.C.: National Academy of Sciences.

The Role of Investments in
Human Capital in Agriculture

FINIS WELCH

Development is talked about and measured only as it affects available opportunities. As such, development is knowledge in use. It is the product of knowledge interacting with and attempting to roll back physical constraints imposed by nature. Useful knowledge is definitionally vested in people prior to vesting in land, machines, or seed varieties, and it is meaningless to discuss development without focusing on people, people not only as benefit recipients but as agents of change.

Investments in human capital occur at all levels of the development spectrum from research to dissemination to implementation and, perhaps equally important, to the production of political-economic environments conducive to change. As such, most authors of papers herein explore some avenue of investments in man. To distinguish my own effort, I concentrate on investments in education and, more narrowly, on the education of farm producers.

I do not consider education of policy makers (this is best left to discussion of the general incentive environment), the education of those who deal directly or indirectly with farmers, or the use of education in the household. By now we are very much aware that the production of personal satisfaction does not end with production of raw materials for consumption. The subsequent transformation is an economic process and has been explored in the literature. More importantly, I do not address the nexus of nutrition, health, and mortality that may be subject to the most immediate changes associated with development and may freely interact with other investments in man, such as those in his fertility and education.

So long as man is the raw material to which investments are added, it must be that the efficacy of these investments depends on health and durability. We have developed a number of conceptual models of the nature of these relationships, but there has been too little empirical work. For example, we know that mother's nutrition during gestation

259

affects a child's birthweight and physical development, and there is some evidence that these effects span more than one generation. There is corresponding evidence linking early nutrition to measured cognitive development. But we have little evidence of effects on subsequent productive capabilities. Similarly, we know that improved health increases life expectancy but we do not know how this affects educational achievements.

There is a recent but large and growing literature of human-resource economics in economic development. Much of the early work concentrated on human fertility, especially on effects of programs disseminating contraceptive information and on effects of reduced mortality (usually infant- or child-mortality) rates. The amenability of these efforts to the investment view and to the "economics of information" is encouraging. There has been (roughly) parallel work linking income returns to investments in education to the pace of agricultural technical change and it is this effort to which I turn.

In doing so, I often use the terms "education" and "formal schooling" interchangeably. I understand that the two are not the same and that in both traditional and modern agricultural environs more is probably learned out of school than in. Yet, in a dynamic setting, school education complements out-of-school learning and, therefore, indexes it. Furthermore, while the distinction is conceptually easy, empirically it is difficult. Other than for fairly crude measures like age or time on the job, we have no obvious measure of investments in education other than time spent in school.

Emphasis is on factors contributing to the productivity of education and, consequently, on incentives for acquiring education. There is no presumption that education is productive independently of other factors. Instead, I assume that farmer education is most of all an ability to capitalize on opportunities for change. It is an ability to learn and, therefore, to speed delivery of the fruit of change.

LEARNING AS AN EQUILIBRIUM CONCEPT

In an essay that draws together more evidence than any other on sources of education's productivity, T. W. Schultz (1975) chooses to call what seems to be the most researched and perhaps the most important attribute of this product "the ability to respond to economic disequilibria." While emphasis is correctly placed on an ability to respond, the response is to economic disequilibria in a narrow sense. It can be smart to be ignorant, and learning—the ability to respond—is very much an equilibrium notion subject to the ordinary optimization calculus. In this section I explore some implications of investments in information. Since I presume that education is an informational skill, investments in education are more productive when information is itself more valuable.

Although there are explicit markets for information—forecasts can be bought—the emphasis here is upon implicit markets where production information is bought by trial and error, by waiting to see how other adopters fare, by giving up otherwise useful time to read about new inputs or techniques, to talk to neighbors or extension agents, and so forth. As a profit maximizer the farmer's job is usually described in the context of perfect information as that of finding the optimal employment level for inputs he is free to vary. With perfect information, the optimal level is that which establishes equality at the margin between revenue and costs and there is no room for a mistake, for failure to hit marginal targets, because mistakes can be costlessly avoided. In contrast, in an uncertain world where information is imperfect, equality at the margins is only a long-range target. It is attained with small probability and in the short run it is not economically efficient.

Consider a farmer who produces a single product and has a history of producing it. He currently is involved in deciding which resources to commit to this period's production. Based on his own experience and perhaps assisted by observations of others or what he has heard or read, he faces a stochastic production relation giving output distributions associated with specific inputs. He does not have a simple deterministic production function but has some idea, conditional on his own actions, of which outcomes are likely. At the time input decisions are made, some prices are known but others, including harvesting costs and product prices, are conjectural.

He would like to use just the "right" quantity of each input but these optimal quantities are unknown. They depend on prices and factor productivities. If price uncertainty alone were at issue his problem would be easier, but factor productivities are themselves uncertain. How much more rice will be produced if one more unit of nitrogen fertilizer is used? It all depends.

Among other things, it depends on seed variety, soil type, water availability, quantities of other fertilizers, planting techniques, levels of all other inputs, light exposure, temperature, and so on and on. The list is long and some elements in it, weather among them, are purely random. Such others as input qualities and the way inputs niche with each other could in principle be known but may not be when current decisions are made. To complicate matters further, whatever the farmer does today will produce responses that contribute to his knowledge of which responses are likely to result from future actions. Thus, the example farmer learns not only from external sources but also from his own actions and what he learns depends on what he does. If he behaves as in the past he may learn little, but if he experiments with new techniques or different input combinations he can learn more.

The standard optimizing rule is to use just enough of each input such that its marginal contribution to revenue is equal to its marginal cost. With uncertainty, the difference between marginal revenue and cost becomes a random variable. For a price-taker this difference for the ith input is $p_y f_i(x) - p_i = u_i$ where p_y is product price, f_i is the marginal product of the ith input which depends on all inputs, x, and p_i is the price of the ith input. The marginal error is u_i and if it is positive too little of the input is used while too much is used if the error is negative. So long as u_i is not zero a mistake has occurred and mistakes are costly. If u_i is perceived as a random variable over which the farmer has a subjective distribution reflecting price and productivity uncertainty, then the cost of this uncertainty is indexed by dispersion in this distribution. Greater dispersion signals larger average errors (both positive and negative) and, since overutilization in one period cannot be compensated by underutilization in another, dispersion is relevant. Furthermore, dispersion in marginal targets has two sources, one associated with imperfect forecasts of what will be and another with imperfect knowledge of what is. This second part, which summarizes the farmer's knowledge, is subject to control, to investments in information.

The farmer's problem is to maximize expected profit or, if he is not indifferent to risk, its utility equivalence. He is in the business for more than one period and recognizes that today's actions not only affect today's profit but add information useful for tomorrow and, therefore, affect tomorrow's profit as well.

By experimenting today he can create information useful for tomorrow but in doing so he will sacrifice part of today's profit. Similarly, he can divert part of his own labor or other inputs from today's production effort to information gathering that is independent of what he does on the farm. He invests in knowledge at the expense of short-run profit. So long as there is an uncertain future such that tomorrow's perceptions are affected by today's actions, it is not efficient to hit all of today's margins even if he could. Global efficiency is attained by sacrificing part of today's efficiency for improved future prospects. What is involved is not only the sacrifice of today's profit in terms of failures to equate marginal conditions, but it also may be economically efficient to sacrifice technical efficiency.

As an example, consider a multiplant firm. The entrepreneur does not know his production function for each plant, but he does know it is concave, that the production function has diminishing returns. He also knows that all plants have the same production function. Based on concavity within plants and homogeneity between plants, he knows that, for given input aggregates, aggregate product is maximized if inputs are uniformly distributed between plants. He also knows that for a fixed input aggregate, an even distribution between plants will minimize the information that *today's* trial generates about the production function of each plant. Because of the inherent trade off between today's profit and information for tomorrow, he will experiment by introducing input variations between plants.

In this case it is economically efficient not to be technically efficient. But the other side of the story is that so long as information is costly, it is economically efficient not to know too much. As in the multiplant example, more information is generated by greater variance between plants in the composition of today's input trials, but the greater is this variance the smaller is today's product.

TECHNICAL CHANGE AND
LEARNING FROM EXPERIENCE

For farmers, improved technologies are more often than not packaged in seeds, pesticides, fertilizers, equipment, or resource-management schemes. They are reported improvements, but the extent of the improvement is unknown (and may be negative). Further, the way they niche with or affect interactions between inputs is unknown. Further still, if the reported improvement has a sizable impact (it is widely adopted, and changes aggregate production as well as input use) there will be derivative market price impacts and even more uncertainty is introduced. If technical change does anything, it not only changes the rules of production but creates uncertainty as to what the rules are.

How does this affect producer incentives for investments in information? The answer is not as simple as may appear at first blush. It is true that a once-and-for-all shock that depreciates old rules creates incentives for learning new ones, but what about steady change?

Any reasonable model of learning behavior will possess diminishing marginal properties such that the informational content of a current experience diminishes with the stock of experience. In a static environment learning will vanish in the long run as the stock of experience accumulates. If the environment is static except for the life cycle of actors, there will be recurrent learning as old actors retire and new ones are brought aboard. But in this case, we would expect avenues for information transmission to evolve that simplify learning. After all, in a technically static environment it is not necessary to know why something works, only whether it works.

The role of steady technical change is to render experience time-dependent. That is, it not only matters which stimuli resulted in which responses, but *when* the experience occurred. With steady change, time serves as an index of technology, of the production rules governing the experiment. Further, technological change proceeds incrementally: with respect to today's technology, yesterday is more relevant than the day before. Thus, in computing the stock of information relevant to today, a steady rate of technical change can be construed as a discount factor for past experience. The more rapid the change, the greater the rate of obsolescence and the lower the stock of experience relevant to today. This says that the informational content of today's observation is greater, the faster the pace of change. It does not say, however, that the value of today's observation is also greater; for so long as change continues, the discount that works backward to reduce the effective stock of knowledge works forward as well to reduce the relevance of today's information for future periods.

A rapid rate of technical change renders past experience obsolete and it increases the informational content of today's experience. But, just as more rapid change renders yesterday less relevant from today's perspective, it renders today less relevant from tomorrow's perspective. So even though more rapid change results in greater learning potential, it reduces the value of what is learned and the implications for investments in information are ambiguous. General statements are impossible unless the technology of learning is itself specified.[1]

What can be said is that in a stationary state, investments in learning will not occur. In a technically steady state they will, but it is not clear that the extent of the investment increases as the pace of change accelerates.

To this point we have considered only the implications of technical change for investments in information when one source of learning exists. Alternatively, we can think of many potential sources of information. Applied knowledge can be gleaned from one's own experience, or, among other sources, from observations of neighbors. More basic knowledge can be acquired through basic principles which in a technically dynamic environment may have lower rates of obsolescence than applied knowledge. Further, in a static environment everyone will be using the same techniques but, where change is occurring, a spectrum of techniques may exist. If everyone is doing the same thing, a new entrant can learn whatever is necessary by observing whoever is cheapest. But if many technologies coexist, then it matters who is observed, and location and costs of travel become important.

A more rapid rate of movement in the technological frontier will change the structure of obsolescence among different types or sources of information. Whereas a static environment may place the highest value on information gained on site or from one's own experience, differential obsolescence raises the value of information that is more basic and therefore more durable.

Consider formal schooling. In a static environment, the comparative advantage of learning in the isolation (and abstraction) of a school is probably least. Even in this case some schooling may be useful. If the production process is complex, something can be said for an isolated environment where a degree of simplification can be attained that may not be possible amongst the "noise" of actual production. But, in a dynamic technical environment where evaluative skills are at a premium, it is likely that the comparative advantage of the schoolroom is increased. Not only is it likely to be more efficient in producing communication skills that are more valuable under change, but it may also be more efficient, relative to on-site experience, in producing forms of knowledge that are durable. In the extreme case, where all forms of information are subject to rapid depreciation, the viable skills are those of learning to learn; and the structure of education would shift toward emphasis of informational sources and the processing of information.

With this in mind, it is perhaps not surprising that most of the research directed toward estimating education's productivity in agriculture has focused on interactions between education and the pace of technical advance. There has been little objection to the notion that schooling may augment worker efficiency although the scope for this type of applied knowledge is limited.[2] But there has been more interest in identifying the role of schooling as an allocative input, one that affects the efficacy with which other inputs are used.

The entire thrust of the allocative-efficiency notion is that allocation is costly. New technologies require evaluation and are not diffused to the farm without investments. As such, it is useful to describe the process of technical change as one of technology for sale. From the farmer's perspective, researchers produce autonomous shifts in technological frontiers; but this does nothing to what is—it only changes what might be. Extension agents and demonstration sites reduce costs of adoption, but some costs remain.

For a particular innovation, the cost of adoption will depend not only on activities of extension workers and availability of demonstration sites, but also on the farmer's own information-processing skills. In addition, evaluation costs depend on proximity to those who have adopted earlier. Since, for successful innovations, adoption rates increase through time, evaluation costs fall through time.

To completely picture how innovations are diffused, we need to have some idea of the returns to adoption, and this is where questions of farm scale arise.

INFORMATION AND FARM SCALE

It is often said that information is scale free and for agricultural technologies this is a useful assumption. The idea is simply that costs of evaluating a new and reportedly improved technique or input do not depend on farm size. For information gained independently of actual farm production, perhaps through extension-agent contacts, visits to experiment sites, observations of neighbors, reading about innovations or the like, this is clearly correct. It is less so for on-the-farm experimentation, but if scalar replication (small-scale experiments whose results can be generalized to the full farm operation) is possible, it remains true even in this case. In contrast to costs being scale free, returns are perhaps best described as proportional to scale. It must be true that the value of knowing that A is superior to B depends on how much A or B is to be used.

Now, to return to the example of technology for sale: suppose that a technical advance has occurred and that diffusion is not instantaneous. To the individual farmer, costs of adoption will fall through time as diffusion increases and evaluation costs fall. Who will be the early adopters? Aside from questions of taste for risk the answer is clear: those who have low evaluation costs, possibly those most educated and those closest to information centers, and those who have the most to gain—those with the greatest potential scale.

There are repeated observations that operators of large farms are early innovators and I think this phenomenon has been too often explained as indicating either that there are scale biases in new technologies, or that innovations require large capital outlays and operators of large farms have easier access to credit markets. I have no idea of the truth of the first assertion, although the second is plausible. I do know that regardless of whether such biases exist from informational considerations alone, I expect a proscale bias in adoption.

This is important. Viewed independently, it is a useful reference for interpreting patterns of change. But, from the perspective of understanding education's allocative role, it enhances our ability to test hypotheses. If education is an allocative input which facilitates adoption of new technologies, then farm scale offers a benchmark for measuring returns to these allocative skills. In many cases the two should have parallel effects and observations that they do add to creditability that education's role is correctly interpreted.

Before examining available studies of education and allocative efficiency, let us further explore the interaction between information and scale.

Assume first that technical change is cost saving and scale neutral, that a particular change will have the same proportionate cost-savings on all levels of production. Second, assume that instead of adoption being an all-or-none phenomenon, partial adoption is possible. This seems reasonable either for change stemming from a variety of underlying small changes for which each component may itself require all-or-none adoption, or from a single "large" change such as an improved seed variety that can be adopted alone, but can be augmented through increased use of fertilizers, more intensive cultivation, or irrigation. If the degree of augmentation is variable, then it is as though the degree of adoption is variable. Finally, assume an evaluation (or adoption) cost function such that costs increase and do so at an increasing rate as the degree of adoption rises. Evaluation costs also depend on evaluation skills, and if evaluation costs fall as proximity to other adopters increases then costs fall as time since discovery increases, but costs do not depend on farm scale. Both evaluation skills and waiting for innovations to "come to you" carry their own costs, and there are optimization questions in these dimensions as well, but the implications for scale are straightforward.

If a firm has an ordinary U-shaped average-cost function when costs include only direct production expenses and adoption possibilities are ignored, the augmented cost function that includes both direct costs of production and optimal (cost-minimizing) outlays for evaluation is also U-shaped. The augmented function necessarily lies below the nonaugmented function (otherwise it does not "pay" to adopt) and since the degree of adoption increases with scale[3] the proportionate discrepancy between the two cost functions also increases with scale.

This in itself assures that, with technical advance, optimal farm size is greater than in a static environment. (It also says that if costs are measured exclusively of investments in information the advantage of scale is overstated.) In this vein, two cases should be distinguished. In the first, technology is initially static. A once-and-for-all advance occurs which is eventually completely adopted, and technology is again static. In the second, there is continuing advance.

Suppose for the first case that before the innovation occurs there is an equilibrium distribution of farm size. Larger farms need not be more profitable. (Recall that the classical example of perfect competition permits replication such that all firms have equal [minimum] average costs but not necessarily equal size.) Also ignore differences among farms in evaluation costs resulting from proximity to information and from differences in evaluation skills. Suppose that there are some fixed costs of adoption so that, initially as the innovation occurs, farms below a given size will not adopt and their output is not changed. Among those which do adopt all will expand output.

This generates product-market responses, a falling price, and leads to product contraction for all farms. In the short run, aggregate output will have increased and its distribution will have skewed toward the initially larger farms. Small farms, especially those not adopting, will have reduced production; and if they use durable inputs, they will receive negative short-run rents. The large, most-intensive adopters will earn positive rents. The short-run effect on income distributions is of reduced income on small farms and increased income on large ones.

In the long run, as adoption costs vanish with increased diffusion, the size advantage evaporates. It may be that all farms return to initial output levels.[4] Whether the income distribution returns to its initial level will depend on aggregate product demand and factor-supply elasticities as predicted by the standard theory, but it will not depend on the size distribution of farms which is crucial in determining the distribution of short-run rents.

I think this case may be useful for interpreting income-distribution effects of the Green Revolution. There have been numerous assertions that the Green Revolution resulted in the poor (farmers) getting poorer and the rich getting richer. This, in turn, has led to an increased emphasis on income-distribution effects and something of a backlash against the apparently resultant regression. I do not doubt that the regression occurred and an understanding of its sources could be useful in designing research and related schemes to reduce these effects. Yet, if such effects are short-run phenomena, duration is relevant.

The second case, that of steady advance, is analytically distinct. In the first case if the initial size distribution reflected but did not affect income distributions, then rents generated by change are eroded by diffusion. With steady change, the erosion forces are not effective. As the technical frontiers shift, scale advantages are maintained. In this case the equilibrium size distribution of surviving farms is shifted toward increased output, and whatever factors contribute to an ability to manage larger scale are important. In the static case, these need not have been viewed as productive factors and need not have earned a return. In the dynamic case they are productive and their scarcity or cost conditions for "producing" them will determine their return and will be important in determining ultimate income-distribution effects. If schooling enhances allocative abilities it presumably enhances the scale over which allocative decisions apply. Thus part of the return to schooling arising from technical advance may be derivative of the implications for farm scale.

EXTENSION, EDUCATION, AND FARM SCALE

By extension, I mean publicly subsidized dissemination of information; and I use education as a summary statistic for farmer abilities to acquire and use information. It is clear in the scenario described that extension, education, and farm scale are interactive in the sense that one affects the productivity of another. In this section I explore questions of the nature of these interactions.

Since it is presumed that information is more productive the larger the scale of activities to which it is applied, I assume that the demand for information increases with farm scale. As scale increases, not only does informational demand increase, but its composition will change with changes in comparative advantage of information sources.

As a farmer's education increases, the ability to receive and decode information improves. It may do so for many reasons, but part of the expanding-horizons nature of education is that improved communication skills augment the number of informational sources to which farmers may usefully turn. As such, farm scale and farmer education are natural complements in the sense that increased scale raises the productivity of education. This, of course, relies on a presumption that information is itself productive, that the production environment is changing.

Are education and extension substitutes or complements? It depends on what is extended. Insofar as extension is one form of information, disseminated at a particular level of complexity, it seems that education-extension interaction is not monotone. It may be that there are sufficiently low levels of communicating skills such that extension does little to augment the productivity of these skills. If so, then increases in education from this level may well enhance the productivity of extension. But as education continues to increase as the scope of informational alternatives broadens, the same forces that initially enhance extension's productivity will ultimately detract from it. As horizons expand, some avenues for learning are outgrown just as others are opened.

The levels of education and extension at which this sort of enhancement reversal occurs depend on the type and complexity of information extended. In general, it is an empirical question but some insight may be gained from speculation.

If it is true that the productivity of information is greater the greater the scale of activities to which it applies and is applied, then there are immediate equity and efficiency implications for extension activities. There would be none if extension information were truly scale free, for one spoken word would be equally heard by all ears. But just as I have assumed that information is only quasi-scale free, *vis-à-vis* farm scale, I make a similar assumption for extension.

For farm scale, I assume that information is not costlessly passed between entrepreneurs. There are losses in transmission. On the other hand, within a farm, there is less loss, and information useful for one plot (plant) is useful for all. For extension, I assume that dissemination occurs in something like teacher-student fashion, and that the usefulness of what is said for any one "student" depends on the size of the "class." If farmers were so geographically dispersed that extension agent-farmer contacts were always one to one, the case would be clearest. The ability to congregate farmer recipients enhances transmission, but diminishing marginal properties can be assumed, both in terms of transport costs in bringing farmers together and within congregations.

To pursue the one-on-one example, efficiency requires that limited extension resources be channeled toward maximum impact. This introduces a proscale bias to dissemination activities which may be partially thwarted by informational investments of operators of large farms. Just as increased education may result in farmers bypassing extension, rising informational investments with farm scale may result in bypassing extension. Furthermore, equity considerations may partially offset this proscale bias. But, if there is such a bias, it is clearly reduced by expanding the scale of extension activities.

In the one-on-one example, with all farmers being equally receptive, if extension agents devote their efforts only to the largest farms, then increased numbers of extension workers will span larger numbers of farms—the marginal contact in each case being to the next smallest farm. Such an allocation pattern assures: (1) diminishing impact of extension, like any other factor, and (2) diminishing productivity of scale with increased extension, as intermarginal farms become intramarginal.

In the classroom example, where one agent contacts more than one farmer (simultaneously or serially, with transport costs), it should be that extension is more productive where agglomeration is cheapest.

This refers both to farm density (which may be contra-scale) and to levels of complexity of the information disseminated. If extension information is of uniform complexity, as it must be within congregations at a point in time, then there are (efficiency) incentives to specify the level of complexity to maximize impact. I presume that this says, more or less, to direct extension information toward the modal educational level.[5]

EMPIRICAL EVIDENCE OF THE PRODUCTIVITY OF EDUCATION IN AGRICULTURE

In his *Transforming Traditional Agriculture*, T. W. Schultz (1964) offered what appeared at the time a novel if not radical hypothesis that in traditional settings resources may be more efficiently allocated than in modern, technically dynamic environments. The idea was that there are always incentives to hit margins, and that margins are more accurately perceived in static situations. By now, this view is generally accepted; but at the time it did much to alter our thinking. It emphasized man as an economic animal who responds to incentives and does the best possible, subject to the resources at hand. The emphasis on development shifted more toward enhancing opportunities under the assumption that economic incentives were sufficient to insure response, and that no other motivation was required. To those concerned with the productivity of education, the Schultzian view raised the immediate question of how education affects productivity. In the U.S. at least, there was plenty of evidence that more-educated persons earned higher incomes. That this is not an artifact, for example of "contacts" or "family ties," was strongly suggested in the work of Griliches (1963a, 1963b, and 1964) on aggregate agricultural production where differences in educational composition clearly affected levels of farm sales.

But behind this there was the fact that studies of production of single commodities fully specified with respect to inputs and climatic conditions rarely turned to education as a source for explaining output. What appeared to be true was that aggregation over diverse activities rendered education important although it was not important in explaining the individual components. This suggests simply that education affects the composition of activities, that it is an allocative resource.

D. P. Chaudhri (1968) supplied important new evidence when he noted that farmer education did not seem to explain differences in production between Indian states if inputs were fully accounted, but that input composition was itself sensitive to education.

Building on the work of Evenson (1967, 1968) and Griliches (1964) demonstrating that differences between U.S. states in levels of agricultural research contributed to explanations of differences in farm production, I (1970) addressed the question of whether differences in levels of research activity affected income differentials among farmer schooling classes. The rationale was that if higher levels of research activity imply more rapid changes in production opportunities, and if the larger the opportunity stream the greater the advantage of discretionary abilities than if education is an allocative input, more rapid technical change implies higher returns. For the U.S., I found positive correlation between research expenditures and the income of persons who had attended college relative to those who had not. Levels of estimated coeffcients suggested that roughly one-third of income differentials between college and high school graduates could be attributed to publicly sponsored agricultural research.

In a separate study (1971) of sources of measured scale economies, I found that farm size and educational levels of farm operators are systematically positively related. This is hardly surprising but is consistent with the view that returns to informational skills increase with scale. More importantly for explaining differences between states in measured scale economies, I found that where scale economy was greatest the rate of change in schooling levels with farm scale was also the highest. Further, the evidence is that the scale advantage of education is higher still in states with higher levels of public research expenditures. In these data increased contacts between extension agents and farmers reduce the advantage of education so that education and extension appear to be substitutes at the sample mean.

In two similarly designed studies, Nabil Khaldi (1975) and George Fane (1975) approach the notion of allocative efficiency through contrast of hypothetical minimum costs of producing realized output and actual costs. For both, hypothetical minimum cost is inferred from first-round estimates of aggregate production functions using the 1964 U.S. *Census of Agriculture*. Khaldi's observations refer to state averages for all U.S. states whereas Fane uses 407 counties for four Midwestern states. Each finds that the proportional difference between actual cost and the hypothetical minimum declines as average farm-operator schooling rises.

Khaldi offers additional evidence that average allocation errors are greater in states where more research occurs. He does not directly address questions of interrelations with farm size nor does he examine the possibility that the effect of education on proportional allocation errors is conditional on levels of research activity. While Khaldi's finding *vis-à-vis* allocation errors and levels of research activity is of marginal statistical significance, it is consistent with the Schultzian view that targets are harder to hit in more dynamic environments.

Fane examines relationships between farm scale and allocation errors as well as the "cost effectiveness" noted earlier. He concludes that average allocative errors are larger on larger farms. I frankly do not know how to interpret this finding for his specification of the scale relation ignores systematic differences in activity mix associated with farm scale.[6]

In two similar papers, Wallace Huffman (1974, 1977) goes to the heart of the allocation issue by focusing narrowly on the use of a single input, nitrogen fertilizer, in the production of a single crop, corn. Huffman reasons that where rapid change is occurring education should speed adjustment. He selected a period, 1959–64, during which prices of nitrogen relative to corn fell 22 to 25% and analyzed the resultant adjustment across Corn Belt counties. Huffman computes a partial adjustment coefficient showing actual changes during the five-year interval as a fraction of the change necessary to hit a hypothetical optimum and relates this measure of adjustment speed to average education, extension, and farm size. The hypothetical target is calculated from an estimated production function for corn.

Huffman's two studies differ only in sample size (the 1974 one includes 122 counties, the 1977 one, 184) and in specification of the form of the adjustment function. While the more recent paper yields estimates that are superior on a priori statistical grounds, the form of the estimated relation is analytically more complex. Further, and not surprisingly, conclusions at sample means are virtually identical. His major finding is that education and extension speed adjustments, but at sample means they are substitutes. Adjustments are also more rapid in counties where average farm size is greater. Based on the earlier paper, Huffman's coefficient estimates imply that a 10% increase in extension reduces the productivity of education by 3%, but a 100-acre increase in average farm size (corn acreage) would increase this one dimension of the return to schooling by 82%!

In still another study of U.S. agriculture, Todd Petzel (1976) explored relationships between farmer education and the dynamics of acreage allocations to soybean production. Unlike Huffman, who calculated optimal allocations based on estimated production relations, Petzel, following Nerlove (1958, 1972), used an implicit optimum based on formulations of expected price. Separately, for 448 counties in nine states, he estimated soybean acreage for the 1948–73 period as a function of expected soybean price, prices of substitute crops, production costs, and one-period lagged soybean acreage. The coefficient on lagged acreage measures (one minus) the speed-of-adjustment factor and Petzel turned to characteristics of farms and farmers described in the 1964 *Census of Agriculture* to explain county differences.

A unique feature of Petzel's specification is that the focus on acreage permits two dimensions of scale. There is composite scale approximated by total resources, in his case land area, devoted to production, and there is unit scale. Some areas have more productive land than others, and the higher the potential product the greater is the advantage of correct assignment. Petzel finds more rapid adjustments in counties where average education levels are highest. He also finds more rapid response associated with both dimensions of scale.

Based on what by now is a large body of accrued evidence, it seems clear that in U.S. agriculture—a particularly dynamic technical setting —education enhances allocation efficiency. Furthermore, increased scale increases incentives for "correct" decisions and results not only in the "purchase" of more education for operators of larger farms but in related investments that enhance response.[7] Do these conclusions extend to farmer education in less-developed countries?

Unfortunately, this is where the lack of data availability takes its toll. Among those examining the productivity of schooling, most do so in a production-function context and, if there is a consistent theme, it is that education is more likely to appear as directly productive in transitional or technically dynamic states. The evidence that education is productive in traditional settings is less convincing.

For example, Clifton Wharton describes his 1958 study of two early-stage areas of Brazil as finding "no relationships between agricultural performance and education as measured by years of schooling completed" (1965, p.207, note 4). For medium-stage developing agricultures, Craig Wu (undated) describes the studies of Tang (1963) for Japan between 1880 and 1938 and the work of Ho (1966) for Taiwan between 1903 and 1960 as offering positive evidence of education's productivity.

More recently, George Patrick and Earl Kehrberg (1973) estimated limited-form production functions for five areas of Brazil based on surveys in 1969. Instead of a gross-product function, Patrick and Kehrberg sought to explain differences between farms in the value product less expenses for purchased inputs other than labor. They noted that this value-added formulation gave more "room" for observing education's productivity than the gross-value function since value added is directly affected by the quality of decisions regarding input purchases.

For the two areas described as traditional, they found no contribution of education. In the two termed transitional, no significant relation was found in one but a positive relation was found in the other. The fifth, described as modern without reference to dynamics, also exhibited no significant relation between education and output. They also examined contributions of extension but found no relation in any of the regions.[8]

In a somewhat similar study, Thomas Haller (1972) collected data for farms in four regions of Colombia (mostly in 1969). In two of the regions, farmers presumably use only traditional resources while in the other two, modern inputs are fairly widely used. Both the traditional and modern sectors are further selected such that each would have one region specializing in a single crop and another in which farms are engaged in a variety of activities. Only for the modern multiple-activity region does he report statistically significant positive effects of education on farm production.

Other than for the value-added adjustment of Patrick and Kehrberg, none of these studies left much "room" for identifying allocative efficiency. In estimating aggregate product relationships where education's product is inferred through statistical attempts to "hold other inputs constant," terms that are derivative of those inputs are not captured. The only room for an allocative effect comes from composition within aggregates. For example, contrast the output measures Haller would have used in his single- and multiple-activity regions. Both were proportionate to market value of total production, but for one crop the proportionality is also to physical output. Therefore, any return associated with picking the "right" level of output (scale) cannot be identified. For the multiple-activity case effects of variations in product mix, holding total production costs constant, can be measured. In this case effects of product composition would be included in estimates of education's product, but effects of choice on aggregate scale would continue to be excluded.

Craig Wu performed a more direct test of allocative effects using data for a sample farm in Taiwan between 1964 and 1966. He first estimated a crop-production function and used it to compute optimal input combinations for maximum profit. Observed profit as a fraction of the hypothetical maximum was then regressed on farmer schooling and a positive coefficient is reported.[9]

Turning to Indian agriculture, Rati Ram (1976) used both total product and value-added specifications to examine the changing product of schooling as the scope of decision-making. His data were farm averages for 150 districts in 1960–61 and in 1970–71. Three specifications are used: (1) gross output, (2) value added by all inputs other than commerical fertilizers, and (3) value added by traditional inputs (all inputs other than fertilizers, tractors, and iron plows). The value-added idea is the old-fashioned one of residual recipients: returns accruing to a residual set of factors are affected by the quality of decisions made concerning the omitted (variable) factors. Thus, differences in schooling's productivity between Ram's gross output and value-added specification which omits fertilizers refer to correlations between schooling and the quality of decisions regarding fertilizer purchases.

Ram's data permit distinctions between schooling of cultivators (farm managers) and agricultural laborers. He argues that to the extent education is an allocative input, this component or product is restricted to persons making allocative decisions. For both years and for all three specifications Ram finds significant positive contributions of cultivator schooling. In contrast, there is no relation between output or value added and schooling of laborers. He also finds that output elasticities of cultivator schooling were higher in 1971 than in 1961 and, for the value-added specification that considers returns to traditional factors, schooling elasticities are higher than for the alternative formulations. Finally, Ram partitions his sample into districts termed "backward" and "progressive." Estimated productivities of cultivator schooling are higher in progressive districts but, under this partition, elasticities in 1961 appear to have been higher than in 1971.

In another study using data for India, Mark Rosenzweig (1977), with a sample of 1,082 landed households from the Rural Incomes Survey, examines determinants of adoption of high-yielding grain varieties. The data refer to adoption by 1971 of varieties introduced in the mid- to late 1960s and he finds that chances of adoption are positively correlated both with farmer schooling levels and with farm size, as is to be expected. This, of course, is direct evidence of schooling's effect on input choice. The implication for agriculture is that the association between income and schooling is not spurious.

A related paper by Surjit Sidhu (1976) contrasts three measures of education's productivity in agriculture as of 1968–69 for Ferozepur, Punjab, India. Sidhu first estimates a production function for the quantity of wheat produced on each of the 150 individual farms in his sample. Even though educational levels are low (the average farmer has 2.6 years of schooling) there is a positive statistical relation between schooling and wheat production even after corrections for labor and other physical inputs are made. However, Sidhu estimates that, controlling for other inputs, an extra year of schooling contributes only 66 rupees to wheat sales. He then examines a gross-sales function, taking all agricultural products into account, and finds evidence of increased productivity of schooling. Finally, Sidhu examines total farm income attributable to adult family labor, land, and education and estimates that an extra year of schooling (at the sample mean) contributes 428 rupees to income. In contrast, an extra adult laborer contributes an estimated 649 rupees. By any standard, Sidhu's estimates suggest very high returns to schooling for this region and his estimate is that most of this return arises from schooling's allocative role in early phases of the Green Revolution.

In sum, the data for less-developed countries concerning ties between technical dynamics and the allocative role of education are more or less consistent with findings for the U.S.: education's productivity is enhanced by a wider range of opportunities for choice.

CONCLUDING COMMENTS

I have only implicitly stayed within the bounds of incentives for investments in human capital. My assumption is that an understanding of factors contributing to returns to investments in human capital by implication reveals incentives for making these investments.

Instead of addressing the variety of facets that constitute investments in man, I have focused on only one—investments in schooling of farmers. I argue that an environment conducive to economic progress, one of emerging opportunities, necessarily places a premium on information and information-processing abilities.

To the extent that information is more efficiently spread within firms (over inputs of firm activities) than between, scale economies are generated by growth in learning opportunities. I expect, therefore, that equilibrium farm size is larger in technically progressive situations. In these situations I also expect that abilities to process information are enhanced by scale simply because larger scale implies a broader scope for applying information.

There are implications for income-distributional effects that differ importantly between once-for-all shocks such as the Green Revolution and a regime of steady advance. The once-for-all shocks generate rents associated with abilities to respond quickly and incentives for response (education and farm scale) that are eroded in the long run as the dissemination process is completed. Steady advance simply adds to the number of factors that are productive and creates incentives for acquiring and maintaining informational skills. There is by now a large empirical literature to suggest that earning capacities arising from scale and schooling are enhanced by technical change. But both schooling and scale are malleable in the long run. As durable traits they are best analyzed in an investment context and equity considerations are likely to be affected by the availability of funds for investments. But, whatever the longer-run equity considerations are, we can be easily misled by the apparent regression associated with the Green Revolution.

I have emphasized determinants for returns to only one form of investment in human capital. Investments in health and nutrition and in contraceptive information are subjects for another day. But I have only touched on one component of the return to schooling of farm families. We now have sufficient evidence that the composition of activities within households is sensitive to schooling to speculate that schooling is productive within the household as well. Further, there is little question that opportunities off the farm are enhanced by schooling. It is fairly obvious that the levels of a society's development can be indexed by the fraction of its total resources devoted to feeding and clothing its people. Aside from opportunities for entering export trade, it is likely that agricultural advance will be associated with a reduced demand for farm labor. And as labor exists on the farm, entry into other pursuits is eased by increased education.

NOTES

Support by the Rockefeller Foundation is gratefully acknowledged.

1. Consider an experiment, X, that costs \$1 and define knowledge, K, as the depreciated stock of all past experiments. Assume that the level of experimentation is constant at X and the rate of technical obsolescence, δ, is the rate of technical change. For accumulated knowledge we have $K = X/\delta$. An experiment of extent X yields information, Y, which depends on the level of knowledge, i.e., $Y = f(K)$. The value of this information is proportionate to Y, but obsolesces at rate δ and is further discounted at rate i, the market rate of interest. The value of the experiment, $V = Y/(i + \delta)$. It follows that $\partial V/\partial \delta \gtrless O$ as

$$-\frac{EY}{EK} \begin{matrix} > \\ < \end{matrix} \frac{\delta}{i+\delta} \quad \text{where}$$

$$\frac{EY}{EK} = \frac{K}{Y}\frac{dY}{dK} \quad \text{defines}$$

learning technology. A sufficient condition for investments in learning to increase as the pace of change accelerates is that $EY/EK < -1'$, that information be elastic *vis-à-vis* knowledge.

2. By worker efficiency I mean the ability to get more from the resources at hand. Schooling for craftsmen may be productive. For agricultural laborers, does schooling enhance abilities to get more work done?

3. If there are fixed costs of adoption, there will be scale levels below which adoption will not pay and will not occur, and for which the augmented and nonaugmented functions are identical.

4. They would if their reproduction functions were homothetic and if the technical change were input neutral.

5. A more precise statement would entail use of the mode from a weighted density where weights would be activity scale adjusted by probabilities of adoption of extension-disseminated information.

6. In my paper on scale economies (1971), I show that both input and product composition change rapidly with farm size. The (homogeneous) Cobb-Douglas production relation Fane posits and estimates necessarily implies that optimal input composition is independent of scale. Outputs are linearly aggregated in Fane's analysis and composition cannot be deduced. Because this relation is misspecified, there is a built-in relation between scale and measured optimality of input mix. Whether the bias is pro- or antiscale is uncertain, a priori, but this specification error makes it difficult to interpret Fane's conclusions regarding farm size.

7. In fact, this point was made before the emphasis on education as an allocative input by John Kadlec and Arthur House (1962) in an investigation of technical efficiency among dairy farms in the Louisville Milkshed: "Continuous rapid change in agricultural technology . . . with differences in human resources [has] resulted in wide variations in technical efficiency among farms. . . . In addition, the low point on the long-run average cost curve may be at larger sizes for farms with greater technical efficiency." (p.1431). I would argue only that they may have reversed causality: larger-size farms have more to gain from lower *average* cost!

8. Patrick and Kehrberg did find positive correlations between education and the quantity of all inputs used, other than those subtracted in defining value added. But since, according to their estimates, agriculture was generally unprofitable in four of the areas, they reasoned that education in increasing scale was counterproductive in these areas.

9. Wu also reports coefficients from regression of observed/hypothetical optimum input ratios on farmer schooling. Since deviations from unity (in either direction) are costly, I do not know how to interpret these estimates.

REFERENCES

Chaudhri, D. P. 1968. "Education and Agricultural Productivity in India." Ph.D. dissertation, University of Delhi.

Evenson, Robert. 1967. "The Contribution of Agricultural Research to Production." *Journal of Farm Economics* 49 (December):1415–25.

———. 1968. "The Contribution of Agricultural Research and Extension to Agricultural Production." Ph.D. dissertation, University of Chicago.

Fane, George. 1975. "Education and the Managerial Efficiency of Farmers." *Review of Economics and Statistics* 57 (November):452–61.

Griliches, Zvi. 1963*a*. "Estimates of the Aggregate Agricultural Production Functions from Cross-Sectional Data." *Journal of Farm Economics* 45 (May):419–28.

——. 1963*b*. "The Sources of Measured Productivity Growth: United States Agriculture, 1940–1960." *Journal of Political Economy* 71 (August):331–46.

——. 1964. "Research Expenditures, Education, and the Aggregate Agricultural Production Function." *American Economic Review* 54 (December):961–74.

Haller, Thomas. 1972. "Education and Rural Development in Colombia." Ph.D. dissertation, Purdue University.

Ho, Yhi-min. 1966. *Agricultural Development of Taiwan, 1903–1960.* Nashville: Vanderbilt University Press.

Huffman, Wallace. 1974. "Decision Making: The Role of Education." *American Journal of Agricultural Economics* 56 (February):85–97.

——. 1977. "Allocative Efficiency: The Role of Human Capital." *Quarterly Journal of Economics* 91 (February):59–77.

Kadlec, John, and House, Arthur. 1962. "The Effect of Technical Efficiency on Optimum Size." *Journal of Farm Economics* 44 (December): 1428–1432.

Khaldi, Nabil. 1975. "Education and Allocative Efficiency in U.S. Agriculture." *American Journal of Agricultural Economics* 57 (November): 650–57.

Nerlove, Marc. 1958. *The Dynamics of Supply: Estimation of Farmers' Response to Price.* Baltimore: Johns Hopkins Press.

——. 1972. "Lags in Economic Behavior." *Econometrica* 40 (March): 221–52.

Patrick, George F., and Kehrberg, Earl W. 1973. "Costs and Returns of Education in Five Agricultural Areas of Eastern Brazil." *American Journal of Agricultural Economics* 55 no. 2 (May):145–53.

Petzel, Todd. 1976. "Education and the Dynamics of Supply." Ph.D. dissertation, University of Chicago.

Ram, Rati. 1976. "Education as a Quasi-Factor of Production: The Case of India's Agriculture." Agricultural Economics Research Paper no. 76:12. Mimeographed. University of Chicago.

Rosenzweig, Mark. 1977. "Schooling, Allocative Ability and the Green Revolution." Mimeographed. Yale University.

Schultz, Theodore W. 1964. *Transforming Traditional Agriculture.* New Haven: Yale University Press (Reprint edition, New York: Arno Press, 1976).

——. 1975. "The Value of the Ability to Deal with Disequilibria." *Journal of Economic Literature* 13 (September): 827–46.

Sidhu, Surjit. 1976. "The Productive Value of Education in Agricultural Development." Staff Paper P76-17. Mimeographed. Department of Agricultural and Applied Economics, University of Minnesota.

Tang, A. M. 1963. "Research and Education in Japanese Agricultural Development, 1880–1938." *Economics Studies Quarterly* 13 (Part I: February; Part II: May).

Welch, Finis. 1970. "Education in Production." *Journal of Political Economy* 78 (January/February): 35–59.

———. 1971. "Scale Economies in U.S. Agriculture." Mimeographed. National Bureau of Economic Research, New York.

Wharton, Clifton R., Jr. 1958. "A Case Study of the Economic Impact of Technical Assistance." Ph.D. dissertation, University of Chicago.

———. 1965. "Education and Agricultural Growth: The Role of Education in Early-Stage Agriculture." In *Education and Economic Development*, ed. C. A. Anderson and M. J. Bowman. Chicago: Aldine.

Wu, Craig. Undated. "Education in Farm Production: The Case of Taiwan." Mimeographed. Department of Economics, University of Alabama, Huntsville.

COMMENT

RATI RAM

Professor Welch's paper is written with his usual lucidity and rigor. I share, for the most part, his major points: that returns to education in production derive mainly from the value of production information, and that the value of such information depends on the pace of technological change, sources of new information, and probably the scale of application of the new information. It is also fairly clear that the empirical evidence from the United States and from several developing countries supports the proposition that education has greater value in agriculture in a state of changing farm technology. Professor Welch has summarized the evidence succinctly. I would share the judgment that greater incentive for acquisition of educational capital in agriculture is likely to be provided by a dynamic technological environment.

I have three supplementary points to make. One is the presentation of a simple conceptual framework suggesting the sort of mechanism which probably generates the observed positive effect of schooling on output. The proposed framework can give some indication of the existence of incentives or disincentives for investment in schooling. The second point involves description of a characteristic of India's agriculture that could be regarded as a significant disincentive to investment in the schooling of farm workers. The third point refers to relationship between health of the farm population and agricultural output levels.

A basic framework pointing out the manner in which, or the mechanism through which, schooling affects productivity[1] is useful in several ways. It can make for conceptual clarity in regard to the sort of role[2] that schooling may play in increasing productivity, in agriculture and elsewhere. Also, it may provide a connecting link between the many investigations concerning returns to schooling in a variety of settings. These studies have made use of the basic human-capital framework, along with distinctions such as those between static and dynamic environments and between "worker" and "allocative" effects of schooling, and responses to economic disequilibria. Professor T. W. Schultz (1961) pioneered the treatment of education as a form of (human) capital. He also first suggested (1964) the important distinction between "traditional" and "modern" settings as a source of differential returns to schooling. More recently (1975) he has investigated the role of education in influencing the rate of adjustment to economic disequilibria. The important distinction between the "worker" and "allocative" effects of schooling was first made and applied by Professors D. P. Chaudhri (1968) and Finis Welch (1970). It seems useful to link these aspects together through a common conceptual framework, which could also provide a basis for other predictions regarding patterns in returns to schooling.

I set forth such a framework recently (1976). The core postulates are quite simple. It has been suggested that a major source of the observed returns to schooling is the effect that schooling has on "production information," which is that schooling raises the (marginal) benefit curves and lowers the (marginal) cost curves of production information. Thus schooling provides incentive to producers[3] to acquire more information, and such increased acquisition of production information is the main source of the observed positive effect of schooling on productivity. Put briefly, the postulate is that education makes production information more useful and less costly and, therefore (elementary economic theory assures us), more educated persons acquire more information and thus are observed to be more efficient "producers" of whatever they are producing. This simple framework can provide explanation for the frequently observed differentials in returns to schooling, and can also generate several other interesting predictions. Working with linear marginal benefit and cost curves of information, it can be shown (Ram 1976) fairly easily that gross returns to schooling are likely to be higher, the less steep is either of the two curves or the higher is the location of the marginal benefit curve or the lower is the marginal cost curve of production information. This simple result enables one to make systematic predictions regarding differential returns to schooling—and hence differential incentives to invest in schooling—on the basis of the likely "height" and steepness of these curves. For example, the difference between returns to schooling in "traditional" and "modern" settings, usefulness of education while one responds to disequilibria, and the primacy of the "allocative" effect when returns to schooling are substantial are easily explained by the proposed framework which can also yield insight in regard to other situations in which returns to schooling may differ. One example of such a situation is given in the following paragraph.

Take the case of India's agriculture. Consider two classes of agricultural workers described as "cultivators" and "agricultural laborers." The former group consists of owner operators and other operators (and their family workers) who take most production decisions. The other group includes wage workers who do not ordinarily participate in such decisions. Hence it is likely that information benefit functions (curves) for cultivators will be located higher than those for agricultural laborers. Therefore, returns to schooling and the incentive to invest in schooling are likely to be higher for the former (cultivators) than for the latter. Thus, existence of this functional dichotomy in regard to the scope for taking production or allocative decisions generates little or no incentive for a large section of farm workers to acquire schooling. Some empirical results for the years 1961 and 1971 provide support for the prediction of a substantially higher return to the schooling of cultivators relative to the schooling of agricultural laborers. Table 1 gives a broad flavor of the differences which are quite striking.[4] Lack of an allocative role for agricultural laborers thus appears to provide little incentive for acquisition of schooling by a large section of farm workers, and constitutes one constraint on expansion of output. The difference between size of the elasticities for the two groups indicates the severity of the difference in the incentives to them.

Further, it is interesting to place the above lack of incentive in a dynamic perspective by considering it along with the issue of optimum scale discussed extensively by Professor Welch. He argues cogently that technological change in agriculture raises the optimum farm size, and that in a state of rapid technical change schooling has a relatively higher return on farms of larger size. If these propositions are valid and applicable to India's agriculture,[5] the consequences of technical

Table 1

Differences in the Elasticity° of Agricultural Output with Respect to Schooling of Cultivators and Agricultural Laborers in India
(absolute values of t statistics are in parentheses)

	1961	1971
Schooling of cultivators	.163	.243
	(2.3)	(2.3)
Schooling of agricultural laborers	.016	−.068
	(0.3)	(0.8)

Source—Rati Ram. 1976. "Education as a Quasi-Factor of Production: The Case of India's Agriculture." Ph.D. dissertation, University of Chicago.

° The elasticities are taken as a generalized proxy for gross returns to schooling. Details of the estimation procedures are given in Ram (1976). The estimated production function has the general form:

$$\text{Ln } Y = \beta_0 + \beta_1 \text{ Ln (LAND)} + \beta_2 \text{ Ln (IRR)} + \beta_3 \text{ Ln (CPTL)}$$
$$+ \beta_4 \text{ Ln (RNFL)} + \beta_5 \text{ Ln (FERT)} + \beta_6 \text{ Ln (EXT)} + \beta_7 \text{ Ln (CL)}$$
$$+ \beta_8 \text{ Ln (AL)} + \beta_9 \text{ Ln (CLSC)} + \beta_{10} \text{ Ln (ALSC)} + U$$

change for accumulation of schooling capital tend to become problematic. Two aspects are clearly relevant here. First, as argued above, return to the schooling of cultivators is likely to be substantially higher than that to the schooling of agricultural laborers (and the differential is likely to be bigger in a more dynamic situation). Second, increase in optimum farm size due to technological change may increase the number of agricultural laborers relative to cultivators. Take a rough example.[6] Suppose initially, return to the schooling of cultivators is ten times the return to the schooling of agricultural laborers (call it X), and the ratio of the number of cultivators and agricultural laborers is 3:1. Then the overall return to the schooling of farm workers is roughly 7.75X. Suppose further that after some time, due to technological dynamism, return to the schooling of cultivators becomes fifteen times that to the schooling of agricultural laborers (which assume unchanged at X), and due to increase in optimal scale or otherwise, ratio of cultivators and agricultural laborers is now 3 to 2.5. The overall return then would be about 8.6X.[7] Therefore, despite a 50% increase in the return to cultivator schooling, increase in the overall return is small. In other words, a structural characteristc of the type discussed here (a) directly implies a much lower return to the schooling of agricultural laborers. and (b) has the effect of dampening the incentive provided by technical change for increased accumulation of educational capital in the farm sector.

My third and final comment deals with some aspects of the relationship between health and gains in output and productivity. We all seem to agree that the human agent at the farm level is important in regard to expansion of output. We also recognize the value of his schooling and training. However, we do not yet appear to have given adequate attention to the importance of health and lifespan of these human agents. Nevertheless, whether recognized as important or not, their health and lifespan are of critical importance, not merely for their own well-being directly but also for increased farm productivity. Health and lifespan of farm workers affect their motivation, their aspirations, and, of course, their capacity for work. Poor health level of workers can impose a serious constraint on increase of farm output; and a longer lifespan is the beginning of the removal of such a constraint.

Over the last two or three decades, dramatic developments have taken place in low-income countries in regard to mortality rates and lifespan. There has been an unprecedented decline in mortality and an increase in lifespan (Ram and Schultz forthcoming). Again, taking India as an example, one finds[8] that life expectancy at birth increased from about 32 years to about 47 years roughly between 1950 and 1970.

During the same period life expectancy at age 10 has increased by about 9 years. Similar progress has been recorded in many other low-income countries.

One consequence of these changes is much too well known—and is the subject of considerable discussion—namely, the growth of population. However, several other very important implications have received scant attention. It is a reasonable belief that the observed increases in lifespan and declines in mortality rates have been accomplished by large improvements in the health of the school-going and working populations (including women working in the household or on the family farm). Two major consequences of these developments should be: (a) rise in the productivity of workers in the form of more output per hour or per day, and also more days per year; and (b) increased investment in education, training, and other skill formations. Very little work has been done to quantify these effects despite the fact that the changes have been large, have covered a very large number of countries, and have far-reaching consequences.

Preliminary investigations attempted with respect to India[9] reveal several interesting features. Considering the investment in schooling alone, it is found that educational outlays (inclusive of expenditures by educational institutions and the "opportunity cost" of students' time) increased from about 5.0 billion rupees in 1950–51 to about 30.0 billion rupees in 1967–68. These outlays, although clearly of the nature of investment, are *not* treated as saving or investment in the national accounts. It is, however, interesting to compare the growth of schooling outlays with the growth of (accounted) capital formation. In 1950–51 schooling outlays were about 35% of the gross domestic capital formation, but in 1967–68 they rose to about 55% of the gross domestic capital formation. While it is not suggested that the entire observed increase in educational outlays is due to increased lifespan and reduced mortality, some certainly is, and the component attributable to these changes could well be quite large.

In regard to the effect of improved health on productivity, we are still trying to get data suitable for a direct assessment. However, it is interesting to note that variations between decades in productivity in India's agriculture and fall in mortality rate are positively correlated. It is observed that despite the Green Revolution in the mid-sixties the productivity increase in India's agriculture was *greater* during 1950–60 than during 1960–70. The reduction in mortality (and increase in lifespan) during the decade 1950–60 was also larger than during 1960–70. Thus there is reason to believe that at least part of the increase in productivity is due to fall in mortality rates and the implied improvement in health and lifespan.

Clearly much more work needs to be done to quantify the role of health and lifespan in raising agricultural output, so as to judge the extent to which low health level and very short lifespans in low-income countries operated as constraints on growth of output, and how far the recent dramatic improvement in lifespan, and probably health levels, has helped loosen the constraints.

In conclusion, let me summarize by pointing to a strange contrast. The crucial importance of human health, vitality, and vigor for expansion of farm production is in some sense obvious. However, surprisingly little work has yet been done on what poor health did to farm output in the low-income countries, and what the recent dramatic changes may have contributed to increasing output. On the other hand, the role of schooling in production is not exactly obvious; but many studies during the last two decades have quantified the contribution of education to growth of output, including agricultural production. Perhaps a similar magnitude of work in the health area requires a challenging proposition of the type which Professor Schultz advanced with respect to education (1961).

NOTES

Professor T. W. Schultz's penetrating comments made me aware of several new aspects of the issues discussed in this paper. The responsibility for all deficiencies is, however, entirely mine.

1. The underlying assumption is to support the "human capital" or productivity-augmenting view of schooling as a major explanation of the observed private returns to schooling. In other words, the screening view (Arrow 1973) and the "job-ladder" view (Bhagwati and Srinivasan 1977) of income-schooling relation are not considered plausible as major explanations, although these views might have relevance and validity in certain special circumstances. It is obviously not possible here to engage in a critique of the various theories of schooling-income relation.

2. Of course, what schools do is not a simple matter to investigate or pronounce upon. Nor is it claimed that the proposed framework seeks to throw light on exactly what schools do. The limited objective is to postulate a mechanism through which schooling probably affects productivity, and all that is claimed is that the proposed postulate appears plausible and is not inconsistent with whatever little is known about what schools do.

3. The terms "production" and "producer" are used throughout in a wide sense and include both market and nonmarket (or household) production.

4. It is not claimed that these results are perfect or final in any sense. If quality of the schooling of agricultural laborers is poorer, the difference may be exaggerated. However, the pattern of the differences in the years 1961

and 1971 does not seem to support the proposition that difference in quality of schooling is affecting the coefficients in a major way.

It should also be noted that the issue of migration of educated persons from rural to urban areas is not quite relevant here. It is true that many educated persons migrate to urban areas; but what is being estimated here is the effect of the schooling of farm workers (cultivators and agricultural laborers) on farm output. The schooling variables measure the schooling of those who *are* working on farms.

5. There is *some* evidence in India's agriculture of the validity of Welch's proposition. For example, in 1970–71, about 23% of the total area under wheat was in holdings of 10 hectares or above, while only about 13% of the area under rice was in holdings belonging to that size group (India, Department of Agriculture 1975, pp.32–33). Since wheat was affected by technological change to a greater extent than rice (in 1970–71) the difference in the size distribution under the two crops may reflect economy of scale of the type suggested by Welch.

6. The example is close enough to the actual situation in India in 1961 and 1971. Making the correction suggested by the Registrar General of India (1974, p.21), the ratio of the number of cultivators and agricultural laborers in India changed from about 3:1 in 1961 to about 3:2 in 1971.

7. The average return would evidently also depend upon the change in the relative schooling levels of the two groups.

8. Details relating to the figures mentioned in this paragraph may be found in Ram and Schultz (forthcoming).

9. See Ram and Schultz (forthcoming) for details of the results mentioned in this and the following paragraph.

REFERENCES

Arrow, K. J.   1973.   "Higher Education as a Filter." *Journal of Public Economics* 2, no. 3 (July):193–216.

Bhagwati, J. N., and Srinivasan, T. N.   1977.   "Education in a 'Job Ladder' Model and Fairness-in-Hiring Rule," *Journal of Public Economics* 7, no. 1 (February):1–22.

Chaudhri, D. P.   1968.   "Education and Agricultural Productivity in India." Ph.D. dissertation, University of Delhi.

India, Department of Agriculture.   1975.   *Report of the Agricultural Census of India, 1970–71.* New Delhi.

India, Registrar General.   1974.   *Census of India 1971: Series 1, Paper no. 1 of 1974.* New Delhi.

Ram, Rati.   1976.   "Education as a Quasi-Factor of Production: The Case of India's Agriculture." Ph.D. dissertation, University of Chicago.

Ram, Rati, and Schultz, Theodore W.   Forthcoming.   "Some Economic Implications of Increase in Life Span with Special Reference to India." Essay for a *Festschrift* in honor of V.K.R.V. Rao.

Schultz, Theodore W.   1961.   "Investment in Human Capital." *American Economic Review* 51 (March):1–17.

———.   1964.   *Transforming Traditional Agriculture.* New Haven: Yale University Press (Reprint edition, New York: Arno Press, 1976).

———.   1975.   "The Value of the Ability to Deal with Disequilibria." *Journal of Economic Literature* 13 (September):827–46.

Welch, Finis.   1970.   "Education in Production." *Journal of Political Economy* 78 (January/February):35–59.

Institutional Innovations

VERNON W. RUTTAN

Economists and other social scientists have made important contributions to the theory and practice of research-resource allocation in the physical and biological sciences and in industrial and agricultural technology (Arndt et al. 1977). They have, however, been shy in extending the analysis to cover the resources allocated to research in the social sciences. Yet, the commitment of public and philanthropic resources in support of research and training in the social sciences and in the related professions, such as administration, planning, social service, and law, implies a judgment that the product of social science research represents a potentially valuable contribution to economic and social development.

A first step in attempting to value the contribution of social science research is to clarify the sources of demand for social science knowledge. The conceptual breakthrough in measuring the returns to agricultural research was to treat the output of research as an input into the process of technical change in commodity production (Griliches 1957). The demand for knowledge in the agricultural sciences and technology is derived from the demand for agricultural commodities. In contrast to the demand for knowledge in physical and biological science and technology, it seems reasonable to presume that a part of the demand for knowledge in the social sciences is derived from a demand for institutional change, a demand including both institutional innovation and more efficient performance of existing institutions. As contributors to agriculture, the public demand that accounted for the establishment of the land-grant colleges and universities and of Rural Free Delivery of the mail are examples of useful institutional innovations. The widely used agricultural situation and outlook reports by the U.S. Department of Agriculture have contributed to the more efficient functioning of agricultural commodity markets.

INSTITUTIONAL INNOVATION DEFINED

A distinction is often made between institutions and organizations. Institutions are usually defined as the behavioral rules that govern human actions and relationships constrained by scarcity of resources. Organizations are the decision-making units—families, firms, bureaus, governments—that allocate scarce resources.[1] What an organization, a household or a firm for example, accepts as an externally given behavorial rule is the product of tradition or decision by another organization—a nation's court system or the practices of organized labor or religion for example.[2]

I find it useful to define the concept of an institution broadly to include that of organization. Accordingly, the idea of an institutional innovation is a change in the actual or potential behavior or performance of existing or new organizations; it entails the relationship between an organization and its environment and the behavioral rules that govern the actions and relationships in the organization's environment.[3]

This definition is intended to be sufficiently comprehensive, with reference to institutional innovation in agricultural development for example, to include changes in the market and nonmarket institutions which govern product and factor-market relationships, ranging from the organized commodity market institutions to the patron-client relationships which often characterized exchange in traditional societies. It is also intended to include changes in public and private sector organizations designed to discover and disseminate new knowledge to farmers; to supply inputs such as water, fertilizer, and credit; or to modify market behavior through price support, procurement, or regulation. It encompasses changes which occur as a result of the cumulative effect of the private decisions of individuals, with respect to fertility behavior and migration for example, as well as those which occur as a result of group action designed to modify public decision-making processes.

D. Gale Johnson (1977, p.2) has argued that "the major world food institutions are the national agricultural and trade policies of the industrial and the developing countries" and that a major goal of commodity policy should be modification of existing world food institutions rather than the creation of new institutions. The definition of institutional innovation employed in this paper includes both the modification of existing institutions and the invention of new institutions. It is inclusive of, but broader than, the set of commodity-market institutions which were the focus of Johnson's paper and of several papers in this volume.

SOURCES OF DEMAND FOR
INSTITUTIONAL INNOVATION

The demand for institutional innovation may arise out of the changes in relative factor endowments and relative factor prices associated with development. Douglass C. North and Robert P. Thomas (1970, 1973) attempted to explain the economic growth of Western Europe between 900 and 1700 primarily in terms of changes in the institutions which govern property rights. These institutional changes were, in their view, induced by the pressure of population against increasingly scarce resource endowments. Theodore W. Schultz (1968), focusing on more recent economic history, identified the rising economic value of man during the process of economic development as one of the primary sources of institutional change.

The suggestion that changing factor-price ratios act to induce institutional innovation is consistent with considerable experience in contemporary developing countries. In Thailand the ruling elite in the royal family and the upper bureaucracy shifted their major economic base from a system based on property rights in man to property rights in land as land prices rose relative to the price of labor in the last half of the nineteenth century (Feeney 1976). In Indonesia, between 1868 and 1928, a period of generally rapid economic growth, changes in patron–client obligations were modified in favor of tenants and landless laborers. Since the late 1920s land prices have risen against wage rates and the balance has again shifted in favor of landowners relative to tenants and laborers (White 1974). In the Philippines rising land prices associated with (a) the introduction of higher-yielding rice varieties and (b) increased population pressure against land are inducing changes in land tenure and harvest-sharing arrangements. Farmers who had acquired leasehold and security-of-tenure rights under the land reform are now finding it profitable to sublease part of their land under share-tenure arrangements. Both owners and tenants are requiring laborers to carry out weeding operations in order to establish a right to share in harvest operations (Kukuchi, Maligalig, and Hayami 1977).

The partitioning of the increases in income associated with modernization and economic growth is a second major source of institutional innovation. In a classical or neoclassical world unencumbered by the use of political resources to achieve income-distribution objectives, the new income streams generated by technical change would be captured in the form of rents by the production factors that are characterized by relatively inelastic supply functions. Advances in technology which generate economic growth can be expected to set in motion attempts by factor owners, social classes, and economic sectors to organize and initiate collective action leading to the redefinition of property rights, to modification in the behavior of market institutions, and to the invention of new institutions for the nonmarket transfer of income among members of society.

In most modern societies, for example, the new income streams generated by modernization have induced a new set of institutions designed to directly alter the functional distribution of income—the income shares accruing to the owners of property and the earnings of labor—to prevent the distribution of income from worsening or to improve the distribution of income. The progressive income tax is a classical example of such an institutional innovation. Similarly, much of the history of farm price-support legislation in the United States, from the mid-1920s to the present, can be interpreted as a struggle between agricultural producers and the rest of society to determine the partitioning of the new income streams that have resulted from technical progress in agriculture.[4]

In the perspective outlined above (a) changes in the factor endowments and factor prices arising out of economic growth and (b) the new income streams arising out of technical change represent important sources of demand for institutional change. The demand for institutional change may also shift as a result of changes in cultural endowments. Even under conditions of unchanging demand, however, institutional change may arise out of improvements in the capacity of a society to supply institutional innovations, that is, result from factors which reduce the cost of institutional change.

SOURCES OF SUPPLY OF INSTITUTIONAL CHANGE

The supply of institutional innovation has not been adequately addressed by either the institutionalist or analytical school of economics. The older institutional tradition treated institutional change as primarily dependent on technical change.[5] Within modern analytical economics there is a tendency to either abstract from institutional change[6] or to treat institutional change as exogenous to the economic system.[7] Neither North and Thomas nor Schultz, on whom we drew for insight on the demand for institutional change, attempted to suggest a theory of the supply of institutional change.

It seems reasonable to hypothesize a close analogy between the supply of institutional change and the supply of technical change. Just as the supply curve for technical change shifts to the right as a result of advances in knowledge in science and technology, the supply curve for institutional change shifts to the right in part as a result of advances in knowledge in the social sciences and related professions (law, administration, social service, planning). In the real world property rights are costly to enforce, market exchange consumes resources, and information is scarce. Advances in knowledge in the social sciences and professions should result in some net benefits from institutional change just as advances in knowledge in the natural sciences and engineering have contributed to the net benefits of technical change.

For example, research leading to quantification of commodity supply-and-demand relationships can be expected to contribute toward more efficient functioning of supply management, food procurement, and food distribution programs (Johnson 1977). Research on the social and psychological factors affecting the diffusion of new technology is expected to lead to more effective performance by agricultural credit and extension services, or to more effective organization and implementation of commodity production campaigns. Research on the effects of alternative land-tenure institutions or on the organization and management of group activities in agricultural production is expected to lead to institutional innovations leading to greater equity in access to political and economic resources and to greater productivity in the generation and utilization of resources in rural areas.[8]

This is not to argue that institutional change is entirely or even primarily dependent on formal research leading to new knowledge in the social sciences and professions. Technical change was not delayed until research in the natural sciences and technology became institutionalized. Similarly, institutional change may occur as a result of the exercise of innovative effort by politicians, bureaucrats, entrepreneurs, and others as they conduct their normal daily activities.[9] The timing or pace of institutional innovation may be influenced by external contact or internal stress. The objectives of institutionalization of social science research capacity include greater efficiency in the allocation of social science research resources (a) to speed up the production of new knowledge that is designed to be used as inputs into those areas of institutional change on which society places a relatively high priority and (b) to apply the new knowledge to bring about a more precise linkage between the institutional changes that are implemented and the objectives of institutional change. If we were satisfied with the slow pace of technical and institutional change which characterize most trial and error procedure there would be no need to institutionalize research capacity in either the natural or the social sciences.

A notable example of the effect of new knowledge in the social sciences on institutional innovation has been the advance in knowledge of macro-economic relationships identified with the Keynesian revolution. No effort has been made to estimate the aggregate economic gains generated by the new knowledge in enabling the developed countries of the West to operate at close-to-full employment for the first quarter century following World War II. We do have the partial estimates made by Arthur M. Okun (1968) of the contributions to

United States' economic growth resulting from the reductions in personal and corporate income tax under the Revenue Act of 1964. Okun's *ex post* estimates indicate that the tax reduction totaling $13 billion in 1964 and 1965 contributed $25 billion during the first two years after the tax cut and an ultimate $36 billion to the growth of GNP. It is increasingly clear, however, that Keynesian fiscal policy is also subject to limitations. The high rates of inflation and of unemployment despite large national budget deficits imply that the fiscal-monetary policy, which is a legacy of Keynesian policy, can have adverse consequences.

In principle it should be possible to estimate the gains (losses) from advances in economic knowledge, for example those from improved knowledge of commodity demand-and-supply relationships on institutional performance. Telser and Higinbotham (1977) have developed and tested a cost-benefit model to explain the emergence of organized futures markets but made no attempt to assess the effects of advances in the understanding of the economics of commodity-market organization on market performance. Peterson and Hayami (1972) have estimated the returns to improvements in the U.S. agricultural statistics system but they did not attempt to attribute a component to the advances in knowledge in survey-research methodology. In the future it seems likely that better information on the returns to social science research will become a necessary input into the research-resource allocation process.

RESOURCE ALLOCATION
IN SOCIAL SCIENCES RESEARCH

The significance of the theory of institutional change proposed in this paper is that it suggests an economic theory of induced institutional change that is capable of generating testable hypotheses regarding (a) alternative paths of institutional change over time for a particular society and (b) divergent patterns of institutional change among countries at a particular time. It is possible to build on this model to develop a theory of induced institutional change that is not only explanatory, in the sense that the present is explained in terms of the past, but is capable of generating testable hypotheses regarding the future direction of institutional change and which can be used to guide economic and other social science research to achieve more effective institutional performance and more rapid institutional innovation.

The premise that the demand for knowledge in the social sciences is derived from the demand for more effective rural institutions places a special burden on the organizations that fund or manage research programs in agricultural and rural development. The demand for knowledge that can contribute to improvements in the effectiveness of the institutions that serve rural areas in the developing economies appears to have risen sharply during the 1970s. In the past, technical constraints on agricultural production have generally represented a more serious barrier to agricultural and rural development in poor countries than have institutional constraints (Schultz 1964). As some of the technical constraints have been removed, institutional constraints have emerged as increasingly significant barriers to the realization of higher levels of productivity in rural areas. The effect is to place research on the social-science dimensions of agricultural and rural development higher on the agenda of research priorities than in the past. If the expanding demand for institutional change is translated into more resources for social-science research on agricultural and rural development the problem of efficient allocation of social-science research resources will become increasingly important.

The response to the demand for institutional innovation and for more efficient institutional performance has often been an attempt to transfer rural institutions from high-income to low-income countries. The effect has frequently been either failure or bias in institutional performance. Failure in poor countries of cooperative production and marketing and credit institutions organized to conform to high-income country models is notorious. The distortion of land-reform programs to expropriate traditional property rights of the landless and near-landless in group production and consumption or to induce the emergence of a new class of subtenants has been widely noted.

It has now been carefully documented and widely recognized that the efficient allocation of research resources to technical change in agriculture involves a choice of research strategy that is consistent with a nation's or a region's resource endowment. In Japan especially so prior to World War II, for example, research resources were efficiently allocated to permit substitution of industrial inputs for the increasingly scarce and expensive land resources. In the United States research resources were allocated to permit substitution of industrial inputs for the increasingly scarce and expensive labor resources (Hayami and Ruttan 1971). In Japan too, during recent decades, the price of farm labor has been rising relative to the price of fertilizer and other inputs that farmers purchase. The institutional innovations that are appropriate in an environment in which the price of labor is rising relative to the price of land will be quite different than the institutional innovations that will be efficient under conditions of increasing pressure of population and labor force against land in rural areas.

ALTERNATIVE PATH OF
INSTITUTIONAL INNOVATION

I have suggested elsewhere (Binswanger and Ruttan 1978) two broad hypotheses with respect to the direction of institutional change. *First, the effect of growth in the income flows available to a community or society is to induce institutional changes that weaken the control of the community or of society over the allocation of resources and the partitioning of income flows.* New income flows may be generated by geographic or geologic discovery, by technical change, or by prior institutional change.

Second, the effect of stagnation or decline in the income flows available to a society is to induce institutional changes that expand the control of the community or the society over the allocation of income flows. Stagnation or decline in income flows may occur as a result of increased pressure of population against resource endowments, technological stagnation or retrogression, or institutional changes such as colonial or other external intervention into a society.

The first hypothesis suggests that during periods when new income flows are being generated at a rapid rate, innovating units are relatively successful in loosening the social constraints that limit their ability to capture the gains from economic growth and in transferring the costs of growth to other economic units and to the community—or society—at large. The history of utopian communities provides a particularly interesting illustration of this hypothesis (Erasmus 1977). The length of time over which such communities have remained viable appears to be inversely related to their economic success. The Israeli kibbutzim have responded to increasing economic prosperity by relaxing their constraints on employment of labor from outside the commune, on diversification of economic activity within the commune, on household consumption patterns, and on family living arrangements. Economic growth has weakened the communal ideology. The kibbutzim appear to be evolving toward a corporate rather than a communal structure, with resultant greater individual control over communal resources and less effective sanctions over the contributions of individuals to communal economic and social development. At the same time, the political power of the organized kibbutzim enables them to continue to receive substantial income transfers in the form of subsidized credit and market protection from the broader Israeli society. The Hutterite communities, which have experienced a particularly long period of communal viability, have successfully used the need for high rates of capital accumulation for the establishment of new communities to maintain rigorous social control over the consumption patterns of the communal membership (Bennett 1967).

From the history of the plantation sector in Southeast Asia we can draw another illustration. In the past, the plantation sector in both the colonial and noncolonial economies of Southeast Asia was relatively successful in capturing the gains from expanded production of staple commodities (Furnivall 1956; Birnberg and Resnik 1975). Plantation owners were also relatively successful in transferring the costs of growth to the peasant and public sectors. As a result, the peasant sector was unable to develop the mass purchasing power necessary to sustain economic growth in the nonagricultural sectors. Moreover, the public sector was prevented from developing the capacity to provide rural areas with the institutional and physical infrastructure that was needed to enable the economy to break out of an enclave pattern of development. More of the experimental political organization in which South and Southeast Asian governments have engaged during the last several decades can be viewed as an attempt to evolve a system of political and economic organization that is capable of mobilizing the region's natural and human resources to achieve more rapid development.

My second hypothesis suggests that a period of economic stagnation or decline can be expected to induce institutional changes that will enable the community, or the society, to force innovating units both to bear the costs of technical or institutional change and to transfer the gains to other economic units or to the community or society generally. Thus, the long period of secular economic stagnation in China during the latter half of the nineteenth and first half of the twentieth century induced a set of revolutionary institutional changes that gave both the local community and the broader society more effective control over local and national resources (Moore 1966). The most dramatic of these institutional changes involved the development of China's capacity to mobilize its labor resources to produce an economic surplus that could be channeled into developing the nonagricultural sectors. As the long period of stagnation is reversed and new growth dividends become available, it seems reasonable to anticipate a set of institutional innovations that will weaken social control over allocation of the growth dividends. Control over these dividends will be captured by the enterprises and individuals providing the sources of growth, as has occurred in the more mature socialist societies of Eastern Europe and the USSR.

This process of technical and institutional change is dialectical rather than linear. The impact of technical and institutional innovations that open up new sources of growth—that generate new income streams—in traditional societies can be expected to induce further institutional innovations that weaken communal and social control over the allocation and use of resources. A period of rapid growth followed by a period of relative decline or stagnation resulting from the exhaustion of either resource endowments or technological potential or from a failure of institutional innovation can be expected to induce institutional innovations that give society greater social control to mobilize the resources of the society. If these resources are directed to the generation of technical and institutional innovations that are consistent with the resource and cultural endowments of the society, a new period of growth will be induced.

The induced institutional innovation hypothesis suggested above implies a strong demand for clarification of the conceptual relationships among resource endowments, cultural endowments, technological change, and institutional change as these bear on the processes of agricultural development:

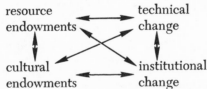

It also calls for the careful testing of those relationships against both historical and contemporary experience. The methodology that will be appropriate in testing the induced institutional-change hypothesis is not yet as clear cut as the rather straightforward econometric tests that have confirmed the robustness of the induced technical-change hypothesis. As our knowledge of the economic forces which condition the rate and direction of institutional change improves, it seems likely that we will be confronted with policy issues that are analogous to those in the area of induced technical change. In technical changes, for example, it has become apparent that distortions of the prices in factor and product markets bias current technology choices. This also affects the technology that will become available in the future. The unfavorable price ratio between wheat and fertilizer or rice and fertilizer has, in some countries, delayed the development of fertilizer-responsive wheat and rice varieties by more than a generation. In a number of countries, the overvalued exchange rates and direct subsidies have resulted in premature mechanization.

The productivity of social science research, under these circumstances will depend on the capacity of research entrepreneurs to penetrate existing bias in the demand for social science knowledge to identify the latent demand that reflects the more fundamental resource and cultural endowments.

PERSPECTIVE

A clear implication of the induced institutional-innovation perspective is the desirability that economists and other social scientists begin to develop greater depth in the positive analysis of the social and political forces bearing on the choice of economic policy.[10] The continuing frustration concerning apparent lack of rationality in trade relationships, agricultural commodity markets, and in the public regulation of economic activity represents in part a failure to utilize modern economics to resolve issues such as the allocation of political resources to effect the distribution of economic resources and the partitioning of income streams generated by technical and institutional change.

NOTES

This paper draws appreciably on Chap. 12, "Induced Institutional Innovation," in Binswanger and Ruttan (1978).

1. According to Frank H. Knight (1952, p.51), "the term 'institution' has two meanings. . . . One type . . . may be said to be created by the 'invisible hand.' The extreme example is language, in the growth and changes of which deliberate action hardly figures; . . . law is in varying . . . degree of the same kind. The other type is of course the deliberately made, of which our Federal Reserve System and this [American Economic] Association itself are examples. With age, the second type tends to approximate the first." Knight's perspective is consistent with that of Samuel P. Huntington (1965, p.394): "Institutions are stable, valued, recurring patterns of behavior. Organizations and procedures vary in their degree of institutionalization. . . . Institutionalization is the process by which organization and procedures acquire value and stability."

2. There is a useful analogy between the concepts of institutions and organization and of external and internal scale economies. Jacob Viner (1932) insisted that the external economies of scale enjoyed by one firm or industry are due to internal economies in some other firm or industry.

3. This definition is broader than that employed by Veblen but is consistent with the one employed by John R. Commons (1950, p.61). The definition used here encompasses the classification system employed by Lance E. Davis and Douglass C. North (1971).

4. This involves an implicit assumption that when shifts in the demand for institutional innovations are induced by new income streams arising from technical change the scope for distributive, in contrast to redistributive, institutional innovations, is widened. It seems apparent that the political cost for distributive institutional change is generally lower than for redistributive institutional change. Under conditions of economic stagnation or decline the demand for redistributive institutional change may be sufficiently strong to divert substantial political and economic resources to the pursuit of redistributive policies. See, for example, the very perceptive article by Anne O. Krueger (1974) on the economics of the rent-seeking society. For insight into the processes involved in the use of political resources to partition the rents generated by agricultural commodity programs see Weldon V. Barton (1976).

5. In the work of Veblen and Ayres "it was the . . . dialectical struggle and conflict between dynamic technology and static institutionalism which caused economic and political institutions slowly to be displaced and replaced, and systems of economic organization to undergo historical change and adjustment" (Zingler 1974, p.331). See also Seckler (1975).

6. According to Paul A. Samuelson (1948, pp.221–2), "the auxiliary constraints imposed upon the variables are not themselves the proper subject of welfare economics but must be taken as given." For a critique of the failure of general equilibrium theory to incorporate institutional change see Martin Shubik (1976).

7. The approach to institutional innovation that is characteristic of much of the reform or planning tradition in economics is illustrated by Abba P. Lerner (1944, p.6): "In this study . . . we shall assume a government that wishes to run society in the general social interest and is strong enough to override the opposition afforded by any sectional interest." Harry G. Johnson (1974, p.9) commented: "The main tradition of welfare economics takes a Benthamite or Fabian view of the state as a dispassionate and all-wise modern equivalent of Plato's philosopher-king, correcting the errors of his subject society by appropriate taxes, subsidies, and lump-sum transfers of income." This point has been made even more succinctly by Irving Lewis Horowitz (1972, p.49): "In the planning ideology all planning is done by a dedicated development-oriented elite supported by loyal, self sacrificing masses."

8. For an interesting analysis of a situation in which modifications in institutional design to achieve greater equity in the distribution of irrigation water represent an essential element in removing the constraints on productivity, see Bromley, Taylor, and Parker (1977).

9. According to Paul P. Streeten (1974, pp.1296–97), "those who take a Marxian rather than a Keynesian view of the relation between the power of ideas and *praxis* see evidence that solutions to social problems are worked out by men and women going about their daily work . . . and that the grand theories distill these practical experiences." P. C. Joshi (1975, p.7) makes essentially the same point drawing on Indian land-reform experience: "The

circumstances which gave an initial stimulus to intellectual inquiry into the land question . . . preceded the professionalization of Indian economic studies. . . . Enquiries into the land problem were thus initiated by those concerned directly with the formulation of land and revenue policies (or the critique of these policies) and not by professional social scientists."

10. "It seems unfruitful . . . to conclude . . . that those policies which did not achieve their announced goals, or had perverse effects . . . are simply mistakes of the society. A policy adopted and followed for a long time, or followed by many different states, could not usefully be described as a mistake: . . . To say such policies are mistaken is to say that one can not explain them. . . . Until we understand why society adopts its policies we will be poorly equipped to give useful advice on how to change these policies" (Stigler 1975, pp.x, xi).

REFERENCES

Arndt, Thomas M.; Dalrymple, Dana G.; and Ruttan, Vernon W., eds. 1977. *Resource Allocation and Productivity in National and International Agricultural Research*. Minneapolis: University of Minnesota Press.

Barton, Weldon. 1976. "Coalition-Building in the United States House of Representatives: Agricultural Legislation in 1973." In *Cases in Public Policy Making*, ed. James E. Anderson, pp.141–61. New York: Praeger.

Bennett, John W. 1967. *Hutterian Brethren*. Stanford: Stanford University Press.

Binswanger, Hans P., and Ruttan, Vernon W. 1978. *Induced Innovation: Technology Institutions and Development*. Baltimore: Johns Hopkins Press.

Birnberg, Thomas B., and Resnik, Stephen A. 1975. *An Econometric Study of Colonial Development*. New Haven: Yale University Press.

Bromley, Daniel W.; Taylor, Donald C.; and Parker, Donald E. 1977. "The Economics of Water Reform: Institutional Design for Improved Water Management in the LDC's." Mimeographed. Madison: Department of Agricultural Economics, University of Wisconsin.

Commons, John R. 1950. *The Economics of Collective Action*. New York: Macmillan.

Davis, Lance E., and North, Douglass C. 1971. *Institutional Change and American Economic Growth*. New York: Cambridge University Press.

Erasmus, Charles J. 1977. *In Search of the Common Good*. New York: Macmillan Free Press.

Feeney, David Harold. 1976. "Technical and Institutional Change in Thai Agriculture, 1880–1940." Ph.D. dissertation, Department of Economics, University of Wisconsin.

Furnivall, J. S. 1956. *Colonial Policy and Practice*. New York: New York University Press.

Griliches, Zvi. 1957. "Hybrid Corn: An Exploration in the Economics of Technological Change." *Econometrica* 25 (October):501–22.

Hayami, Yujiro, and Ruttan, Vernon W. 1971. *Agricultural Development: An International Perspective.* Baltimore: Johns Hopkins Press.

Horowitz, Irving Louis. 1972. *Three Worlds of Development.* 2nd ed. New York: Oxford University Press.

Huntington, Samuel P. 1965. "Political Development and Political Decay." *World Politics* 17 (April):386–430.

Johnson, D. Gale. 1977. "World Food Institutions: Policy Perspectives—A Liberal View." University of Chicago Agricultural Economics Research Paper 77:2. [Also in press, *International Organizations.*]

Johnson, Harry G. 1974. "The Current and Prospective State of Economics." *Australian Economic Papers* 13 (June):1–27.

Joshi, P. C. 1975. *Land Reforms in India.* New Delhi: Allied Publishers.

Kikuchi, Masao; Maligalig, Luisa; and Hayami, Yujiro. 1977. "Evolution of Land Tenure System in a Laguna Village." Mimeographed. Los Baños, Philippines: International Rice Research Institute.

Knight, Frank H. 1952. "Institutionalism and Empiricism in Economics." *American Economic Review* 42 (May):45–55.

Krueger, Anne O. 1974. "The Political Economy of the Rent Seeking Society." *American Economic Review* 64 (June): 291–303.

Lerner, Abba P. 1944. *The Economics of Control.* New York: Macmillan.

Moore, Barrington. 1966. *Social Origins of Dictatorship and Democracy: Land and Peasant in the Making of the Modern World.* Boston: Beacon Press.

North, Douglass C., and Thomas, Robert P. 1970. "An Economic Theory of the Growth of the Western World." *Economic History Review* 23 (2nd Series) 1–17.

———. 1973. *The Rise of the Western World.* London: Cambridge University Press.

Okun, Arthur M. 1968. "Measuring the Impact of the 1964 Tax Reduction." In *Perspectives on Economic Growth,* ed. Walter W. Heller, pp.25–49. New York: Random House.

Peterson, Willis L., and Hayami, Yujiro. 1972. "Social Returns to Public Information Services: Statistical Reporting of U.S. Farm Commodities." *American Economic Review* 62 (March):119–30.

Samuelson, Paul A. 1948. *Foundations of Economic Analysis.* Cambridge: Harvard University Press.

Schultz, Theodore W. 1964. *Transforming Traditional Agriculture.* New Haven: Yale University Press (Reprint edition, New York: Arno Press, 1976).

———. 1968. "Institutions and the Rising Economic Value of Man." *American Journal of Agricultural Economics* 50 (December):1113–22.

Seckler, David. 1975. *Thorstein Veblen and the Institutionalists.* London: Macmillan.

Shubik, Martin. 1976. *Beyond General Equilibrium.* Discussion paper 417. New Haven: Cowles Foundation for Research in Economics at Yale University.

Stigler, George J.   1975.   *The Citizen and the State: Essays on Regulation.*
Chicago: University of Chicago Press.
Streeten, Paul P.   1974.   "Social Science Research on Development: Some
Problems in the Use and Transfer of an Intellectual Technology." *Journal
of Economic Literature* 12 (December):1290–1300.
Telser, Lester G., and Higinbotham, Harlow N.   1977.   "Organized Fu-
tures Markets: Costs and Benefits." *Journal of Political Economy* 85 (Oc-
tober):969–1000.
Viner, Jacob.   1932.   "Cost Curves and Supply Curves." *Zeitschrift für
National-Ökonomie,* Band III:23–46.
White, Benjamin.   1974.   "Agricultural Involution: A Critical Note." Mim-
eographed. Jakarta: Agro-Economic Survey.
Zingler, E. K.   1974.   "Veblen vs. Commons: A Comparative Evaluation."
Kyklos 27, no. 2:322–44.

PART VI

THE QUEST FOR EQUITY

Approaches to "Basic Needs" and to "Equity" that Distort Incentives in Agriculture

G. EDWARD SCHUH

Policy makers and world opinion leaders have become increasingly sensitive to the problems of social justice and equity. The World Bank's sector policy paper (1975) on *Rural Development* was an important landmark in the recent emergence of a concern for the world's poor. The World Employment Conference, held in Geneva in June, 1976, with its *Declaration of Principles and a Programme of Action*, was another.[1]

The empirical basis for this concern is by now well known. Despite important caveats about the data, it has become an accepted belief that more than 700 million people around the world live in acute poverty and are destitute and that some 450 to 500 million people suffer from a severe degree of protein-energy malnutrition. There are also "estimates" that nearly 300 million persons were unemployed or underemployed in Third World countries in the mid-1970s (International Labour Office 1977, p.1).

There is a wide range of policies which have been devised to deal with these problems; some of these policies are of rather long standing, and resources are being committed on an increasing scale. This belated recognition of the severity of the poverty problem on a world scale is long overdue. However, many of the policies designed to deal with poverty are misdirected, and waste precious and scarce development resources, often with little payoff in terms of attaining their avowed objectives.

My main emphasis here is that many policies designed to deal with "basic needs" and/or equality have strong resource-allocation effects both within the agricultural sector and between the agricultural sector and the rest of the economy, often with serious adverse effects on output. First, I will illustrate a number of such policies. Second, I shall argue for a different set of policies to deal with poverty—policies

307

which actually promote growth rather than inhibit it. At the end I shall have some concluding comments.

EQUITY-MOTIVATED POLICIES THAT DISTORT INCENTIVES FOR AGRICULTURE

Agriculture bears a disproportionate share of the deleterious consequences of equity-motivated development policies because food is a wage good and makes up a major share of the budget expenditures of the poor. Policy makers prone to deal with symptoms of problems and/or interested in a "quick fix" logically turn to doing something about the price of food. That the bulk of the poor around the world, even in the advanced countries, are located in agriculture also makes this sector a likely target for policies designed to deal more directly with poverty. Some of these latter policies are in my view as misguided as are those that deal more directly with food prices.

In this first section I consider four sets of policies that represent rather divergent approaches to dealing with the equity or basic needs problem. Two of these policies involve manipulations of relative prices: the food and price policies in India and the trade and exchange-rate policies in Brazil. The other two deal more directly with the "structure" of agriculture, and include land reform, in which case I draw on the Chilean experiment under Allende and the recent emphasis on rural development.

Price and Food Policy in India

India is an important example of a country that has intervened heavily in the food and agriculture sector in an attempt to take care of basic needs of the "vulnerable" section of her society. These interventions have involved particular price policies for the food grains, plus direct participation in the marketing system.

Features of the policies prevailing since 1960 and that are of interest to us include the following[2]:

(1) Restrictions on the interstate movement[3] of food grains—the so-called "zonal restrictions";

(2) Operation of a public distribution system through a network of "fair-price shops" and rationing;

(3) The use, for producers, of a two-tier price system, consisting of a minimum price announced in advance of the sowing season and a procurement price at which the government buys grain; and

(4) Operation of a system of compulsory procurement of a part of the marketable surplus at less than market prices.

The "fair"-price shops were, until recently, located predominantly in urban areas. The government provides grain to these shops at a subsidized price. An informal rationing system is in effect, with the consumer buying a part of his total consumption from the fair-price shop at the subsidized price and the remainder at the prevailing market price. Hence, at least in the urban areas there is a two-tier price system for consumers.

The procurement operations by means of which the government acquires grain to sell to the vulnerable groups have taken several forms. There have been at different times and places a levy on producers and/or millers and traders at less than market prices, monopoly procurement of the marketed surplus, and market purchases. Overall, however, the policy has been to procure a part of the production, mainly of rice, directly from farmers by means of a compulsory levy at less than the market price and then to permit producers to sell the rest of their output in the semicontrolled market.

In essence, this system of procurement is nothing more than a system of taxation in kind. In principle, there could be little objection to such a tax, since farmers pay very little by way of a monetary income tax. Similarly, the sale of food grains to consumers at subsidized prices amounts to an income transfer to these consumers. This should increase the overall demand for the food grains, with the result that an uncontrolled market price of these cereals would be higher under the procurement scheme than in its absence.

There are rather obvious distortions to incentives in other directions, however. In the first place, the tax is discriminating in the sense that only crops subject to procurement (for the most part, rice and wheat) are taxed, while other crops remain outside the system. This in itself should serve as a disincentive to produce the very crops that policy makers believe the vulnerable groups should have greater access to.

Second, procurement is undertaken primarily by the states. Again, the taxation is discriminatory. In fact, the zonal restrictions which prohibit interstate shipments are designed to enable the state governments to "trap" the grain within individual states so that they can acquire the required quantities at the specified procurement price.

Clearly, there are two effects on incentives in this case. The first is the effect on the price of the product; it reduces the incentive to produce. This is largely a consequence of the zonal restrictions and the relatively low price at which procurement takes place. Second, there is the discriminatory tax effect which comes about because producers in some states are taxed heavily, while those in other states are not taxed at all. Hence, the policies should reduce the supply of work effort, with a differential effect among states.

Unfortunately, the effect of both of these incentive effects will tend to be most adverse in the very states that have the greatest production potential. Although population density is important in determining where a production "surplus" will exist, the quality of the "land" in terms of soil characteristics, rainfall, and temperature is also important. In effect, the policies act to reduce the incentives to produce in the very areas where the production potential is the greatest.

The policies pursued have also had a discriminatory effect between the two food grains. Rice is by far the most important food grain. Hence, policy has been more severe with respect to this crop. Schultz (forthcoming), for example, notes that on the world market a unit of rice typically sells for double the price of wheat, whereas in India they exchange at approximately a one-to-one ratio. This, of course, is an enormous distortion in relative prices.

It is interesting to note the source of this distortion. Sukhatme (1975) provides data which indicate that the Indian domestic wholesale price of wheat was between 50 and 55% higher than the world price of wheat between 1964 and 1972. The wholesale price of rice, on the other hand, was between 7 and 55% lower than the world price in the same period.

These differences between Indian and world prices (a measure of nominal protection) suggest that the production of wheat has been protected, at least in this period. A more interesting concept, of course, is the level of effective protection, which takes account of taxes or subsidies on purchased inputs. Sukhatme's preliminary calculations suggest that the effective protection for rice between 1960 and 1972 ranged between +4% and −62%, with the rate being negative after 1964. For wheat, on the other hand, the effective protection was positive for the entire period 1960 through 1972 and ranged between 26 and 100%. Clearly, the distortion between the two crops is large.

The important point to note here is that more producers grow rice than wheat. Moreover, the land committed to the production of rice has few production alternatives. Hence, producers of rice have little opportunity to escape this tax within agriculture, so its effect is to lower agricultural output in the aggregate. Moreover, the tax provides incentives for producers to leave the rice sector (which in large areas of the country is synonymous with agriculture) and seek employment elsewhere.

There are other aspects of Indian policy which could usefully be discussed. The takeover of the wheat trade in 1972–73 and the long-time use of P.L. 480 imports from the United States, for example, are important examples of policies designed to help the poor which have ultimately had sizable negative effects on agricultural output. However, instead of considering these policies, I shall turn to an alternative means by which basic needs and equity goals have been handled, and which also has important incentive effects.

Trade and Exchange-Rate Policies in Brazil

Brazil has used trade and exchange rate policy as the primary means to extract the surplus from her agricultural sector (see Bergsman 1970, chap. 3; Doellinger et al. 1974; Leff 1968, chaps. 2 and 3; and Veiga 1974). Contrary to the case of India, there have been only limited attempts to transfer food directly to low-income groups. Rather, policy has been directed to shifting the internal terms of trade against agriculture, primarily through trade and exchange rate policy.

The policies pursued involved a complex, ever-changing, and at times bewildering maze of interventions. However, the "core" of the policy during most of the post-World War II period consisted of three main elements: (1) High protective tariffs for the industrial sector as the basis for an import-substituting industrialization drive;[4] (2) a "vent-for-surplus" export model;[5] and (3) an overvalued exchange rate. The first of these policies had little to do with basic needs or equity so I shall concentrate on the other two.

The "vent-for-surplus" export model has as its basic precept that only the excess above domestic needs should be exported. This basic idea has dominated Brazilian export policy through most of the post-World War II period. Its tenets were adhered to less rigorously in the period following 1967 but not abandoned entirely. Exports were controlled for the most part through licensing arrangements. The decision rule for granting an export license was that the domestic price not be rising. In a situation in which inflation was chronically between 20 and 60 to 70%, the obvious result was for exports to be constrained.

In addition to these licensing arrangements, much use was made of export quotas, periodic embargos on all exports of a given product, and explicit export taxes. The consequence of these policies, of course, was to channel output to the domestic market by foregoing export possibilities. This had the effect of causing domestic prices for the agricultural export products to be less than their world market opportunity value. Such discrimination, in turn, was a disincentive to production, especially as high levels of protection pushed prices of industrial products well above international levels.[6]

It is important to note that the explicit objective of these trade-restrictive policies for agricultural products was to keep food prices low in the chronic battle with high rates of inflation. The production disincentive of the policies was severe, often with the result that imports had to be brought in to offset some temporary food shortages which arose as a consequence of the government's restrictive policies. Ironically enough, Brazil more often than not ended up paying more to foreign producers for the imports than she was willing to pay her own producers.

The other policy which has had a substantial effect on agriculture as an export sector is the chronic overvaluation of the Brazilian currency. The cruzeiro has been overvalued throughout most of the post-World War II period, with the amount ranging from 10 to 20% most of the time, but at times being much greater.[7] Only in 1970–72 was it close to equilibrium.

An overvalued exchange rate is, of course, an implicit export tax. In the immediate post-World War II period, it appears that the main rationale for its use was to exploit Brazil's dominant position in the world market for coffee.[8] Later, most observers seem to agree that its main rationale was to assist in the continual battle to check the rise in cost of living (e.g., see Bergsman 1970, chap. 3). Policy makers were quite aware that a devaluation would raise the domestic price of both export commodities and imports. Both of these were important most directly to urban consumers, with foodstuffs being especially important to industrial workers. Hence, policy makers resisted the devaluation as long as they could. The result was a persistent tax on agriculture.

Mauro Lopes (1977) has used the model Floyd (1965) developed for an analysis of U.S. agriculture to analyze the effects of the implicit export tax on Brazilian agriculture. The results of his analysis provide estimates of the consequences of the discriminatory policies, and at the same time provide important insights with respect to certain puzzles of Brazilian agricultural development.

Lopes made the rather conservative assumption that the effect of the overvalued exchange rate and other restrictions on exports was to lower the relative price of agricultural products by 10%.[9] In the aggregate, his results show that the effect of this shift in the internal terms of trade is to reduce employment in agriculture by 18%, that of capital by 27%, and land use by 6%, other things being equal. Clearly, the policies had a major disincentive effect on agriculture. Moreover, these policies also appear to have played a major role in pushing labor out of agriculture and causing it to accumulate in the urban centers.

Lopes also analyzed the effects of the discriminatory policies by size of farm, and these results go a long way to explaining why large farms are cultivated so extensively in Brazil while small farms are cultivated relatively more intensively. In contrast to only a 3 to 4% decline in employment of labor among small farms, the reduction is between 22 and 26% for medium-sized farms and between 32 and

34% for large farms. A similar relationship holds for capital, with reductions of 23 and 26% for medium-size farms and between 36 and 43% for large farms. What these results suggest, of course, is that the large farms are more able to escape the tax than the small farms. In the final analysis, moreover, it is the agricultural worker who has to bear the bulk of the burden of the tax.

Both the export policy and the exchange-rate policy in Brazil have been predicated in large part on keeping the price of food down for urban consumers. The consequences of the policies has been a relative shift of labor and capital out of agriculture. In effect, agricultural resources have been substantially undervalued in relation to their international opportunity value, with the result that the major share of poverty in the Brazilian economy is today concentrated in the agricultural sector.

Needless to say, Brazil has the potential to be a major source of agricultural products on world markets. To date it has sacrificed a large share of that potential by pursuing restrictive trade policies.

Land Reforms

The redistribution of land is one of the most frequently proposed solutions to the equity problem in agriculture. In Latin America this is partly because the distribution of land holdings is in fact highly skewed. Moreover, land ownership is the key to political power, and land redistribution is viewed as much as a means of redistributing political power as it is of redistributing income.

Land reform is also often viewed as a means of increasing agricultural output, however. This proposition rests on three arguments, at least two of which can be questioned. The first is the long-held belief that sharecropping led to a misallocation of resources. Cheung (1969) has challenged the analysis which led to this belief, and there is growing empirical evidence in support of his revised formulations of the problem (see Reid 1976).

The second argument is based on the empirical finding that small farms tend to have higher land productivity than do large farms. This leads many to conclude that breaking up large farms into small units would raise overall output. Needless to say, whether it does or not depends importantly on why farms have the particular size they do, and why the productivity relationships take the particular form they do.[10]

Finally, there is a common belief that it is the eye of the master that fattens the cattle. Hence, providing the means whereby the tiller is the owner of his own land is viewed as a way of raising overall resource productivity and efficiency.

A final reason why land reform is a common policy prescription for

dealing with both efficiency and equity problems is the land fundamentalism that dominates so much thinking about agriculture. Despite
the considerable evidence to the contrary,[11] and the emergence of a
rather robust theory of human capital, increases in land productivity
are viewed as the sine qua non of agricultural development,[12] and as
the main source of income streams for rural people. The importance
of human capital is still widely neglected when it comes to thinking
about agricultural development.

As an example of how a land reform can distort production incentives and in the end be counterproductive, I shall examine briefly
the Allende land reform of Chile. The Chilean experience is useful
not because it is representative of land reforms, but because it is a
pointed example of how incentives can be distorted by programs designed to deal with equity.

The Allende land reform was a massive attempt to redistribute both
income and power within the rural sector.[13] Interestingly enough,
especially in light of its ultimate consequences, it was also expected
to eliminate economic irrationality in land use, and to improve the
productivity of agriculture.

Contrary to the case with many land reforms, Chile was quite well
equipped to undertake a redistribution of assets on the scale proposed.
It had the best cadastral survey in Latin America, a modern tax system, a technical assistance program accompanied by the best financial backing and highest technical level of any poor country which has
instituted a massive agrarian reform program.

Despite these favorable preconditions for a successful reform, the
results were little short of a disaster. Output declined 3.6% in the
1971–72 crop year and 13.7% in the 1972–73 crop year. Moreover, imports of food increased by 60% in 1971 (compared to 1970), 91% in
1972, and 27% in 1973. As a consequence, net farm imports, which
on the average used the equivalent of 18% of the total annual value of
national exports during 1965–70, increased to more than 50% of the
total value of Chile's exports. This land reform generated a serious contraction in output and employment in the rest of the economy.

These serious balance-of-payments consequences were in part de-
mand-induced. The income policy of the Chilean government substantially increased the effective demand for food, as did price policies.
But the decline in agricultural output was not due to bad weather
nor to the lack of government support for agriculture. Although private
investment in agriculture was practically eliminated, financial transfers through public investment and credit were increased dramatically.
Whereas on the average, during 1960–70, official credits to agriculture

amounted to about 20% of its gross product, this figure reached approximately 80% in 1972.

Valdés (1974) argues that the reorganization at the farm level was probably the principal reason for the decline in production and the high financial cost of the program. The *Unidad Popular* intended to inhibit in every way possible the development of private property and to avoid the physical subdivisions of farms. The land and fixed capital was to belong to the State, and the goal was to have at least 80% of the land worked collectively and the rest assigned individually in pasture and farming rights.

It was here that incentives became distorted. Each member was required to work a minimum number of days for the collective, and was paid in advance, generally at the minimum wage, for this work. The advance was made on account against the final profits of the agricultural year. But the campesinos could share individually in the surplus only up to a maximum not greater than 20% of the total surplus. Ten percent went to the formation of an internal investment fund and the rest was for a community development fund.

Clearly, these institutional arrangements designed to develop collective work and equality of income in fact encouraged members to concentrate their attention on their own individual farm plots. Since these plots represented only a small portion of the total area of the collective unit, the result was an inefficient allocation of labor effort between individual and collective cultivation and a consequent loss in output. The bulk of the land received very little labor input, while a small proportion of the land received a major share of the labor. The subsidized capital inputs presumably were for collective activities, but one can well imagine that much of it ended up on the individual plots.

Perhaps the most serious criticism of the Allende reform is that it did not come to grips with the problem of rural poverty, despite the high costs incurred in public resources, sacrificed output, and wasted foreign-exchange earnings. Chilean wage earners in the agricultural sector tended to be better off than the small farmer or *minifundiario*. Moreover, the wage earners were better organized. As was to be expected, therefore, they were the principal beneficiaries of the agrarian reform. The poor small farm owners, who constituted about 50% of the campesinos, received no benefit from the reform.

The Allende experiment was in a sense unique.[14] But its lesson for programs designed to establish equity through collective work activity and the collective sharing of the surplus is that such policies can badly distort incentives. In effect there is little incentive to supply work effort to the collective activity. The result is very similar to the classic free-rider problem associated with public goods. And the analogy is direct. Equity in a very real sense is a public good.

There are other disincentives associated with land-reform programs, depending in part on the particular form and character the reform takes. One of these has to do with the supply of entrepreneurial talent. When a land reform is inflexible and rigid, as in the case of the *ejidatario* system of the Mexican land reform, for example, there is little incentive to develop such talents. The system ties the worker to the land while at the same time limiting the potential for internal growth of the farm. Consequently, there is little incentive or opportunity to develop the entrepreneurial skills for a larger unit.

Under alternative reform arrangements, the entrepreneurial skills may be misdirected rather than stifled. This occurs in particular when the reformed sector is put in a straitjacket of bureaucratic control, as it was in the Chilean reform under Allende. Much of the entrepreneurial talent becomes directed to extracting resources from the system, or more generally, to "beating the system." This is a misuse of the very skills and talent that are all too scarce in a developing agriculture.

The final distortion to incentives associated with land reforms is that pertaining to investment in land and fixed structures on the land. In Brazil there currently is much talk about a partial or limited land reform. The difficulty in establishing credibility for such a limited reform is rather obvious. Once owners realize that the land may no longer be theirs, their discount rate becomes quite high. Hence, they turn to exploitation of the land and the physical capital on it, rather than investing in its future.

Rural Development Programs

Agricultural development efforts around the world have in recent years focused increasingly on what is called rural development. The World Bank has committed a major share of its efforts and responses to such programs. The Ford and Rockefeller Foundations are devoting larger shares of their budgets to similar efforts and the U.S. Congress has directed the U.S. aid agency to give rural development greater emphasis in its programs.

Probably no two people would agree on a definition of rural development. But in contemporary language it has become a "buzz word" for working with the rural poor. Ruttan, in his skeptical evaluation of such programs (1975), uses rural development to refer only to relatively comprehensive or integrated programs devoted to the income and well-being of people living in rural areas. He excludes activities such as a crop production campaign, the organization of cooperative credit institutions, and the adoption of family planning. He also excludes activities directed primarily toward single objectives, such as the intensive agricultural districts' program in India, and the Puebla Project in Mexico.

Project Puebla (see International Maize and Wheat Improvement Center 1974) focuses on small farmers in the state of Puebla, Mexico, who produce primarily maize. The central thrust of the project is the diffusion of a technological package among the farmers, with the package consisting of the increased use of fertilizer, a higher plant density, and a split application of fertilizer. The project has an applied agronomic research program associated with it, and also attempts to organize the farmers so that they have greater access to credit and fertilizer.

For our purposes, I prefer to take a somewhat broader definition and include the Puebla-type projects, since they are becoming increasingly popular in their own right. Mexico in particular has replicated Plan Puebla on a rather extensive scale, and other countries in Latin America and elsewhere have also initiated similar projects. Moreover, many rural development programs have the production and distribution of new production technology as a central thrust.

The motivations for this recent shift in program emphasis differ somewhat by institution. Agencies such as the World Bank seem to rest the bulk of their case on the argument that agricultural output can be increased in the aggregate only by working with the large number of small farmers (see World Bank 1975). Hence their interest derives in part from a concern with the world food problem.

The mandate by the U.S. Congress, on the other hand, appears to derive primarily from more direct income-distribution considerations. Critics of foreign aid have pointed out that in the past the major beneficiaries of foreign aid tended to be the middle or upper income groups rather than the poor. The political process therefore forced a shift in program emphasis. Not only are we now committed to the poorest of the poor in terms of countries, we also focus on low-income groups within individual countries.

Programs such as Plan Puebla are predicated in large part in the now familiar pleas for an "appropriate" technology. The objective is to devise a technological and institutional package for the small, disadvantaged farmer. Still other programs are predicated on participatory decision making, or political development per se.

In the face of all the rhetoric in favor of such programs, a number of rather important paradoxes stand out. First, as Ruttan has noted, previous experience with such programs, both in the United States and in developing countries, has proven disappointing. Despite success with the individual pilot projects, attempts to generalize them on a broader scale led to widespread disillusionment.

Second, Plan Puebla—a motivating force behind much of the recent emphasis on technologically-based rural development programs—has been quite disappointing, even as a pilot project. It has fallen far short of the yield goal it set for itself, and after seven years of concentrated effort, only 27% of the farmers in the region had adopted some element of the package (International Maize and Wheat Improvement Center 1974).

Finally, there is the paradox of the United States having long neglected its own rural poor and small farmers,[15] only to self-righteously lecture other countries on the need to do something about theirs. Admittedly, the U.S. development process has been quite wasteful of human resources, and one would hope that other countries could avoid some of our mistakes. But the paradox remains that we urge other countries to do what we ourselves were not able to do, either for technical or political reasons.

At the risk of taking a very unpopular position on what has now become accepted policy, I submit that many, if not most, of the current rural development programs are misdirected. Moreover, they are wasting scarce talent and development resources, with little potential for attaining their avowed objectives.

My position is based on four points:

(1) *Most of such programs are predicated on keeping people on the farm.* This is most shortsighted. As Johnston (1970) has noted, perhaps the one universal law relative to agriculture is that the agricultural labor force has to decline as development proceeds. The relative conditions of demand in general require (trade being the exception) that labor be transferred out of agriculture if per capita incomes in the rural sector are to keep up with those in the nonfarm sector. If there should be rapid technical change in agriculture, the need to transfer labor out tends to be even greater. To fly in the face of these forces of economic development is to doom the policies to failure and, more importantly, to condemn the rural poor to chronic poverty.

(2) *Such programs fail to deal with the basic problem, which is misguided economic policy.* Rural poverty in many if not most low-income countries is a result of severe discrimination against the agricultural sector. Moreover, economic policy has tended to induce a capital-intensive development path for the industrial sector, and at the same time to impede the performance of the labor market. To promote

industrialization, the prices of capital and capital goods are lowered below their true cost to society. Credit for investment in the industrial sector is highly subsidized, import preferences are granted for capital goods, and overvalued exchange rates lower the cost of such goods in terms of domestic resources.

At the same time that the price of capital is made artificially cheap, the price of labor to private firms is made artificially dear. Minimum-wage laws set wage rates above their market-clearing levels. On the misguided premise that private capitalists will have to pay for them, social welfare programs are financed by payroll taxes. The truth of the matter is that these costs are passed on to the workers in the form of reduced employment opportunities.

With such distortions in the price of capital and labor, it is little wonder that industrialization develops along capital-intensive lines and that the economy does poorly in creating new employment. In effect, development policy has a very strong antiemployment bias to it. Moreover, rural populations are poor, as are those in the informal labor markets of urban centers, because the labor markets are badly clogged and the workers do not have the human capital to obtain alternative employment.[16] The solution to the problem is to change these policies, not to settle for second-best policies which offer palliatives, but which in the longer run will be counterproductive.

(3. *It is asking too much to expect that new production technology be a major instrument for dealing with the equity problem.* The production and distribution of new production technology can be an important means of dealing with some classes of income problems. After all, new production technology is an important source of income streams, and when there is generalized poverty associated with low productivity, as in northeast Brazil, the diffusion of new technology can be an important means of alleviating *absolute* poverty.

But to ask production technology to bear the brunt of efforts to deal with problems of the *relative* distribution of income is asking too much, except in a rather limited sense. The issue here is one of *efficiency* of policy instruments. Some policies lend themselves to attaining one policy goal, while others lend themselves to others. We would not expect that a negative income tax would be an efficient means of raising the level of technical efficiency in agriculture. Similarly, we should not expect that production technology would be an efficient means of dealing with the equity problem.

This is not to deny, of course, recognition to the deleterious relative income-distribution consequences of technical change nor to rule out implementation of complementary policy measures to offset these consequences.[17] But to channel a major share of the expenditures for producing new production technology to dealing with *relative* income problems is to badly distort economic incentives, and to distort them in a very counter-productive way.[18]

(4) *Finally, such programs can be quite wasteful of human resources.* Ruttan (1975) has noted that intensive rural development projects tend to be highly skill-intensive. In fact, he argues that this aspect of these programs may be the main reason why there has been so little success in generalizing the successful experiences. Few countries have the skilled manpower to replicate successful projects on an extensive scale.

Such efforts therefore constitute a serious misallocation of resources, and often a misallocation of those resources which are scarcest in the individual country. The plant breeder who uses his time and talent producing an improved variety that, even if adopted, will have little impact on total output has been sadly misused by society. The opportunity costs of output foregone from such misallocations can indeed be large. Similarly, the economist who uses his time and talent analyzing misspecified problems will fail to diagnose the appropriate policies, and it is the latter diagnosis that could really make a difference. Again, the cost in terms of foregone output or in terms of an improved distribution of income is large.

Another serious issue here, of course, is that the international community is contributing to distortion of the incentive system and thereby to a serious misallocation of resources. The loss of credibility that we eventually reap from this misdirection can have serious longer-term consequences. More important, however, is that we are wasting scarce talent and development resources, not just our own but those of other countries as well. The people who will ultimately pay for these mistakes are those the policies were initially designed to help—the poor.

To close this section, I would like to emphasize that my objective is not to take issue with the concern for the poor, nor to argue that the poor should be left to fend for themselves. Rather, it is to argue that many policies and programs designed to deal with the equity problem can seriously distort incentives, and thereby serve as a serious constraint to output expansion. Moreover, current program emphases have little potential for effectively dealing with the problem of rural poverty.

Next I turn to a discussion of policies that are more appropriate for dealing with poverty and "basic needs."

POLICIES TO DEAL WITH EQUITY

Poverty is rooted in an inadequate accumulation of resources at the household level, and in unsatisfactory performance of the factor markets. Household resources may be in tangible physical form, or in the more intangible human capital of skills and abilities, health, and nutrition.

The major failings of the policies outlined above are threefold. First, they attempt to deal with problems that are rooted in the factor markets by inappropriate interventions in the product markets. Such policies are not only inefficient in dealing with the basic poverty problem, but they have serious deleterious consequences to output as well.

Second, they tend to ignore the considerable body of knowledge that has been developed with respect to human capital. Perhaps the most disappointing note in contemporary discussions of development policies is the failure to recognize the importance of training and schooling for the poor. Rural people are poor in most countries in large part because their governments have seriously underinvested in their human capital. Educational disparities between the rural and urban sectors are very large. Publicly supported health centers predominate in urban centers, but such centers are few and inadequately staffed in rural areas. Only in the case of nutrition do rural people tend to come off better, and typically that has little to do with government policy.

Third, the policies discussed tend to deal with symptoms rather than fundamental causes. Instead of increasing agricultural output to lower prices of agricultural products, the prices are kept low by decree. Efforts are made to increase employment in agriculture rather than to attack the fundamental problems causing low labor absorption in the industrial sector. And the magic of rural development blinds us to the inadequacy of concept in most programs that are given that label.

Finally, there is a failure to sort out goals and objectives and to relate them to a specific set of policy instruments.[19] This has especially been true of intensive rural development programs, which often are a mishmash of multiple attempts to be all things to all people. Such intellectual "mush" offers little as a basis for economic and social policy.

All too often there is also a failure to recognize that the major constraints affecting the development of a region have little to do with what goes on in the region itself. Northeast Brazil, for example, is poor in part because trade policy has discriminated severely against it, thereby siphoning resources toward the more well-to-do South. (See Baer [1964] and Martin and Schuh [undated].) Local development efforts that do not deal with this major constraint on the region are likely to have a low payoff.

More generally, we fail to recognize that the introduction of new production technology is appropriate for attaining one set of goals, but not for others. Similarly, nutrition and health programs can accomplish certain goals, but not others. And finally, institutional changes are as much induced by changes in economic forces as they are likely to induce such changes.

In my view our major policy failing has been in not recognizing that to deal with the relative-income problem requires a different set of policies than to deal with the output problem. Clearly, the introduction of new production technology is a necessary condition for alleviating generalized poverty in an agricultural sector. And the introduction of that technology can be an important source of expanded output for the economy as a whole.

But the introduction of new production technology is an inefficient means of dealing with most problems involving relative-income problems. In fact, despite the potential of such new technology as a source of expanded income streams for society as a whole, it may worsen the relative income position of the farm sector as a consequence of its general equilibrium effects,[20] and through its effects on the comparative advantage of particular regions within a country.

These consequences of new production technology have been the source of caveats which social scientists place on agricultural development policies that are strongly technology biased. This dimension of the problem tends to be poorly understood by biological and physical scientists, and therefore constitutes a source of serious misunderstanding between the physical and social scientists. It is to be regretted that there are some social scientists who would have us throw the baby out with the bathwater by abandoning technical change altogether, rather than devise alternative policies to deal more directly with the deleterious income-distribution consequences.

Any positive program to deal effectively with the problem of rural poverty must recognize that under a fairly general set of conditions labor has to be transferred out of agriculture as modernization and development proceeds. Moreover, in general, the faster this transfer can be accomplished, the less the incomes of rural people will tend to lag behind those of urban people. Hence, policies for alleviating rural poverty must be directed to giving rural workers the skills they need for alternative employment, to promoting more efficient labor markets, and to removing the antiemployment bias of development policy by reducing the factor-price distortions in the economy at large. Efforts to decentralize the industrialization process can also play an important role in producing more efficient factor markets.

An important point to note is that skill-intensive rural development programs seldom focus on those elements of policy which I have just cited. Hence, they fail to come to grips with the basic problem. A redirection of scarce development resources to these more fruitful lines of attack on the problem of rural poverty is long overdue.

Moreover, we should not burden the biological and physical scientists with the double task of simultaneously raising production possibilities and dealing with the relative-income problem. The proper role for these scientists is to provide the sources of expanded real-income streams. The relative-income problem can be dealt with more effectively and more efficiently by other means.

The important point here, of course, is that the attainment of multiple policy goals requires the use of multiple policy instruments. The challenge to policy makers is to relate the correct policy instrument to the correct policy goal.

CONCLUDING COMMENTS

In closing, I would like to make three points. The first is that many of our mistakes in policy ultimately trace to failures of analysis. Price policies directed to product markets are used to attain income objectives when in fact the problem is more properly one of poorly performing factor markets and the lack of investment in human capital. Technology is saddled with solving problems of equity, when its more proper function is to provide a larger supply of real-income streams as a whole. And, in general, we do not distinguish clearly between problems of absolute poverty and those of relative poverty.

Second, many of the policies that are designed to transfer income from one group to another through interventions in product markets—redistribution policies that have a deleterious impact on output—are used in lieu of an effective tax system that mobilizes resources more directly. Brazil has extracted the surplus from its agricultural sector through trade policy largely because, either for political or administrative reasons, it was unable to implement an effective income or land tax for agriculture. The key to dealing with the equity problem in a more appropriate manner is to have a more efficient tax system.

Finally, too much has been made of the presumed tradeoff between equity and efficiency, with the implication that a more equitable distribution of income can be had only by growing at a lower rate. In most low-income countries this is a false dichotomy. Appropriate policies to raise the income of the poor, either in an absolute or relative sense, will raise overall resource efficiency in the economy at large. Greater investments in human capital of the poor, the removal of distortions that create an antiemployment bias, and the promotion of more efficient labor markets all make for a more productive economy.

If a tradeoff does in fact exist, it is most likely because inappropriate policies are being used for dealing with the equity problem.

NOTES

1. For a brief synthesis of this conference and a summary of its main conclusions, see International Labour Office (1977).

2. This section draws heavily on Sukhatme (1975). For a penetrating analysis of more general social policy in India and its consequences for economic growth, see Johnson (1977).

3. There have also been restrictions on the interdistrict movement of grains within individual states.

4. Baer (1965) and Bergsman (1970, chap. 3) provide useful analyses of these policies.

5. See Leff (1969) and also his discussion (1967) of its role in Brazilian development policy.

6. After 1971 some part of this discrimination was offset by a massive infusion of cheap credit.

7. Estimates of the disequilibrium in the foreign exchange market have been made by Bacha et al. (1971), Bergsman (1970, chap. 3), Doellinger et al. (1974), and Homen de Melo and Zockun (undated).

8. Brazil's limited ability to import during the war years meant that its physical plant had deteriorated seriously while its reserves of foreign exchange had grown rapidly. After the war the exchange rate was kept low to facilitate the rebuilding of the industrial plant. When the reserves were exhausted, however, the cruzeiro was not devalued, largely out of a desire to exploit the downward sloping demand curve Brazil faced for its coffee.

9. Bergsman (1970, chap. 3) and Bergsman and Malan (1971) estimate that the implicit export tax rate from the overvaluation of the currency alone ranged from 22 to 37% between 1954 and 1966, with the rate being 28% or greater in all but three of these years. Homen de Melo and Zockun (undated) present data from a study by Fishlow (1974) which shows an implicit tax due to an overvalued currency of 48 and 49% in the three-year period 1952–54.

10. For an analysis of this phenomenon in the case of India, see Bardham (1973). For an analysis of productivity relationships in the context of agricultural development, see Schuh and Thompson (1977).

11. Research with the metaproduction function for agriculture has tended to show a relatively unimportant role for land either as a source of output expansion or as source of differentials in productivity. See Hayami and Ruttan (1971), Ogg (1974), and Thompson and Schuh (1975).

12. This bias towards land fundamentalism was reflected in the 1975 amendments to the U.S. Foreign Assistance Act of 1961, in which Congress mandated that foreign aid should be directed (among other things) to raising the productivity of land, with no mention made of labor productivity.

13. The material in the paragraphs that follow is based on Valdés (1974).

14. It should be noted, however, that many of the same problems had arisen under the less-radical measures of the Frei government. See Valdés (1974).

15. Charles Hardin (1977) notes how deficient even the New Deal programs were in assisting small farmers in the U.S.

16. For an analysis of this problem in the case of Brazil, see Schuh (1976).

17. Schultz (1961) has cogently discussed policies that might be used to redress the injustices associated with economic progress.

18. Eckaus (1977) has made a careful analysis of the "appropriate technology" question for the U.S. National Academy of Sciences.

19. The classic formulation of the policy problem argues that there has to be at least one policy instrument for each policy goal. See Tinbergen (1956).

20. These general equilibrium effects are for the most part realized in the product markets, where the increase in the output due to the new production technology causes product prices to decline. For a general analysis of this problem, see Martin (1975).

REFERENCES

Bacha, Edmar Lisboa; Barbosa Ararizo, Aloisio; da Mata, Milton; and Lyrio Modenesi, Rui. 1971. *Análise governamental de projetos de investimento no Brasil: Procedimentos e recomendacões.* Relatório 1. Rio de Janeiro: IPEA/INPES.

Baer, Werner. 1964. "Regional Inequality and Economic Growth in Brazil." *Economic Development and Cultural Change* 12 (April):268–85.

———. 1965. *Industrialization and Economic Development in Brazil.* Homewood, Ill.: Richard D. Irwin.

Bardham, Pranab K. 1973. "Size, Productivity, and Return to Scale: An Analysis of Farm-Level Data in Indian Agriculture." *Journal of Political Economy* 81 (November/December): 1370–86.

Bergsman, Joel. 1970. *Brazil: Industralization and Trade Policies.* London: Oxford University Press.

Bergsman, Joel, and Malan, Pedro S. 1971. "The Structure of Protection in Brazil." In *The Structure of Protection in Developing Countries,* by Bela Belassa and associates. Baltimore: Johns Hopkins Press.

Cheung, S. N. S. 1969. *The Theory of Share Tenancy.* Chicago: University of Chicago Press.

Doellinger, Carlos von; de Castro Faria, Hugo B.; and Casterta Calvalcanti, Leonardo. 1974. *A politica Brasileira de comercio exterior e seus efeitos, 1967–73.* Relatório 22. Rio de Janeiro: IPEA/INPES.

Eckaus, Richard S. 1977. *Appropriate Technologies for Developing Countries.* Washington, D.C.: National Academy of Sciences.

Fishlow, Albert. 1974. "Foreign Trade Regimes and Economic Development of Brazil." Mimeographed. New York: National Bureau of Economic Research.

Floyd, John E. 1965. "The Effects of Farm Price Supports on the Returns to Land and Labor in Agriculture." *Journal of Political Economy* 73 (April):148–58.

Hardin, Charles M. 1977. "Agricultural Price Policy in the United States: The Feasibility of a Market-Oriented Policy." Mimeographed. University of California, Davis.

Hayami, Yujiro, and Ruttan, Vernon W. 1971. *Agricultural Development: an International Perspective.* Baltimore: Johns Hopkins Press.

Homen de Melo, Fernando, and Zockun, Maria Helena G. P. Undated. "Exportacões agricolas, balanca de pagamentos e abastecimento do mercado interno." Mimeographed. Fundacão Instituto de Pesquisas Economicas, São Paulo.

International Labour Office. 1977. *Meeting Basic Needs: Strategies for Eradicating Mass Poverty and Unemployment.* Geneva.

International Maize and Wheat Improvement Center. 1974. *The Puebla Project: Seven Years of Experience, 1967–1973.* El Batán, Mexico.

Johnson, Harry G. 1977. "Economic Growth with Social Justice." Mimeographed. University of Chicago.

Johnston, Bruce F. 1970. "Agriculture and Structural Transformation in Developing Countries: A Survey of Research." *Journal of Economic Literature* 8 (June):369–404.

Leff, Nathaniel H. 1967. "Export Stagnation and Autarkic Development in Brazil, 1947–1962." *Quarterly Journal of Economics* 81 (May):286–301.

———. 1968. *Economic Policy-Making and Development in Brazil, 1947–1964.* New York: John Wiley and Sons.

———. 1969. "The 'Exportable Surplus' Approach to Foreign Trade in Underdeveloped Countries." *Economic Development and Cultural Change* 17 (April):347–55.

Lopes, Mauro de Rezende. 1977. "The Mobilization of Resources from Agriculture: A Policy Analysis for Brazil." Ph.D. dissertation, Purdue University.

Martin, Lee R. 1975. "Market Effects on Income Distribution." In *Externalities in the Transformation of Agriculture: Distribution of Benefits and Costs from Development,* ed. Earl O. Heady and Larry R. Whiting, pp.22–58. Ames: Iowa State University Press.

Martin, Marshall, and Schuh, G. Edward. Undated. "Brazilian Trade Policy and Its Impact on the Regional Distribution of Income." Mimeographed. Purdue University, Lafayette, Indiana.

Ogg, C. 1974. "Sources of Agricultural Productivity Differences in North America." Ph.D. dissertation, University of Minnesota.

Reid, Joseph D. Jr. 1976. "Sharecropping and Tenancy in American History." Mimeographed. University of Chicago.

Ruttan, Vernon W. 1975. "Integrated Rural Development Programs: A Skeptical Perspective." *International Development Review* 17, no. 4:9–16.

Schuh, G. Edward. 1976. "Imperfections in the Labor Market and Policy for the Rural Poor in Brazil." Mimeographed. Purdue University, Lafayette, Indiana.

Schuh, G. Edward, and Thompson, Robert L. 1977. "Assessing Agricultural Progress and the Commitment to Agriculture." Mimeographed. Purdue University, Lafayette, Indiana.

Schultz, Theodore W. 1961. "A Policy to Redistribute Losses from Economic Progress." *Journal of Farm Economics* 43 (August):554–65.

———. Forthcoming. "On Economics, Agriculture, and the Political Economy." Elmhirst Lecture. In *Proceedings, 16th International Conference of Agricultural Economists, Nairobi, Kenya, 1976.*

Sukhatme, Vasant. 1975. "Government Policy and Agricultural Development in India." Mimeographed. University of Chicago.

Thompson, Robert L, and Schuh, G. Edward. 1975. "Sources of Regional Differences in Productivity in Brazilian Agriculture." Mimeographed. Purdue University, Lafayette, Indiana.

Tinbergen, Jan. 1956. *Economic Policy: Principles and Design.* Amsterdam: North-Holland.

Valdés, Alberto. 1974. "The Transition to Socialism: Observations on the Chilean Agrarian Reform." In *Employment in Developing Nations*, ed. Edgar O. Edwards, pp.405–18. New York: Columbia University Press.

Veiga, Alberto. 1974. "The Impact of Trade Policy on Brazilian Agriculture, 1947–1967." Ph.D. dissertation, Purdue University.

World Bank. 1975. *Rural Development.* Washington, D.C.

COMMENT

EMERY N. CASTLE

Schuh's major thesis is that policies to promote the generation of additional income streams should be uncoupled from policies to redistribute income or wealth. He draws on the experience of three economies where intervention, designed to promote income- or wealth-distribution objectives, has negatively affected incentives for agricultural production. I found his survey of the experience of these countries as well as his skeptical comments about rural development exceedingly interesting.

Schuh was probably wise in limiting his discussion of the meanings of "basic needs" and "equity." He substituted increased production and increased income for "basic needs" and seemed to assume that a more egalitarian distribution of income was more "equitable" than a less egalitarian distribution.

His and Ruttan's critical comments concerning multiple-purpose rural development efforts should not mean that group decision-making needs at the rural community level are nonexistent or unimportant, for we have identified the following significant group problems:

Production infrastructure: irrigation and drainage, declining ground water levels, and grazing rights.

Factor markets at the community level: education and rural industrialization.

Externalities in agricultural production: excess usage of plant nutrients, erosion, and insecticides and pesticides.

Quality of life: rural water systems and waste disposal.

This brief, incomplete list serves three purposes here. First, it suggests that not all of the significant problems of agricultural development can be faced in the context of the agricultural firm. Second, it permits comments about social science research and education, and third, it facilitates discussion about rural institutions.

Much of the research on the organization of public-sector research and education has focused on the natural sciences. This, of course, is understandable because that is where the bulk of the investment has been and it is where the tangible products of research can be more easily identified and measured. However, as the constraints to increased agricultural production and distribution shift more from the physical and biological to the economic, social, and political, greater

328

emphasis may need to be placed on the social sciences and their role in development.

One of the major benefits of the social science research is the effect on the person doing the research. The increased capacity of those who have participated in that research to perform a diagnostic function in the identification and analysis of important social problems provides one example of such a beneficial effect. Tangible research products that are capable of being generalized are rare in the social sciences although they certainly exist and should continue to be emphasized. Perhaps one reason that multiple-purpose rural development efforts have tended to have difficulty while single-purpose efforts have tended to be somewhat more successful is because of faulty problem identification in undertakings of the former kind. Greater attention has been focused on the importance of problem identification and analysis at the firm level in farm management and at the national level in agricultural policy than at the community level. Nevertheless there is a real need at all three levels of decision making for such expertise. This need should be recognized in recommendations on the organization of social science research and education.

There is a growing awareness of the importance of institutions and institutional analysis. The underlying concepts may well be too broad and encompassing to be of much assistance in social-problem diagnosis. In any meaningful problem diagnosis it is necessary to distinguish between those rules which govern social relationships, such as property rights and entitlements, and social behavioral entities, such as the family, a unit of government, or an organized market. In some recent discussion there has been a tendency to equate property rights (rules) with institutions. Even within property rights greater precision is needed for many purposes and the subdivision of property rights into entitlements protected by *property rules, liability rules,* and *inalienable entitlements* is often required (Calabresi and Melamed 1972). A body of literature is developing which relates changes in property rights to changing economic values commanded by the factors of production (Demsetz 1964, Furubotn and Pejovich 1972, Schultz 1968, and Ruttan 1971). This important development provides a useful view of economic history.

It is, of course, quite a different matter to anticipate and then predict the probable consequences of institutional changes. So long as the economist or social scientist chooses to work on obstacles that inhibit the working of existing institutions, he can expect at least a modicum of support for his efforts. Nor should great controversy be anticipated from efforts to provide an economic interpretation of history. If, however, he anticipates and analyzes the type of development that will change institutions (property rights) he can expect the potential value conflicts to be sharp and severe.[1] Changes in property rights may adversely affect those who view, say, property entitlements as the means to protect their claims to income and wealth as well as those who view the institution as an end in itself. There are numerous historical examples of organized religion being aligned with vested economic and political interests.[2]

I now return to the Schuh paper and the larger message it conveys. His paper and others in this volume document in a most convincing way that government policies, often adopted for the announced purpose of promoting greater equity, distort producer incentives. The consequence is that income generation is suppressed and that neither the relative nor the absolute position of the "poorest of the poor" has been improved.

But why is this the case? Why is it that both developed and developing societies have so much difficulty adopting policies that make economic sense, given even an intermediate time frame as a planning horizon? I believe this question must be addressed if we are to proceed very far with the "equity-basic needs" conflict.

There are many possible explanations for the existence of these perverse policies, and two occur to me. One is that economists are very poor teachers and educators and, while we know the "best" policies, we just have not marshaled the right evidence or presented it in a convincing way. Yet there are problems with this explanation. Following Schultz (1964), economists generally believe that the individual entrepreneur on the land is able to select wisely from among many alternatives, given his objectives and opportunities. Do public sector decision-makers not have comparable capacity to choose wisely from among alternative public policies even when they have (or perhaps despite) the assistance of economists? If not, why not? Economists do seem to be fairly successful in selling certain macro policies pertaining to government spending and taxation. Thus, this explanation seems to lack force.

A more promising explanation is based on an understanding of the objectives of the alternatives available to those in the public sector who formulate and make policies affecting agriculture. To this end, the following observations are offered:

(1) Public-sector decision makers can be expected to act in their own self-interest. The literature of public choice is based on the self-interest hypothesis, and while this literature is still quite underdeveloped, the empirical evidence suggests there is a great deal to it. George Stigler (1975) has said "there is, in fact, only one general

theory of human behavior and that is the utility-maximizing theory" (p.137)[3] and also "if incentives can be contrived to persuade people to act voluntarily to the goal of reform, we can be confident that our reforms will be crowned with success" (p.32).

(2) For numerous reasons, the self-interest of public sector decision makers will not automatically lead to the greatest public good. There are numerous reasons for this which have been identified in the political-science literature (Haefele 1973, Niskanen 1971). I suggest that a particularly important reason relates to time and planning horizons.

(3) Those who have responsibility for public-sector decisions are typically under pressure to satisfy a clientele in a relatively short-run context. Elections may be faced frequently by elected officials and comparable short-run accountability may exist for civil service-type personnel. Instead of future returns being discounted at, say, 15% in accordance with economic analysis, a more realistic planning horizon for the public-sector decision-maker may be three to five years. An ideal policy from his viewpoint may be one that promises returns in less than, say, three years but defers apparent costs for more than three years.[4]

It is not clear that public-sector decision makers are either more or less devoted to equity than are others in the populace. If we ask people to define equity, we should not be surprised if it turns out to be consistent with the maximization of their own self-interest.

What to do? Two possible approaches seem logical. One might be called structural reform which would focus on designing incentive systems for public-sector decision makers with the "public interest" being served as public-sector decision makers look after their individual interests. The market-failure literature in economics details the ways in which the private sector may fail to serve the public interest and offers suggestions as to what can be done to avoid such failures. To my knowledge a comparable literature does not exist for public-sector performance, although it is needed. I wish the public-choice people and others who are trying to do something about this every success.

There are more mundane things which may also be done. Economics has some very explicit ways of dealing with time. Indeed, supply response has little meaning unless time is given explicit treatment. D. Gale Johnson makes the point that improvement in basic agricultural production capacity takes considerable time. However, as Schuh observes about the experience in Chile, production response, in this case a negative response, may occur in a much shorter run. I suggest, therefore, that a major problem facing public-sector decision makers involves the substitution between and among policies that have alternative patterns of costs and returns over time. It is perhaps an over-simplification to say that public-sector decision makers select from among short-run policies while economists concerned with agriculture and natural resources recommend long-run solutions. Yet there may be a kernel of truth embedded in the exaggeration.

But there is a danger here. If economists simply adopt the time frame of public-sector decision-makers and propose only those policies consistent with this time frame, they may become apologists for the political status quo. In principle, this is little different from taking income distribution as given and deducing an efficiency solution, when we know that a different efficiency solution will result if the income distribution is varied. Either approach runs the risk of making the analyst the handmaiden of those who are in power or those who have income. However, fundamental reform is less likely to result in significant improvement if it occurs in the absence of knowledge about the existing situation. A distinction needs to be drawn between the acquisition of knowledge and the use to which that knowledge is put. A better understanding of public-sector motivation and performance may be used either to reform the system or to justify the status quo.

Regardless of what one thinks about this or alternative approaches, there is a fundamental point that should not be neglected in discussions of this subject. The economist typically believes the application of his body of knowledge to an actual situation in the private sector will permit him to make predictions about the effect of policies on per capita incomes. He then typically makes the assumption that if per capita income is increased, public-sector policies can be adopted which can better accomplish equity objectives. From this we get the "uncoupling" type of recommendation which is found in Schuh's paper. Yet if income distribution is to be uncoupled from income generation, the public sector will need to be involved.

Economists have the tools to stipulate both the necessary and sufficient conditions for the accomplishment of policy objectives related to the private sector. With respect to the public sector, they typically have to be content with establishing only the necessary conditions. This is insufficient as a basis for policy change, because the behavioral theory for the public sector is not comparable to that which exists for the private sector.

NOTES

1. Certain economists can take some justified pride, I believe, in anticipating early in the 1960s (1) the effect of changing income elasticity of demand

for leisure (Stevens 1966a, 1966b) and (2) the increased scarcity of certain resources held in common resulting from the negative side effects of mass use of modern technology (Clawson 1959, Kneese 1962, Stoevener 1963, and Stoevener et al. 1972).

2. There is a methodological distinction between an ex post explanation of changes in property rules as reflecting changed economic conditions and an ex ante evaluation of possible change. In the former case, the economic historian can say that the benefits of change outweighed the obstacles to change, otherwise the change would not have occurred. This is obviously true, given the historical power structure which existed. An anticipation of such change, however, places the analyst, ex ante, in the position of evaluating, implicitly or explicitly, the probable consequences of change.

An ex post evaluation of rates of changes in property rules over time and across nations would undoubtedly reveal a great deal about historical power structures. It is hypothesized that the society most conducive to economic progress will be the one that balances a degree of certainty in property rules with a capacity for rule changes in response to emerging economic conditions.

3. See Rawls (1971) for a statement of and an attempt to resolve the inherent contradictions in ultilitarianism.

4. This is not to argue that all public-sector decision makers have a high rate of discount. It would appear plausible, however, that many of those in a position to choose from among agricultural development policies have a limited planning horizon.

Economists have devoted a great deal of attention to theoretical reasons why the social rate of discount may be different than rates of discount used in the private sector. In addition there have been attempts to measure returns earned over time in the private sector. To my knowledge there has been little effort made to ascertain discount rates and planning horizons of public-sector decision makers as they choose from among alternative policies. This, of course, is very different from the rate of discount used for benefit-cost purposes on public investment projects.

One of the major criticisms of the market has been its failure to anticipate long-run resource availabilities and needs. It is not clear that public-sector decision making, influenced as it is by short-run political forces, reflects a longer run point of view.

REFERENCES

Calabresi, Guido, and Melamed, A. Douglas. 1972. "Property Rights, Liability Rules and Inalienability: One View of the Cathedral." *Harvard Law Review* 85 (April):1089–1128.

Clawson, Marion. 1959. *Methods of Measuring the Demand for and Value of Outdoor Recreation.* Reprint no. 10. Washington, D.C.: Resources for the Future.

Demsetz, Harold. 1964. "The Exchange and Enforcement of Property Rights." *Journal of Law and Economics* 7 (October):11–26.

Furubotn, Eirik G., and Pejovich, Svetozar. 1972. "Property Rights and Economic Theory: A Survey of Recent Literature." *Journal of Economic Literature* 10 (December):1137–62.

Haefele, Edwin T. 1973. *Representative Government and Environmental Management.* Baltimore: Johns Hopkins Press, for Resources for the Future.

Kneese, Allen V. 1962. *Water Pollution: Economic Aspects and Research Needs.* Washington, D.C.: Resources for the Future.

Niskanen, William A., Jr. 1971. *Bureaucracy and Representative Government.* Chicago: Aldine-Atherton Publishing Co.

Rawls, John. 1971. *A Theory of Justice.* Cambridge: Belknap Press of Harvard University Press.

Ruttan, Vernon W. 1971. "Technology and the Environment." *American Journal of Agricultural Economics* 53 (December): 707–17.

Schultz, Theodore W. 1964. *Transforming Traditional Agriculture.* New Haven: Yale University Press (Reprint edition, New York: Arno Press, 1976).

———. 1968. "Institutions and the Rising Economic Value of Man." *American Journal of Agricultural Economics* 50 (December):1113–22.

Stigler, George. 1975. *The Citizen and the State: Essays on Regulation.* Chicago: University of Chicago Press.

Stevens, Joe B. 1966a. "A Study of Conflict in Natural Resource Use: Evaluation of Recreational Benefits as Related to Water Quality." Ph.D. dissertation, Oregon State University.

———. 1966b. "Recreation Benefits from Water Pollution Control." *Water Resources Research* 2, no. 2:167–82.

Stoevener, Herbert H. 1963. "An Economic Evaluation of Water Pollution Control Alternatives: A Progress Report." In *Water Resources and Economic Development of the West,* pp.47–59. Report no. 12, Western Agricultural Economics Research Council. Pullman, Washington: Committee on the Economics of Water Resource Development.

Stoevener, Herbert H.; Stevens, Joe B.; Horton, Howard E.; Sokoloski, Adam; Parrish, Loys P.; and Castle, Emery N. 1972. "Multi-disciplinary Study of Water Quality Relationships: A Case Study of Yaquina Bay, Oregon." Special report no. 348, Oregon Agricultural Experiment Station. Corvallis.

Contributors

Martin E. Abel
Schnittker Associates

Randolph Barker
International Rice Research Institute
Los Baños, Philippines

Gilbert T. Brown
The World Bank

Emery N. Castle
Resources for the Future
Washington, D.C.

Sir John G. Crawford
Australian National University
Canberra

Robert E. Evenson
Yale University

Keith W. Finlay
International Maize and Wheat
Improvement Center,
El Batan, Mexico

Roger W. Fox
International Food Policy Research
Institute, Washington, D.C., and
The University of Arizona

Earl O. Heady
Iowa State University

Reed Hertford
The Ford Foundation

W. David Hopper
The World Bank

D. Gale Johnson
University of Chicago

P. A. Oram
International Food Policy Research
Institute, Washington, D.C.

Sir Charles Pereira
Ministry of Agriculture, Fisheries
and Food, London

Rati Ram
Illinois State University, Normal

Vernon W. Ruttan
University of Minnesota

G. Edward Schuh
Purdue University

Theodore W. Schultz
University of Chicago

Howard A. Steppler
Macdonald College of
McGill University

Paul E. Waggoner
Connecticut Agricultural Experiment
Station, New Haven

Finis Welch
University of California at
Los Angeles and
The Rand Corporation, Santa Monica

Joseph W. Willett
U.S. Department of Agriculture

Name Index

Abel, Martin E., 173, 181
Adams, Dale W., 89, 98, 123
Anden, Teresa, 12
Anderson, Jock R., 166
Arndt, Thomas M., 89, 228, 230, 290
Arrow, K. J., 287
Atkinson, L. Jay, 131

Bacha, Edmar Lisboa, 324
Baer, Werner, 321, 324
Baker, H. G., 49
Bardham, Pranab K., 324
Barker, Randolph, 12, 35, 43, 103, 141, 143, 145, 189
Barlow, Colin, 158
Barton, Weldon V., 301
Beall, H. W., 39, 61
Becker, S. L., 257
Behrman, Jere R., 101
Bene, J. G., 39, 61
Bennett, Gae A., 138
Bennett, John W., 298
Bergsman, Joel, 311, 312, 324
Barry, Albert, 123
Bhagwati, J. N., 287
Bieri, Jurg, 119, 130, 138
Binswanger, Hans P., 158, 249, 297, 300
Bird, Richard M., 97
Birnberg, Thomas B., 298
Biswas, Basudeb, 203
Booth, Anne, 150
Boserup, E., 40
Boyce, James, 224, 225, 226, 232, 234, 240, 241, 242
Bromley, Daniel W., 301
Bunting, A. H., 29
Buringh, P., 37, 51, 52
Burton, G. W., 53

Calabresi, Guido, 329
Chaudhri, D. P., 271, 283
Cheung, S. N. S., 313
Clark, Colin, 40
Clark, Sara, 131
Clawson, Marion, 333
Clay, E. J., 148
Cline, William R., 99, 103
Cock, James H., 247
Commons, John R., 300
Côté, A., 39, 61
Crisostomo, Cristina M., 141
Cummings, Ralph W., Jr., 163

Dalrymple, Dana G., 35, 89, 228, 230
Davis, Lance E., 300
De Datta, S. K., 27
de Janvry, Alain, 138
Demsetz, Harold, 329

Dillon, John L., 165, 166
Doellinger, Carlos von, 311, 324
Drilon, J. D., 37
Dudley, Leonard, 124, 125, 127
Duff, Bart, 145, 158
Dupree, A. Hunter, 251

Easter, K. William, 173
Eckaus, Richard S., 325
Eckert, Jerry B., 88
Erasmus, Charles J., 297
Evenson, Robert E., 16, 224, 225, 226, 228, 230, 232, 234, 238, 240, 241, 242, 250, 271–72

Falcon, Walter P., 16, 87, 173
Fane, George, 272, 273, 279
Feeney, David Harold, 292
Fettig, Lyle P., 133
Fishlow, Albert, 324
Fitzharris, Joseph C., 252
Flores, P. M., 238
Floyd, John E., 312
Furnivall, J. S., 298
Furubotn, Eirik C., 329

Gans, D. U., 255
Gibson, A. H., 63
Goolsby, O. Halbert, 171
Griffin, Keith B., 166
Griliches, Zvi, 17, 248, 271–72, 290
Gutierrez, Nestor, 123, 128

Haefele, Edwin T,. 331
Haller, Thomas, 275
Hardaker, J. Brian, 166
Hardin, Charles M., 325
Hardy, W. F., 63
Hare, F. K., 50
Haswell, M., 40
Hathaway, Dale E., 119, 217
Hayami, Yujiro, 40, 44, 88, 89, 103, 141, 146–47, 152, 158, 228, 238, 292, 295, 296, 324
Hazell, P. B. R., 119
Herdt, Robert W., 35, 43, 101, 143, 156–57, 158
Hertford, Reed, 15, 123, 128
Hesselmark, O., 102
Heyer, Judith, 13
Higinbotham, Harlow N., 295
Ho, Yhi-min, 274
Holsendolph, E., 255–56
Homen de Melo, Fernando, 324
Horowitz, Irving Louis, 301
Horsfall, J. G., 255, 257
House, Arthur, 279
Howard, Albert, 31

336

Subject Index